Adventures of a Gentleman's Gentleman

GUY HUNTING

Adventures of a Gentleman's Gentleman

THE
QUEEN,
NOEL
COWARD
AND I

Published by John Blake Publishing Ltd, 3 Bramber Court,
2 Bramber Road, London W14 9PB, England

First published in hardback in 2002

ISBN 1 903402 94 8

British Library Cataloguing-in-Publication Data: A catalogue record
for this book is available from the British Library.

Design by ENVY

Printed and bound in Great Britain by CPD (Wales)

1 3 5 7 9 10 8 6 4 2

Papers used by John Blake Publishing Ltd are natural, recyclable products
made from wood grown in sustainable forests. The manufacturing processes conform
to the environmental regulations of the country of origin

I was twenty-one years old, queer and a Buckingham Palace footman in 1967 when, for the first time, I found myself drawn to a political figure who was neither Lady Violet Bonham-Carter nor Bessie Braddock. With his dark good looks, flamboyant personality and taste for fussy clothes, I also thought that in Jeremy Thorpe I had identified a kindred spirit. In fact, as he bestrode the nation's stage, the gay world in general – always hungry for an icon – could see that he had far more potential than Mr Heath, whose bachelor status was starting to look as if it was a blind alley leading to a damp squib.

At the age of thirty-nine, and after only ten years in the House as the member for North Devon, Mr Thorpe jumped to the head of the small queue that was the Liberal Party to replace the greatly respected Jo Grimond as its leader. No profile of him at the time was complete without mentioning that he was unmarried and that his long-dead Tory MP father had sent him to Eton. His flare for publicity and skills as an orator were becoming well known, but those with more intimate knowledge also knew that he was a collector of fine porcelain and a talented violinist. As a superb mimic he was also much admired and his devastating portrayal of Lady Dorothy Macmillan was enthusiastically received in a number of drawing rooms.

As leader of the third largest political party, his new eminence soon provided him with his first invitation to Buck House. The occasion was an official dinner given by the Queen for the two leaders of the Soviet Union, Mr Krushchev and Mr Breshnev. No Russian supremo had been received by a British sovereign since the Revolution, and the protocol boys and Foreign Office bigwigs were thrown into confusion by this unprecedented diplomatic situation. If their presence in the country had been regarded as a state visit, the Queen, as a matter of course, would have given a full-blown banquet in the ballroom with about a hundred and fifty guests. As it was, the compromise was to be a formal dinner in the state dining room for about sixty VIPs and Brits with Russian connections. Lounge suit, not white tie, was the order of the day and round tables were to be used rather than the huge horseshoe that was the norm for more serious feasting. The room itself had been closed for many months while it underwent a complete facelift. All the faded nineteenth-century curtains and carpets had been faithfully copied and replaced and the walls re-hung with a very brave crimson damask.

I was on dinner-serving duty that evening and most anxious to know who would be on the receiving end of my wobbly entree dish and unsteady sauceboat. Knowing from past experience that I would not be allowed too close to anyone with an HM or HRH in front of their names, I was delighted to see on the table in front of me Jeremy Thorpe's place card – even though it was next to that of the Master of the Household. Not much chance of a mild flirtation with that placement, I thought.

With the candles lit and flunkies in position, the doors opened to admit the sound of the Guards String Orchestra playing in the picture gallery and all the guests, except the royal party. As the table plan had been closely scrutinised in the blue drawing room, table-finding was a relatively easy process. A few famous faces, of which Margot Fonteyn's was far and away the most attractive, passed by me. I turned my admiring glance from her as a voice in front of me boomed:

'What a beautiful room! The walls are such an amazing colour.'

Imagine my nervous excitement when I saw that these observations came from the smiling face of the Leader of the Liberal Party.

'Isn't it wonderful? It's just been completely redecorated and this is the first time it has been used for ages,' I gabbled.

At that he stood back, subjecting me to a searching look.

'Well I must say your uniform is pretty magnificent too,' he exclaimed. 'I'm going to a fancy dress ball at Edward Montagu's next week and would love to borrow it.'

I forbore to point out that the height difference between us was probably about six inches.

'How long have you worked here?' he asked, with great interest. 'Do you like it?' With increasing confidence, I confided, 'I am leaving after Christmas.'

'What are you going to do next?' he enquired.

'I hope I've got a job in the news room at the BBC,' I told him.

'How marvellous,' he retorted, 'but you must let me know if you need any help. I've got good connections at the BBC.'

During this little exchange I had failed to notice that the Queen and her principal guests had not only processed into the room, but had actually taken their seats. To my horror, I was suddenly aware that Mr Thorpe and I were standing alone in the middle of the room, and that Elizabeth Alexandra Mary's notorious laser beam was boring into me. My dilemma was compounded when a completely composed JT, taking his seat, pointed me out as the new Richard Dimbleby to an emphatically unamused Master of the Household, Sir Mark Milbank. Jeremy's position next to the baronet, Guards officer and Yorkshire landowner who was my boss made further exchanges difficult, but we did manage the odd amused glance. In fact, we had no further contact that evening and more than a year was to pass before we spoke again.

I didn't join the BBC in the end, but went instead to work for Noel Coward in Switzerland. However, that is jumping the gun. I think my story should begin at the beginning.

2

As a child I knew very little about the person called Ivor Novello, but I sometimes used to wonder if he removed his dentures before eating. What seems now to be a ludicrous idea started life as an occasionally recurring question whenever we sat down as a family to eat. My father was a vain man whose favourite boast was that he had the same striking good looks as that aforementioned pillar of the musical theatre. As I had never seen a likeness of Mr Novello it was impossible for me to judge, but the business of the teeth often made me wonder. The sleight of hand necessary for their removal was always a tense moment for onlookers in the know, and this was made much worse if anyone from outside the family was present. I suppose more sophisticated people would have talked more loudly or made witty remarks as a distraction, but sadly mealtime conversation was not encouraged. Shortly after settling himself at the table a large white handkerchief would be pulled from a trouser pocket and held momentarily to the lower half of his face. Was he blowing his nose or simply wiping sweat from his top lip? Years of practice meant that the operation was completed in seconds, the square of cotton and its presumably faulty contents tucked out of sight, to enable eating to begin.

My brother, John Francis, and I were bastards. Dad, fifty-one years old at the time I was born, was married to someone whose name I never knew and whose whereabouts were unknown. After the birth of my brother two and a half years before me my mother, Nora Louisa Jobson, changed her name by deed poll. She was an attractive woman of forty-two when I appeared on the scene. Many years later she confessed to me that although she had had other gentlemen admirers, Francis Gilbert Hunting was the only man she had ever 'known'. Dad's family were from Northamptonshire. All I know about them is that they ran a number of butcher's shops and counted a Lord Mayor of Peterborough among their number. I did once visit that fair city and saw some empty premises with our name across the front. A cousin canon at the cathedral was also mentioned on socially assertive days.

My mother's family were from Hampstead in north-west London, where my grandfather had his builder's business. As well as his yard in West End Lane he also owned two houses in Sarre Road and a block of four flats in Fordwich Road. According to my mother he had once been commissioned to build a house, although I never discovered its whereabouts. His two great interests in life were his garden and radical politics. With his friend and fellow Hampstead dweller Ramsay MacDonald, he helped to form the Independent Labour Party. Mama had fond memories of playing with the MacDonald children – Ishbel in particular. Great-grandfather had been an artist of the Thames School and I treasure a photograph of this venerable old man with a long beard and wide-brimmed hat sitting at an easel. That said, the three pictures of his that I own would be more loved if they portrayed fewer dahlias and slightly fatter peaches.

My mother, in fact, I never actually called her that. She was 'Mummy' until my teens and then 'Mum'. In later life we both preferred the more affectionate 'Mama', with a long first 'a'. Mama had two brothers – Douglas and Kenneth. Dull Douglas, who had a troubled relationship with Mama, took over the business, married twice and had two sons. Kenneth, by all accounts good looking, was blown up in a tank he was commanding in Egypt. My aunt Ruby, Douglas's wife, once suggested that Kenneth and I might have been quite alike. Was he gay, I wondered? No, apparently he was drawn to older women. Not a shrewd judge of character, my aunt!

There was no love in the house at number 10 Sarre Road. My grandmother, Edith Jobson, was completely in thrall to her Victorian husband. The boys had a formal, occasionally hearty relationship with their father but poor Nora was completely ignored. She was told that if she ever met her father in the street he would not acknowledge her. After school she took a secretarial course and later, with good qualifications, got a job with Vauxhall Motors. As well as office work she was sometimes roped in to stand beside the latest little black family saloon for publicity pictures. I have a photograph of her in Princess Margaret shoes, self-consciously opening a car boot. Although by then presumably the possessor of some confidence, she was still a soft target for the silver-tongued motor salesman, ten years her senior, who was to become the father of her children.

The Second World War began soon after my parents got together. FGH joined the Royal Air Force and was posted to Transport Command at RAF St Mawgan in Cornwall. Like a dutiful common-law wife, my mother followed her man and found lodgings in the nearby little town of Lostwithiel. Eventually they moved into a rented house of their own in time for John's birth. In 1945 I was born and FGH was demobbed.

My parents had become very fond of the West Country and decided to settle there. Dad managed to get a job selling cars near Exeter and we moved to a little thatched cottage with no mains water or electricity in a tiny village called Chawleigh, near Chagford, in a beautiful part of North Devon. I hope that in my rapidly approaching dotage I will have some memory of that early period of my life, but for now all I know is that Mummy said I once stormed out of the house in high dudgeon, aged three, vowing never to return. All I took with me in those pre-dolly days was a pile of building bricks. At the appropriate age I joined John at the village primary school, but barely had a chance to carve my initials into my desk before we were on the move again.

Our destination this time was a far cry from the primitive surroundings of Chawleigh. We moved into the old rectory on the Baring Gould estate at Lewtrenchard, just south of the A30 between Oakhampton and Launceston. There was no village as such, just the Elizabethan Lew House, the parish church of great antiquity nearby and a scattering of houses and farms. For no reason that I ever discovered our new home was called The Ramps, although according to legend it had once been Rampenstein. As far as I was concerned it was the grandest place I had ever seen – although, of course, I was only four at the time. But for the Reverend Newman and his wife Eulalia it was considered not nearly grand enough. On taking up his new parish they refused to move into it, and a new eight-bedroom rectory had to be built.

The formal garden of Lew House has a tiny gate at the end of it. Beyond lies a narrow path bordered by wild garlic and lily of the valley that skirts a deep lake. In fact, the inky black water lies at the bottom of an ancient quarry that created the huge escarpment upon which The Ramps was built. But the real puzzle is, when? Like the majority of people with an interest in their surroundings I like to think that I can recognise most periods of architecture, but The Ramps completely defeats me. Its basic construction is brick and timber with a slate roof. The windows are lead lights. On the roof sits a little figure on horseback, probably terracotta, whose significance was once explained to us – but sadly remembered no more. The arrangement of the interior leads me to believe that it was designed for the comfort of one man, possibly even Sabine Baring Gould himself, who served his time as rector there and wrote the hymn 'Onward Christian Soldiers'. This wonderful bachelor pad had one enormous bedroom with a long run of windows on two sides. Across the corridor was a large bathroom. On the half-landing below was a small room that might have been a dressing room. For his use on the ground floor was a morning room, drawing room and dining room. The staircase hall led out to a loggia and garden. The other half of the house was approached through a stone flagged hall with a cloakroom, thence to the kitchen and scullery. Upstairs was a big bedroom (John's) with a door to a wide passageway (mine) beyond which was the landing outside the main bedroom. As a boisterous child I soon discovered that nothing is more delightful than a house with two staircases.

And then there was the garden. Somehow or other my father had agreed to maintain the grounds, paying only a 'peppercorn' rent to the estate for the pleasure of living there. Although it extended to about four acres, some of it was woodland and the rest grass with no flowerbeds. Having bought a serious mowing machine for the majority of the work, he concentrated most of his efforts on the long-abandoned vegetable garden sited just below the house. Rich soil and Herculean efforts soon paid dividends. But for me the glory of the garden was the profusion of daffodils and the white strawberries that grew on the bank in front of the house.

My father's proper job took him to Launceston each day, where he managed a motor car and tractor showroom. John and I were enrolled at Lewdown Primary School, half an hour's climb back to the A30. The school, an Edwardian building, was about a mile from the village centre, sitting at what once may have been an important crossroads. If life's foundations are laid in the early years of school, my thanks must go to Mr and Mrs Millward, who had about them something of Kurt Hahn, Bedales and the Royal Academy of Dramatic Art. They were a Welsh couple in their forties, with two sons. The only other help they had was from Mrs Doige, who fed us. In the best tradition of their homeland, the beginning and end of each day were marked with sturdy hymns – 'Now The Day Is Over' always a favourite. A certain amount of serious learning also took place, but the lynchpins of the year were the season of maypole dancing and the long run-up to the Millward-conceived pantomime, in which everyone at school was given a singing, speaking or dancing part. Mothers rallied round to make costumes for their little darlings, and mine was certainly never outdone when it came to elaborate creations. Whether it was 'Cinderella' or 'Puss in Boots', Mr Millward always adapted the story to include local issues or places, and his considerable songwriting skills were used to pepper lyrics with puns on family names. The single performance at the village hall was a thrilling and nerve-wracking occasion, but was always received with thunderous applause.

I expect most village schools today possess a television set and probably a computer as a matter of course, but I would be surprised if a maypole was regarded by many of them as an essential piece of equipment. In the early 1950s, Lewdown Primary had one that was state of the art. A hole in the middle of the tarmac of the playground was specifically designed to receive its slender, white-painted length. Several afternoons a week, from the end of April to the middle of June, the pole, with its long, brightly coloured ribbons, would be put in place. Research by Mrs Millward had yielded a great number of specially written dances, both for couples and solo dancers. With one eye on the plait, as it worked its way down the pole, we tripped the light fantastic to the accompaniment of a portable gramophone.

That same playground was also the source of a quite different kind of entertainment. Sex. One corner of it had been turned into a makeshift tent. It was low slung with an almost impenetrably dark interior created by layers of old potato sacks. Without exaggeration, it was more difficult to pass through that flap than it is to enter the smartest clubs in St James's. To the envy of everyone else, the only people allowed anywhere near were handsome George 'Buster' Dawe, the pretty blonde brother and sister Richard and Heather Kearsey, and me. The Dawe and Kearsey families owned large adjoining farms called Foxcombe and Beechcombe over towards the edge of Dartmoor. Buster's older brother, Trevor, was a friend and contemporary of John's.

Apart from a few sacks to sit on, the only other thing kept in the tent was a carefully concealed torch. Every dinner hour the four of us would troop into our little hideaway to take part in the daily ritual. The routine was always the same. Heather would lie on some improvised bedding, lift up her skirt and hike down her knickers. One by one each boy would take a turn with the torch, using its strong beam to peer at the lower half of Heather's body. No coercion was ever required – Heather was as curious about her anatomy as we were. Only once did we become more adventurous, and that was when a lavishly illustrated pamphlet was found on a rubbish tip. I seem to remember it being called *Breast-Feeding Baby*, and to our amazement and delight it contained close-up photographs of nipples being scrubbed and babies with happy faces enjoying a milky snack. Needless to say, this revelation necessitated even more undressing for poor Heather. However, a close examination of her hitherto unexamined upper part led us to conclude that Buster stood more chance of satisfying a mewling infant than she did.

During my six years as a pupil at Lewdown we only twice played host to visitors from abroad. The first was a large, happy lass from West Africa whose family was staying temporarily in the area. Her presence was responsible for a great deal of head-scratching among the potato sack research team, as we had never seen a coloured person before. After much debate we decided against Richard's idea of inviting her to join one of our torchlight vigils, settling instead for close observation in the classroom and playground. After several days' persistent eye-balling, especially during PE, we reached the conclusion that although her skin colour was largely brown, her private parts must definitely be white.

The other foreigner arrived in the aftermath of the Hungarian Revolution. She was a bright, plain girl called Gizella Zverko, and was not regarded as torch-fodder by the Privates on Parade. Twice over the years I have read about her in the newspapers. The first time was when she was revealed as the leading scientist in her particular field, and then again when she married a peer of the realm with an ancient title.

Turning right out of the gate from Dad's vegetable garden, the road led up the gradual incline past the Lew House walled garden, and the turning to the church and main gates of the house. Getting steeper, it passed the new rectory and a few hundred yards further on encountered a Y-junction. The right-hand fork was our route to school, whilst the one to the left led to the village of Lewdown. Just beyond that point was the new house of our GP, Dr Stephenson. Although she went to a private school and led a rather sheltered life, his daughter Jane and I had become good friends. I called to see her quite often and we played together in the garden. It was all very innocent, until one day we found ourselves sitting on the roof of the summerhouse. To my great surprise she turned to me and uttered that immortal line, 'I'll show you mine if you show me yours!' Little did she know that I was no stranger to a vagina, but I went along with the suggestion nevertheless. After all, no one before had ever shown the remotest interest in what I might be hiding. We duly carried out our inspection and, as was customary on these occasions, no physical contact actually took place. I can't help thinking that had I been older (I was about eight) or wiser I might have started wondering how sexual intercourse ever happened. We 'did it' again a couple of times and then she was sent away to another school and I never saw her again.

However, I did hear that soon after these events took place her father abandoned medicine and took Holy Orders. Overreacting slightly, I would have thought.

Meanwhile, back at the school my sexual journey was going off in a completely different direction. Looking back it is obvious that Buster was the first in a long line of completely heterosexual, butch blokes on whom I had a crush. Having said that, it is also true that he sought my company; but probably only because I represented the other side of the coin from his 'silence and strength'. In the course of the school day we moved around the building for different lessons. As it was all very informal we could sit where we liked and best friends often chose to be side by side. Buster and I did just that whenever we could. Knowing how, as an adult, I shrink from the concept of making the first move, it still amazes me that during one particular lesson my hand worked its way up the inside of his trouser leg (the short variety, it hardly needs to be said) until it made contact with his willy (the long variety, I am happy to say). And there it remained for the duration of the lesson. When the need to write arose I would discreetly withdraw, only to slip greedily back as soon as the coast was clear. Although there were many of these exciting encounters there was never even the hint of an erection on either side, nor word exchanged, just my hand paying mute respect to his manhood (or having a great time holding his dick, which is how I really want to think of it). No reciprocal gesture ever took place, but neither were my advances rebuffed.

Following the 11-plus examination Buster, like a number of the sons of wealthy local farmers, went off to boarding school. I once heard that in later life he became a policeman and won the George Medal for an act of great courage.

My friendship with him and the Kearsey children was also a great part of my social life out of school. For the most part it was centred on Beechcombe, the Kearsey family farm about three miles from Lewtrenchard. The road to it passed behind the gardens of Lew House and in front of the entrance to some deep, dark caves I had only once had the courage to enter. Having pedalled furiously away from that part of my journey I would freewheel down into the valley once more and through the tiny hamlet of Lewmill, which nestled around the Dower House. This, the loveliest of Baring Gould tenanted houses, was occupied by a family called Nelson. After about half a mile Beechcombe Farm hove into view, sitting beneath the foothills that were the edge of Dartmoor. There was never any traffic except occasionally the giant black Kearsey Humber, CUP 419, oozing its way between hedgerows, forcing me to flatten the cowparsley and ragwort. The best time to be there was late summer, when the barns were full of mountains of sweet-smelling hay bales, a sight no intrepid climber could resist. With the harvest safely gathered in, attention turned again to the fields whose crop had just been given up. Men with flaming torches attacked the stubbly ground – 'swaling' they called it – filling the air with plumes of smoke. The lines of flame criss-crossed hundreds of acres, clearing the ground and thrilling child onlookers.

Until I decided to trawl seriously through the tattered remnants of my memory, I had always looked back on those years at The Ramps and thought of them as representing the first of the rather solitary periods of my life. I can see now that although I was only ever alone by choice, I spent a great deal of time living in my head. My mother, always keen for us to have an outing together – her on a bike, me propelling my scooter – had warmth but no communication skills. She and my father had nothing in common and he looked to John for any sort of companionship. It was only Fritz and Franz, the dachshunds, and Percy, the cat, for whom we all cared.

What I loved doing best was staking out my own little kingdom, and reigning over it as the all-powerful 'Atzikana'. Beech trees, with their fat, low branches, were the best territory and I would climb to dangerous heights to mark out my claim. Long sections of the river bank were also mine and nobody else's. When bad weather forced me to stay inside, I held meetings of the AAAA (the Actors, Authors & Artists Association) in the little room on the half-landing. To give her credit, my mother saw the direction of my interests and hoped to satisfy my imagination by buying me a small theatre and glove and string puppets. At first they were an absorbing diversion, but in the end the limitations of their appearance and movement frustrated me.

Nothing daunted, my mother's next move was to enrol me in the first of the ballet classes arranged by Mrs Millward to be held each week in the ballroom at Lew House. I should point out at this stage that the House was being run as an hotel by Mr and Mrs Paynter and their son Alan. Elsie Paynter was a warm and wonderful human being, whose twin loves were animals and cooking. Her many dogs included a giant St Bernard, which gave me rides and fought with a gang of cats that shared with me a fascination for the kitchen worktops where many a titbit could be found. Her husband and son were never much in evidence and she seemed to run the place with only the help of Ken the rather morose Scots waiter.

I was the only boy in a class of about eight girls. We were taught by Miss Negus, an elegantly slender creature with the trademark bone structure and tight bun. I enjoyed the lessons and was very pleased when Miss Negus said I had a natural aptitude for the subject. After two or three months she suggested that I might even think of taking up dancing as a career. Why not try for a scholarship to the Royal Ballet School? I rushed home to tell Mummy what she had said. Initially she was thrilled, but her face clouded slightly when she trotted out the familiar phrase, 'I'll have to discuss it with your father.' The vehemence of his reaction – along the lines of, 'No son of mine' etc. – took even my mother by surprise and scuppered my chance of a life in tutu and tights. As it happens, I grew to be six-foot four, which meant that even the New York City Ballet might only have found a role for me as *The Nutcracker*'s Christmas tree.

To make up for that little artistic setback I threw my energies into The Junior Drama League, the cadet branch of something, probably now defunct, called The British Drama League. They received my application for membership with great enthusiasm, even suggesting that I become the West Country delegate. I regarded this as a great honour and morale booster, even after it later emerged that I was the only paid-up member in the whole of Devon and Cornwall. Sadly my pocket money never stretched as far as a train ticket to London to attend any of their jollies, but I did enjoy receiving all the bumf.

Whilst I was doing all this nancying around, John was happily engaged in sticking stamps into albums and 'blowing' birds' eggs. The two-and-a-half-year difference in our ages was by no means the only thing by which we were separated. John was much taller than myself, well built and rather conventionally good looking. Whereas his name was sturdy, mine was odd and cissy – moreover, both he and my parents called me Bim. John's eyesight was perfect, whereas mine required distinctly unglamorous National Health wire-framed spectacles that clung to big sticky-out ears. Understandably, he made damned sure our paths seldom crossed during schooltime. However, when one day in the playground I saw him being provoked into a fight by a couple of notorious bullies, my sense of injustice propelled me into their midst with flailing fists. Believe it or not, they fled. This was a completely uncharacteristic thing to have done, not least because most of the time I longed for him to fall fatally out of a tree, or witness his outstretched hand slip beneath the waters of the lake, thereby ensuring that I was the only son and heir. Though God knows what I thought I was going to inherit.

Quite unexpectedly the opportunity to put him to death myself arrived when Dad gave us each a Webley air pistol one Christmas. Bizarre presents for two young boys at the best of times, let alone in the Season of Peace and Goodwill to all Men. To begin with we set up targets in the garden and competed to score the most bull's-eyes. Needless to say, John won every time, but I considered my lazy left eye a great handicap. Once that novelty wore off we took to the woods, pursuing each other through the trees, having agreed beforehand that shots were to be wide of the mark. These were games that could so easily have ended in disaster, especially given the volatility of our relationship. However, the worst that happened was that we both suffered slight pellet wounds to our arms. When Mum discovered what we had been doing and inspected the damage, our weapons were immediately confiscated.

My father actively discouraged visitors to the house, and there was certainly never any question of guests for lunch or dinner. The absence of a social life must have been quite tough for Mummy, who really only had Elsie Paynter as a friend to call on occasionally. But it was the Women's Institute, that remarkable network of 'Earth Mothers', that kept her occupied outside the home. She never missed the weekly meeting ('all jam and Jerusalem' as someone once described them) held in Lewdown Village Hall. When news of an invention called the knitting machine reached our far-flung outpost she ordered one immediately, putting it to work making sweaters for her menfolk. So proficient did she become that she was even persuaded to demonstrate her skills in front of the other ladies at a packed session. In no time at all her ability as a performer came to be known by other branches in the area and she was invited to be a guest speaker. I sometimes went with her to give moral support and to model the chunkier numbers.

Probably as a result of these experiences, the first stirrings of an interest in clothes were just beginning to arise in me. But unfortunately, the ones I wanted to wear were my mother's. Lack of money meant that her wardrobe was not extensive. Sadly, she also wore trousers quite often – no fun there for me. However, I found one or two frocks and blouses quite acceptable and even a couple of tweed suits, albeit bordering on the severe. But my all-time favourite was a heavily pleated paisley skirt in which I'd twirl for ages in front of a full-length mirror. I am sure I must have avoided being 'dragged' up in front of Dad or John, but Mummy was no problem at all. In fact, she was very pleased that I had a new hobby and even produced some outfits that I hadn't considered. Although not interested in jewellery herself she had inherited some from her mother, which was kept in a rather nice leather-covered jewel case. The versatility of her poppets were a constant fascination, as was a long necklace of seed pearls. Among the other treasures were a large cameo brooch and a plain silver bangle. Oh how much I must have needed make-up! But Mummy kept very little. I did dabble with a little lipstick and foundation, but decided I didn't like having a sticky face.

The frequent visits to play with my friend Jammy provided marvellous excuses for appearing 'costumed' in public. He shared my interest in uninhibited fantasy and role-playing, though to a more controlled extent. During the long summer months we put on regular carnivals as well as circuses with the reluctant assistance of the three pets. The climax of any of these performances was always my appearance as Queen of the May. Sitting, arrayed in almost everything that Mum wasn't wearing at the time, on a chair on top of Dad's four-wheeled garden barrow, I would be hauled around the garden by a sweating Jammy as the cheers of loyal subjects rang in my ears.

In spite of a healthy dislike of my father and the countryside, Grandma Jobson came sometimes to stay. She was a charming old lady and a keen knitter who always presented her grandchildren with home-grown socks and a one pound note on birthdays and at Christmas. As far as I was concerned the real pleasure of her visits was the chance to wear amber and jet and adopt the older look. Not content with that, Jammy and I even made money out of the old girl by arranging jumble sales for which she was the largest contributor. On sale days suitable items were collected from Mummy and Grandma in the morning and laid out on a trestle table in the garden ready for the afternoon's fun to begin. At three o'clock I would declare the jumble sale open and then take my place behind the stall to deal with the rush of eager purchasers. Although prices were very reasonable we had to contend with a lot of consumer resistance, especially when the two of them were asked to part with good money for things they thought they had owned for years.

Jammy was one of the three sons of Maurice and Marcia James and they lived in a rented bungalow near the village of Coryton, about three miles' hard pedalling from The Ramps. He went to Lewdown, but was a year or so younger than me and not considered tent-worthy. In spite of that we were very close, spending a lot of time at each other's houses. Maurice had once been handsome, but never successful. Like FGH he had had to move around in pursuit of poorly paid selling jobs. The last of these that I remember was with a firm making boxes of matches. In spite of having very little to live on, they were a warm and friendly family who gave me honorary membership. They also provided me with a diet to which I was not accustomed: rich cakes. Many's the time, as a famished cyclist, I burst through the kitchen door to find Auntie Marcia attacking one of those large, yellow mixing bowls with a wooden spoon until its contents were beaten into submission. The mixture was often chocolate, certainly always delicious. When the process moved on to the next stage, spoon and bowl were passed to me for a major licking.

Approaching The Ramps by car meant negotiating a manky pot-holed drive. It started at the remains of entrance gates that stood beside a little thatched cottage. This was wonderfully rustic, but gate lodge it was not. Further along, the road meandered past a couple more houses until it petered out at a ford over the river, a tributary of the River Lyd, at the valley's bottom. This was definitely one of my favourite playing places – an old footbridge and gravelly beach providing lots of entertainment. Anyone venturing as far as this had just been through a minefield, the road in front of Ramps Farm, home to the Horn family. The main danger was the pack of sheepdogs that approached strangers at speed, barking furiously and giving chase to any motorist who tried to evade them. On foot you risked slithering ankle-deep through cowshit, for the Horn cows produced the juiciest pats I have ever encountered. The feathered members of the livestock community also contributed to the general squalor, when they were not tearing at the last vestiges of lawn beneath the giant monkey puzzle in the front garden. Judging by the quality of the glorious brown eggs, this was a diet that suited them very well. Any that could be spared were bought by John or I when one of us made the daily journey to collect a small churn of milk. On a good day, which meant arriving clean and unscathed, we were met at the back door by a careworn Mrs Horn who doled out the goodies. Although not an old woman, she had little concern for her appearance. Her long face might have been conceived by Modigliani and her lumpy body painted by one of those early Dutchmen. By contrast, Mr Horn smiled and bellowed rather a lot. We knew that the raised voice betokened anger, but at a normal level it made very little sense at all. When they were not at school, he was helped around the farm by his sons Roger and Edward. Although they were our contemporaries, John and I did not find them exactly riveting company. In spite of that we managed to get into a few scrapes together and humped some bales with them at harvest time.

I never knew what sort of work FGH did as a flight sergeant in Transport Command during the war, but I suspect it was to do with wireless and communications. Certainly he was always very interested in that sort of thing, telling us that as a young man he had made crystal sets and fiddled for hours with short-wave radios (whatever they are). The obvious extension of this was his fascination with the idea of television. Some time during 1952 he arrived home from work one day, staggering under the weight of an enormous box that proved to contain what was known as a TV set. As none of us had ever seen one before, I guess we all expected different things from it. Aged seven I was sensible enough to know that it would be a bit more sophisticated than my puppet theatre, but on the other hand how were lots of little people going to survive in such a small space? Sadly, the reality was bitterly disappointing. On the rare occasions when there was any picture at all it usually showed a waterfall, a potter's wheel or a grinning schoolgirl. The rest of the time the screen seemed to be filled with the image of a boring fat man called something like Dotheboy or Bumblebee.

As far as I was concerned the advent of television was not a life-changer. I still preferred to let rip with my imagination rather than stare at a little grey screen. However, in the summer of 1953 my attitude changed dramatically with the announcement that the Queen's Coronation was to be televised as it happened. Thanks to Mum, a staunch royalist, I had for some time been interested in the doings of the Royal Family. A glimpse of Queen Mary at the Festival of Britain and a closer encounter with the Duchess of Kent at the Royal Cornwall Show had probably set me off. To my great surprise, Dad was persuaded to allow us to invite some of our friends to watch with us on the great day. We knew that we had the only set for miles around and people were thrilled to be asked. The response was so great that we could have sold tickets. Thirty-five loyal subjects crammed into our little sitting room on 3rd June and I for one was spellbound.

Only two invitations were spurned, and that was by Guy and Eulalia Newman. The reverend gentleman declared that they would not be coming because they thought that it was black magic. Did he mean the coronation service or the television transmission? We hoped it was the latter. In point of fact, my poor sensitive mother thought there might have been another reason for his refusal. It had lodged in her memory that when he had first come to call upon us, I had behaved discourteously. When she greeted him at the door she had introduced herself and urged me, as her son Guy, to shake hands. He reacted by saying, 'My name is Guy, too.' He stayed for about an hour, taking tea and quizzing Mummy about her religious beliefs. As he left, saying goodbye to my mother, he turned to me with the words, 'Goodbye Guy.' Without hesitation I replied, 'Goodbye Guy.' He didn't look best pleased.

Mummy had two great-aunts, Kitty and Etta, who shared a house in Torquay. Kitty had married a surgeon and spent many years with him in India. Etta had never married, a fact that surprised me not at all. Even allowing for her being ninety years old when we first met, it was inconceivable that at any age another human being could have found her attractive. When her sister, for many years a widow, died she accepted Mummy's offer of making her home with us at The Ramps. The morning room, ground floor and close to the loo, was filled with her possessions and arranged as a bedsitting room. With the seaside house sold, all the bigger pieces of furniture went as well. She brought with her only the smaller things, as well as pictures and ornaments. Unfortunately for their heirs, Aunt Kitty shared a passion with her husband, Mr Pearson, for benevolent mutilation. In his case, the tool was a scalpel. For her it was a chisel. Among the many pieces of furniture that surround me at this moment are an eighteenth-century longcase clock, a seventeenth-century oak coffer, a corner cupboard and a mirror framed in walnut. All these much-cherished things would have been even more pleasing to the eye if dear old Kitty had chosen embroidery as a hobby rather than wood carving.

Aunt Etta's grey hair was scraped back into a tight bun. Although the rest of her body was not under strict control, the look was beefy rather than blubberous. Slightly bowed legs (not so much as to fail to stop a pig in a passage) were assisted by a silver-topped ebony cane. This instrument was used to agitate a perfectly happy fire or for prodding Fritz or Franz when she thought they were about to show their 'rudies'. Not once did a kind or friendly word escape her lips and, thanks to an electric bell rigged up by Dad, Mummy was at her beck and call twenty-four hours a day. When she died, after two years with us, Mummy's health had deteriorated to the extent that she was sent off to a sanatorium with suspected TB.

Aunt Etta's death was a first for both of us, and I am sure I thought at the time that it should have been a good deal sadder. But for a while at least the Huntings reaped the benefit. Mummy's illness proved to be only a shadow on the lung, and she made a full recovery. In her will, Aunt Etta left her estate to Mum without a mention of cats home or parish church. With this new-found wealth my father decided to go it alone and start his own business, ponderously named 'Hunting's Agricultural Supplies'. Like so many of us, before and since, he may have always wanted to run his own show and saw it as a route to riches. But before long he was made aware of the fact that a silver tongue and an easy manner are no substitutes for a grasp of accountancy and a degree of business acumen. Mummy supported him all the way. While he was criss-crossing the county chatting up the farmers, she was at her typewriter sending out letters and publicity material. For a while things went quite well. Small farmers, notoriously wary of change, liked dealing with someone whose track record they knew. Orders for parts for ploughs and hoeing machines flooded in. But the big boys who ordered tractors and combine harvesters by the brace had discovered the discount word, and there Dad just couldn't compete.

The cameo brooch was the first thing I missed. This was followed by Aunt Kitty's silver gilt dressing-table set, which always looked rather out of place. When asked about these things Mummy explained that they had been sold to help Dad's business. She went on to say that other bits and pieces would have to go as well. A kind jeweller in Plymouth was taking them off her hands in return for 'large' sums of money. I went with her on the train to Plymouth one day, armed with the black-and-gold lacquer mah-jong set, a dagger with a curled blade in a gold-and-silver scabbard and a long-barrelled rifle inlaid with ivory. I imagine the proceeds from their sale kept the show on the road for a few more weeks.

In due course, everything with an obvious value had been sold. I suppose I should be grateful that there was no market for 'later decorated period furniture' or the daubs of an amateur late nineteenth-century artist in oils. My flat would be bleak without them.

My father admitted defeat, just before the creditors moved in. Although by now in his early sixties, he managed to find a job as manager of a showroom selling motorcars in the town of Liskeard, just over the border in Cornwall. A house in the nearby village of Doublebois – always pronounced Dubbleboys – was included in the deal. For my part, although I was sad to leave my enchanted valley, I knew it was time for a change. Aged eleven, I had failed the 11-plus and followed John to a hideous secondary modern school in Oakhampton. It was a Philistine establishment with no maypole and a heavy emphasis on the twin horrors of rugby and showers. I loathed it and could not wait to leave.

Our new home was The Slate House, a nondescript three-storey building faced with slate, that sat beside the main Paddington to Penzance line, close to the station. Of the house itself only a few memories survive, and they are mostly, as an unseasoned traveller, entwined with my first impressions of the glamour of travel. The house sat at the summit of a very steep railway incline, and as *The Cornishman* or *The Cornish Riviera Express* in gleaming chocolate-and-yellow livery passed by, braking heavily or gasping for breath, I was presented with a clear view of the smart folk sitting at their candle-lit tables in the dining car. I was happy if a cheery wave was returned. Less vicarious pleasure was derived by standing, enveloped in oceans of steam, on the nearby bridge that straddled the line.

Without the benefit of trees or a large garden I found myself in strange surroundings with nothing much to pass the time. John had moved in to cigarette cards in a big way, and I briefly considered the idea of something called autograph hunting. But after some thought I came to the conclusion that west of Plymouth there were very few names to pursue. Little did I know that A.L. Rowse and Daphne du

Maurier were near neighbours – and how lucky they were that I had never heard of them. The origins of the next hobby that finally came my way are lost in the mists of time. I can only think that life beside a railway line pushed my imagination into travel mode and thoughts of foreign lands. As a family our only knowledge of the world beyond our shores was gleaned from the *Daily Telegraph*. Mummy and Dad read it avidly and I riffled through it from time to time. But at some stage I must have decided that newspapers would be an introduction to foreign lands. I remembered from visits to London that in those days newsagents stocked only the home-grown varieties, with exceptions like the *New York Times* and *Le Figaro*. The only alternative I could think of was to write begging letters to the embassies in London asking for examples of their finest newsprint. The response was almost always immediate and very rewarding. Our postman must have been very intrigued by the quantity of packages that arrived, addressed to me, on an almost daily basis. I found the whole process terribly exciting and treated each new arrival with great reverence. The yield was usually one paper, presumably the equivalent of *The Times*, per embassy. But communist countries, desperate perhaps for a contact in the Royal Duchy, would overwhelm me with magazines and pamphlets containing photographs of marching boy soldiers and children swinging Indian clubs. Every new arrival had its pages turned with great solemnity before it was consigned to the growing number of heaps in the corner of my bedroom. Bound with string, these small forests were loyally moved around by Mummy from house to house, long after they had been forgotten by me. When she finally left Cornwall, we had a big bonfire of them.

Doublebois was too small to contain any possible playmates, which meant that I spent most of my spare time in the much larger nearby village of Dobwalls. Here there was a small council estate, a church, a filling station and a village hall that turned itself into a cinema on Saturday nights. But most importantly it had its own industry; a factory making fat, gutsy buses called Rowe Hillmaster. Mr Rowe, the man behind the business, also owned the petrol station and lived beside it with his wife and two children. The son, Kenny, was about three years younger than me, whilst Wendy must have been about five years older. Wendy was attractive and fancied by all the young bucks. But she was also the apple of her father's eye and was being groomed to take over the business. He carefully monitored her social life, fending off unsuitable advances. In spite of that I was always sure that she was sweet on Tony Brenn, a handsome young motorbike-riding mechanic. I expect I was quite keen on Mr Brenn myself, especially when, as his pillion passenger, he urged me to hold onto him tightly.

This was the nearest thing to a sexual encounter I had achieved since those precocious episodes with young Buster. All that early promise had petered out. However, at about this time I added yet another layer to my inner confusion by falling in love. The object of my devotion was a sweet-faced girl called Diane Yeo. The mental picture I have of her shows short curly hair, large eyes and big bosoms. An interest in ladies' upper chest areas had been quietly brewing for some time; I am not sure if it could be regarded as healthy or unhealthy. Although Diane and I spent a lot of time together, the physical side of the relationship never got beyond hand-holding. She may well have been itching for a bit of fumble and caress, but if she was, it was left to another member of my family to do the business. At the same time that her interest in me was on the wane, kind friends were quick to point out that she was often to be seen in the company of my brother. Sure enough, they did have a fling, but it was cut short when he achieved the first of his ambitions. Having reached the age of fifteen he went off to RAF Cosford as a boy entrant. His departure signalled the end of what little closeness there had been between us. Periods of leave brought us together from time to time after that, but we would meet almost as strangers. The close proximity of childhood was left behind and there were no common interests to bind us as young men.

Dad's employers in Liskeard were an old established business called Blamey & Morcom, run by members of two prominent families. John Morcom, a fat man with a bald head, was the senior partner. He was known to have several wives as well as an interest in 'rough trade'. A rather more predictable passion was for flashy cars, with the favourite being a two-tone black-and-red Consul with tail fins.

Philip Blamey was a much more patrician figure, whose sons I used to play with. His wife is a talented painter of flowers and widely acclaimed.

After a couple of years we moved from Doublebois into Liskeard itself. I have no idea if this meant promotion for Dad, but it certainly represented a huge leap in our standard of accommodation. Our new home was a colossal Edwardian pile, the embellishments of which included towers, cupolas and ornamental balconies. It had been built for his own occupation by a local builder called Mr Cubitt. Although he called it, rather endearingly, 'Pencubitt', I would have thought 'Whirlpool' more appropriate, as it swallowed all his money before he was able to move in. It was taken off his hands by B&M and used to house their senior staff. I realise now that the vast majority of families in those days never owned their own homes. Like us, they either rented or lived in a tied house that went with the job. At least we were lucky enough to have a few sticks of furniture, although not nearly enough to furnish our new Xanadu. Mummy, who was always a keen arranger of furniture, did her best to provide a degree of comfort in the smaller rooms on the ground floor. Upstairs, beyond the well-proportioned rooms on the first floor, the house became a maze of attics and large cupboards. Tucked away there was the sole, and pretty basic, bathroom. My father used to use this facility once a week, emerging to proclaim, 'I am the cleanest man in the house.' One evening as the ritual progressed, I stole up to the door and lowered myself in front of the keyhole. I will never know if the urge to spy on a portly gentleman in his sixties, who was also my father, was based on sexual desire or simple curiosity. Through the steam I could see him standing in the bath, facing towards the door. His right hand was wielding the bar of soap with great vigour, while the left made his 'tackle' available for cleansing and unwitting display. I remember it being pretty impressive. However, although I may resemble my father in some ways, sadly, the likeness is confined to facial features!

At Liskeard County Secondary School I was once again a member of an informal gang that consisted of five other boys: Chris Taper, Alec Stephens, Brian Kent and Philip Ugalde. My best friends were the tall and handsome Chris and Alec. Philip was chunky and taciturn, whilst Brian had a chirpy jack-the-lad personality. Nothing even vaguely sexual took place between us, and in fact we spent our dinner hour walking round the town, buying sweets and ice-creams. I had a dark side to me at the time when it came to self-financing. As this was a time of no pocket money from my parents, I resorted to helping myself to the change in my father's trouser pockets as they hung behind his bedroom door at the end of each day. These ill-gotten gains supplied me not only with confectionery, but also the means to add a new excitement to my life. This came in the form of magazines with names like *Spick 'n' Span*, which showed close-up photographs of busty ladies in revealing poses. Having smuggled them into the house, they were studied closely, but never with any accompanying release on my part. When the collection outgrew the limited number of hiding places in my bedroom I resorted to sliding them under the lino on the floor of any number of rooms that were never used.

As far as schoolwork was concerned it was by now perfectly obvious that I was a dead loss. Basic arithmetic was certainly beyond my grasp, and even interesting subjects like history and geography defied my powers of concentration. It was only English and Drama for which I showed any prowess at all. In these I was aided and encouraged by the formidable Miss Osborne. She was a woman whose age was always a source of speculation and even confounded someone like me who had older parents to use as a yardstick. I suppose clues must have been there in the carefully applied make-up and tight chestnut perm that was just a shade too dark. Her dignified presence was enhanced by a twinset and discreet skirt that touched base well below the knee. Jewellery consisted of a short rope of pearls and delicate flower earrings and a brooch made of what looked like hand-painted china. In spite of her age no other female member of staff was better presented or had such a terrific figure, a fact that was not lost on the wretched menfolk with whom she enjoyed the occasional flirtation. Poor young, unattached Mr Gilbert blushed to his roots whenever they met in front of the class. The worldly art master, Mr Tynan gave her a wide berth.

Miss Osborne and I got along famously, even though my feelings were sometimes mixed when I was chosen yet again to stand up and recite a poem for the enjoyment of my peers. Her topic for essays, I like to think, inspired us all and no one could have been unaffected by her enthusiasm for the works of good, readable authors.

I greatly regret that many years later I passed up the chance of meeting her again. The opportunity presented itself on a platform at Truro Station. As a nineteen- or twenty-year-old footman I was sitting on the royal train waiting for the Queen to return after opening the new hospital. In those days the Sergeant Footman rather sweetly chose a chap with local connections to go as part of the entourage if the Queen was doing a bit of business in the area from which he came. Among the crowd milling around and trying to peer through the window I suddenly caught sight of an unmistakable figure. I rushed out into the corridor and watched from the door as Miss Osborne marshalled her group of pupils. As so often happens in my life, courage failed me at the last moment. Only my eyes followed that distinctive hair-do as it disappeared into the distance.

In 1958, when I was thirteen years old, FGH found yet another purveyor of cars and tractors who was prepared to take him on as the main man. Our destination this time took us deeper into Cornwall, and close to some distant relations of Mum's. For the duration of this assignment we were installed, close to the centre of St Austell, in a pretty house on East Hill next to a petrol station that was part of Dad's bailiwick.

My very last school was a nasty modern building in which I was to learn four things that were to equip me for life in the world of work. They were how to light a Bunsen burner, decorate a Christmas cake, the rudiments of ballroom dancing and the part of Shylock in *The Merchant of Venice*.

Mevagissey, a picture-postcard fishing village, was on the coast a few miles away. It had been home for years to Mum's second cousin, Jim Weston, and his wife Marjorie. Jim was a bit of a mystery, not least because his name should have been Jobson, the same as Mum's. They lived at Polkirt House, a fine Georgian building that dominated the hill on the 'money side' above the harbour. The 'sunny side' opposite was made up of terraces of quaint little cottages. One of the narrow streets that threaded its way between them was called Shittyalleyup. With very little help from her husband, Marjorie ran the house during the summer as a renowned bed-and-breakfast business. When not drinking with his fishermen friends Jim acted as a keen auxiliary coastguard. Marjorie's glorious sister, Pat, spent her last days living in a little cottage next to Polkirt House. She was a stalwart lass from Maida Vale who dedicated her life to SSAFA, the forces charity. Paralysing arthritis overwhelmed her in the end; a lengthy *Times* obituary paid her great tribute.

During our time at The Ramps, Dad had apparently learnt that his wife had died. This information was joyous news for Mum, who had always been unhappy about her common-law status, especially when her inquisitive son questioned her about wedding photographs. Under pressure from Mum he agreed that there was nothing now to prevent them legitimising their relationship at Tavistock registry office. Although she persisted he always made excuses, and the deed was never done.

Soon after our arrival in St Austell it became perfectly obvious that all was not well in the Hunting household. Dad would often arrive home late in the evening and, though they tried to conceal it, major rows took place. The worst part for me was the telephone calls Mum received that would reduce her to tears. One day, in great distress, she confided that they were being made by a woman Dad was seeing. The object of the calls was to plead with Mum to leave Dad, as they were very much in love. This sorry state of affairs went on for many months, but somehow they patched it up and life returned to an uneasy normality.

I suspect the reason for our last move as a family was not unconnected to the crisis that had disrupted our lives. With Melton Mowbray in Leicestershire as our destination it certainly looked as if distance was meant to be part of the healing process. It was also probably not just a coincidence that Dad was returning to the part of the country where he had been brought up.

All of a sudden, aged fifteen and a half, I was finally old enough to leave school, an event to which I had been looking forward for some time. What I was not so excited about was the prospect of finding a job when my only qualification was a Royal Society of Arts pass in English. In recent years I had reluctantly decided that I had neither the looks nor the ability to consider acting, although it had always been my dream. Funnily enough, in the light of subsequent events, it was the idea of butchery or buttling that appealed most. As it turned out, the only job I was able to find, once we had been in Melton Mowbray a couple of days, was one for which I was physically, mentally and sexually completely unsuited. The organisation rash enough to take me on was a business with a familiar ring to it. They were called Sharman & Ladbury and their stock in trade was tractors and cars. But not for me the easy money and sharp suits of the showroom. Oh no, I was chosen to do something quite different. Anyone wanting a flange or sprocket would find me wearing a dirty grey overall, standing behind the counter of the agricultural stores doling out spare parts. As jobs go I couldn't have hated it more and it was only the fleeting smile of a handsome mechanic that got me through each day. After six interminable months I found alternative employment that was rather more my cup of tea. I was taken on by Teals, MM's swankiest gents' outfitters. As a shrine to DAKS and a temple of cavalry twill my new surroundings could not have been in greater contrast to the utilitarian world I left behind. The High Priest was a Franklin Engleman lookalike, skilled in the use of a tape measure and expert at re-folding an unwanted shirt, complete with its twenty-eight pins. His acolyte, Mrs Moore-Coltman, was married to a policeman (she must have pioneered the use of the more acceptable 'officer') and would rather not have been working in a shop. I kept to myself the fact that she was my first encounter with a living double barrel. The work was pleasant enough, and with an hour for lunch I was able to zip home to eat with Mum. It is rather frightening to think that I might actually have found my niche. Had 'things' not been different, I suppose I could easily be there to this day.

But once again all was not as it should have been at Chateau Hunting. Dad had taken against me, big time. He was probably missing his girlfriend and resented having to put up with Mum and me. As we had never been very close, I was the obvious target for his pent-up frustration and general unpleasantness. Even though I tried to avoid him as much as possible, the house was too small for our lives to be lived separately. The last straw came one evening when I heard him loudly complaining about me to Mum. He didn't, in fact, refer to me by name, but called me 'the creature' instead. At that moment I decided that I had no choice but to leave home. I packed what few clothes I had into a small suitcase, wrote a letter to Mum and slipped quietly out of the house. It was about eight o'clock when I arrived at the station and thankfully I didn't have too long to wait for a train. I sank into a seat, my mind racing. Everything had happened so quickly that the enormity of the step I had just taken was only just beginning to sink in. In spite of that I could not suppress a frisson of excitement at the thought of being in London in just a few hours.

Moving to London had always been an ambition of mine, but of course I had expected to do it after careful planning and with a job and a home to go to. Having relations there was a great help when it came to the visits we had made over the years. Usually we stayed with Grandma at her flat in Fordwych Road, but on one epic occasion we took over Uncle Douglas and Aunt Ruby's house in Hampstead Garden Suburb for a week while they were on holiday. They lived quite comfortably, but there was an understandable air of sadness about the place. A wall in the dining room was covered in a mural painted by their talented son David. He had been studying medicine at university when he discovered that he was suffering from a rare and incurable disease. One fateful day while he was staying with his parents at 51 Meadway, Ruby returned home from the school where she was head teacher, to find David lying dead on the floor of the sealed kitchen, with his head in the gas oven. Michael, their other child, had a difficult birth that left him with irreversible brain damage. Although much loved by his parents, he is happiest at his special school, where the care and facilities are first rate. Whilst it is difficult for me to understand how people come to terms with two such terrible tragedies, I know that Ruby and Douglas enriched their lives with the support of close friends and through their work in local politics and for good causes.

Having arrived at St Pancras I used my limited knowledge of local geography to find my way to the big YMCA in Tottenham Court Road. I was happy that my bed for the night cost only seven and six, as it was just about all the money I had. The next morning I set off on foot to see Grandma.

Fordwych Road would be best described by estate agents as 'a quiet, tree-lined residential street'. They would almost certainly not add that 'its proximity to Kilburn would never allow it to be smart'. But it has seen better times, flourishing again with the wholesale gentrification that took place in the seventies and eighties. The flats were built by Granddad with the compensation he received after the war when the old house was destroyed by a bomb. Grandma occupied the one on the first floor. She was obviously pleased to see me and welcomed me with a big hug. I used her telephone to ring Mum and tell her that I was in good shape. She sounded relieved and asked if there was anything I needed. The only thing I could think of was my bicycle, and she promised to send it down on the train when I had found somewhere to stay. Grandma gave me some money – a gift not a loan, she insisted. Looking around her cosy sitting room, I couldn't help remarking that I thought it looked different. Had she, I asked, rearranged the furniture? No, she replied, some things were missing because she had not had a chance to replace them since the two burglaries. She had been robbed twice in the last six months, the last time only a week ago. Returning from shopping one morning, just before lunch, she reached the path that led to the main entrance to see a man carrying a TV set and a suitcase struggling to get through the double doors. She rushed forward to help and managed to hold open one of the doors, enabling him to squeeze through. As he did so, she exclaimed brightly, 'How funny, I've got a television set just like that.' When she reached the first floor and saw that the door had been kicked in, she realised that she hadn't any longer.

With my new-found wealth I indulged in a bus to the West End. In my search for a job and somewhere to live I decided to target the big hotels. After all, they might provide accommodation as well as work. For some reason the Savoy was top of my list of grand hostelries, and so I started there. Having walked past the wonderfully elegant main entrance in the Strand, I found my way to the back, where the surroundings were rather less salubrious. I negotiated overflowing dustbins before reaching a scruffy door marked 'Staff'. Just inside, a man stared at me from behind a glass partition.

'Can I help you?' he enquired unconvincingly.

'Yes please,' said I, 'I'm looking for a job.'

Looking puzzled he continued, 'What sort of job?'

'I'd like to be a page boy,' I replied innocently.

'You are too tall,' he told me, happily. In fact, in flat shoes I was a tad under six foot.

'What about a job as a porter?' I persisted.

'How old are you?' he responded, in a voice now consumed with boredom.

'Fifteen and a half,' I told him.

'You're too young,' he exclaimed, triumphantly.

It was many years before I returned once more to the Savoy Hotel, but it was a visit I infinitely preferred to the first. The occasion was a cabaret performance in the restaurant by that feisty little French broad – no, not that one, the other one whose name I can neither spell nor pronounce. I was there with my girlfriend Sue as the guest of her uncle. Sadly for Sue she had been orphaned at quite a young age and left in the care of her mother's brother, who acted as guardian. Sue shared a flat, opposite a pub in Earls Court called The Coleherene, with a very upmarket piece of goods whose lover at that time was Eddie Kulukundis. (Now if I can manage Kulukundis, why can't I do Matthieu?) Sue let me sleep with her there from time to time; she also distinguished herself by being the only person to ever take my dick out in the back of a taxi. Soon after we met she said that we had been invited to spend a weekend in Hove at the house her uncle shared with his friend. She had told him about me and he was keen to give me the once-over. We drove into Hove on a Friday evening and walked straight onto the set of 'La Cage aux Folles'. Naughty Sue had not really prepared me for the fact that her uncle and his friend were openly gay, although I suppose heavy hints had been dropped.

As far as she was concerned, knowing about my sexual proclivities, there should be no problem at all. Out of the corner of my eye, I was aware of her watching me with wry amusement. But I was, of course, concerned that they would think I was a rampant queen, there under false pretences, and out to deceive the darling niece. In order to prevent this happening I realised I had to do a bit of heavy role-playing. With unusual restraint I stopped short at hearty back-slapping and overarm practice in the sitting room. But I certainly did not ask where the fabric came from for the drapes round the four-poster in my bedroom, or if a decent hairdresser was difficult to find on the south coast. On Sunday afternoon I collapsed, drained, into the motor car and was driven back to London by Sue. We remained good friends for quite a long time; the last news I had of her was that she had married a chap in the Green Jackets.

After my rejection by The Savoy I decided to try my hand downmarket and along the Strand at the internationally unknown Charing Cross Hotel. Like The Savoy, it had nether regions that left a lot to be desired, but at least there was a pleasant enough bloke to answer my enquiries. Not only did he do that, he also arranged for me to be seen, there and then, by a nice young assistant manager. The upshot of the interview was that he took me on as a bit of a hybrid, neither page boy nor porter, but a cross between the two. If I had been prepared to wear a frock (which I probably was) and work as a chambermaid, I could have had a room as well. Instead of that, he gave me the address of a hostel in Eccleston Square that provided accommodation for lads in the hotel and catering trade. I thanked him profusely and headed for Victoria.

The Square was made up of handsome late nineteenth-century buildings on three sides, with a central garden enclosed by railings. The stucco of number 33 could have done with a touch up, but it did not otherwise stand out from its neighbours. Happily there was a vacancy, and I was given a guided tour of the dormitories, the lounge and canteen. I spent one more night at the 'Y' and moved the next day.

Life at the hostel was relaxed and very friendly. The only thing that it took me a little while to get used to, as a light sleeper, was living in a dormitory. Unlike my public school friends, I had never before experienced communal sleeping and the horseplay that seemed to go with it. Although 'lights out' was at ten, that did not mean that all activity ceased. After all, my companions, none of them over eighteen, were experiencing their first jobs and life in the wicked city, giving them lots to talk about. As well as the nightly pillow fight, there was a certain amount of bed-hopping, in which, sadly, I was not included. On the other hand, had I been leapt on by a priapic sous-chef, I might have screamed the place down.

As much as possible I joined in the postmortem at the end of each day, when we exchanged stories about our respective establishments. But there were some things I chose to keep to myself. My crush on Enzo, the Italian porter at the Charing Cross, was definitely one of them. He was tall and well built, with olive skin, beautiful eyes and a crowning glory of black curly hair. His off-duty hours were spent at a language school learning English. As luck would have it, we started work at the hotel on the same day, which meant being thrown together rather a lot. My days were spent trailing along behind him, glowing with devotion like an elderly Jack Russell. It would have been impossible for him not to realise that my interest extended beyond a delight in helping him with his pronunciation. But I hope I was more discreet than the dreadful old queen whose pursuit of me was nothing short of relentless. Cyril was his name, and he ran the cocktail bar on the ground floor opposite the lift and main staircase. He was the first obviously gay bloke I had ever encountered, and as such I viewed him with a certain amount of curiosity. I suppose he mistook this interest for rather more than it was. In any event, he made his first move one morning when I was relieving the liftman for his lunch break. He wandered over to where I was standing, dutifully waiting for passengers.

'Hello, Guy,' he said, 'I must show you something funny than happened to me one day when I was working the lift.'

'Oh really,' said I, suspiciously. With that, he led me through the doors and pressed the 'close' button.

'Yeah, the lift was very crowded,' he explained. 'All of a sudden, in the crush of people I felt this hand squeezing my goolies. Like this it was.'

Quick as a flash he did just that to me.

'How awful for you,' I exclaimed, brushing his hand away. 'I bet you thumped him.' At that moment the doors opened as we arrived at the second floor. 'You go on,' I said, tartly. 'I'll walk down.'

If he hadn't been so revolting, more like Enzo perhaps, I might have enjoyed the experience. But it was a clever little ruse and I filed it in the memory bank.

I had worked in a hotel once before, while I was on holiday from school in St Austell. The Carlyon Bay Hotel, at the famous local beauty spot, took me on as a waiter. I suppose it was a life that in lots of ways resembled the theatre. Certainly, an ability to act was useful when dealing with the foibles of wealthy customers. And the staff had a strong cast of players. The Charing Cross was very much the same. My boss, the Hall Porter, was a leading seaman-type figure who ran a very tight ship indeed. He bitterly resented having to cede some of his authority to the effete bunch who ran Reception just across the hall. But in general everyone got along famously and created an atmosphere that was appreciated by the guests. Its proximity to the station meant that lots of customers were literally just passing through – having perhaps a cup of tea or a quick drink before catching a train. Even if the railway service was lousy, British Rail in those days had a good name for running hotels. This was appreciated by lots of successful businessmen, some of them big tippers, who maintained permanent rooms. Another group of people who were regular visitors were parliamentary delegations from the islands in the West Indies. I suppose it was handy for Whitehall, where they discussed independence and trade. The memory of these big black men with smiling faces has always stayed with me.

I kept closely in touch with Mum during this time. She always managed to sound quite cheery on the telephone, but I could tell by her voice that she was far from happy. One day when I rang I told her that thanks to my job and the hostel I was now ready to receive the bike. It arrived by train from Melton Mowbray some days later. In those days cycling in London meant freedom – not helmets, masks and little red sticks poking out to ward off evil cars. It also meant that the journey between Eccleston Square and the hotel took no time at all. The route could not have been more direct. Buckingham Palace Road, passing the entrance to the Royal Mews, negotiating the Victoria Memorial; The Mall; Trafalgar Square and I was there. There was something about cycling past the Palace that always gave me a thrill – not that I ever saw the Queen or anything – it was just solid grandeur and emanations of history. One day I left the hostel earlier than usual, cycled to the front of the Palace and parked my bike against the railings. Summoning a degree of boldness I had not known I possessed, I approached a policeman standing beside one of the huge wrought-iron gates.

'Excuse me, constable, can you tell me how I go about getting a job in there?' I asked politely, indicating the building behind him.

'Well sir,' he replied thoughtfully, 'you would probably have to write in. But you had better go and ask somebody at the trade door in Buckingham Palace Road.'

I thanked him, climbed aboard my trusty steed and retraced my steps round the corner. The trade door itself is set into a large arch close to the Ambassadors Entrance, where the public is admitted when the Palace is open. In a little room just inside the door I found an elderly man in battledress with a large red 'ER' on his pocket. I put to him the same question that I had asked the policeman.

'Well', he said, 'what would you like to do?'

'I'd like to be a page,' I replied.

'Ah well, you couldn't be one of those just yet. You see, pages are rather important folk around here. Anyway, the best thing you can do is to drop a line to the Master of the Household and he'll sort you out.'

With those reassuring words ringing in my ear I pedalled off towards Trafalgar Square.

Some time during the summer of 1960 I wrote my letter from the hostel in Eccleston Square to the Master of the Household at Buckingham Palace. With the benefit of experience I discovered that regardless of who you write to at BP, you always get a reply from someone else. The acknowledgement I received was from the Deputy Comptroller of Supply, Michael Tims. (We were destined to meet again many years later through a dear mutual friend called David Petrie, banqueting king of The Dorchester.) The Deputy Comptroller expressed an interest in my letter and set a date for an interview. At the appointed hour I strode (nervously) into his office to be received by a man not too much older than myself, with nineteenth-century good looks and who was even more shy than I was. Having questioned me about my background and aspirations he then suggested that I should be seen by the Palace Steward, whose role was equivalent to butler to the Queen. A meeting was arranged for a few days hence. By this time, with all this interest going on, I started to wonder whether I was being considered for a really important post, like Lord High Executioner or even Mistress of the Robes. After a few minutes with Mr Oulton, the suave Palace Steward, such ideas were soon dispelled. He announced that because of my age the best position they could offer me was the post of Silver Pantry Assistant, with a wage of seven pounds a fortnight, plus seven shillings a week board wages and a blue suit and a pair of black boots annually. The appointment was subject to the approval of the Yeoman of the Plate and a once-over by the Master of the Household. The Yeoman proved to be a dear, more concerned about the effect on my mother of our separation than he was about my suitability for the job. With a hand on the shoulder he led me off to meet the man who ran the Queen's Household. We passed along miles of corridors flagged with stone and then later linoleum, until he pushed open a green baize door to reveal carpet in rich red as far as the eye could see. Our route was lined with probably not very important paintings framed in gilt, and Edwardian showcases stuffed with porcelain and royal bijouterie. We paused in a passage overlooking the quadrangle. The Yeoman squared up to the big door ahead of him and knocked timidly. I was ushered in. The most important interview of my life found me in front of the imposing figure of Major Sir Mark Milbank. In true military fashion he went straight to the heart of the point.

'Ah Hunting. You're coming to join us. Welcome aboard and good luck.'

I think I managed a 'thank you, sir' before I was removed from the scene by a sweating Mr Evitts.

I moved to the Palace in July 1961. The Liveried Porter, on duty at the trade door, telephoned the Yeoman of the Plate to tell him that I was there and then pointed me in the direction of his office. After only two previous visits I wasn't at all sure that I knew where I was going, but I went off with as much determination as I could muster. But I soon found myself lost in the labyrinth of ill-lit corridors that make up the Palace's basement. Apart from one door labelled, rather enticingly, 'Swimming Pool', all the others were unmarked. I retraced my steps until I reached the foot of a staircase and heard the sound of whistling. With previous experience, I associated this with Mr Evitts, and found his office on the landing above. In the weeks ahead I got to know that he was famous for declaiming the full works of Joe Loss's repertoire.

He welcomed me to my new job and took a few minutes to point out some of the many advantages I would enjoy. As well as the clothing and board wages allowance, he told me that a barber came in every month and that the resident doctor held regular surgeries. The Trade Door was closed each night at eleven o'clock, and the duty policeman was not keen on being disturbed thereafter. Visitors were allowed in staff rooms, but only admitted by a pass signed by the Palace Steward. Spiritual needs were in the hands of the Sub-Dean of the Chapels Royal and refreshment provided by Mr Cuff, who ran the licensed canteen. (Not that it mattered, but he was one-armed, and had scant regard for conventional licensing hours.) This remarkably self-contained community was linked to the outside world by the switchboard, manned by Mr Jones and his cheery voice, and his band of centennial telegram-senders who ran the Court Post Office.

After our chat Mr Evitts led the way out of his office and back down the stairs again. Another long passageway and staircase led us to the Silver Pantry itself: two large rooms around which my life was to revolve for the next couple of years. The first room was dominated by a pair of colossal wooden sinks, with which I was about to begin a long and intimate relationship. At its centre the adjoining room had a huge scrubbed table and walls lined with deep cupboards. Work was in full swing, but Mr Evitts introduced me to the underbutlers, who were Alec Metcalf, Freddy Mitchell, Victor Fletcher and Michael Perry. My fellow assistants were called Charlie Barton, David Hutcheon and Richard Wood. The only man I didn't meet that day was Walter Fry, who ran a one-man gold pantry. He was responsible for the dazzling displays of gold and silver gilt plate that decorated the ballroom for state banquets. As a young man he had been on the staff at York House, as valet to the Prince of Wales. He and the other servants had great affection for their young master, and indeed for most of the girlfriends he brought into their lives. The glaring exception, of course, was Mrs Simpson. It was not the fact that she was foreign or divorced or untitled that rankled, it was simply that she did not seem to know how they should be treated. The worst example of this was her behaviour at the table. At lunch or dinner most people react immediately when they are aware that someone is standing beside them holding a dish of meat or vegetables. The well-mannered turn slightly, without breaking off conversation, and help themselves to whatever is being offered. Wallis Simpson's habit was to ignore poor bent (no pun intended) footmen for as long as possible. When Walter realised that this was a game she enjoyed playing at every opportunity, he decided that she must be taught a lesson. During dinner one evening he waited patiently beside her to see if she was up to her usual tricks. When she failed, yet again, to acknowledge the presence of the large dish of roast pheasant that was getting heavier and heavier, he moved it slightly to the left until it brushed gently against the bare flesh of her upper arm. The heat of the silver generated an immediate response, and a withering glance from the lady from Baltimore. After that little incident she played by the rules, and Walter was a hero. Later in his career he moved to Queen Mary at Marlborough House, joining the Palace staff when she died. By the time I met him he was semi-retired and although quite deaf, always good for a yarn.

Mr Evitts took me up to the room that was to be my home for the next two years. I loved it on sight. It was a big, square, sparsely furnished room with a large window looking onto the quadrangle. Anyone coming through the arch from the forecourt could see my little eyrie perched on high, above the left-hand corner of the Grand Entrance.

I woke up early the next morning, determined not to be late for my first day at work, and also to allow time to find it. After only a couple of wrong turns I rolled up on time. During that morning I was shown how the Pantry worked by Alec Metcalf, the Senior Under-Butler. I also had the chance to size up my new colleagues. The two older assistants, Charlie and David, didn't say much and were obviously just the sort of people the powers that be preferred to employ. Their horizons were low and they appreciated the security of the Palace cocoon. But Richard was quite different. He was ten years older than me and had started work there just a few months earlier. Although he was well built, with reddy gold hair and a high colour (if I say Christine Trueman, you will probably get the picture), the thing that was most noticeable about him was his charm and personality. His voice was full of laughter, and he spoke in a way that was better suited to the other side of the green baize door. To a shy lad from the shires, like me, he embodied an urbanity and sophistication that I could never hope to emulate. Because we seemed to come from such different worlds I was fully prepared for him to ignore me completely or, at best, treat me with friendly disregard. But I am happy to say that this was not to be the case. For whatever reason, he saw in me something that he liked, and he proved it by counting me among his best friends. At last I had a role model.

My working day began with breakfast in the Servants Hall at seven-thirty a.m. By eight a.m. I was expected to be tied into my long white apron and ready for action. The Pantry would be clean and uncluttered; no question of leaving the washing-up till the morning in this establishment. Soon after opening for business our first visitors would be the footmen responsible for breakfast. The Queen's Footman, the Nursery Footman and the two roster footmen took away with them the large wooden high-sided butler's trays that had been prepared the night before and left covered in cloths. With that out of the way we got down to cleaning the silver from the previous day and anything that might be required for today's meals. The Queen and the Nursery had their own sets of silver, whilst the every day stuff was kept for the Household and large-scale entertaining. My colleagues and I, the assistants, shared out our tasks on a rota basis. One day in four I was responsible for doing the knives, the thing I hated most. It entailed taking these large weapons with beautiful silver handles and stained blades down to a dark room under the Pantry stairs. It was musty there, with a strong smell of Goddard's Plate Powder in the air. The room's only occupant was an ancient knife machine that had a sturdy handle and four slits for the offending objects. The principle was obvious and the process short lived, but it was all so horribly Dickensian. On another day my job would be to supply the silver needs of the Kitchen, the Coffee Room and the Pastry. Although I came to regard this as rather a social outing, in the early days it was fraught with anxiety. Mr Aubrey, the tall and plump Head Chef, was usually too committed to organising his troops, piping mashed potato or flicking ash from his cigarette to have much truck with the likes of me. Even when I did manage to catch his eye, it was very difficult at first to understand his language. The words he used most often were 'flats', 'ovals', 'entrée dishes', 'boats' and even 'Argyll'. As there was never any question of writing anything down, by the time I had walked the many yards back to the operations room my memory would be in turmoil. Thankfully the demands of the Royal Pastry were far more modest. I was always able to understand a request for cream jugs, even when it was made in the heavily accented English of Mr Roux, the aptly named presiding genius. Ample Miss Smith from Bristol reigned supreme over the Coffee Room and her gaggle of toast-making matrons. She never allowed a discussion about the size of a teapot to interfere with a kind enquiry about my health.

By ten o'clock the Pantry was at full stretch. The breakfast things were being washed up, Michael Perry was mixing a large bowl of mustard for the day's needs, Freddy Mitchell busied himself with the tray of things for Royal Lunch, Victor Fletcher regaled us all with an account of the latest play he had seen and Alec Metcalf was thinking about his first pint of Guinness.

My first glimpse of that part of the Palace beyond the linoleum was the Household Dining Room. Together with our colleagues from the lesser pantries – Glass and China – we descended on it mid-morning to set the table for lunch. On a typical day the number of places might be ten or fifteen. The Queen, by contrast, usually lunched alone. On the first day of my responsibility for her requirements I carried my tray up the stairs outside the Pantry to the first floor. I put my shoulder to a heavy door, which opened to reveal the full glory of the Picture Gallery. Bathed in golden light, I walked its length, taking in a few Dutch masterpieces on the way. At the far end, beyond a vestibule, I reached the little corridor that led to the Private Apartments. This suite of rooms, on the north-west corner of the Palace overlooking the garden, consists of the Audience Room, the Dining Room, Sitting Room, Bedroom and Bathroom. Opposite the Sitting-Room door, by the lift, is the little Duty Room of the Queen's Page and Footman. I made myself known to Mr Bennett, the Page, who led the way into the Dining Room and fussed with the table while I held the tray. As HM was known never to take more than half an hour for lunch I was back there by one-thirty p.m. to scoop up the debris. At the sound of a bell Mr Bennett entered the room to clear away. Waiting outside I just caught sight of the monarch between the hinges, sitting alone at the table.

After lots more washing-up, the first half of the day drew to a close at about two-thirty p.m. The Pantry was then abandoned until five p.m., when the tea things had to be dealt with and preparations made for dinner. Happily the tea ritual was a very low-key affair. Apart from the Queen and the Nursery, the only other partakers were the Lady-in-Waiting, who took tea in her sitting room, and the Household, for whom it was a moveable feast in the Equerries Room. As long as HM was dining alone, dinner was also not very labour intensive. The Duty Equerry, in black tie, ate in solitary splendour in the Household Dining Room, whilst on the top floor Miss Peebles, the Governess, had a tray in her suite. That left the Nursery which, in those days, comprised the fat infant Andrew, baby Edward, Mabel Anderson and the Nursery Maid. Prince Edward was actually born not far from the Pantry during my time there. The exact location was a set of rooms on the ground floor known as the Belgian Suite, normally reserved for visiting heads of state. A few weeks after his birth, an afternoon was set aside so that the massed ranks of servantry could make his acquaintance. When the time came we formed an orderly queue at the far end of the Grand Hall and were hustled through in quick succession. I was disappointed that he was not to be seen bouncing around on his mother's knee, but lying out cold at the bottom of a large and over-draped cradle. Once in the royal presence, all sense of protocol deserted me. I paused for a second, peered and walked on. It occurred to me later that His Little Royal Highness might have expected a bob or a curtsey. Oh well, he had plenty of those to look forward to.

One weekend in four I had to do my tour of duty at Windsor Castle. This entailed leaving London on a Friday afternoon with a small group of fellow workers. We travelled in a strange vehicle, part-bus part-van, known as 'the Grey Lady'. I could quite see that the Castle at weekends provided a wonderful retreat for the royals, but for the skivvies it felt strange rattling around in a building that was designed to hold hundreds of people. The Pantry, under the control of Freddie Mitchell's father, Freddie Mitchell senior, was much further from the Royal Dining Room than the one at BP. They were separated by a labyrinth of stone-flagged corridors that were very confusing for a first-timer. Added to this, my bedroom, at the top of the Lancaster Tower, was as remote as it was possible to be. However, in spite of all this enforced exercise, Windsor weekends provided a chance for unprecedented access to those closest to the Royal Person. If I was lucky, the duty Queen's Footman would be my new friend Malcolm Wakefield. We had started to exchange approving looks and I longed to get to know him better. His opposite number, Basil Stibbs, was very charming, but he was also the father of two. It was once said of Basil in his ordinary footman days that ambition had driven him to wear a pork chop in his uniform, making him irresistible to the Queen's four-legged friends.

As far as I was concerned, the Castle at weekends had a very intimate side, in spite of its size. This was also true, of course, of Balmoral and Sandringham, where the business of monarchy was kept to a minimum. The Private Secretary had a house within the Castle precincts but did not bother HM on Saturdays or Sundays. As in London, access to Her Royal Highness was jealously guarded by the Queen's Page, whose official title was Page of the Back Stairs. He held court behind the ubiquitous green baize door in a room next to the Dining Room. Once dinner had been served the weekend crew, including the representative from the wine cellar, would settle in for a good natter.

A few weeks after my arrival, travel arrangements were announced for the annual August migration to Balmoral. This ten-week royal holiday is divided for the staff into two five-week periods, allowing a complete change-over in the middle. A special train is chartered to move the vast quantities of people, animals, cars, silver, china and glass all the way to the station at Ballater. The army provides lorries at both ends. The trip was doubly exciting for me, as I had never been to Scotland before or spent the night on a train. Not only did the journey turn into an all-night party, it also provided me with my first ever seducer. Quite how a Spaniard came to be working as one of Her Majesty's kitchen porters was not a question that concerned me at that moment. All I knew was that he was a swarthy young buck called Santos with a very determined streak. Sadly, our brief liaison did not increase his desire to stay in royal service and he moved to Paris a few weeks later. I heard that he died there as a result of wounds he received in a brawl.

Unfortunately, my first sight of Balmoral as we drove through the Castle gates, was not an image that made the spirits soar. It was a long, low hut that was to be my home for the next five weeks. Along with a series of others, it was a temporary structure thrown up in 1840 to house part of the enormous retinue the Tsar brought with him on his visit to Queen Victoria. I suppose if I had been a hairy-arsed Cossack I might have found the extremely Spartan conditions quite salubrious, but as it was I was cold and uncomfortable. I warmed up each morning by dashing across the grass to the sanctuary of the Servants Hall, where a marvellous breakfast of porridge, kippers and warm baps gave me a new lease of life. The layout of the comparatively small castle meant that the Silver Pantry, just off the corridor that led to the Ballroom, was right at the heart of things and a popular meeting place. Our big table was used for afternoon table tennis tournaments, sometimes graced by the presence of Charles and Anne.

Each year the Palace staff was augmented by a resident company of soldiers from one of the Scottish regiments, who acted as porters and beaters. Happily, their sexual services were also sometimes available when logs had been carried and grouse shot, for which many a housemaid and silver pantry assistant were deeply grateful. Taking into account the relative isolation of the estate, the powers that be went to considerable lengths to keep the 'troops' happy with a variety of entertainment. There were coach trips to Aberdeen, weekly hoolies in the recreation hall, Gillies Balls and film shows. Films were shown in the Ballroom and timed to coincide with the end of the royal dinner. The seating arrangements were not exactly on a first-come, first-served basis and woe betide anyone who put a Philistine bottom in the wrong place. Two or three rows of huge, comfortable easy chairs were set out in the front for the Family and house party, with a table and bellpush where HM would sit. At a distance behind were dining chairs for the officials, and finally lines of benches for the likes of me. An hour or so into the performance the soundtrack was often interrupted by loud snoring from a squaddie who had overdone the McEwans Export. For the hapless equerry and Queen's Page this would be the second time they had sat through the picture. A morning viewing would be laid on so that they could check it for anything that might offend the royal sensibilities.

The hierarchical system was much less evident at the Gillies Balls, where the Family danced with the servants, estate staff and soldiers alike. At one of these do's I like to think I made a bit of history by being one of the few men who, simultaneously (or even separately) held hands with the Duke of Edinburgh and Lord Snowdon – albeit while dancing the Paul Jones!

The Queen and her Court (to a much lesser extent) returned reluctantly to London at the beginning of October and settled back into the routine of life at BP. The next major upheaval was the move to Sandringham for Christmas. But unlike the Balmoral exercise, this did not involve the mass movement of every sort of artefact and appurtenance, as the House was used more often and kept in a permanent state of readiness. Nevertheless, the little railway station at Wolferton on the edge of the estate was the scene of constant comings and goings. Behind the red-brick Edwardian facade of Sandringham there lies a very glamorous country house, but once again the servants' quarters left a lot to be desired. It must be fun for the ruling classes, secure in their period houses with antique furniture and pictures, to pretend that they are living in another era as long, of course, as the central heating is at full blast and logs are thrown, like lambs to the slaughter, onto ravenous fires. Behind the double-glazed green baize doors however, comfort was harder to find. Shared rooms, coal fires and a queue for the bathroom was about all we had. But the compensation for this material lack was a strong community spirit and a warm and happy atmosphere.

I had a sneaking sympathy for the Queen on Christmas Eve when she had to spend a couple of hours on her feet beside the tree in the Ballroom distributing her presents to the faithful. I am sure she tried to muster a child or two to support her, and I can imagine their reaction. 'Oh Mum, do we *have* to?' In the event only a grim-faced Prince Philip stood by her side. Outside the Ballroom a queue was drawn up in strict order of precedence, which meant that I was almost standing in the garden. At long last I found myself in the doorway with the Palace Steward announcing, 'Guy Hunting, Silver Pantry Assistant'. The length of the floor between myself and the sovereign appeared to be never-ending, but she very discreetly studied the little package she had been handed by the housekeeper as I made that enormous journey. This was to be our first full-frontal encounter, and when she looked up I was completely gobsmacked by her dazzling smile. In common, I like to think, with almost everyone who meets her for the first time, I was so overawed that I have no recollection of what she said to me – it might have been, 'Your breath smells of garlic', for all I can remember. I stumbled past her, after mumbling something about the time of year, only to have my hand grasped firmly by her husband as he said, '…New Year'. Imagine my delight when I unwrapped the present to find not one, but two pairs of socks in real wool. An appropriate use was found for them at once, and they remained about the only royal mementoes that my mother found difficult to either frame or drink out of.

With two blue suits and two pairs of boots to my credit, a

restlessness came over me. I suppose it was sparked originally by my burgeoning friendship with Malcolm and the glamour of his job. But although I knew I could never emulate him and be the Queen's Footman, I thought that being tall and seventeen I might stand the chance of a job as an ordinary footman. The Sergeant Footman, Mr Candy, (known inexplicably as Chuffchuff) was receptive and sympathetic but told me frankly that there was no vacancy at the moment. Frustrated and unhappy, I decided that the only alternative was to try my luck in the outside world. That was all very well, but of course I had no idea how to go about it. It was only when I confided in Richard Wood that he told me about an old established domestic agency called Mrs Hunts that might be able to help.

Having put myself on their books I didn't have long to wait before I was taken on as a footman by a couple called Sir Rowland and Lady Robinson in Carlton House Terrace. The house, number 24, was just up the Mall from the Palace – an attraction I would have found it difficult to overlook. Sir Rowland was MP for a Blackpool constituency and a popular but not very prominent backbencher. As far as I could see, his only claim to fame was that he had married an American called Maisie Gasque, who was a Woolworth heiress through some family connection. It was presumably her money that enabled them to live in such a smart street where there were only two other private houses: the vast mansion of the Marquess of Lansdowne and the official residence of the Foreign Secretary. (Sadly the house was demolished in the mid-eighties to make way for an office block.)

By today's standards the number of living-in servants employed by the Robinsons may come as rather a surprise, but at that time such a complement was not unusual. There was the butler, Mr Matson, Isobel the ladies maid, Hilda the housemaid and Pepino the chef. He, at various times, was also helped by his wife and his brother Alfredo. Joe Matson was an austere Yorkshireman and a professional to his fingertips. On top of all his other work he also got up at five a.m. at least twice a week on dinner party days to buy flowers at Covent Garden. He would then spend several hours arranging a vast display on the dining room table and elaborate creations in the hall, morning room and drawing room. His duties also included looking after Sir Rowland's clothes and cleaning the silver – which he did like a man possessed. Although I had hoped for a job with flashy uniforms, I had to be content with a black jacket and striped trousers covered, most of the time, by a large white apron when not on parade.

In an uncharitable moment I might describe Hilda, also Yorkshire born, as the original drudge with a grudge. Although in many ways a character, she was never exactly surrounded by an aura of happiness and her only pastime was smoking cigarettes. Her daily Hoover-led assault on the various rooms was a task made harder by the need to remove traces of her own presence. Cupped hand and ash did not always coincide.

Like Hilda, Isobel was also fairly permanently down in the dumps – although that, apparently, was largely due to troublesome gums. But she also had a grievance. She knew that her presence in the house was resented by Lady R. It appears that in her youth Maisie had been provided by her doting parents with the services of a French maid, who was much prized – probably for being a status symbol as much as anything else. She stayed with her overweight mistress for many years before finally, with the onset of old age, hanging up her bustiere. The trouble for Maisie was that with French maids being rarer than hen's teeth she had to choose as her replacement someone rather less exotic. Enter the whey-faced lass from the Highlands.

As far as Her Ladyship was concerned the only servant who was beyond reproach was Pepino, the elfin Italian with the radiant smile. He was certainly attractive, but when it came to sex appeal he was knocked into a cocked hat by his swarthy, monosyllabic younger brother. Encouraged by the Mistress and much to the annoyance of Mr Matson (who called his food 'foreign muck') he produced main courses piled high on silver dishes that had to be paraded around the dining table to receive the acclamation of the guests. On good days my buttling boss performed this task with a look of grim resignation, saving his best grimace for the puddings. In the best Italian tradition these were usually mounds of ice-cream surmounted by a web of spun sugar, brilliant with fairy lights.

Lady Robinson was the sort of woman with lots of money who goes through life looking for trophies. Although her marriage to a middle-class Member of Parliament was a bit of a gamble, she was sensible enough to select one who was bright and ambitious. As an American I am sure she also knew that no union is stronger than the relationship between money and politics. Between them the Robinsons used a fine house and lavish hospitality to win Sir Rowland powerful friends and influence, albeit from the back benches. He may not have made office, but he was knighted in the days before such honours became two a penny. The title, I am sure, added lustre to the social life they enjoyed at their house in the Bahamas, a dependency he went on to govern, as Lord Martonmere, when he retired from the Commons.

Pause for a postscript. During my time with the Robinsons I saw very little of their two grown-up children, Richard and Loretta. But whenever Loretta was at home her beauty and charm always attracted a stream of admirers. Among the most persistent of these was the handsome young scion of a famous banking family. Many years later I opened the front door of a house to this man again. In a changed world, it was a house I had just sold to his son.

With limited means and only an attic bedroom to call my own, any social or sex life was pretty thin on the ground during this time. Having said that, I did briefly enjoy a relationship with a strikingly handsome young German called Gerd, who insisted on showing his affection for me by trying to hold my hand in the street. This of course was a deep embarrassment and almost certainly a hanging offence in the mid-sixties. But in the end it was his lack of English that ground me down. Our affair must have lasted for about six months and during that time he met the few friends that I had. Ironically, the one he liked most was Malcolm, the Queen's Footman, and he looked forward to our visits at the Palace. As it turned out, bringing them together was probably the most successful introduction I have ever made. Initially without my knowledge they became romantically involved and decided to set up home together. When all was revealed they announced that they were going as a 'couple' to work for the three elderly bachelor Leveson-Gower brothers at their house, Titsey Place in Kent. Thirty years on I know that the old boys are long dead and that the house and its beautiful garden are open to the public, but perhaps there is a little cottage somewhere on the estate where the Anglo-German alliance continues to flourish.

In an unusually friendly gesture, Mr Matson encouraged me to ask the occasional chum to join us all for staff supper. Naturally it was Richard Wood who came most often and was a very popular guest, forcing smiles to appear on even the saddest face. But one evening, much to everyone else's surprise, an acquaintance of Mr Matson's took the spare place at the table. He was a Devonian called Peter Drury and worked at the Mansion House with what was, for me, the impressive title of Sergeant Footman. His description of city pomp and ceremony made it sound as if life with London's First Citizen might be a substitute for what I had only glimpsed at the end of the Mall. And when he went on to explain that footmen's liveries were redesigned each year with the arrival of a new incumbent, I was convinced.

In the course of a conversation with Peter several days later, he mentioned that the next Lady Mayoress was looking for a new footman. I applied for the position at once. It was towards the end of 1963 and I was interviewed at their flat in Eaton Square by Sir Ralph and Lady Perring, who were due to assume the mayoral mantle that November. The bedding shop proprietor proved to be nice enough, but Mary his wife was in a class of her own when it came to style and charm. She explained that being her personal footman meant looking after her on all official occasions, standing behind her chair at dinners and banquets and riding beside her chauffeur when she travelled to engagements. She made it all sound like a fairy tale and I couldn't wait to be part of it.

The reality, needless to say, was somewhat different. But things did get off to quite a good start. I moved to EC4 in time for the Perring inauguration on Lord Mayor's Show Day. That was fun, but meant an awful lot of rushing around with trays of drinks for thirsty aldermen. The glory bit came two days later at Guildhall when I stood, in full State livery, behind the Lady Mayoress's thronelike chair during the Lord Mayor's Banquet. The high point of the proceedings, a keynote speech by then prime minister Harold Macmillan, was shown live on television – with my face clearly visible above his left shoulder.

The Mansion House is an extraordinary building. Behind its ancient walls, the rooms used for a rich variety of purposes include a magistrate's court, ornate state rooms for grand occasions, suites for visiting dignitaries, offices and a comfortable flat for the mayoral family. One little-used room, but about the biggest, is the double-height Old Ballroom, which has a gallery running round it. Along with the other staff rooms my little bedroom led off it – and pretty dismal it was too. My next-door neighbour was an unprepossessing character who, as deputy steward, was my immediate superior. As he had never known a footman (or probably anyone else) to be called Guy he decided, with the baffled agreement of the Perrings, that I should be known as John. If I had had any choice in the matter I would have gone for Bert or Sid – after all, there are only so many Johns a small family can take.

With the exception of that one man, all the other staff, including Captain Shaw the private secretary and Elizabeth Gilliat his deputy, were extremely nice. And I liked the Perring children too. There were three of them, all grown up. But the work was exhausting. In common, I am sure, with most men who achieve this pinnacle of success, Sir Ralph was determined to make full use of the well-run establishment for which he held the tenancy for just twelve months. And to be fair, a great deal of his own money had been spent to get him there and a lot more would be needed before the year was up. Whenever there was a lunch or dinner in a livery hall that did not require the attendance of the mayoral couple, the Mansion House's private dining room was filled to capacity with everyone they had ever known or sought to impress.

As the year wore on I began to feel constantly tired and was told that I looked pale and thin (not pale and interesting, you understand). In fact, I wasn't just knackered but was going down with pleurisy.

When the illness developed I went to stay with Mum for a couple of weeks in the house she had just moved into in Sarre Road. After I left Melton Mowbray her relationship with FGH deteriorated rapidly, until she decided one day to follow my lead and move to the big city. In a moment of rare compassion, Douglas suggested that she should take over an empty flat in one of the pair of houses the family owned in West Hampstead. Once her furniture and possessions were installed, life looked up a lot. The next task she set herself was to see about finding a job, something she hadn't done since well before John was born. For a girl who had been out of circulation for so long and was in her late fifties, this might have been a daunting prospect. But, nothing ventured, she soon had a couple of interviews under her belt – one with a firm of solicitors in Piccadilly. All went well until it came to the question of a test of her shorthand and typing. Without going into too much detail (like the fact that she hadn't done either for twenty-five years), she confessed to being 'a bit rusty'. To her understandable delight, however, she passed with flying colours and got the job.

The time I spent away from the Mansion House gave me a chance to think seriously about the future. Taking stock, I accepted that although the job had aspects that I quite enjoyed, my daily encounters with the ghastly deputy steward were too much to bear. I decided to give in my notice and, not only that, to write to Mr Candy at the Palace at the same time. In his reply he told me exactly what I wanted to hear. Yes, there was a vacancy in the Footmen's Room, and no, he saw no reason why I should not fill it. The only proviso was that I would have to be seen by Lord Plunket, the Deputy Master.

Although dear old Chuffchuff made it sound like no more than a formality, I did have some concerns about my interview with the noble lord. The main one was that he was known to prefer the attentions of the sturdier sort of manservant who got his kicks from 'bulling' boots to a high gloss, rather than the sensitive ones who took too long to 'lay-out' the right tie with a shirt. I would have to butch up for our encounter. The job of Deputy Master was not one of the plum positions in the Household, but Patrick Plunket had influence that stretched way beyond the confines of his office. As children, he and his brother had lived in Piccadilly in a house next door to the Duke and Duchess of York and their two daughters, Elizabeth and Margaret

Rose. The four of them played together and began a friendship that was to last throughout their lives. With the death of Lord and Lady Plunket in a plane crash, the two young boys were taken under the wing of their kindly neighbours. Happily there was no shortage of money as their mother had been a member of the Guinness family. After service with the Irish Guards, which he left with the rank of major, Patrick joined the Household and remained with it until his untimely death in 1975. Although a very social man, with a passion for the arts, his personal life was lonely and unfulfilled. The Windsors were his family.

His office was next to the one occupied by the Master, outside which I had waited so nervously four years before. This time, instead of Mr Evitts, I was led to my fate by the Palace Steward, Charles Oulton. To my great relief, His Lordship could not have been more charming and he expressed great pleasure at welcoming me back into the fold. Oh happy day!

As I already had a knowledge of the territory and some of the ropes, the prospect of starting my new job was very exciting. The only downside was that my great friend and mentor was no longer there to stimulate and amuse, for Richard had moved on.

4

Richard Wood was born, the youngest of eight children, in a small village near Tewkesbury, where his family had been for generations. Long before he and I embarked on our life-long friendship in London, his brother and mine were stationed together at RAF Cosford. But unlike us, these two lads were never destined to be great mates. The former was commanding officer and the latter a boy entrant.

After school he went to work in a grocer's shop in the village of Coleford in the Forest of Dean. His personality and way with the customers soon made him a popular figure. He joined the Young Conservatives and went as a delegate to party conferences. National Service took him into the army, where he rose to the rank of lieutenant. After that experience, which was by all accounts a considerable eye-opener, he returned to Coleford to manage the shop. He restored his links with the YCs and at the same time was asked to help with the local branch of the Army Cadets. There was even talk of standing for Parliament!

To the interested observer it must have looked as if Richard was enjoying a rich and rewarding life. But something was missing. He knew what that 'something' was, and that rural Gloucestershire was not the place to find it. In due course his photograph appeared in the local paper above the announcement 'Mr Richard Wood, well-known local resident, pillar of the Church and Army Cadets and leading light in the Young Conservatives, will soon be leaving for London to take up an appointment at Buckingham Palace.' Three months later we met beside the sinks in the Silver Pantry.

The first big public occasion at which Richard made an appearance was one of the summer garden parties. Catering for the masses at these events is provided by Joe Lyons, but in the Royal Tent silver and damask is complemented by rich delicacies from the Coffee Room and Royal Pastry. At the last moment, to coincide with the Queen's arrival, silver kettles on stands with little burners are borne across the lawn. Richard, resplendent in long white apron, was making his careful progress between the flowerbeds when his name was called from among the crowd. He stopped for a moment, turning his head gently so as not to disturb his precious burden, to see the unmistakable figure of his local Rural Dean bearing down on him. It took only a split second to decide that the best course of action was to get behind a canvas flap at the earliest opportunity.

Richard loved being with and observing people. After only a few months into his new life he had made many friends among the personalities in most of the departments of the Palace and enjoyed a burgeoning social life. Although he saw very little of his Pantry colleagues outside working hours, there were two or three footmen whose company he sought. One of them in particular, blessed with aristocratic good looks, was the son of a chauffeur at Mereworth Castle in Kent, called David Walters. Dark and handsome he certainly was, although he was thought by many to be cool and arrogant. He and Richard would go out together to pubs and to the theatre, either on their own or with an old girlfriend of David's. When an old girlfriend of Richard's from Gloucestershire arrived to work in London she would occasionally join them to make up a foursome. But for Richard, the happiest times were spent alone with David on long walks at Sandringham and Balmoral. They talked for hours, but Richard was at pains to conceal the true depths of the feelings that were dominating his life. He did, however, have an outlet for his emotions and that was to be found in the gay pubs and parties of Earls Court. Even in those days Kangaroo Valley was fast becoming Fairy Grotto. A leading player on the scene was an outrageous character called Tony Parfitt and in him Richard had found the perfect foil. He was older than Richard by only a few years, but in that time he had come to terms with his sexuality, stormed out of the closet and shut the door firmly behind him. When David was away they spent as much time together as possible, with

Tony urging Richard to be more positive in his approach to his emotional turmoil. Emboldened by this advice Richard decided to allow Tony and David to meet by taking them to see *The Sound of Music* at the Palace Theatre. (Something of a Constance Shacklock groupie, he had already seen it seven times.) The evening was a huge success. Tony and David got on like a house on fire.

In the days that followed that fateful night, Richard began to realise that David was avoiding him. David was ill at ease when confronted by this observation. Seemingly at a loss to know what to say, he finally blurted out, 'I've moved in with Tony.'

Years went by and wounds were licked. Eventually Christmas cards were exchanged. One day Richard rang to say that 'we' had been invited to a party to celebrate Tony and David's tenth anniversary.

'We must go,' he exclaimed. 'I bet they are both looking pretty dreadful.'

Well, to say that I was surprised is to say nothing at all. On the one hand I was delighted that he felt he could cope with such a situation; on the other, I was damned sure that David, who openly disliked me, would never have included me in the invitation. That being said, I could not expect Richard to go on his own.

On the day of the dreadful event he asked me to arrive at his flat at about seven p.m. wearing a dinner jacket. He greeted me at the door similarly attired and thrust a glass full of amber liquid into my hand. He explained that he had rung our hosts to say how much we were looking forward to the evening, but that we would arrive late after a dinner party. That way, he said, we would make an entrance, cut a dash and be suitably merry. Well, I thought, that sounded like a cunning ruse. But unfortunately the only gesture he had made towards a 'dinner party' was to buy a bottle of a lethal substance called Dry Fly Sherry. The first few glasses cried out for a pinched nose and a narrowing of the eyes, but in what seemed like no time at all we had drained the bottle – surely a first for that particular brew. It was ten o'clock and we headed for the street to find a taxi. The chill night air knocked me sideways but I managed to regain my balance and climb into the cab. Even the next day (and thank God there was one) I had no recollection of the journey. Miraculously, when we reached our destination I was able to alight unaided, but prompted by many 'pull yourself together'-type mutterings from my fellow passenger. As the front door opened I was struck again by a blast of air, but this time it was hot and fetid. Having got as far as the hallway I sank to the ground at the feet of a bald-headed man with a paunch – a caricature of the once-handsome footman. Completely without ceremony he bundled me back out onto the pavement and shut the door. Within minutes Richard was bending over me with a concerned look. The door slammed behind him and we went home.

After two years of daily contact with large quantities of Fairy Liquid and Goddards Plate Powder, fingers begin to suffer and when Richard reached that stage he decided to take his leave of the Silver Pantry. As luck would have it, he had heard on the skivvies' grapevine that a job might be coming up at St James's Palace. This was no backstairs drudge assignment, but the position of second valet to the Duke of Gloucester. The Duke was in his early fifties and from the time he came out of the army, thirty years before, the intimate details of his life had been attended to by his personal servant, Mr Amos. Although he must have had a Christian name it was never used and remained largely unknown. He shared his work with a deputy, as did all of those who worked most closely with the senior members of the Royal Family. Their number also included pages, footmen, dressers and housemaids. In the case of Mr Amos, whose retirement was on the horizon, the importance of getting the right man for the job was even more significant.

In spite of being lowly pond life in royal hierarchy terms, Richard sailed through his interviews and was offered the job. He told me later that he thought he had got on particularly well with the Duchess. And the Duke may well have been impressed by his service in the Army.

The Gloucesters' London home, York House, was the large chunk of St James's Palace to the right of the sentry at the bottom of St James's Street. One of the capital's few surviving medieval buildings, it had once been a leper hospital and was divided into separate apartments between the wars. The Duke of Windsor lived there until his accession and it is now home to Prince Charles. Although there were one or two decent rooms on the ground floor, the rest of it was a dark and narrow rabbit warren. With nothing else to think about, the Duke, in common with his father and grandfather, was obsessed with dress etiquette and the minutiae of uniforms and decorations. Although his public engagements were few he would reach eagerly for his Field Marshall's baton at the first note of a bugle call. The Queen could always rely on him to be there when things were looking a bit military. As the only uncle she had ever really known she had a special place for him in her affections. But by many he was regarded as a buffoon, an impression not helped by a tendency to hide his shyness behind bursts of high-pitched giggling. He aged very quickly and had some difficulty controlling his movements towards the end of his life. I remember being on duty at a grand Palace dinner when soup was served as the first course. When everyone else had finished eating, the room fell silent and all eyes focused on the difficult journey the Duke's hand was negotiating between plate and mouth. In their own minds his fellow diners were urging him to succeed, but every spoonful arrived empty at its destination. Only the Queen, with her great experience and understanding, behaved normally through this ordeal. Choosing her moment, she turned and whispered something to her father's younger brother, they both smiled and she signalled for the plates to be removed.

Across the courtyard from the Gloucesters was that part of the Palace that was home to Mary, the Princess Royal, the Duke's only sister. Once again shyness was the key to her personality. In private she was known to have a wicked sense of humour, but to the outside world she presented a solemn and austere figure still suffering from an unhappy arranged marriage. Like her brother she was deeply attached to the Queen and loved being involved in the life of her family. Her own two sons were regarded as a disappointment. Her butler, Mr Groom, became a great friend of Richard's and they shared many a teapot together discussing the doings of their employers. One day Richard rang me to ask if I would like to join him and his eight-year-old godson to watch the return of the Princess from the State Opening of Parliament. My work in the Silver Pantry gave me little chance to see the Royals at close quarters and I said yes at once. During the speech from the throne Mr Groom provided us with cups of coffee before leading us through to the Dining Room to await the arrival. When questioned about the rather unusual venue for our encounter Mr Groom explained that on ceremonial occasions HRH could glide down the Mall, swish in through the gates of Clarence House, home to her neighbour and sister-in-law the Queen Mother, and alight outside her own apartment. Little James became very restless and was not reassured when told that he was about to meet the Queen's aunt. Knowing the clockwork precision of Royalty on parade Mr Groom left us, rather to my surprise, within minutes of the arrival of the royal car. We stood in a line of three in front of the big mahogany sideboard. Suddenly an engine purred and gravel crunched. Stepping through the French windows came a tall figure in a shiny dress and shimmering tiara. Without expression she extended a white-gloved hand three times – 'How do you do... How do you do... How do you do.' Without pausing for a moment she disappeared through the Dining Room doorway.

When the Princess Royal died the Buckingham Palace establishment, always conscious of the costs of a pension, gave Mr Groom a job as general factotum at the Queen Mother's Royal Lodge in Windsor Great Park. For those who have never seen it, this house is best described as a pink William IV version of one of those 'cottages' beloved of the American super-rich at Newport, Rhode Island. It is comparable in size to Clarence House and Birkhall on the Balmoral estate, providing an awful lot of space for one old lady living alone. For Mr Groom being a backroom boy was rather a comedown after running the show – albeit rather small one – for the Princess Royal. But he had a blind devotion to the Royal Family and so long as he was working for them he didn't mind what he did. It was his proud boast after a series of grand tea parties presided over by his employer that he had 'boiled water for five queens'.

For a little winter sun the Gloucesters and the Princess Royal decided to go to Barbados one February. A small group of servants led by Mr Groom waited by the car to wave them off. As they bundled in and headed for the airport the Princess was heard to remark;

'Oh dear, I always wonder what they'll get up to while I am away.'

To which the Duke replied, 'I wouldn't worry about that. Just be grateful they are there when you get back.'

The Gloucesters regarded their main home as being Barnwell Manor in Northamptonshire and they went there every weekend. It is a large rambling house set in beautiful countryside with several thousand acres farmed on the Duke's behalf. They were well liked in the community and did a lot for the church and local charities. Before the days of tight security they would set off on a Friday afternoon in the distinctive grey Rolls-Royce with its 'Flying Lady' mascot on top of the radiator replaced by a miniature tank gun turret. If the Duke decided to dispense with the services of a chauffeur he would drive, with the Duchess sitting beside him. Richard was obliged to sit in solitary splendour in the back.

Weekend life at Barnwell was remarkably similar to that in manor houses all over the kingdom. The neighbour's geese made nuisances of themselves all over the lawns (much to the Duke's annoyance). A strict routine was carefully adhered to when it came to meal times and the ritual dressing for dinner. On only one occasion was the Duke known to break his own rules by leaving his dressing room a few minutes early to go down to drinks before dinner. This sudden and unprecedented move came as a hapless housemaid was finishing a little evening brushing on the staircase. Hearing the royal footsteps approaching she dashed for cover into a cupboard on the half-landing, shutting the door behind her. Her heart missed a beat as the footsteps stopped outside. Suddenly the door opened enough for the Duke to say 'Goodnight' before he closed it again and carried on with his journey.

They enjoyed a lifestyle that was expensive to maintain, even in those days of generous allowances from the Civil List. In order to keep costs down, the ducal pair practised economies that could be regarded as petty in some quarters. The Duke's contribution to frugality was to lay out his handkerchief to dry after use, while for her part the

Duchess trawled the bathrooms for used soap, after the guests had departed.

Royal valets and dressers had the best time when they accompanied their employers to stay at Windsor, Balmoral or Sandringham. As visiting staff they were given comfortable rooms in the closest tower or wing to their bosses' suite. They ate in style in the Stewards Room and swanned around in smart clothes. All a far cry from a bed in a cubicle, snatched meals in the Servants Hall and a serge suit and lace-up boots. Their close proximity to the Royal Family set them apart from the other servants and made them an elite group. The only royal who exceeded the one-to-one ratio was the Queen Mother, who always travelled with a troupe of four. They were her page, footman and two dressers. William, her page, had risen over a great number of years from dishing out food in the Servants Hall, by way of Brusher (or third valet) to the King, until his present eminence. Miss Suckling, the senior dresser, was very grand and had taken on something of the appearance of her mistress. It was always difficult to imagine her doing anything with Thawpit. Miss Field, her number two, was a much more down-to-earth figure who loved her food and had a reputation as a fine needlewoman. She was even rumoured to be responsible for covering with matching fabric all those hundreds of handbags without which the royal arm is incomplete. If you were lucky enough to be in the Grand Corridor at Windsor quite early of a morning you might catch a glimpse of a small procession as it left the Queen Empress's Bedroom. In the lead would be Miss S. carrying the glorious confection that had been worn the night before. In her wake, Miss F. bore the undergarments shrouded from view under a cloth kept specially for that purpose. Further along the corridor, a somewhat less dignified scenario was being enacted. Behind a closed door, Princess Marina was sipping a cup of black coffee and enjoying her first cigarette of the day. Between bouts of coughing she could be heard calling in vain 'Edith! Edith!', for her deaf but delightful dresser, Miss Hinman.

The undisputed stars in the royal firmament through the mid-sixties and seventies were Princess Margaret and Lord Snowdon. Their unassailable position as darlings of the popular press came about largely because of the absence of anyone else on the scene. The Queen's children were too young to be seen leading glamorous lives and the older royals were still stuck in their traditional ruts. The one possible exception was the popular figure of Princess Alexandra, but she suffered by being regarded as too far from the throne.

The Snowdon court was centred on the apartment they occupied next to Princess Marina at Kensington Palace. The official term 'apartment' was misleading in the extreme, as it was in fact a large house on four floors. It had been completely remodelled for them by the Ministry of Works under the exacting direction of Snowdon himself. They moved to it from their first home, 1A Kensington Palace, which was subsequently rearranged to accommodate the Waleses and the Michaels.

To run the establishment and provide for the comfort of its occupants a large team of people was required. These included a resident housekeeper and housemaid plus two dailies, a chef and kitchen maid, two chauffeurs, a butler and footman and the dresser. Lord Snowdon also brought with him the old secretary from his bachelor days to act as his ally against the hostile forces of the Princess's office staff, who were housed in a separate part of the Palace.

During a family gathering at Windsor, Richard, valeting Uncle Harry, met for the first time his Snowdon counterpart, a rather silly young man called Malcolm Higgins. (Richard, who never used a male first name when a female one seemed more becoming, immediately christened him 'Molly'.) In spite of his obvious shortcomings, Malcolm was sturdy and not unattractive. But what Richard admired about him was that in spite of receiving a pittance he worked bloody hard in his dual role of butler/valet for his two very demanding bosses. What Malcolm may not have realised, but what Richard saw in due course, was that Snowdon was adept at charming people into carrying out his wishes and sweetening pills with treats. Thrown together, largely because the alternatives were so dull, the two valets struck up a friendship. By the time their stay at the Castle came to an end, Malcolm had persuaded Richard to leave the Gloucesters and move to Kensington Palace as second butler/valet. The suggestion of a change had come at a time when Richard was seriously considering a move from the Gloucesters, fond of the family though he was, to a household that was a little more lively.

Richard's new home was a room on the top floor of the Palace above a guest bedroom and Lord Snowdon's dressing room and bathroom. Its window looked south over the sizeable garden, across Kensington Gardens to the eastern end of the High Street. The room next door was occupied by Miss Isobel Mathieson, the Princess's dresser, a feisty character from the west coast of Scotland. She had been in service all her working life. Before joining Princess Margaret she had been ladies maid (only the Royals have dressers) to Mrs Soames, mother-in-law of Lady Soames, and also Lady Churchill. Isobel and Richard soon became firm friends. And it was a relationship, unlike some, that survived exhausting official visits to Uganda, Japan and the United States. To those of us left behind, travelling with the Snowdons represented the last word in glamour and excitement, but at the sharp end it meant constant changes of clothes that had to be pressed, packing and unpacking and climbing in and out of small aeroplanes whilst keeping an eye on a mountain of luggage.

During her many years with PM the biggest challenge Isobel faced each day was separating the royal body from its bed. On a non-engagement day (and there were many) the ten o'clock tray of tea seldom did the trick. Opening the curtains produced a moan but no serious movement. Only after the teapot was replenished two or three times was the order likely to be given for the bath to be run.

I went to Isobel's funeral with Richard a few years ago. She had been retired for a long time and lived in a grace-and-favour flat on the Duchy estate in Kennington. Miss Sumner, the elderly Snowdon nanny, was there, but apart from her it was very poorly attended. Sadly, the few floral tributes to a fine old lady did not include a contribution from her last employer, Princess Margaret.

The Butler's Pantry is in many ways the control room of an important house and its smooth running requires routine and organisation. Chez Snowdon, Richard soon discovered that a combination of Malcolm's lack of experience and His Lordship's crusade to be unconventional meant that both these elements were missing. Rather to his surprise, the Princess seemed to go along with the general relaxation of standards. Her golden rules were that no one ever addressed her as anything less than 'Ma'am'; that VAT 69 and ginger ale were on tap from the moment of sundown, and that dinner was served at her command some time between eight p.m. and midnight. She was still basking in the glow of the relative newness of her marriage and was prepared to concede a certain amount of leeway to the man who had made her his wife.

With no intention of trying to change the status quo, Richard got on with what he regarded as the traditional side of the job, leaving Malcolm to his 'eye service'. By mid-morning the silver was gleaming and the china and glass polished ready for use. For the first time the house was filled with flowers as Richard demonstrated his skill as a latter-day Lady Pulbrook. The stone-flagged hall was an obvious contender for one of his more exotic displays, and the table facing the front door a perfect position for it. Unhappy though he was with floral restraint, he had to be careful not to conceal too much of the rather flat Annigonni portrait of the lady of the house that hung there.

PM shared with her sister a complete lack of interest in gardens (have you seen what they are like at Balmoral?) and flowers – as a result, no doubt, of having unwanted bouquets thrust into their hands at a very early age. Richard was never complimented on his efforts or even given much in the way of acknowledgement. For one particularly lavish party the Snowdons gave he had decorated the rooms to perfection, work that took many hours. As the guests arrived several of the ladies rushed up to the Princess to say how lovely the arrangements were and to ask who did them – hoping against hope, of course that a blushing princess would coyly admit to doing them herself. At first these enquiries were brushed aside or ignored, but finally one persistent young thing exclaimed, 'Oh Ma'am, your flowers are so gorgeous. You must tell me who did them.' The royal countenance froze for a moment, but without turning she hiked a thumb over her shoulder and muttered, 'He did.' Richard, standing behind the buffet, could not resist a small beam of pleasure.

Of course, Princess Margaret's flair for the put down is well known. Another example of the genre took place at the Royal Opera House during a gala. Dinner was served in the Retiring Room behind the Royal Box during the course of the evening. The performance on stage was as of nothing compared with the production required to dish up a bit of cold food for six people. China, glass, silver, linen and flowers were ferried across from Kensington Palace during the day. As the curtain came down for the first interval, Richard and I stood behind the chairs, braced for the arrival of the Princess and her guests. When she came through the door of the rather ornate little room, the woman beside her said.

'Oh Ma'am, what a charming room.'

'Oh really,' the Princess responded, 'it was my great-grandfather's loo.'

After five years at Kensington Palace, Malcolm decided to leave while he was still young enough to take up a new career. Happily, he found something in a completely different world and has made a great success of it.

Although Malcolm and Richard had not always had the most harmonious relationship, for the most part it worked well enough. His departure left Richard's head alone above the parapet at a time of burgeoning internecine warfare in the camp. There were times when the atmosphere in the house, above stairs and below, was openly hostile. The core of the problem was that Princess Margaret and Snowdon, having had their two children, were bored with each other. The fact that they were both supremely selfish and determined to have their own way did not help. He began to plead pressure of work to avoid accompanying her on royal engagements and used similar excuses for staying with her, only fleetingly, on the obligatory visits to the in-laws. Although his study was on the ground floor next to the drawing room he was more often to be found in the basement where he kept his dark room and workshop, next to Dorothy Everard's office. The Princess never set foot in that part of the house, only going as far as the top of the stairs to call down, 'Darling, where are you?' if something needed to be discussed. In fact, thanks to a particularly stinky eau de toilette called Zizzani with which he drenched himself, finding Snowdon was always pretty easy.

As well as the mutual animosity between Princess Margaret and Mrs Everard, Snowdon for his part disliked Miss Sumner, the nanny, although she was widely regarded as good at her job. Not to be outdone, Miss Mathieson had no time for Miss Sumner or Lord Snowdon. In this she was continuing a tradition that encompassed the dressers of all the royal ladies. Further down the pecking order it was a well-known fact that Miss Foley, the housekeeper and Leo Groden, the chef, could barely bring themselves to speak to each other. However they were all united in disliking the Princess' favourite, John, the handsome chauffeur. In spite of all this, Richard, easily the most volatile of all of them, somehow managed to keep the peace.

Only in his direct dealings with Princess Margaret was his patience sometimes put to the test. He did not care how often she asked for a bowl of hot soapy water so that she could wash the china in a display case, or ask for the television to be put on the dining table if she was alone for dinner. But he did object, as the person in charge, when he had to find out from the chef how many people were coming to dinner. He quite rightly maintained that the chef's daily meeting with the Princess was to plan menus, not discuss the guest list. Her favourite trick was to say, as she passed through the hall on the way to the theatre, 'Richard, we shall be six for dinner at eleven o'clock.' As if this was not bad enough, more often than not he would receive a phone message during the evening to say that the number had increased to eight.

By far the worst example of the Princess's behaviour in this regard occurred on the Queen Mother's birthday in 1968. This was in the days when the anniversary of the Queen Mother's birth was considered interesting, rather than remarkable. The high point of the celebrations would be a quiet dinner with her family rather than a carnival in the Mall.

Princess Margaret told Richard in the course of the day that there would be eight for dinner at eleven o'clock after the theatre. Knowing the significance of the day he had his suspicions and rang Billy Tallon at Clarence House to ask what the Princess was doing that evening.

'She is coming to you after the theatre, of course, with the Queen,

Prince Philip, the Gloucesters and Prince Charles,' Billy replied, with some incredulity. In spite of having spent most of his life under the same assorted roofs as Princess Margaret, Billy never ceased to be amazed at her behaviour. At his own establishment the preparation for such an important dinner would have gone on for days, involving a staff of fifteen.

Although Richard was furious with his employer for not saying, at the very least, 'Oh Richard, as it is a special dinner tonight for Queen Elizabeth's birthday, I hope you will make the table look particularly nice', he spent the day doing exactly that. As well as arranging a low-rise floral centrepiece (the Royals hate view-obstructing flowers in the middle of the table), he found places for the few decent gold figurines and boxes in the Princess's meagre collection. His close observation over many years of the Dowager Queen in dining mode had taught him that there were various things she liked to have on the table in front of her. These included a small Thermos of ice with silver tongs, a swizzle stick for her champagne and a silver note pad and pencil. She also expected to have a chair with arms and a footstool. By the time I arrived that evening to help, the stage was set. We spent the next few hours in the staff sitting room watching the telly. Soon after eleven o'clock we heard the sound of cars pulling up outside.

'Oh God, they're here,' I exclaimed, 'we'd better go upstairs.'

'Stay where you are,' Richard commanded, 'she's got a key.'

A few moments later footsteps and voices were clearly audible in the hall above our heads. Just as Richard was turning up the volume on the television the door burst open to reveal the happy band of chauffeurs and detectives, their duties temporarily discharged. This awestruck group of men were horrified to see that we were not hovering eagerly upstairs, but their protestations were interrupted by the buzz of the internal telephone. Richard moved not a muscle. With the second ring he sauntered over and picked up the receiver. 'Oh really,' was all he was heard to say. Having hung up he turned to me and declared:

'Well, I suppose we had better go and light a few candles.'

In a state of some panic I scooted along behind him as he headed for the kitchen to see if the food was ready. From there we processed to the pantry to open white wine and fill the water glasses. I lit the candles while Richard took what seemed to be an eternity making last-minute adjustments to the table. At long last, as I stood rigid with apprehension, he approached the double doors, saying over his shoulder, 'Let battle commence.' As the doors opened to reveal the brightly lit drawing room, a hush came over the assembled senior members of the Royal Family and all eyes turned towards the figure framed in the doorway. Looking directly at his employer Richard, in a firm voice, announced:

'Dinner is served, Your Royal Highness.'

In response the Princess, standing beside the Queen, turned to her sister and with a hint of steel in her voice said:

'Come on, we'd better go in or there's going to be a row!'

In spite of the occasional turbulence in their relationship over the years, the Princess and Richard had an affectionate respect for each other. When the day finally came that he told her he was giving in his notice, she did her very best to get him to change his mind. But her entreaties were to no avail, as he was determined to see more of the world and receive the sort of salary that was his due. His ability and experience proved to be much in demand, his skill and knowledge greatly sought after. One particularly grateful employer even bought him a house to be sure of retaining his services. He buttles at present in an ancient moated East Anglian house, which has been in the owner's family for seven hundred years. Always ready to adapt, he starts his day by lowering the drawbridge and raising the flag.

My new room was on the top floor at the back of the Palace, on a landing where all the ordinary footmen slept. Although it wasn't as big as the bedroom that overlooked the quadrangle, it did have a washbasin and slightly superior furniture. But the best thing about it was the huge window and its view of the setting sun and forty-five acres of garden. It was astonishing to be right in the middle of London, but with a completely rural outlook and hardly a sound to be heard. At night, the quietest time of all, there was only the occasional crunch of an army boot on gravel to disturb the peace. By day, when there was noise at all it was deafening, and always the result of a take-off or landing by one of the red helicopters. Each time the culprit would be one or other of the two royal 'copterholics, Prince Philip or the Queen Mum, for whom no journey would be considered too short for an airborne ride.

On day one, my first appointment was with the Deputy Sergeant Footman in the 'dressing-up room' to sort out my uniforms. During the war the day-to-day uniform of the scarlet tailcoat worn with stiff white shirt front and wing collar was replaced by more practical battledress. Mercifully, the practice of powdering the hair or wearing a wig was also abandoned. As scarlet is still worn in front of visitors I was measured for this and for its replacement. In order of importance the next livery is a scarlet tailcoat again, but one that buttons across the chest, with epaulets and a stand-up collar stiffened with gold wire. This is worn on the Yacht with black trousers and at Windsor with blue plush knee breeches. Only the grandest occasions, thank God, warrant the appearance of shoulder-buckling full State livery. The heavily interlined coat for this, when not richly red, is sewn with gold and huge crested brass buttons. The right sleeve carries a badge that bears the royal cypher, and a jabot decorates the throat. As if all this was not enough, plush breeches are red and worn over pink tights – two pairs for the hairy. Black patent buckled pumps complete the picture. As far as the last two uniforms were concerned there was no question of them being tailor-made. The huge cost involved in producing them meant that over the years they were simply altered to fit. Before the session was over I was presented with a large leather trunk and filled it with an assortment of accessories. These included a sword, gloves, white bow tie and stiff shirts, a black and gold-encrusted waistcoat and something called a travelling cord that hung across the chest and originally had a pistol at the end of it. Three hat boxes contained a blue velvet jockey cap to be worn with state livery on carriages, a tricorn hat for less splendid outings and a black silk topper. The largest item of all was an ankle-length scarlet coat with layered cape shoulders.

The Footmen's Room was our headquarters and it was the noticeboard there that controlled our lives. Our daily roster was pinned to it, along with movement orders for the year ahead and the names of those chosen for foreign trips. The other centre of our activity was a room beside one of the entrances from the quadrangle, known as the Kings Door. On the other side of the doorway was what had once been a rather smart waiting room, but was now the office of the Keeper of the Privy Purse. The duty footman's first task each morning was to collect a copy of the airmail edition of *The Times* from the Privy Purse Door and place it neatly on a table in the Keeper's Office. As far as I know the paper was never looked at or opened by anyone. Out of curiosity I once asked one of the old timers why it was there. The only explanation he could think of was that the room had once been used by the Prince of Wales (later Duke of Windsor), who must have asked for it to be delivered. The financial whizzkids must have been apoplectic when the bill for that little item was scrutinised. Beyond the entrance hall was the Equerries Room and the curving flight of stairs that led to the first floor and Prince Philip's part of the private apartments known, rather quaintly, as 'the Duke's end'. He used The Door for all his official outings, as did the prime minister when he came for his weekly audiences.

As the morning hotted up, with the members of the Household arriving at their offices, the duty man had to inquire of each one whether he would like lunch that day. The numbers were then passed through to the Comptroller of Supply. An extended version of passing the parcel came next. This was the serious business of moving documents and papers, some of them undoubtedly top secret, between offices. As none of them was ever allowed to travel naked, the ubiquitous red box was brought in to play. All the bigwigs had their own keys to the boxes, which meant that none ever passed into the wrong hands. The only office we never entered in the course of our deliveries was the Queen's. Boxes for her were always handed to the Queen's Page. She never received more than two or three each day and the poor old Duke never had any at all.

After lunch the pace of life slows appreciably, especially on Fridays when the Queen heads for Windsor and 'Flaggy' (the nickname of the orderly in charge of the pole) lowers the Standard. This is the signal for which her courtiers have been waiting, and before you can say 'green wellies' they are speeding away to their country estates.

One particular Friday afternoon I was sitting at the desk at the King's Door, trying hard to stay awake, when I saw through the window the figure of a stout, well-dressed woman walking purposefully towards the Grand Entrance. As far as I knew, no visitors were expected, and if they had been it was the Privy Purse Door at the front to which she should have gone. When I caught up with her and asked if I could help she explained that she was the Duchess of Brighton and that she had come to have tea with the Queen. She added that she must sit down soon, as the screwdriver sticking into her back was very painful. Knowing that Her Majesty was safely on her way to Windsor, I guided the newcomer towards the King's Door and suggested she wait in the office whilst I told the Queen that she had arrived. Having settled her into a chair I shut the door and flew across to my desk to telephone the police lodge and put them in the picture. My next move was towards the Equerries Room where I knew that

Lord Plunket, as duty equerry, was having tea. Although I was sure that this was not a time when His Lordship would be happy to be disturbed, there was part of me that was looking forward to witnessing his reaction. His copy of *Country Life* was slowly lowered as I coughed and made my entrance. It was only when I got to the bit about the screwdriver that scented tea and magazine shot across the room as he clambered to his feet. With introductions out of the way, His Lordship and I were just being shown the embedded screwdriver when the sound of cars screeching to a halt interrupted our inspection. Minutes later the unfortunate old lady was led away by a horde of burly policemen. I was told the next day that she had escaped from an asylum and had a history of self-mutilation – born out of time I would say! How she got so far beyond the Palace gates was something I never discovered.

For tourists and Londoners alike, one of the most colourful and unexpected sights that London has to offer on an ordinary weekday morning is the procession of carriages taking a new ambassador and his staff to the Court of St James to present his credentials to the sovereign. It was rotten luck, and in my view unfair, that the footman usually chosen to be part of this spectacle was the one who was off-duty that day. In my case this meant enjoying only a brief lie-in and missing breakfast, which was a great mistake. With minutes to spare I would climb into my battledress, cover it with the caped coat and whirl round to the Royal Mews carrying my black topper and white gloves. The little cortège comprised three closed carriages with coachmen and grooms, a car for the ambassador's spouse and another containing the Crown Equerry. With an escort of mounted policemen we headed for our first port of call, the home of the Marshall of the Diplomatic Corps at St James's Palace. For the tenure of his office his 'tied cottage' was that part of the Palace beneath the clock, with a view directly up St James's Street. From there our destination might be almost anywhere in central London, depending on the wealth and status of the country concerned. A representative of somewhere relatively insignificant might be holed up in one of Bayswater's small hotels; a place with more clout could afford a suite at a grand establishment in Park Lane, and then there was the big league with long-established embassies in places like Belgrave Square and Kensington Palace Gardens. From the old hands I soon discovered that East European countries were the flunkies' favourites, as they wanted all those involved to enjoy their ambassador's great day. Not only would everyone receive a large tip, but we were also asked in to the party afterwards. I vividly recall the morning we returned to the Polish Embassy in Millionaire's Row after the ceremony at the Palace. On the other hand, I do not clearly remember leaving. His Excellency invited the Marshall, as was customary, to go inside for a drink. But he also extended the invitation to the police and everyone from the Palace. As we trooped into a brightly lit reception room we were met by waiters bearing trays of mixed drinks and caviar canapés. After about an hour the slightly ill-at-ease Marshall looked around the room and announced that it was time we were going. As we took our leave the Ambassador presented each of us with a bottle of plum brandy and a manila envelope. Once Earl Cairns was safely aboard, the smiling head coachman whipped up his team and headed for the open road, or more precisely Kensington High Street. Rarely can a carriage and four have exceeded the speed limit in a built-up area, but we certainly did that day. Standing on the box at the back of the first carriage, with only a strap to hold on to, it was all I could do to avoid losing my bottle (in every sense), let alone keep my balance.

When Mr Candy was promoted to Page of the Presence his place was taken by a much younger chap called John Taylor, who had spent all his working life at the Palace. Chuffchuff's new eminence meant black battledress with gold epaulettes and the company of four others under the command of the Page of the Chambers. As well as running the Household dining room and the Privy Purse Door, they also presided over the Grand Entrance and Hall when the Queen had morning appointments. Two of them would be on duty there, with the Equerry and Lady-in-Waiting, to receive official visitors. Sometimes this little reception committee would be joined by the curmudgeonly figure of the Queen's Pipe Major in full Highland regalia – to the amazement of some of the arrivals. Although he obviously resented having to stand around like a spare prick, his only other job was to play the bagpipes each morning beneath the Queen's bedroom window.

Over many years the new Sergeant Footman had known and worked with the small group of senior footmen, like him mostly married, who represented the core of the Footmen's Room. In spite of always being very pleasant to me, I do not think he ever regarded me as a real insider. Nevertheless, early in my first year I was chosen to be in the party accompanying the Queen and Prince Philip on their state visit to Ethiopia and the Sudan. For someone who had never been anywhere more exotic than Lloret de Mar, this was a very exciting destination. The rest of the party included the Foreign Secretary, two private secretaries, the Duke's Equerry, the Captain of the Queen's Flight, two ladies-in-waiting, two detectives, office staff, three dressers and two other footmen. Along with mountains of luggage we filled an RAF VC10 that had been specially converted to provide the royals with a sitting room and bedroom. I was to act as valet to the Equerry and the Press Secretary.

We drove away from Addis Ababa airport in a long cavalcade of motor cars towards the centre of this small African city. Our route – a broad, straight highway – was decorated with triumphal arches that were adorned with the flags of the two countries and images of HM and the emperor. On either side, what must have been a good percentage of the population jostled each other for space, whilst waving with every impression of excitement. For the duration of the visit the Royals were housed at the palace with the Emperor and his family, while the rest of us stayed at a reasonably modern hotel nearby. The Queen and Prince Philip had a heavy schedule of engagements, doing all the things they have done so often before in other countries. The staff were left with lots of time to explore and see the sights. We were lucky in that the ambassador, Sir John Russell and his charming Greek-born wife had gone to a lot of trouble to see that we were not bored. Sadly, after three days of excursions around Addis we were forced to conclude that there was very little there for tourists to enjoy. The only things of interest were the enormous highways that ran through the city and then petered out to become dusty tracks. These were built by Mussolini's army of occupation as part of a grand design that was nipped in the bud. But it was left to the emperor to provide one of the most enduring memories of the trip – the sight of the two leopards flanking the steps at the entrance to his palace.

On day three we flew to Asmara, a provincial city where the old man also had an impressive pile. The enthusiasm here for the Queen and the emperor was even greater than it had been in the capital. It underlined the fact that although he ruled his kingdom as an absolute monarch, he was revered almost as a God by his people. I use the word 'almost' because in fact Ethiopia has been an island of Christianity for hundreds of years. The highlight of our brief stay was an enormous reception given by Haile Selassie in the grounds of his palace. Everyone in the royal party received a very stiff invitation to attend.

From Asmara we flew across Ethiopia to a place called Gondar, high in the mountains, where the Imperial Family went to escape the heat. It turned out to be nothing more than a vast plateau hundreds of feet above a deep gorge that was part of the Rift Valley. In this inaccessible spot an extraordinary tented encampment had been built, more like The Field of the Cloth of Gold than anything you would expect to see on top of an African mountain. Set apart from the canvas dwellings was a group of highly sophisticated air-conditioned caravans for the use of the two royal families. If she felt like writing, the Queen had the use of an open-sided tent complete with Persian rug and desk and chairs. Although there was no sign at all of anything like a pot over an open fire, marvellous food was served on bone china in what can only be described as the dining-room tent, by white-gloved waiters. These attentive young men also made sure that our glasses were constantly replenished with chilled French wine.

On the morning of our last day at Gondar, the emperor led his family and the Queen and Prince Philip out of the camp to stand in front of the gateway. The rest of us were rounded up and herded in behind. Ahead of us lay the vast expanse of the sun-baked plain. After a while, there was what sounded like distant muffled thunder, accompanied by a dust storm on the horizon. As the noise grew louder and the cloud darkened we could see that what was bearing down on us at great speed was an army of men on horseback, waving guns and hollering at the tops of their voices. Even as they drew nearer there was no slackening of pace and it looked as if they would gallop straight through us. As the dust swirled all around, I thought for a moment of making a dash for it, and I could see that those around me had the same idea. Suddenly, with only feet to spare, they reigned in their mounts and slithered to a halt in front of the man they called The Lion of Judah.

Back in Addis once more for the last day of the visit we were all summoned to be received at the palace. I climbed the steps rather nervously between the sentries and the pair of leopards. But I need not have worried because on closer inspection they looked as if they might be sedated. On our way to the imperial presence we passed through any number of rooms filled with thrones, until we arrived at the biggest and the best. Dwarfed by his surroundings, the little emperor dressed in a khaki uniform, stood on a raised dais with his court around him. He shook hands and presented each of us with a pair of rather vulgar cufflinks in the shape of a tribal shield, crowned by the imperial arms.

Khartoum was baking hot beside the cool waters of the Nile when we arrived there for the next leg of our journey. At first sight it seemed to be a much more interesting and exotic city than poor old Addis. Its inhabitants thronged the streets in elegant white djelabahs, and I spotted lots of men walking in pairs and holding hands! But apparently it had not always been such a tranquil place. Religious and political differences had riven the country for many years. In remote areas fighting was still going on, even during the royal visit. Nevertheless it had obviously been decided that the situation was stable enough for some serious Union Jack-waving to take place. Government was in the hands of a committee of twelve men, who took it in turns to be boss. It was the February President who acted as host to the Queen and Prince Philip. Once again, the Royals stayed at the palace while the rest of us were either in a hotel or at the embassy residence. The house provided for 'our man', Sir David Scott Fox, was a nasty concrete-and-glass box reminiscent of Terminal 2 at Heathrow.

A fleet of cars was laid on so that we could all move easily between our various lodgings, but that did not always mean that journeys were without incident. This was mainly due to the presence in the city of fanatical followers of the Mahdi, whose famous ancestor had been a thorn in British flesh a hundred years before. They were quite literally up in arms about the royal visit and saw the official cars as obvious targets. Once or twice my driver had to turn into a side street to dodge a potentially hostile crowd. One time he was unable to avoid a noisy mob who surrounded the car, chanting and waving fists. As they surged forward to see who was inside my sturdy companion clasped my hand but only, I suspect, for reassurance. Once they had seen that the passenger did not resemble the Queen, nor less the Duke, we were allowed to pass. A sequel to this little incident was our trip the next day to the site of the Battle of Omdurman, where the forebears of my protagonists had fought our boys to the death. It proved to be a vast expanse of desert that had not been disturbed since the last soldier had fallen. Walking away from the rest of the party, my imagination went into overdrive, just as it would when I stood in the fields at Waterloo on another occasion. With eyes half closed I could picture the scene of the cavalry and tribesmen locked in bloody conflict, the noise of battle ringing in my ears.

Sir David had a very lively, high-spirited daughter in her late teens who organised a picnic for the staff whilst the royal party was away one day on an engagement. The location she had chosen was an island at the junction of the White and Blue Niles, just outside Khartoum. In what proved to be an idyllic setting we ate well and lazed around beneath shady trees. But not for long. Suddenly our hostess suggested that some of us might like to water-ski. In the deafening silence I heard my own voice saying that although I had never done it, I was prepared to have a go.

'Oh good,' she responded. 'And I am sure you're a strong swimmer.'

'Well, not really,' said I, 'but my Monte Carlo crawl is pretty powerful. Is it strong currents that you are worried about?'

'Not exactly,' she replied, 'it's just that there is the occasional crocodile in these parts, but they are usually much too lazy to attack anybody.'

To hoots of laughter I backed down as gracefully as I could. As an alternative we went off for a less risky walk along the riverbank. Along the way Sir David's daughter said that as her parents were dining that evening at the Presidential Palace she had asked some friends to join her for supper and would I like to be included. Even if I had wanted to, it would have been difficult to plead a prior engagement. The evening turned out to be the best time I had had since we left London, and certainly a pleasant change from hotel dining rooms and the company of some of my colleagues. Needless to say I stayed far too long and, to my horror, was still there when the ambassadorial couple returned from dinner. My first reaction was that they would be horrified to see their daughter playing host to a footman, even a royal one. But I need not have worried; whether it was Foreign Office training or natural good manners, they could not have been more charming.

The presidential gifts we were all given to commemorate the visit were an ivory cigarette holder and a snakeskin attaché case.

Soon after we got back to London I found myself one morning, in scarlet, waiting at the Grand Entrance to do a little car door opening. Lo and behold, who should be the first to arrive but Her Majesty's Ambassador to Khartoum. To my great surprise not only did he remember me but we spent so long chatting that the Equerry, waiting uncomfortably in the background, must have thought Sir David had mistaken me for someone rather more important.

On another investiture day I was on duty in the Grand Hall when a man in a morning coat came up to me and asked the way to the loo. I was slightly taken aback when he added that he would like me to go with him. I led the way, quietly congratulating myself for having washed my hair that morning. Once we reached the seclusion of the Gents he explained that his braces had broken and he was afraid that when he rose from the knighting stool in front of the Queen his trousers would be round his ankles. Although I thought to myself that this was the sort of diversion the Queen would adore, what I actually said was that he could have my braces and I would be careful to stand with my legs well apart. After a quick swap he scuttled away a happy man. The next day I was rung by the page on duty to be told that a chauffeur was waiting to see me at the Privy Purse Door. When I got there the smartly dressed man handed me a parcel and then drove out of the forecourt in a Rolls-Royce. The package proved to contain my braces, wrapped in tissue paper, and a hand-written letter from the outgoing High Commissioner for Australia thanking me for my kindness on the most important day of his life.

In the 1960s, the time about which I am writing, English society was still very carefully structured and everyone 'knew their place'. This hierarchical system, the status quo, was seen by many as a contributing factor in our ability, as a nation, to lead and to inspire. But in that decade changes started to take place: class divisions became less rigid and where jobs and establishments like universities were concerned the emphasis switched from background to ability. However much this was true of an increasing number of areas, the last redoubt would be the armed forces, the civil service and the Royal Household. Of these three, the first two were an unknown quantity as far as I was concerned, but I observed the third with great interest.

At Buckingham Palace there were two obvious sets of people: the aristocrats who were members of the Household, and the servants who were the Household staff. But sandwiched between that great divide was another layer of people known as the Officials. The women tended to be upper middle class and known as lady clerks rather than typists or secretaries. The male of the species, mostly lower middle class, were certainly not called gentlemen clerks. The majority of them worked for either the Chief Clerk, Private Secretary's Office or the Chief Clerk, Master of the Household's Office. When it came to retirement the difference in background was reflected in the DCVO for the Private Secretary's Chief Clerk and the MVO for the Master's man. Tucked away in a corner of the Palace, running a department of her own, was the redoubtable Miss Peggy Short, Lady Clerk to the Lady-in-Waiting, whose output of letters was considerable. The missives were all a variation of the same theme, beginning 'I am commanded by Her Majesty to thank you.'

The arrival of a new female recruit to any department was always a topic of great interest to those of my colleagues who studied this sort of form. In the case of Rosemary Eden their excitement was even greater than usual, for she was a very attractive young lady. For a start she was at least ten years younger than the other girls in the Private Secretary's Office. She was slightly built, with reddy gold hair and a shy smile. During the course of a day at the King's Door I bumped into her quite often as she flitted between her own office and the one occupied by Sir Edward Ford, who was her boss. She always gave the impression that she was very friendly, and so after a while we paused in the corridor for a chat. One evening we met for a drink after work and found that we had lots of common interests, as well as a shared sense of humour. Rather to my surprise she told me that she lived with her parents in Surrey and had a regular boyfriend. I was even more surprised at how easy I found it to tell her that I did not have a boyfriend, and she made sympathetic noises. As neither of us earned very much money our outings were rather restricted, but we saved up for the occasional trip to the theatre and a cheap supper. One day I took her home to meet my ever-so-delighted mother and one evening, by way of a trade off, she introduced me to her less-than-delighted boyfriend. I was forced to confess that the person she had described as wet and boring seemed to me to be remarkably attractive.

On the day of my twenty-first birthday I had arranged to take Mum to the ballet at Covent Garden in the evening and I had asked Rosemary to lunch with me at The Caprice. As we were having a drink at the bar I saw to my horror that Princess Margaret was in a party at one of the tables. This was a scenario that could have been very embarrassing for Rosemary, but fortunately when we moved to our table we were placed some distance from where she was sitting. With luck PM wouldn't have spotted us. But of course, I should have remembered that she shares with her sister the knack of taking in a room at a glance. Sure enough, later that afternoon I was telephoned by Richard, sounding somewhat confused, from Kensington Palace. He had no idea where his employer had been that morning, but as soon as she got out of the car she greeted him with the words, 'Guess who I've been having lunch with at The Caprice?' Met with a blank look, behind which Richard was thinking she'd overdone it again, she added, 'G-u-u-u-y. He was at a table with that nice secretary of Sir Edward Ford's.'

Although there were no obvious repercussions of our being seen together in public, we both knew that our friendship was well known within the Palace. Who knows, perhaps it was even mentioned by Princess Margaret during her daily telephone call to Her Majesty. After all, their relish for servants' tittle-tattle was well known. But in the end it was only Sir Edward who gave the merest hint that he knew that something was up. It happened when I entered his office one day with a red box, as usual. Rosemary was sitting opposite him at the desk, taking dictation. As I placed the box on the table inside the door he paused, looked at me over his glasses and said, 'Ah, Hunting,' before glancing at Rosemary. The poor girl blushed deeply.

In August we were together at Balmoral. The lady clerks' accommodation there was inherited from Queen Victoria's Indian retainers. It was an extraordinary bungalow called Karim Cottage, which the old queen had had built at the bottom of the garden to house the Munshi and his happy band. As a footman I literally went up in the world, changing the hut for a cubicle in a room at the top of the massive tower that dominated the Castle. Our friendship blossomed on long walks beside the Dee and cycle rides around the estate. On one of my days off I waited until dusk had fallen and then crept over to the cottage where Rosemary was alone and had prepared supper. After a lovely evening together I very nearly stayed a little longer but in the end stumbled off into the darkness.

That year the resident company of soldiers was from the Black Watch, under the command of a young South African major called Richard Orde. Now it just so happened that Major Orde was very dishy indeed, and as soon as I had my first glimpse of him I rushed off to tell Rosemary that her future was assured. She must set her cap at him without delay.

Many years later and on the other side of the world, my sister-in-law Susan was in a military hospital in Singapore. After a couple of days the woman in the next bed, who was very friendly, asked Susan if she was related to someone called Guy Hunting. When Susan explained our relationship and asked why she had asked, she said that we had once been close friends but had lost touch. With a wry smile she told Susan that she would like me to know that she had four children, was married to a colonel in the Black Watch and that her name was Rosemary Orde.

One of the most interesting trips I was allowed to go on started with a flight to Cardiff with HM and HRH to join *Britannia*. It was the first time I had seen this beautiful boat and she was even more spectacular than I had imagined. Although not large by naval standards, she still required a crew of two hundred – and they weren't all washing napkins and polishing silver. With the Royals on board space was at a premium, which meant the stewards had to relinquish their cabins to the Palace staff. The poor things had to sling their hammocks, hugger-mugger, with the ordinary seamen. We had our own mess and a bar that sold duty-free booze, and bought an awful lot of friends. With an escorting frigate we sailed that day for the Firth of Clyde, where the Queen was to review the Home Fleet. When we awoke the next morning, through the rapidly clearing mist we could just discern rows of ships covered in flags and bunting. At the appointed hour the yacht sailed slowly along the lines of the Fleet at anchor, with only the Queen and Duke visible on the upper deck. The rest of us were hidden behind the net curtains in the dining room. As *Britannia* approached, each ship's company lining the rails doffed their caps and gave three cheers. After the Review the Queen gave the order 'splice the mainbrace', which meant that everyone, including civilians, had an extra tot of rum. Great fun was had by all.

We sailed from there to Scrabster in the north of Scotland, where the Queen's last engagement was a large cocktail party on the main deck for local bigwigs. With practised skill the crew erected a vast canopy, the galley produced lovely little things to eat, stewards and footmen glided around with trays of drinks and the royal barges ferried guests to and fro. HM flew back to London the next day, leaving the Duke with a greatly reduced entourage to set sail for the North Sea. The object of his solo mission was a review of the Hull fishing fleet, an exercise that was easier said than done. The contrast with what had taken place in the Clyde could not have been greater. I did not envy the task the Admiral had of finding something to be reviewed, for although the fishermen knew that the Duke was coming, their prime reason for bobbing around in that hostile bit of water was the pursuit of fish. However, we did catch sight of a couple of vessels and got close enough for the Duke to give them a friendly wave from the bridge. Most crews looked as if they were too busy to wave back.

Weather conditions worsened dramatically and by early evening we were in the teeth of a force nine gale. Although the yacht is fitted with stabilisers it is still very uncomfortable when the going gets rough. One by one cabin doors closed behind the sick and queasy. It soon emerged that the numbers for royal dinner were reduced to two: the Duke and his unfortunate RAF equerry. The dining room is big enough to seat thirty or forty people, and it looked rather empty with a small table and two chairs in the middle of it. This arrangement also meant that Mr Childs, the Duke's page, and I had a great distance to cover from the safe haven of the sideboard to the support of a chair back. In order to prevent me from ending up on the floor in a heap of vegetable dishes Mr Childs, a veteran of the royal yacht *Victoria & Albert*, had an immortal phrase that was my watchword: 'Wait for the roll, old boy.' Prince Philip's appetite, always hearty at the best of times, appeared to be unaffected by the violent motion, but his poor companion's face was turning greener by the minute. He had given up eating altogether and obviously found conversation a problem. When the ordeal was finally over the defeated airman swayed uneasily out of the room and away to his bed, where he joined almost half the ship's company – in a manner of speaking.

We had been told that some time during the night we were due to sail close to Surtsey, a new volcanic island that had sprung out of the seabed a few months before. At about four a.m. I was roused by a steward who came to say that we were approaching a huge mass of light and fire. The sight of a volcano spewing molten lava and showers of sparks into the night sky was one of the most amazing sights I have ever seen. During our airborne return journey we saw the island again in daylight and circled round it so that its red-and-gold core was clearly visible.

Our reason for being in this part of the world was that the Duke was on his way to pay the first official visit of a member of the royal family to Iceland. As we sailed into the harbour, what looked like Great Yarmouth out of season proved to be Reykjavik, the capital city. But on closer inspection it turned out to be quite a jolly place, with friendly people speaking excellent English who were very handsome in a Nordic sort of way. While HRH went off to inspect hydro-electric schemes and to mingle with wild geese, the crew of *Britannia* and the Household staff toured the island in coaches. Not a lengthy excursion.

To appreciate the extent of the exciting things that were pointed out to us, it is best to describe what was billed as the highlight of our expedition. The coaches stopped beside a rock formation perched on top of what proved to be our last remote and windy headland of the day. In spite of the urging of our guides there was some reluctance among the passengers to disembark. Those of us who braved the elements were handed soap pellets and shown how to drop them into holes in the surface of the rock. After a short pause a jet of water shot into the air. This was known as a geyser. After the show was over we rushed back to the warmth and comparative comfort of our transport to find that those we had left behind had slept throughout the entire performance.

Traditionally, on the last day of a visit to a foreign land, the royal guest returns the hospitality of his host. Iceland was no exception and so a dinner party for the president had been arranged. The domestic arrangements for this were in the hands of a chief petty officer with the ponderous title of Keeper and Steward of the Royal Apartments. He was a sort of butler and housekeeper rolled into one. His deputy, the Assistant Keeper, was a junior petty officer called Peter Ford, who was a good friend of mine. Peter had a way with a crochet needle and a stiffened napkin, but his great flair was for arranging flowers. On big occasions the state rooms were always filled with his wonderful displays. But his artistry was about to meet its biggest challenge. The trouble began when we realised that although parts of it had a green covering, Iceland was not a country where trees and clumps of vegetation grew very happily. With the dawn of our final day panic ensued in the flower room. A state dinner with empty vases was unthinkable, and so Peter decided that he had no choice but to scour the island for floral decoration. I agreed to accompany him, and we set off by barge for the quay and a waiting Embassy car. After a lengthy cruise round the streets we tracked down Reykjavik's florist and purchased their entire stock of greenery and potted chrysanthemums. On our way into the countryside we paused in front of any house that displayed a cheese plant in its window, or a farm with a few cloches dotted around the garden. But finally we found that part of the country that was given over to a degree of market gardening. To Peter's great relief the greenhouses there yielded a reasonable number of the sort of cut flowers and plants that he could work with. He bought anything that might be suitable, and when the owners were told of the use to which they were going to be put they proudly threw in all the rest as well. By now the car was beginning to resemble a float in a festival of flowers, with very little room for passengers. Somehow or other we squashed in and headed back to the harbour. When the barge came alongside *Britannia*, crowds of crew and staff were lining the rails – all laughing, some applauding. From their vantage point the sight of two men in a boat shoulder-deep in flowers must have looked like the start of a honeymoon on an Amsterdam canal.

That night the dining room looked magnificent and Peter glowed with pride as the double doors were opened and the President of Iceland and his wife made their entrance escorted by the Duke of Edinburgh.

My two weeks on the royal yacht had been a great adventure, and something of an eye-opener too. It was the first time I had been confined in a world that was unutterably masculine, rubbing shoulders each day with friendly, handsome men in a sexy uniform. At first I put it down to wishful thinking, but I soon accepted that there really was a sexual undercurrent where some of the 'Yachties' were concerned. This feeling was also confirmed by Peter Ford and some of the Palace old hands. During that particular voyage one or two of my workmates retired early to their cabins, armed with quantities of cheap booze, ready to receive naval visitors. Although I was much too gauche and shy to do the same, I have to admit that a taste for men in uniform had been acquired.

6

A stone's throw from the Barracks, just off Knightsbridge Green, there stands a hideous modern pub called Tattersalls Tavern. Pubs of that name have stood on that site for hundreds of years, as it was next to the ring where horses were traditionally bought and sold. Commerce of a rather different kind took place there when I used to frequent it in the mid-sixties. London, like every large city, had always had pubs with a gay bias and in those days the principal ones were the Golden Lion and the White Bear in the West End, and the City of Quebec (known as the Elephant's Graveyard) at Marble Arch, Earl's Court's Coleherne and the Queen's Head in Chelsea. Docklands pubs were in a world of their own, the emphasis being on bawdy entertainment. Cabaret for the night would be provided by an extravagantly dragged-up docker of the hairy-arsed variety tottering along the top of the bar miming to records by Mae West or Marilyn Monroe. North London had the William IV in Hampstead and the Black Cap in Camden Town. Before I discovered the delights of Knightsbridge my favourite of all these was the Queen's Head in Tryon Street. It was poorly lit (thank God) and had linoleum on the floor, but against one wall was an upright piano, the ivories of which were tinkled by a curious old man called Mac who wore a kilt. I don't remember ever picking anyone up there but I enjoyed the ambience. The place flourishes to this day and is still an interesting mix of queens from every walk of life. The only real difference is that Mac has been replaced by a CD player, and the lino covered by close-fitting carpet in a nasty shade of Brewers Brown.

But Tattersalls was different. It wasn't really a gay pub like the others I have mentioned. For a start, it consisted of a single enormous horseshoe-shaped bar, with its patrons split into two groups at either end. Rather like a village hall hop before the beer has started to flow. The area by the loo and closer to the Barracks was the preserve of troopers from the Life Guards and the Blues and Royals. Chatting in groups, they looked for all the world like men having a quick pint before going home to long-suffering wives. To the customers on the other side of the room, however, they were fantasy-fulfilling sex objects, who for the price of a few beers and a gift of a fiver would allow you to make free with their bodies. Contact was made in a choice of ways. It had very little to do with the meeting of eyes that signals interest in most gay places. When a man one liked the look of moved to the central part of the bar to get a drink, the punter stepped in to do the honours and introduce oneself. More often than not the offer was accepted, but with a round to pay for rather than a single pint. Once that contact was made, your new friend would stay with you rather than going back to his mates. A bolder approach was to follow your quarry into the loo, where at least the goods could be inspected before being bought. I was never brave enough to adopt either method, and only went to the pub with people who had what it took. At six-foot four, and very often taller than the boys, it was impossible to be inconspicuous, but I lurked in the background smiling and laughing as if I was thoroughly at ease. When I was brought into the conversation at all it was usually because someone had asked 'What does he do?' One squaddie even suggested that I looked like Lord Normanton, one of their officers.

The pub had its regulars on both sides of the divide. Star turns among the gays were the comic actor Richard Wattis, the Canadian 'swingometer' man Bob McKenzie, and the actor Charles Gray. Their familiar faces and skill with the chat-up lines were a guarantee of good but thirsty audiences. When it came to refilling empty glasses all three were notoriously sluggish in the wallet-producing department. I suppose they were arrogant enough to assume that half an hour of their witty company was the only generosity that was required, whereas we all knew that most lads were drawn to the place because they were so appallingly badly paid. For the better-looking among them – not, alas, necessarily the ones who came most often to Tattersalls – an enterprising Corporal of Horse provided a sort of 'male order' service in which big money and hot dinners were the order of the day. Over the years he had built up a client list of wealthy and sometimes well-known gentlemen who did not want to be seen hanging around a four-ale bar.

Sex, in terms of physical contact, was not apparently the motivating force for all of these encounters. Several clients simply enjoyed taking a soldier out to an expensive dinner just for the pleasure of being seen with a good-looking man in public. Others liked to cook for them at home. A not-exactly-typical example was the politician who delighted in serving up his own delicious food, but insisted that his guest condemn each course as being filthy or disgusting. A famous ballet critic was prepared to pay for his trooper to bring his full dress uniform to change into for dinner. When the last course, a large dish of profiteroles, was placed on the table in front of the breast-plated son of Stoke-on-Trent, the order was given to 'Fire'. Within minutes the happy scourge of Covent Garden was covered in the creamy contents of a hundred pastry balls.

My own experiences, by comparison, were very low key but at the time gave me some satisfaction. By the end of a typical evening in the pub the handsome hunks would be whisked off to a late supper at a Knightsbridge restaurant or straight back to a bottle of Scotch at a Belgravia mews house. The ones that were overlooked and left behind were happy to settle for a chat over a few drinks. My two regulars were Mick, who lived with his wife and small daughter in the married quarters tower block of the barracks, and Dave, who was single and shared the dormitory. Mick was slight of build and to my eyes very attractive. He loved to escape for a few hours from humdrum domesticity and sip a few beers with someone he described as a 'silly young queen'. Our hour or so in bed was not exactly an earth-moving experience; as his white body lay there in a state of semi-rigor mortis I took him into my mouth, as his wife never did. I found him a fiver whenever I could.

Dave, on the other hand, was not remotely good-looking, but we shared a sense of humour. Before leaving the pub I would apologise for not having any money. He would say that was okay as long as I didn't tell anybody. In bed he was capable of the tenderness of the lonely, sometimes even surprising me with a kiss.

The short-term pleasures of encounters like those were very important at the time. After all I was sleeping with men who were – to use the parlance of the gay lonely hearts column – 'straight-acting and-looking'. But it has been quite difficult for me in later life to come to terms with relationships in which passion might be involved. Simply because I was not accustomed to being regarded as physically interesting, some of my more recent lovers may have thought me cold and unresponsive, especially when their tongues paid court to certain of the more sensitive bodily areas.

There were three soldiers, only occasionally seen in a bar, who excited my interest more than most. Of these the odd one out was a powerfully built fellow from Somerset, nicknamed 'Cider'. A warm personality and a ruddy complexion containing a big grin were what was revealed to the outside world. But the word among his peers – a group as given to gossip as a small village or a ship of the line – was that he was the possessor of the Household Cavalry's most significant arrangement of genitalia. Although embarrassed by the attention he received, he was a good-natured man who accepted with great courtesy the many offers of drinks he received. But he was above seduction. By ten-thirty p.m. he was heading back to the old iron bedstead across the road.

Number two was a Greek god called Chris, a product of London's suburbs and an accomplished amateur athlete. His good looks were combined with charm, an ability to converse and bisexuality that seemed not to worry him at all. On the face of it we had very little in common, but we were the same age and shared an employer, the Queen, who paid us very badly. The friendship that developed between us, with no sexual complication, endured through his subsequent career as a cab driver, two marriages and the tenancy of a couple of pubs. At his peak, and when his contemporaries were heading off for a two-week stay at Butlins, Chris was enjoying the hospitality of Malcolm Forbes at his ranch in California. Persuaded to stay for a few more days, our hero had to telephone his company commander with an explanation for his absence.

Trooper Smith: 'Sir! I've got food poisoning and won't be able to report for duty for a few days.'
Major Ferguson: 'How did you get it, Smith?'
Trooper Smith: 'At Elizabeth Taylor's birthday party, sir.'
Major Ferguson: 'Where exactly are you, Smith?'
Trooper Smith: 'California, sir.'

It may have been difficult in those days for a junior and unknown officer to come to terms with the holidaying activities of his men. But at least in Major Ronald Ferguson's case it was the shape of things to come as far as his family was concerned.

Cherry was not the only colour of the blazer invariably worn by the last of the trio; it also became the name by which he was known. It said something about his self-awareness that it complemented so perfectly the blond of his hair and the freshness of his complexion. Like Chris, he was tall and powerfully built, but he lacked his colleague's warm personality. Only when we were alone together did he reveal a dry sense of humour. We had several of the predictable commercial, restricted-movement bedroom encounters and became quite good friends. To my great surprise he suggested one day that I might like to meet him at Horse Guards for a drink after he came off guard duty. Naturally I jumped at the idea, flattered on a personal level and thrilled to be invited to enter one of the British Army's holiest of holies. This small group of buildings beside the famous parade ground was designed by William Kent and resembled the sort of grand stable block that might be found at top of the range houses like Blenheim or Stowe. In the nineteenth century it was the command post of the Duke of Wellington. Today his office is occupied by the general officer commanding the Household Division, and is placed at the disposal of the Queen Mother and her guests for Trooping the Colour. I had stepped inside the door twice before when, two years running, I had occupied the seat beside the coachman on the barouche that followed the Queen Mother as she went to witness her daughter's Birthday Parade. In those days her fellow passenger was usually Princess Margaret, before she slipped down the pecking order and was supplanted by the Princess of Wales. The cheers and applause that was directed at them petered out pretty quickly when the crowds lining the route failed to recognise the elderly couple trundling along behind. Only the smartest royal watchers would know that they were HM's Treasurer, Major Sir Ralph Anstruther, who was always wheeled out on military days, and beside him the always erect figure of a lady-in-waiting. Until quite recently this group of well-born women, contemporaries of Lady Elizabeth Bowes-Lyon, had attended her since she first joined the Royal Family as Duchess of York. But old age has taken its toll, and one by one they have either died in harness or asked to be relieved of their duties. As no one else has ever been present when they have asked permission of their mistress to stand down, it is impossible to know what transpired at the interview. However it is reported that the last empress of India, renowned as having the stamina of a small herd of Highland cattle, had been aghast at the mention of the 'retire' word. 'Retire!' she claimed, 'I can't possibly retire, and I don't see why you should want to.' But in the end she would always relent and this dwindling band of the members of the inner circle were visited in hospital and sent flowers on their birthdays. In the last quarter of her century QE enjoys the attention of ladies-in-waiting who are younger than her elder daughter.

My tryst with Cherry took me through the gates in Whitehall to a door on the right, just in front of the main archway. In these security-conscious times it seems extraordinary that I was able to enter such a place without even a body search, but all I had to contend with was a trooper who asked me the name of the soldier I was going to see. The canteen was rather steamy and brightly lit. Khaki-clad men were sitting at half a dozen tables. No one was in civvies, as it wasn't the sort of place you patronised if it wasn't part of your duty period. A cheerful woman dispensed coffee, tea and sandwiches from behind a bar in the corner. My level of nervousness quadrupled as conversation stopped and all heads turned as I walked through the door. I was rescued from terminal embarrassment by Peter, an openly gay soldier, who beckoned me over to his table and provided me with a cup of coffee.

The secret world of the barracks behind closed doors was very much meat and drink to Peter and it was from him that I heard the hushed-up story of Lord Mountbatten's ADC. In the last few years of Lord Mountbatten's remarkable life he was appointed Colonel of the Life Guards, a unique honour for a non-royal. As a colonel he was entitled to the services of a captain to help with his military duties. Whether the officer in question was selected by Lord Louis personally or imposed upon him, I do not know. But soon after his appointment stories began to circulate about wild parties at the Mountbatten house in Kinnerton Street. It was well known that the ADC had formed an attachment with a young member of his regiment from the 'other ranks'. After some time it was announced that the gallant captain had resigned his position and left the army to concentrate on the running of his estate in Ireland. In the months that followed this revelation it emerged that a certain Bugler Bunn had raised the money to 'buy himself out' and had gone off to work in Ireland.

Engrossed as I was in Peter's gossip I had failed to notice that the Guard had just changed and that the magnificent figure of Cherry had come into the room. With glinting breast plate and clanking spurs he came over to our table. I already knew him to be a man of few words but I could tell from his expression that he was not pleased with the company I was keeping. Poor Peter was damned in the eyes of his colleagues for having sex for pleasure rather than profit.

'I've got to go and feed the horse. Do you want to come and see him in the stable?' he asked.

We left the bar together to the accompaniment of what I thought were good-natured noises from his mates. The stable was dimly lit and smelled like the West Country barns of my childhood. As if in greeting, several of the occupants tossed their manes and made throaty noises. Cherry took me over to the fine specimen that had borne his weight for the last few hours and we stroked his neck and patted his nose. As Cherry went in to his stall with a bucket of feed and some fresh straw I began to feel a sense of closeness to nature and sexual arousal. Brushing past me as he left the horse to his supper he walked over to a dark corner. Although few words had passed between us, my pounding heart convinced me that he was going to say something now.

'I've been dying to have a piss,' was what he said. Not, on the face of it, the most romantic remark I have ever heard, but significant nevertheless. The evidence of the magnitude of his need was all too obvious as a small cloud of steam came up through his open legs. When the flow had ceased he half turned towards me, the extent of his manhood a splendid profile. It would have been churlish of me to ignore a man at a moment like that.

The last I heard of Cherry was that one day he was sitting on his horse in Whitehall when a beautiful girl slipped a piece of paper into the top of his boot. It contained her name and telephone number. She was the daughter of an American millionaire who had taken a fancy to the handsome face under the helmet. They married and live in Chicago.

The day The Beatles came to an Investiture to collect their MBEs generated more excitement than anything that had happened at the Palace in living memory. In recent times only the visit of Yuri Gagarin was its equivalent. Never before had so many off-duty footmen volunteered to work, or so many housemaids made themselves available to hand out tickets in the cloakroom. On Investiture mornings everyone always seems to arrive at the same time, making the Grand Hall a scene of great activity. Those of us doing the shepherding usually have no difficulty moving the guests towards the staircase and their little gilt chairs in the Ballroom. But on Beatles Day everyone wanted to stay close to the Entrance, hoping to get a glimpse of the lads from Liverpool. The sound of wild screaming beyond the railings added to the air of expectation, and when it reached a crescendo we knew that their arrival was imminent. As they passed through the doorway, and entered the vastness of the marble-columned sanctum, the Grand Hall witnessed its first ever mobbing.

Not surprisingly, John, Paul, George, Ringo and Brian Epstein looked bewildered and very vulnerable as they stood there in fashionable suits, waiting to be given some guidance. Help was at hand in the shape of the Groom of the Chambers who broke through the throng and led them up the Grand Stairs to the Green Drawing Room. It had been decided that they should be given private instruction in the mysteries of bowing and conducting themselves in front of the monarch by no less a person than the Comptroller, Lord Chamberlain's Office, Sir Eric Penn. Even to those of us who were used to such people, Sir Eric was an awe-inspiring figure in his Guards ceremonial uniform. Thin as a reed, six-foot four, clipped moustache and devilishly handsome, he was almost a caricature of a senior army officer. As the little group waited in the ante-room for the rehearsal to start I took the bull by the horns and approached them, my crested notepaper at the ready. Nervously I explained that Princess Anne was disappointed not to be there to meet them, but had asked me to get their autographs. Naturally they were only too happy to oblige. Ringo's enthusiasm was so great that I only just prevented him from inscribing, 'To Anne with love from Ringo.'

British Week in Milan was my next overseas assignment, but for the Duke of Edinburgh it could only be British forty-eight hours. In an Andover of the Queen's Flight we flew into the airport at the height of the evening rush hour. At the best of times motorised activity in an Italian city is frenzied, but at five-thirty each day chaos reigns supreme. However, our carefully arranged timetable had been devised with the co-operation of the police, which meant that every crossing point and junction was suitably manned. As our little motorcade zoomed into the heart of the city it was made apparent that the population did not take kindly to having their homeward journeys interrupted in this way. The sound of car horns was quite deafening. By contrast, our hotel – the Principe e Savoia – was a haven of luxury and calm.

Even by the frenetic standards favoured by the Duke of Edinburgh the programme that evening was astonishing. At seven-thirty we arrived at La Scala for the first act of the Royal Ballet's *Swan Lake*. By nine p.m. we were en route for a stadium to witness the second half of a football match between Chelsea and Milan. At ten-thirty p.m. the Duke took the salute at a military tattoo given by bands of the British Army in a floodlit arena. A more varied evening's entertainment would be difficult to devise, and it left most of us feeling pretty shattered. Back at the hotel I tried to persuade James Macdonald, the Duke's valet, to have a nightcap before turning in, but he was anxious to have an early night, knowing that he would have to be up with the lark in the morning. His master kept to a strict routine and James was happy to go along with it. They had known each other since the day the impecunious young prince had arrived at Buckingham Palace with nothing but a small suitcase and the elderly sports jacket that he was wearing. As the king's second valet he was given Prince Philip to look after, but it was not a job that he enjoyed. On duty one cold winter's day at Sandringham in 1952, it was James who had knocked on the king's door and, receiving no answer, entered to find that the sovereign had died in his sleep. With the new reign Prince Philip inherited both James and Mr Jerram the senior valet. When Mr Jerram retired, James became top dog and, over a period of time, grew to respect the Queen's demanding young husband. The Duke was lucky to have such a man.

The next day was spent sight-seeing and visiting British Week exhibitions, before we took off that evening for London. For some reason there was no comfortable Andover to take us home, just an RAF transport plane with the novelty of backward-facing seats.

Sometimes on a day off my exploration of London and thirst for knowledge of its institutions took me to the House of Commons to listen to debates, in the hope of seeing Sir Winston Churchill. Although by that time he had retired as prime minister, I knew that he occasionally appeared in the House. But unfortunately my visits never coincided with his. During his last long, lingering illness I also went one evening to join the world's press and the silent crowd as they waited outside his home in Hyde Park Gate for news of his condition. After his death I stood for hours in the long queue outside Westminster Hall waiting to file past his body as it lay in state. I thought then that it was the closest I had ever been to him, and it provided the last chance I had to pay my respects. Little did I know that my association with the Grand Old Man was not yet finally over.

As the funeral was to be a state occasion, the Earl Marshall sought the permission of the Queen to use the carriages from the Royal Mews for the procession. Her coachmen and grooms were naturally included. To my great surprise I was detailed to ride on the first carriage and look after the principal mourners. The horribly grey February day dawned and proved to be one of the coldest that anyone could remember. Much discussion had gone on about the sort of uniform we should all wear, but it was eventually decided that in view of the outside temperature the scarlet caped coat would be most appropriate. Underneath that I was to wear my ordinary battledress, which would be hidden from view. The more experienced among my colleagues suggested that the best way to keep the cold out was to wrap brown paper around my chest. But I thought that was a silly idea, and settled instead for a heavy woollen sweater over my shirt. Lo and behold, the carriages had not got very far down Birdcage Walk before my teeth were chattering to such an extent that I thought I might frighten the horses. The first leg of our journey took us to the Palace of Westminster, where we clattered into the courtyard to collect my three passengers. I jumped down, opened the carriage door and lowered the folding steps. As the ladies approached I placed my foot on a corner of the bottom step and pressed down hard so that the carriage wouldn't sway. I gave Lady Churchill my arm as she climbed aboard, and was treated to an enchanting smile. She was followed by Lady Soames, who was elegant and serene. Behind her came Sarah, Lady Audley, reputedly Churchill's favourite child, her face carrying a great deal of make-up. Because the old carriage had no form of heating, the Mews had provided both stone and rubber hot water bottles as well as a pile of rugs. When all three were comfortably seated I tucked them in as best I could, and climbed up to the platform just behind them. As the cortège moved off we slotted in immediately behind the gun carriage bearing the flag-draped coffin. At a snail's pace we headed out into Whitehall to begin the last great journey of England's great twentieth-century hero. Every inch of pavement and thousands of doorways and windows were jammed with a multitude of muted people most of them, like me, numb with cold. Some had bowed heads, others held handkerchiefs to their eyes, but the majority gazed with a mixture of fascination and sympathy at the passing cavalcade. Viewed from my lofty position, the sight of all those sad, proud mourners was remarkably moving. The silence was only disturbed by the sound of church bells, marching feet and horses' hooves. By the time the gun carriage arrived at St Paul's the vast congregation, including the entire Royal Family, was in its seats. The Queen had broken with tradition to attend the funeral of a commoner and, unusually, arrived not last but just ahead of the Churchill family. After my passengers had alighted at the foot of the steps the carriages moved to the south side of the cathedral to wait for the service to end. I had been told in advance that a special van from the Mews would be waiting nearby. To my horror I saw that the van, in its distinctive dark green livery, was parked on the north side of the cathedral. Although the distance between me and it was only the width of the West Front, it meant running the gauntlet of the rows of servicemen who formed the guard of honour. Cold and bored, I could imagine how much they were looking for an amusing diversion. Sure enough, the sight of me passing in front of them in an ankle-length scarlet coat bearing a collection of hot water bottles was the sight for which they had been waiting. I am sure it was only the solemnity of the occasion that made the wolf whistles sotto voce and the giggles slightly muffled.

With the service over we drove off again through the streets of the City towards the Tower of London, where my part in the proceedings would end. At Tower Pier the coffin was put onto a barge for the short journey to Waterloo Station. I helped the Churchill ladies to descend the carriage steps once more, and as I did so Lady Churchill squeezed my hand, smiled gently and said, 'Thank you.' On the journey back towards the Palace our little empty procession saw the barge sailing majestically up river in front of rows of idle wharves the cranes of which, with heart-stopping dignity, lowered their arms in a last salute.

* * *

The Commonwealth Games for 1968 was to take place in Jamaica, with Prince Philip and Princess Anne as the guests of honour. They were also to be joined by Prince Charles, from his school in Australia. Also in the party was a group of the Duke's polo-playing chums who were due to have some matches against local teams. We left Heathrow in a special aeroplane with the British team filling the economy compartment and the royal party ensconced in the front. On the way we stopped for an hour in New York, and then again at Nassau, where Prince Charles came on board to a coolly affectionate welcome from his father and sister. At about four o'clock in the morning we touched down at Kingston, and as we left the aircraft the amazing heat hit us like a wall of damp cotton wool. On the ground I was contacted by an English major in the Jamaican Regiment, who commanded the baggage party. He seemed terribly eager to take charge of the mountain of luggage, and I was just as pleased to abdicate my responsibility. When everything was loaded onto a couple of army trucks we headed for the foothills of the Blue Mountains and the former plantation house that was to be our home for the next week. The old building was owned by an expatriate couple who had built cabins in the garden and ran it as an exclusive hotel. As the suitcases and trunks were disgorged onto the lawn they were carried off to the appropriate rooms by the rugged young soldiers. Everyone by this time was exhausted – the long flight and great heat had finally beaten us. Once the lawn was clear again I went off to find my own room, and was just starting to unpack when a young lady clerk appeared in the doorway. She said that she had not got her suitcase. Luckily I just managed to catch the major and his men as they were about to leave. He and I assured her that all the luggage had been distributed, and that her case must have been put in the wrong room. Dawn was just beginning to break by this time and it was decided that a thorough search would have to wait until morning. I returned to my cabin and collapsed onto the bed, but realised that sleep would be impossible if I didn't do something about the air-conditioning. With the machine on, the noise was like a road drill in the hands of a demented Irishman; with it off, the temperature rose to an uncomfortable level in only a few minutes. In the end I decided not to use it, and slept in a moist heap.

A ravishing Caribbean morning greeted me when I opened the shutters the next morning. The gallant major reported for duty and once breakfast was out of the way a detailed search began in earnest. I was amused at one stage to see that the major even peered under shrubs and bushes, just in case one of his lads had thought 'fuck it' and thrown the wretched thing in the undergrowth. By the middle of the morning, desperation had set in and the hotel's proprietors were unlocking rooms that were empty and unused. It was in one of these that the recalcitrant object was finally run to ground, and not a moment too soon. Not only was my credibility as baggage master at risk, there were also questions of finance to be addressed. The BOAC big cheese in the area was standing by to jet in to sort out the airline's possible involvement, and the disadvantaged young lady was looking forward to heading into Kingston with two hundred pounds to spend on a new wardrobe.

We all went to the opening ceremony of the Games, which was a wonderful mix of ceremonial and slapstick. My three lasting memories are of the sound of drinks sellers in every part of the stadium crying 'Red Stripe!' And then there was the colour party from the Jamaican Regiment, trying awfully hard, but looking slightly ridiculous in scarlet uniforms that didn't quite resemble those of the Brigade of Guards. The third image is of the party on the Royal Dais, where the Governor General played host. He was the first native-born islander to hold that position, and he and his good lady were very popular – and hugely overweight. Once she was lowered into her chair, with supporters on either side, she was stuck there until heaved out again. She sat through the proceedings looking very happy with a bag of peanuts and her legs at ten to two.

After a week we moved from our base in the mountains to a very special hotel on the coast called Frenchman's Cove. It was a remarkable place in that it occupied an entire headland, with its own private beaches. A central building provided elegant dining rooms and bars, while guests were accommodated in comfortable houses, with their own maid and butler, that were dotted around the grounds and set into the side of cliffs. Each house had a fully stocked bar and a refrigerator bulging with goodies, as well as a brace of golf carts waiting by the door. It was conceived, so the story goes, by the Canadian millionaire Garfield Weston as a playground for his super-rich friends. They paid a whopping great one-off sum that covered all the amenities and every trapping of luxury. I only hope that we stayed there as guests of the proprietor and not the unfortunate Jamaican government.

During my three years as a royal footman I made two further forays into foreign lands, and they were about as far removed from exotic Jamaica as is possible to imagine. The first was a flying visit with the Queen to Northern Ireland, where we stayed with the Governor at Hillsborough Castle. In those distant low-security days a group of us spent the first evening sampling Guinness in a nearby pub and chatting with the locals. Back at the Castle a large crowd of Loyalists had taken up position outside the main gates and gave vent to their emotions by banging something called the Lambeg Drum. To the horror of everyone inside this noise persisted throughout the night, making sleep almost impossible. I can only imagine that the authorities allowed it to happen because the alternative might have been uproar on a different scale. The poor Queen had to endure an investiture the next morning, followed by a series of engagements in Belfast. To everyone's relief the day passed off without incident, apart from a minor encounter between the royal Rolls and a poorly aimed brick.

My only other outing was the state visit to King Baudouin and Queen Fabiola in Brussels. Our three days there were spent at the Royal Palace in the centre of the city. Entertainment not on the official programme was provided one evening by one of our friendly Belgian counterparts who was keen to show us the night life. With Edward, my handsome ex-Welsh Guardsman colleague, and Roy the shy Queen's footman we headed for our first bar of the evening. Brussels in those days felt like a small and rather dull provincial town, but by eleven p.m. we had gained access to its only gay club. So carefully did it conceal its identity, it was only because our guide knew the owner that we were allowed in. Once again I found that my sanctuary was a dark, smoke-filled room with a few slightly sinister men lining its walls. After a few drinks and the sound of universal gay music, Edward and I shuffled around between the tables to the strains of Frank Sinatra and his hit 'Strangers In The Night'. Just when I was beginning to think that it was my turn to lead, the door burst open and three armed policemen forced their way into the room. In the ensuing confusion the club's owner sought us out and pushed us towards a rear exit, using words like 'scandal', 'against the law' and 'the palace' as we moved. Once outside we followed our friend in a panic-stricken dash through the back streets until we could see the Palace in the distance.

The Queen's thank-you dinner on the last night of our stay was given at the Ambassador's residence. It was a handsome eighteenth-century house with room for only a limited number of guests. Those of us from the Palace were there to help the Ambassador's staff, and we did so in our full state liveries. The dining room was lit only by candles, mounted on the walls in sconces and suspended from the high ceiling in enormous chandeliers. When it was all over and the clearing up had begun I was selected, as the tallest person there, to extinguish the overhead lighting. Two ridiculously large chandeliers later I returned to earth with the whole of my upper body encased in rapidly stiffening wax. A hoot for my friends and a challenge for Sketchleys.

Another state visit that sticks in my memory is the one paid by the king and queen of Greece to London. It took place against a background of increasing hostility, in her adopted homeland, to the German-born Queen Frederika. We were told that the king was seen to be weak and that his wife was thought to be too interested in politics. With this in mind the police were worried that there might be a reaction from London's Greek community as the Queen escorted her guests in a carriage procession from Victoria Station to the Palace. Although on the day I was not on a carriage but safe from any danger in the Grand Hall, I was subjected to a certain amount of harassment from a member of the king's own family. The Hall that morning was filled with senior members of the Household and friends and relations of the visiting royal family. Stationed just inside the door, I was there to lend colour to the scene, not to converse with any of the guests. As the time ticked by I was approached by a man I knew to be Major Richard Brandram, husband of the king's sister Lady Katherine. She was there too, a large plain woman who had forfeited her birthright to marry an English Guards officer. As far as I knew, they had a son, lived in Hampshire and kept a pretty low profile. He started by asking me my name and how long I had worked at the Palace. Very conscious of my surroundings I kept my responses to a bare minimum, but even so he was still beside me when the royal party arrived on the scene. He was in the midst of asking me when he could see me again when I noticed that the all-seeing eyes of the Queen had spotted us together. I mumbled an excuse and walked away while he went over and paid court to his relations. He remembered my name and rang me the next day in the footmen's room to ask me what I was doing that evening. When I replied that I had a prior engagement he responded like a true Guards officer by asking if I knew someone I could send in my place.

Three royals, two of them granddaughters of Queen Victoria, remain in my memory from those years. The first is Princess Alice, Countess of Athlone who was the Queen's great-aunt. She was very elderly even in those days, took little part in public life and lived quietly at Kensington Palace. As a minor member of the Royal Family she was always roped in when the full panoply was on parade. The only time I ever saw her was on the occasion of a state banquet.

With the feasting over, the Royal Family and their principal guests moved into the White Drawing Room for coffee and refreshments. After the formality of the banquet this provided an opportunity to move around and meet more people. The Queen was devoted to her great-aunt and always greeted her with great warmth, stooping to kiss her on both cheeks. But this was not before Princess Alice had executed the deepest curtsey in front of her sovereign. When it came to curtseying Princess Alice had a rival in my other favourite, her cousin Lady Patricia Ramsey. She had been born Princess Patricia of Connaught, the daughter of Queen Victoria's third son the Duke of Connaught. Lady Patricia dropped out of royal circles when she married a young naval officer, Alexander Ramsey, who subsequently became an admiral. Their appearance at court was confined to an invitation to one garden party a year. My only sighting of them took place on one of those days, and very remarkable they were to behold too. Although once tall, they were both now quite stooped and leaned heavily on walking sticks. I opened the door for them at the Garden Entrance when they arrived to join the royal party. Waiting with them for the Queen to arrive was Princess Alexandra and her husband and the duty members of the Household. Dead on time the sound of a small bell pressed on the floor above by the Queen's Page foretold the imminent lift-borne arrival of the sovereign. As the door slid open the smiling Queen was received in the usual way by the assembled company. Poor Lady Patricia tried her best to keep up and execute a deep curtsy, but unfortunately she got into a bit of a muddle with her stick and her husband's arm that she was holding onto. In the end the best she could manage was a sort of shuffle and a dip, much to the delight of everyone watching. The Queen rushed forward, a big grin on her face, to embrace her, saying, 'Oh Patsy, I think that was very clever!'

The death in an aircrash of Prince William of Gloucester robbed the Royal Family of one of its most glamorous figures. He was tall and fair and knew how to turn on the charm. Seen in the company of his brother he appeared even more attractive, as Richard was short, dull and plain. On his twenty-first birthday his doting parents gave him a huge party at their Northamptonshire home, Barnwell Manor. I was on the royal train that was used for the journey and also for overnight accommodation in a nearby siding. William was surrounded by scores of beautiful women during the celebrations, even though he was suspected in some circles of being queer. In the end it was acknowledged that he did have a sexual hang-up, but about older women, an aberration he shared with successive generations of Windsor men.

After three years as a footman I knew that it was time for a change. Although still fascinated by royalty, it was only the Queen's Footman's job that I wanted, and I knew that it would never be mine. But I had also reached the stage where I wanted to walk into a room and be acknowledged as an individual rather than a flunky with a tray of drinks. As ever, it was my mother who came up with the solution. She paid for me to be 'vocationally guided', a process that concluded that I might be suited to journalism. She passed on this information to a friend of hers who worked in the news room at the BBC. After meeting her she told me that provided I learned to type and take shorthand she would have no difficulty finding me a job at Broadcasting House. Mama agreed to pay for me to take the appropriate course and so, towards the end of 1966, I gave in my notice to the Sergeant Footman. In the time that was left to me I had to face one more royal Christmas and my last state occasion.

Because of a huge refurbishment job at Sandringham my last Christmas was spent at Windsor Castle, where on Christmas Eve I received my final present from the Queen. As she handed me the parcel containing a Spode half-calling set (or was it a Spode calling half-set?) she said:

'May I wish you a very happy Christmas. I hear you are moving on.'

'Yes, Your Majesty,' I replied, rather taken aback.

'And joining the BBC, I understand.'

'Well yes, I hope to eventually.'

'From one large organisation to another! Well I can only wish you all the luck in the world,' she said, smiling sweetly.

Boxing Day at Windsor means shooting pheasants and the mobilisation of armies of people to make sure that the stupid birds make themselves available for slaughter. For the kitchen staff it means preparing hot, tasty dishes that are sealed in silver boxes and packed by the Silver Pantry into heavily lined hampers to be transported by the Mews to the footmen who are waiting at the luncheon venue. On that particular day the site that was chosen was the small community hall in the model village that sits in the middle of the Great Park. A party of us, the advance guard, arrived there in time to put up trestle tables, a bar and serving tables and to cover it all in acres of white damask. It was a room that had obviously not been used for a long time, which meant doing what cleaning we could with brooms and dusters. With minutes to spare before the arrival of the ladies from the Castle, footman Robert went into the loos with hand towels, soap and bog rolls. Seconds later he emerged screaming for Harpic and Ajax. 'Come and have a look at this,' he cried. 'You won't believe it!' We rushed passed him into the Ladies, to be confronted by the sort of graffiti that you imagine only exists in public lavatories – and in the Gents at that. Rather to my surprise there wasn't much in the way of writing. The good ladies of Windsor seemed to prefer imagery to words. It was too late to send back to the Castle for powerful cleaning agents, so we rubbed away as best we could using what was to hand. Our efforts were cut short when the cry went up, 'They're here.' Dashing back into the Hall we were just in time to relieve the ladies of their outer garments and to offer them a drink. I think it was the Duchess of Kent who 'went' first. We tried to keep busy, we really did, but the door marked 'Ladies' had become compulsive viewing. After however long it takes, the Duchess emerged, head slightly bowed, to be reunited with her glass, which she promptly drained. She was followed by Princess Alexandra who disappeared briefly and then strode back into the room without catching anyone's eye. Princess Margaret, ridiculous in a trendy pink plastic crash helmet, went next and returned with a slight smile on her face. She went again twenty minutes later. It seemed as if it was only the seasoned troupers, the Queen and the Queen Mother, who had heeded their nanny's advice and 'been' before they came out.

In 1967 Noel Coward was playing in the West End in a production of his own triple bill, *A Suite In Three Keys*. At the age of sixty-seven he was not in particularly good health, and this was to be his last stage appearance. I was halfway through my secretarial course at Pitmans in Kingsway, and had already been defeated by the mysteries of shorthand. Typing I found much easier and pressed on with it in the hope that at last I would have a skill to put to good use. As the only male in a class of forty, I was an object of some curiosity – a dubious honour I shared with a zany girl whose identity her famous father was obviously determined to keep a secret. Her name was Maxine Bygraves.

One day I was telephoned by a friend, who knew of my interest in the theatre and informed me that Noel Coward was trying to find a young man to work for him at his house in Switzerland. The search was on for a chap with secretarial skills and a flexible attitude to working practices who would fit into an unconventional household. If I was interested, I was told that I should contact Cole Lesley, Noel Coward's secretary, at the Savoy Hotel. When my call was put through to Coley's suite he sounded charming and soon put me at my ease. After I told him a little bit about myself he said that he and the Master would like to see me as soon as possible. I think he sensed my enthusiasm when I said that I could be there in half an hour. Sadly, he said, an interview in the next few days was out of the question as the diary was full until they returned to Switzerland at the end of the week. *A Suite In Three Keys* was ending its run on Friday and they were leaving at the weekend. The obvious answer, said Coley, was for me to come out to Les Avants, the Master's Swiss home. He would arrange airline tickets that I could collect from their Shepherd Market travel agent. Having given me his

Swiss telephone number and confirmed once again how much he wanted to meet me, he said goodbye.

A few days later I found myself, almost elegant in a rather over-pressed dark blue suit, on a Swiss Air flight to Geneva. In twenty-two years of living this was, undoubtedly, the most exciting adventure I had known. After all, how often do people get to meet Switzerland and Noel Coward for the first time – and together too. When the pilot announced, as we began our descent, that snow was falling heavily, I was less concerned about a safe landing than the fact that I had not brought anything with which to protect my precious interview suit – let alone snow shoes. The details of how Coley and I were to identify each other are lost to me now, but I do recall a warm and friendly welcome. When we reached the waiting car outside the terminal building he introduced me to Guido, the Coward chef, who doubled as driver. Snow was falling steadily as we drove along beside Lake Geneva, on the road to Lausanne. Conversation flowed easily between us, and the white countryside flashed by. After a while he suggested that as it was such a cold night we should stop at a friendly hotel for a little warming refreshment. Evidently encouraged by my enthusiasm for this idea he rummaged deep into his voluminous shoulder bag and produced a shiny hip flask. A strong burning sensation hit my tongue and throat as I swallowed the first of the evening's many tots of whisky. I like to think that the Beau Rivage at Ouchy was our only port of call on the journey, but I could easily be mistaken. Over drinks in the comfortable bar Coley put me in the picture about life at the Chalet Coward, and explained what being his assistant would mean.

As well as the Master and Coley, the cast list also included their great friend Graham Payn, who had once been a star of many Coward shows. Apparently he had virtually given up acting and was now a full-time member of the company. The chorus, as it were, consisted of Guido the chef, his lover Giuseppe who played the butler's part, and their child-substitute apricot poodle. The only female cast member was Madame Monod, who came in daily to keep house. For thirty years the Coward 'organisation' had been run in London by the Master's trusted friend Lorn Lorraine and her part-time assistant Joan

Hirst, who also worked for Michael Redgrave. This arrangement left Coley free to run the Swiss house and to act as Master of the Revels. However, Lornie had been in poor health for some time, which meant that Coley had been forced to take on the bulk of the office work and administration – quite a responsibility for a man no longer in the first flush of youth. Master was aware of the problem and decided that they should employ somebody to help with the workload. The man selected for this task was an erstwhile actor called Calvin Darnell, whose sister Linda was a great friend. From what Coley said I got the impression that Mr Darnell's stay in Switzerland was a briefer encounter than he might have liked, largely due to his preference for the cocktail shaker rather than the typewriter. Seemingly few lessons were learned from this mistake for, hot on CD's departing heels, there came another thespian, albeit a more celebrated one this time. His name was Peter Arne. Coley was a little more reticent when it came to an explanation for his short run, but I was told much later by Guido that Mr A's idea of recreation was a visit to a building site or roadworks to watch men and their tools in action. When he started extending invitations to some of them to visit him chez Coward, it was decided that enough was enough. The poor man was murdered in London a few years later. By this time the Master and Coley realised that it would make more sense to hire a chap with at least some secretarial skills and only a passing interest in martinis and rough trade.

All this was quite riveting, but Coley's chat about the background chez Coward was interrupted by Guido, who came in to say that he was increasingly worried about the weather and the state of the roads, bearing in mind that the rest of the journey was to take us up into the mountains. Coley paid the bill and we walked, arm in arm, out to the car with as much dignity as we could muster. Above Montreux the road narrowed appreciably and became steeper by the mile. Coley and I huddled in the back under travelling rugs, sipping and giggling, largely unaware of what was going on outside. Suddenly the car slithered to a halt, jolting us back to reality. An anxious Guido pointed out that there were no chains in the car, and that without them he could drive no further. Coley and I thought this was great fun, but remonstrated with Guido for suggesting some sort of bondage at this early stage in our relationship. Ignoring, or perhaps not understanding, this merry jest, our doughty driver got out of the car, opened the rear doors and heaved us out onto the road. As I sank up to my calves in freshly fallen snow I heard Guido explaining to Coley that Les Avants was only about two miles away, and that we might be able to make it on foot in about an hour. The freezing temperature did its best to bring me to my senses and succeeded to the extent that I was able to drape a rug over Coley's head and round his knitted blazer and the ubiquitous shoulder bag. Having similarly shrouded myself we waved goodbye to Guido and trudged off into the night. Progress was uncomfortably slow, and not helped by frequent stops for warm draughts of the amber liquid. The prospect of our supply drying up remained an unspoken anxiety. After what seemed like an eternity, twinkling lights appeared in the distance, prompting Coley to exclaim that the village must be only about half a mile away.

The streets of Les Avants were deserted, but this was after all midnight, and I was soon to discover that anywhere in Switzerland was dead after seven o'clock in the evening. We shuffled past the railway station, a row of shops and an imposing building Coley said was a girls' school. The odd chalet displayed glowing windows, and the smell of wood smoke hung in the air. It seemed an unlikely setting for a house that was home to Noel Coward and with a neighbour, according to Coley, in the person of Joan Sutherland. He pointed towards a hill at the far end of the village, on top of which their two houses sat, quite close together. We paused for breath, bracing ourselves for the final assault. A rectangle of light fell onto the drive when the front door opened as we approached. Giuseppe, who had been watching out for us from a window, fussed around removing sodden drapery and jabbering away about the lateness of the hour and dinner keeping hot in the oven. The cloakroom I was shown into had its walls and ceiling lined with sheet music of the Master's compositions. My appearance in front of the mirror presented a very sorry sight, which no amount of washing, combing and brushing was able to improve. My trousers were wringing wet and had shrunk a couple of inches. Having decided that come what may the show must go on I returned to the hall to find Coley with a large drink in his outstretched hand. Clasping it gratefully, I followed him into the drawing room. Just inside the door I passed a huge grand piano smothered in framed photographs of familiar faces, and the longest and purplest sofa I had ever seen. At the far end of the forty-foot room, comfortable chairs were grouped around a blazing fire. Two figures got to their feet as we approached. I had always imagined that at whatever time we met, Noel Coward would be wearing a dressing gown, and I wasn't disappointed. He greeted me with an emphatic 'Dear Boy' and waved me to a seat beside his own cream leather wing chair. Graham shook hands warmly before they both sat down again and carried on with the *Daily Mail* crossword. This they obviously found completely absorbing, in spite of polite enquiries as to the comfort of my journey. After a while I was even able to help with one of the clues. Eventually Coley suggested that we should retire to the dining room for a spot of supper. Only when we subsequently climbed the stairs to my bedroom did I realise how exhausted I was after my eventful day. Thankfully, Coley said that there was no point in having a lengthy discussion that night, as there would be plenty of time tomorrow. I had just fallen into bed when he returned with a dressing gown and toothbrush, having realised that I had left my bag in the abandoned car.

Brilliant sunshine flooding into the room woke me from a deep sleep some hours later. Suddenly realising exactly where I was, I walked to the window for my first good look at La Belle Suisse. Beneath the chalet the little village was going about its morning routine, the half-remembered dim shapes from last night now clearly defined against the white background. Hundreds of feet below, the dark waters of Lac Leman shimmered under the majestic backdrop of a large chunk of Alp. No cloud was visible in the vivid blue sky. Coley came in with a cup of tea and told me that the time was ten o'clock. My bag was apparently on its way and the Master would like to see me at eleven. He said that there would be some breakfast in his office on the ground floor when I was ready. Having donned, once again, my sad little ensemble, and with my hangover firmly in place, I let the aroma of coffee lead me to a little room, next to the drawing room where Coley sat at his desk. The decor was deeply Victorian, and at a glance I guessed the typewriter on a table in the corner also sprang from that period. The only incongruous note was struck by a three-storey battleship-grey filing cabinet that dominated one wall. It was crowned with affectionately inscribed photographs of smiling ladies, Marlene Dietrich and Kay Kendall well to the fore. We chatted for a while, and then he announced that it was time for my interview. Taking a sheaf of letters with him, he led the way up the stairs to the top floor.

Master lay propped against a mountain of pillows in an emperor-sized bed, the padded chintz headboard of which matched the curtains at the window. Opposite him, at the other end of the room, a wall of mirrored glass reflected his every move. I was later to discover that it concealed his not inconsiderable wardrobe, including a cherished collection of dressing gowns. After referring the Master to some correspondence to be read, Coley left me to my fate. Having invited me to sit on a corner of the bed, he launched into a discussion that can only be described as wide ranging. The Duke of Edinburgh and Lord Mountbatten, as well as my sex life, were two of the topics we covered at length. When the conversation turned to the prominence of my ears I told the only small untruth. According to mother, they were like Bing Crosby's but I told the Master that she thought they resembled his, and thought what a lucky boy I was to have such a role model. In no time at all he asked me when I could start work, as Coley needed someone as soon as possible. We agreed that a mutually convenient date could easily be decided, and I took my leave. When I told Coley that I thought I had been employed he gave me a big hug and then went back upstairs to confer. When he returned we finalised things such as salary and timing, just as Graham came into the room. He too seemed pleased with the news and suggested that we drive to Montreux to celebrate. After all, he pointed out, my flight was not until the evening, which meant that we had the whole of the afternoon to play.

In daylight the mountain road, with its sheer drop on one side, was quite spectacular. Snow ploughs had been working through the night to clear our route. Montreux had a sort of Edwardian charm and a discreet air of prosperity about it. We made our way to an open-air bar, a favourite of theirs, on the lakeside. When our drinks arrived I was amused to see our invigorating companion from the night before emerging from its hiding place to bring the alcohol content of our glasses up to strength. Sitting there contentedly in the warm sun I was able to observe my new friends at close range. They were both men who would never see fifty again. Their pink cheeks, suggestive of an expensive lifestyle, glowed from behind a permanent suntan. Although beautifully groomed, it is true to say that their clothes might have been designed with slightly younger, slimmer bodies in mind. The influence was definitely more Sunset Boulevard than Savile Row. Coley spoke French fluently, whilst Graham, who was South African, had no difficulty reading menus. But the thing that intrigued me most was the knack they shared with the Master of slipping French words into English conversation. With my knowledge of the language I found it challenging enough to use French words in French conversation. As I came to know Coley better, and to appreciate his humour and intelligence, it was easy to see why he had retained the friendship of a demanding personality like the Master for so long. Graham had great charm, but I was never to find him stimulating company.

After several drinks Coley asked if I wanted to go off and do some shopping, as they had one or two purchases to make. Leaving them to their own devices I sought the shops, where I found it difficult to avoid buying a Swiss lawn blouse for Mum and a watch for myself. We drove to Geneva later in the day, and I caught my flight to London.

Two weeks later I returned to start my Alpine adventure. The Chalet Coward – or Covarr as it was known locally; Swiss Cottage or the Shilly Chalet to friends – was unique. Although traditional in outline, the conventional oiled wood exterior had been covered with a sort of Suffolk pink render. It stood in about three acres of terraced garden, with a staff cottage that housed the two Italians. The chalet's lower-ground floor consisted of the large kitchen and wine cellar, as well as the dining room and my bedroom and bathroom. The ground floor was made up of the drawing room, the cloakroom and the office. The first floor had Coley and Graham's bedrooms as well as a guest room, all with their own bathrooms. The top floor was entirely given over to the needs of the Master, containing his bedroom, shower room and study.

My day would begin at about eight-thirty a.m. with breakfast in the kitchen, where Guido would be doing chef-like things while Giuseppe prepared breakfast trays and waited to be summoned by bells. By nine a.m. I was in the office and dealing with the large quantity of post that arrived each day. I opened everything except the obviously personal material, and when one of the boys passed the door bearing Coley's large pot of coffee it was my cue to follow with the day's batch of goodies. For the next hour or so I sat on Coley's bed discussing plans for the day and going through the mail. After that, I returned to the office, while Coley performed his toilet. I dealt with any request for autographs or signed photos, letters that only required a yes or no, and cheques to be paid into the bank. On good days royalties from Coward plays, books and music amounted to a great deal of money; even an old cynic like NC was quietly thrilled to be paid for a production of *Hay Fever* performed in Japanese at a Tokyo theatre. When Coley joined me he dictated letters, which I took down in my own personal shorthand. The system failed if I delayed too long before hitting the machine and couldn't remember the gist of what he had said. Apart from all this, there were two huge tasks that occupied my time at Les Avants, and kept me at the typewriter for as long as my fingers would allow. The most important was to transcribe the hand-written foolscap sheets that the Master rather intermittently produced. They represented the work he was doing on his third volume of autobiography, and a long gestation period it was too! Thankfully Coley was usually around to help me decipher the idiosyncratic handwriting and NC's confusing use of odd place names and even odder nicknames. I suppose it is not surprising, after thirty years with the Master, that all this was so familiar to him. He was even proficient at writing in exactly the same way and producing a flawless NC signature to boot. The first two autobiographical instalments, *Present Indicative* and *Future Indefinite*, had both been bestsellers, covering the

Master's life and career up to the 1950s. For some reason the third one was proving more difficult to deliver – possibly because it encompassed the wilderness years when his work was regarded as unfashionable and dated. It wasn't finished during my time with him, and I do not know if it ever was.

I soon discovered that the office's large filing cabinet contained almost every letter he had ever received, but mostly the ones from celebrities or the well-known. Some of the most significant names of the twentieth century were represented, including GBS, Lawrence of Arabia, Charlie Chaplin and Lord Mountbatten. My job was to type a copy of all this correspondence, so that the originals could be sent to a bank vault in London; in those pre-photocopier days, it was the only way to do it. For a not very skilled typist it was a laborious task, but made fascinating by the obvious pleasure of reading, for example hand-written thank-you notes from the Queen Mother and other members of her family, exchanges of ideas from Cole Porter and Laurence Olivier, detailed accounts of travels and holidays from Marlene Dietrich and Ian Fleming, as well as reams of gossip from Ivor Novello and Gertrude Lawrence. But by far the wittiest and most numerous letters in the archive came from the Lunts and someone I had hardly heard of called Benita Hume. Alfred Lunt and Lynn Fontane were two of the Master's oldest friends and always wrote with great warmth and affection. Rather endearingly, letters from them always began, 'Dear Little Rabbit's Bottom'. The only thing I knew about Benita Hume was that she had been married to George Sanders. I discovered in her letters that even when describing darkest depression she still managed to produce some of the funniest writing I have ever seen.

Thirty years on I am lucky enough to be asked to parties by a friend called Zoe Richmond Watson. Among the many people I have met at these great do's is an American couple called Jules and Jim. They were living in Majorca when we first met, but more recently they have moved to Thailand, where they keep their boat. Jules's father was a film star called Ronald Coleman. As luck would have it, we have never had much of a chance to speak. However, quite recently, Zoe rang to ask me to supper and said that it would be just her, Jules and me. As the wine and conversation flowed, during the course of the evening, Jules suddenly said that she had only recently heard that I had worked for NC. As a child she had known him, through her parents, quite well. She seemed interested to know about my work for him. Without boring her, or Zoe, with too much detail I simply mentioned the filing cabinet and all the letters. I told them that lots of them were fragments of history and that some of the correspondents wrote quite brilliantly. At the risk of going on too long I finished by saying that the most amusing were written by someone called Benita Hume.

'Oh Guy,' she said with a big smile, 'you're just saying that.'

'No, really,' I continued, 'she was brilliant. I have even tried to find out if someone has written her biography.'

'You mean you didn't know?'

'Know what? Oh, my God. Do you mean she was your?'

'Yes, she was my mother.'

By far the largest file in the letter cabinet was the one that contained correspondence between the Master and Coley when they were separated for any length of time. This was usually when NC was making one of his periodic solo journeys to far-flung corners of the world. He liked to depart as soon as one of his new productions had opened, leaving behind him the pain and anguish of giving birth. As far as possible his itinerary, containing dates and destinations, was left with Coley so that any news was forwarded. In his own meticulous way Coley made sure that no port was reached without a letter having arrived in advance. As a belt-and-braces move, a copy of the same letter would be sent to the destination after that, to allow for dodgy postal services. As I waded through the sheaf of thin Air Mail paper it became clear that Coley always gave as good as he got. In fact, dare I say it, his letters to the Master were often much funnier and more interesting than the ones he received. After the Master's death, I was very disappointed when it was announced that James Pope Hennessy was to be his official biographer. With the untimely demise of Pope Hennessy himself I was in turn thrilled when Coley was not overlooked a second time. On the day of publication I received a very special copy of the book.

At about noon each day our routine would be interrupted by the arrival of Graham, the effects of a sleeping pill worn off, needing coffee and a chat. As lunchtime approached he invariably re-appeared with brimming glasses of mind-numbing bullshot or Bloody Mary, signalling the end of the morning's work. It was the Master's habit in those days not to come downstairs at all. He spent the time reading in bed and smoking menthol cigarettes. Lunch was served on a tray and washed down with several glasses of his favourite white wine. Needless to say, this was not a sensible regime for an elderly gentlemen with buggered circulation. One morning, to everyone's amazement, he announced that he was finally going to heed his doctor's advice and take some exercise. At noon that day, we were told, he would go for a walk. As the appointed hour approached the occupants of the house assembled at the foot of the stairs to mark the epic occasion. When he appeared on the landing above us, spontaneous applause burst forth to accompany his final descent. Judging by his shining and slightly contorted face, I wasn't at all sure that he should venture any further, but with a small adjustment to his cravat he tottered gamely through the front door. His last audible words, addressed to Guido, were instructions to collect him from the *buffet de la gare* in half an hour. With that he was gone, a whiff of Chanel a lingering memory. Moments later five very anxious faces pressed their noses against the windows of a first-floor bedroom, to follow his progress down the steep incline to the village. As he disappeared from view behind the row of shops it dawned on us all that we might not see him again – or at least, not for twenty minutes. Guido was the first to recover his composure, a profound sense of responsibility resting on his shoulders. Muttering something about getting the car started he moved proudly towards the door. Soon afterwards the loud purr of a powerful engine interrupted our thoughts. Outside on the driveway sat a recently delivered cream convertible, ready for the off. It was an example of one of Mr Mercedes's and Mr Benz's latest and largest creations. Sitting with his head just below the top of the steering wheel, in bright sunlight, surrounded by quantities of scarlet leather upholstery, the diminutive chef looked eager and determined; like a man with a mission. The journey to the station bar and back again took ten minutes, but we all thought the wait was worthwhile when the beaming countenance of our patron hove once again into view. Climbing awkwardly out of his new toy, he paused to regale us with an account of his adventures. The bar had been crowed with local people, as well as a few tourists. He had ordered and consumed a cup of coffee and two large brandies. Three autographs had been signed, and Adam the young postman had blushed handsomely in response to a mildly flirtatious observation. All in all, if that is what exercise is all about he could not have enjoyed it more, and was looking forward to a repeat performance the next day. Sadly this initial enthusiasm was short-lived, and after two more outings the idea was abandoned in favour of his bed.

At about this time, just when it looked as if the Master's morale was at a pretty low ebb, a much-needed boost arrived in the form of an offer to star in a film with Richard Burton and Elizabeth Taylor. The script was an adaptation of one of Tennessee Williams's least-known plays, *The Milk Train Doesn't Stop Here Any More*. Master's reaction to the script was less important than the enormous fee involved, and the opportunity to work alongside two of the cinema's greatest box-office attractions. Joe Losey was to direct and location filming was due to start in Sardinia, towards the end of the summer. From the very beginning, however, enormous problems beset the production. For a start, the title of the play was considered too long for the cinema, and after lengthy discussions between the interested parties, including its very strong-willed author, 'Goforth', the name of the character played by Elizabeth Taylor, was chosen. Several months into filming, the title was changed once more. It became bafflingly, *Boom* and it was under this banner that it was released for the entertainment of the great cinema-going public, who stayed away in droves.

In the play the Master's character was actually a female witch – not an insuperable challenge for an actor of his calibre – but instead of getting him into drag, heated debate took place as to whether he should be known as a warlock, a devil, a sorcerer or a wizard. In the end it was agreed that he should be a male witch, and wear a wonderfully understated brown dinner jacket made by Dougie Hayward of Mount Street. He was allowed to keep this suit when the film was completed. It became his favourite party outfit, one that he wore at every opportunity.

My only role in the proceedings was to telephone his hotel in Sardinia to inform the manager that Mr Coward would like his suite (overlooking the sea, of course) to contain a king-size bed with twenty-four pillows.

Early in September, Master, Coley and Graham set off for Sardinia, leaving me behind to carry on with my work and cope with letters and phone calls. When they returned four weeks later Coley said that although it was a ghastly film, the Burtons and the Master had become bosom buddies and everything had gone very well. The only major disaster had occurred when a freak wind had struck the set, a sprawling villa on a rocky headland. As luck would have it, the biggest casualty had been Miss T's luxurious caravan/dressing room, which had broken loose from its moorings, plummeting from its clifftop position onto the beach below. When informed of this disaster, she had rushed to the scene, her grief inconsolable. Given her reaction, it was assumed that a life might have been lost – an old retainer perhaps, or an adored Pekinese – but no, peering down at the wreckage it was easy to see that the casualty had been six cases of her old friend, Jack Daniel's. Only the generosity and quick thinking of the Aga Khan saved the day. When he heard about the catastrophe and the distress it was causing, a jet was at once dispatched to the mainland for fresh supplies. Much to everyone's relief the crew did not return empty-handed.

One activity that seemed to be ignored by the inhabitants of the Chalet Coward was sex. Of course, Graham and NC had once been lovers, but I guess that any sexual relationship had long since turned into warm affection. As far as Coley was concerned I can only assume that they had both been his sleeping partners at some stage. The only affair he ever mentioned was a lengthy one with the handsome American crooner Johnny Ray. Then, one day, quite by chance, I discovered a clue to Master's sexual fantasies.

One side of his bed was dominated by a handsome mahogany chest of drawers, eighteenth century with five drawers. Set into the frieze around the top was a small brass plate with a well-rubbed inscription that said it had been the sea chest of an admiral. Bending to read it more closely I noticed that what it was fixed to was in fact a shallow drawer with no apparent means of opening it. After a bit of gentle pushing, I found that if pressure was applied to one end it yielded to the touch and sprang open. I thought at first that it must contain private papers or valuables, and so I was not prepared for the sight that met my eyes. When I say that it was a collection of photographs and magazines that I should like to have studied more closely, you will probably get the picture. However, I left them undisturbed and never again touched that particular piece of furniture – just in case. I only hope Madame Monod's polishing was not too vigorous.

In my own case, familiarity with long periods of sexual abstinence had sort of prepared me for a frustrated life on a mountain with three old queens. But as it happened the outlook was not as bleak as I had expected. Just before I left London I was told by an old friend and lover that he was moving back to his flat in Berne. A year or two earlier he and I had encountered each other in a pitch-black basement club that called itself The Place. It was to be found in a street in World's End at a time – the sixties – before the area was discovered by the upwardly mobile. I regarded it as the most exciting place in town, not least because admission was only after eleven p.m. Having paid your seven and six pence to the Greek at the door, you descended a narrow flight of stairs and then attempted to pass through the doorway ahead of you. This often proved to be a push-and-shove affair, as the mass of humanity at the entrance was reminiscent of rush-hour on the Tokyo underground. Once all dignity had been abandoned there was only the lack of light to contend with. After a few minutes your eyes would adjust sufficiently for shapes and even features to be identified. There was deafening music (mostly The Supremes), no bar and absolutely no rules. It seems almost unnecessary to mention it, but the idea was that if you thought you saw someone you fancied you wormed your hand through the throng until it was in a position to give him a good grope. It was by these means that my friend and I met. He originally told me that he was Swiss, which surprised me as he had crinkly black hair and olive skin. With hindsight, his name too should have been a clue. After all I don't suppose many Swiss cantons can boast a family with the name Manjaka, or for that matter a Swiss family with a son called Naim. Once our relationship got into its stride he admitted that he was Jordanian and told me that he was studying chemistry in Berne. I think I loved him rather a lot. He was fond of me too, but in a pretty unfaithful sort of way.

A couple of hours of squeezing, sweating and salivating at The Place meant that I did not return to my home at the end of The Mall until well after the drawbridge was raised for the night. A bell by the gate allowed late-comers to summon the duty copper, who was almost always not best pleased to be roused from his sneaky slumbers. Having said that, the band of policemen permanently attached to the Palace were generally a very friendly bunch who, in some cases, spent their entire career lurking in and around its walls. In the summer they moved en masse with the court to Balmoral, greatly enjoying the social life of the Castle.

During his stay in London, Naim lived with friends in South Kensington, which made it difficult for him to entertain. Consequently he came often to visit me in my room. Coming from a country with its own royal family, he was terribly interested in ours. He was thrilled one day when I took him on a tour through the state rooms that culminated in a gawp at the gold with Walter Fry. After we both moved to Switzerland I used to look forward to weekends at his little flat in the old part of Berne. We also explored together, staying the night in lovely places like Ascona and Gstaad. He went down (in a manner of speaking) very well with the Master and 'the boys', who encouraged him to stay as often as he liked. Sadly, our relationship had probably run its course by the time I returned to London. We lost touch, and our paths were not to cross for several years. I was in New York, lunching with a girlfriend named Pat in the restaurant at the Metropolitan Museum, when I suddenly saw him across the crowded room. Quite naturally we greeted each other like old friends, and he joined us at the table. He explained that he had moved to the States soon after I had left Les Avants, had found a good job and lived in a tiny flat next to Carnegie Hall. I thought he had gone off quite a lot, except for the eyes, and they made up for everything else. He suggested that for the rest of my stay I should move in with him – it would be more fun than a hotel. This sounded like a great idea, and I arranged to call round with my belongings later that evening. After lunch Naim went back to work and Pat and I decided to go to the movies. We wandered through the downtown area, seeing what the various cinemas were showing. Something new with Laurence Olivier, based on a Peter Shaffer play, looked as if it was going to be our choice when we suddenly saw a large illuminated sign advertising *The Devil In Miss Jones*. It was perfectly obvious from our reaction that we had both heard of it and knew something about what it contained. However, just in case Pat was under any misapprehension that it was about the occult and starred Charlton Heston in drag, I pointed out that it was what is known as a porn flick. Without further ado we headed for the box office and sold our souls. As we took our seats I made it clear to her that if at any time she felt uncomfortable, she was to nudge me and we would leave. After all, I had to bear in mind that she was a well-brought-up English woman of a certain age – albeit with two grown-up children. Once the projector started doing its work we began to see images that could only be described as revelatory. The story line may have been thin, but the bodies of the actors and actresses were richly endowed. A high point arrived when the eponymous heroine was shown reclining in a bath only half submerged. At first she caressed herself quite playfully, and then with more intimacy. Bored with this, she extended her hand towards a large bowl of fruit on a table by her shoulder. A grape was plucked and rolled around her breasts until it trickled down her body, before disappearing into the water somewhere below her navel. Several more followed in hot pursuit. The ritual was repeated with three plums, two apricots and a banana. At this point my companion, who had appeared to be rigid beside me, whispered in my ear, 'What a good thing there isn't a melon in the bowl!'

I stayed with Naim for the rest of my holiday. On the passion front it was gratifying that roles were rather reversed. In spite of that, we have lost touch once again. But I did hear that he had got married.

Weekend visitors were few and far between during my year in Les Avants. NC set great store by his many friends, and adored entertaining, but for one reason or another only three came to stay. Personally, if I had been feeling under par I would not have allowed any of them to cross the threshold. The first, Ginette Spanier, did not draw breath for a moment; the second, Robin Maugham, talked a lot too, but only about his health; and the third, Joyce Carey, was charming but stone deaf.

Ginette came from her home in Paris for a couple of weekends. She was as stylish and elegant as you would expect from a former directrice of the House of Balmain. You would have to read her autobiography, *Make Mine Mink*, to discover how she made her way from Hampstead to the top of the French rag trade, but I suspect her colossal personality played a part in her rise. In spite of being married to a distinguished doctor, she was rumoured to have been a lover of Marlene Dietrich – through whom she met NC.

I suspect that Robin Maugham's invitation to stay was self-extended. As well as talking ill, he certainly looked it, and had no discernible personality whatsoever. The only respectable link between him and NC was the fact that they were both heartily disliked by Robin's uncle Willie.

Joyce Carey's credentials for Coward friendship were impeccable. Her mother, Liliane Braithwaite, had been a distinguished actress and Joyce, in turn, had acquitted herself on stage very well. Although seldom a leading lady, she had featured prominently in lots of early Coward productions. Even with her disability she was still in work at the age of ninety. Her London home in Chester Street, just off Eaton Square, was a scaled-down version of a much bigger Belgravia house and was known to her friends as 'The Baby Grand'. She was a delightful woman and always showed me great kindness.

In the Spring, when the alpine snow is melting, it is replaced on the slopes surrounding the village by drifts of white narcissi. They are admired not only for their fragile beauty, but also for their delicate fragrance. Young ones are picked, packed tightly into boxes and sent all over the world. While the rest of the chalet's occupants indulged in a siesta, I would often spend the afternoons walking in the countryside, relishing the clean air and marvellous scenery. On the slopes around the house I would sometimes be accompanied by the sound of one of the world's greatest sopranos rehearsing at home. Her hectic international programme meant that she spent very little time in Switzerland, basing herself instead at her house in Sydney, or her flat in Cornwall Gardens in London. Richard Bonynge, her husband, either travelled with her or carried out solo engagements as a leading conductor. By comparison with the set-up next door, their domestic arrangements might have seemed conventional. But on the other hand there probably aren't many wives who travel everywhere with their aunt, while at the same time the husband is accompanied by a close male friend. Not to be outdone, their young son Adam enjoyed the company of a Swiss-German nanny, who doubled as housekeeper. Although the Chalet Bonynge had a happy atmosphere, walking into it was rather like entering a shrine to high Victoria art and decoration. Richard was an obsessive collector of anything from that period – even the house itself. Despite the fact that the two neighbouring households had friends and interests in common they had very little social contact. Not many people know, however, that The Diva and The Master got together to make an LP, called *Joan Sutherland Sings Noel Coward* – a curious conjunction of talent that could have been a joy, but which failed in the end to do justice to either singer or composer. There was no question of opening new numbered accounts at the Montreux Banque Suisse as a result of that little collaboration.

During Master's bed-bound phase he would usually dine in his room, either alone or with 'the boys'. Having tucked him in at about nine-thirty p.m. they would return to the drawing room to indulge in their favourite pastime of the moment. Some years before, all three of them had a passion for painting in oils. Suitably besmocked, they would stand for hours at their easels dabbing away at stretched canvases. Sadly it was only the Master who showed any real talent, whilst 'the boys' would have undoubtedly benefited from some coaching in perspective and composition. The house was decorated with many works in the Master's hand, his style slightly reminiscent of L.S. Lowry. Unlike Lowry, though, Master chose brightly lit port and beach scenes as a setting for his crowds of small figures. Nuns and sailors were usually well to the fore, though never too closely juxtaposed. But painting was *vieux chapeau* in my day; the needle had replaced the brush and embroidery was all the rage. Whether point was gros or petit I am not sure, but they certainly turned out some vivid cushions and chair covers. Although invited to participate, my plea of failing eyesight and pudgy fingers was reluctantly accepted. Instead I played records and distracted them with requests for stories from the good old days. Rather to my surprise, a light-hearted suggestion that they should apply for membership of Queen Mary's Sewing Guild was met with an enthusiastic response. I hope they didn't follow it up.

I had been back to London a couple of times during the year, and friends had been to stay. As well as Naim in Berne, I enjoyed the company of Susanna, a teacher, and Lesley, a secretary from Chatelard, the posh girls' school in the village. But, ludicrous though it may seem at the age of twenty-two, I was homesick. If I am honest, I suppose I also felt that I was missing some action. When I plucked up courage to confide in Coley he couldn't have been sweeter or more sympathetic. Even when he told me that they had hoped I would go with them to the house in Jamaica for Christmas and the New Year, I still stuck to my guns. Finally, after a few more attempts at persuasion, he accepted that I wanted to leave. From that moment on he became terribly excited about the prospect of finding me a fun job in London. His first thought was that Binkie Beaumont was looking for a new secretary to replace his old faithful, who was retiring. Sadly this idea came to naught when it emerged that the office skills required were far in excess of my limited ability. In the end, he suggested that until something amazing came along I could help Joan Hirst run the office in Milner Street.

My last day at the Shilly Chalet was one of very mixed emotions. In spite of looking forward to my new beginning I hated the thought of saying goodbye to my dear friends. When the farewell phase began the big surprise was that Guido and Giuseppe seemed genuinely sad to see me go. For the most part they had been kind and friendly, but sometimes I had sensed a little resentment and jealousy. With my luggage in the hall I climbed the stairs for the last time to take leave of my remarkable employer. At Coley's suggestion I took with me a photograph of the master for him to sign. I had deliberately selected a large close-up of his face that was not normally given away.

'Tell me,' he asked, 'why have you chosen such a horrid photograph?' 'I like it because it is just you and no boring body,' I explained boldly. 'And what is so boring about my body?' he enquired with a big grin. He inscribed it to me nevertheless, as I sat beside him on the bed. With the deed done he leant forward and whispered conspiratorially, 'I have something to confess. I have a nickname for you, but no one knows what it is as I haven't told a soul'. (Which I certainly didn't believe.)

'Oh dear,' I said nervously, 'what can it be?'

'Large Lord Fauntleroy,' he declared with heavy emphasis. We laughed like drains and hugged each other, but then the mood changed and eyes had to be dabbed. As I got up to leave he thrust an envelope into my hand which contained, he said, 'something to tide you over'. In a state of confusion I walked out of the room, unable to look back. At the airport Coley and I embraced and the expression on his face spoke volumes, which set me off again. Not much composure was regained until the aircraft was well on its way to London.

Thanks to Master's generosity I was able to have a two-week break with my mother and catch up with old friends before starting work in Milner Street. Although Joan and I had spoken on the telephone we had never actually met, but we soon became firm friends. After a long illness Lornie had died during the last weeks of my time at Les Avants – a loss that was felt greatly by NC. The large, gloomy house (opposite a pub called The Australian) had been her home for many years, with the ground floor given over entirely to the Coward office. Its new owner, Lornie's son, decided to sell it in due course, with the prospect of a giant upheaval for poor Joan, who only worked for NC five afternoons a week. The rest of her time was spent dealing with the affairs of Sir Michael and Lady Redgrave, who lived in Rossetti Mansions off the Kings Road. For the next few months I turned up each day just after lunch ready to help in any way I could.

Joan lived with her husband Geoff, a dedicated Yorkshireman with an impish smile and a keen sense of humour, in a tiny flat in Mallord Street. They had no children of their own, although Joan had a grown-up son from an earlier marriage. Great company themselves, they loved being with people of all ages. During her long association with the Redgrave family Joan had become a close friend and confidant of both Michael and his wife Rachel. When I knew them they spent many an evening with Rachel in a favourite local restaurant. Sometimes I was lucky enough to be invited to join them. Joan, who had known Vanessa, Corin and Lyn for most of their lives, was fond of them too, but did not care for the revolutionary political causes that the first two espoused. I escorted her one evening to the first night of a Henry James play, *The Aspern Papers*, at the Theatre Royal, Haymarket, where the cast was led by Vanessa and Christopher Reeve. Michael had adapted it many years ago as a vehicle for himself, and he was there that night to be seen in public for the last time. When the outing was suggested Joan had told me, 'You won't want to go to the party afterwards, will you? I'm afraid it will be full of all those terrorist friends of Vanessa's.' What could I say? We didn't go.

The problem of finding another office when the house was sold resolved itself when it was decided to move it and the Hirsts to a larger flat in Cadogan Square. It was on the top floor, light and airy and approached by a coffin-sized lift. I helped them to move in and to arrange the second bedroom as Joan's rather overcrowded workplace.

In December 1969 a week of festivities took place to celebrate the Master's seventieth birthday. As well as lunching at Clarence House he was knighted by the Queen and appeared as guest of honour at a midnight gala at the Phoenix Theatre. For this occasion I sat in the dress circle with the Coward 'family', just behind the Snowdons who had relinquished the Royal Box in favour of the birthday boy. Flanked by Merle Oberon and Joyce Carey he looked as if he was having the time of his life. But no one seemed to enjoy it more than Princess Margaret, who led the applause and got to her feet at every opportunity.

One function to which I was not invited, and probably did not expect to be, was the celebratory dinner at The Savoy. But as luck would have it, a nasty flu epidemic was sweeping the capital at the time and guests dropped out in droves. At the last moment not only was I invited to attend myself, but I was asked to bring two friends as well! The River Room proved to be so full of famous faces that it was difficult to imagine exactly who had been forced to languish in their sick bed. In the case of my own table I could only think that I was meant to be a woman, and probably a ballerina. My fellow diners were the dancers Anton Dolin and John Gilpin, the founders of the theatre museum Raymond Mander and Joe Mitchenson and an elderly beauty called 'June' who was famous before the war for doing something that required ravishing good looks, before she married Lord Inverclyde. With her came her companion, Peggie Dear. But the identity of the eighth person at the table will have to remain a mystery. Long and hard have I studied the menu, signed by them all, but the most I can come up with is 'George'. God knows, if he had been famous I would have remembered him like a shot but I suspect that, like me, he may have been only a tiny cog in the great machinery of the Master's life. We ate four delicious courses washed down with fine wines and culminating in a Veuve Laurent-Perrier Extra Dry for the Loyal Toast. There followed appropriate speeches by the lords Nugent and Mountbatten and a rambling dissertation from Laurence Olivier, who tried too hard to be clever. The Master, of course, spoke too but only briefly and then sat to receive a long line of well-wishers and signature seekers. I joined the queue behind Frankie Howerd and nervously prepared to explain my identity. But I needn't have worried, for I was greeted with a warm embrace and a whispered 'Large Lord Fauntleroy!'

As a result of that evening I kept in touch with only two of my fellow guests – after all, 'George' didn't stand a chance. Raymond, an unsuccessful actor, and Joe, an ex-dancer (known to the Master as Gog and Magog) had, over many years, turned themselves and their house in Sydenham into a repository of theatrical knowledge and memorabilia. They also published books that became the standard works on every aspect of theatrical history. Within the profession they were regarded as outrageous as a couple and outstanding as a source of reference. At one stage they asked me to help with the administration of the Collection, which they intended to present to the nation, but I declined. Their parties were numerous and chaotic, with thespian guests often outnumbered by marble busts of the likes of Garrick and Irving. After one such shepherd's-pie-on-the-floor evening I gave a lift back into town to Judy Dench and Michael Williams and the legendary broadcaster, Audrey Russell. Over a nightcap in what Audrey described as her Brownhart Gardens 'slit trench', it rapidly emerged that while I was losing luggage in Jamaica or fighting off the Mahdi's followers in Khartoum she was there too describing, inimitably, the bigger picture for the folks back home.

When I came to the end of my usefulness as far as Joan was concerned, Coley surprised me with another idea for a job. Knowing how much I loved books he had asked Handyside Buchanan, who ran Heywood Hill in Curzon Street, if there was an opening for me there. The upshot was not an offer of a full-time job but a fortnight's work while John Saumarez Smith was on holiday. This venerable institution, where Nancy Mitford had once been a partner, is unquestionably London's smartest book shop. But so understated is its presence that in common with only one other establishment I can think of (Stephen August, the hairdresser in Chester Row) its name is not advertised outside. The Master must have been one of its best customers, regularly placing orders for the latest novels and biographies. Although in two weeks I was hardly ever able to suggest a good read for any of the regular customers, I did succeed in getting on reasonably well with the other long-term employee, who was known as 'the admiral's daughter'. At the end of my stint Handyside presented me with a thesaurus and a novel by Gaia Servadio.

A couple of weeks before I left Les Avants I decided to take the bull by the horns and write to Jeremy at the House of Commons. After all, he had said he might be able to help where the BBC was concerned, and anyway I had been thinking about him rather a lot. By return, a hand-written letter on House of Commons paper arrived saying that of course he remembered vividly the enormous figure in scarlet who helped to make his first visit to Buckingham Palace so memorable. He insisted that I ring him at his office when I got back to London. Within a matter of days I was reunited with my mother at her house in West Hampstead. Reaching Jeremy by telephone at the House proved to be remarkably easy and an invitation to drinks there at six the next day was soon forthcoming.

Just as I was leaving home a message came through from Jeremy's private office to say that he would be leaving the House early and would I go instead to his flat at Marsham Court. At first I was sorry to miss the chance of a first visit to the Houses of Parliament, but on reflection I guessed that we would both be more relaxed in his own home.

I crossed London by bus and walked from Westminster Abbey down Marsham Street towards the river. Marsham Court is an imposing block of flats built, I should think, in the late fifties with the needs of the occupants of the Palace of Westminster very much in mind. It is in the division bell area and close enough to the Commons for members to walk there when summoned. Having negotiated the surprisingly uninquisitive porter I took the lift to the third floor, my heart pounding in my chest. The door opened as the bell rang and a warm welcome was immediately extended. As he showed me into the small sitting room he apologised for the lack of space, explaining that it was only a base in London since his main home was in the constituency. With drinks liberally dispensed we settled down to begin a conversation that can only be described as wide-ranging and hilarious. At first I was daunted by Jeremy's flare for words and eloquence, but as he also possessed the rare good listening gift, my ability to contribute soon came into play. He relished any snippet I could dredge up about life with the monarch or the Master, obviously fascinated by both. When he said how much he would like to get to know them better I had to explain that my influence with the former was such that I didn't think I was able to bring them closer together. However, some months later I was able to arrange for him to meet the Master.

When we got on to the subject of Jeremy's political life it was obvious that not only did he revel in every aspect of it but that he was also extremely ambitious. He even hinted that to gain power the Liberals would work with the Labour Party of Harold Wilson, a man for whom he had some regard. Not so Ted and the Tories. Jeremy said that his attempts at friendship with Ted were always icily rebuffed. Image consciousness was in its infancy in those days, but even so he was aware that potentially damaging rumours were circulating about his unmarried status and had to be silenced. To that end, a suitable spouse candidate and a move in that direction would soon be made. He and his friend David Holmes, who was almost as ambitious as Jeremy, had a woman acquaintance in common and straws were about to be drawn to decide which of them would ask for her hand. Amazed though I was that Jeremy would reveal so much to someone who a few hours before had been a complete stranger, his next admission made me realise that he had a very real problem. With sex as the subject he admitted that late at night he was in the habit of driving down certain streets that were the known haunts of rent boys and unscrupulous rough trade. I couldn't decide whether his motivation was driven by sex itself or plain loneliness. What I did know was that he was playing a very dangerous game and putting his career at risk. It seemed astonishing that a highly intelligent man who aspired to be prime minister in a Liberal government, or rather more probably home secretary in a coalition, could act so irresponsibly. But I suppose such behaviour is a well-established tradition in British political life. It was very late when he suggested we should have some supper. We moved into the little kitchen and working together produced passable scrambled eggs and bacon. Several hours later I returned by taxi to West Hampstead. This was the first of many such evenings, sometimes two or three a week.

As a temporary Christmas job I worked at Fortnum and Mason selling hampers and groceries on the ground floor. My presence there in a public and exotic place allowed Jeremy to wander in and see me during the day. If we were to meet in the evening following one of his visits he would buy something delicious like smoked salmon or potted shrimps to eat as a first course before we had the scrambled eggs that had become traditional. Occasionally he would suggest varying the routine by taking me to dine at Locketts, the restaurant on the ground floor of the Court. One memorable evening we went instead to his club, the Reform, a well-known haunt of politicians generally and Liberals in particular. With his usual bravado he chose a table in the centre of the dining room so that we could be clearly observed by the other diners. All went well until he lowered his voice to say that the leader of the Welsh Liberals had just walked in and that as he was on his own he must be asked to join us. Responding to the greeting, Emlyn Hooson came to the table and accepted Jeremy's invitation with a tepid smile. To my horror I was introduced as a constituent and aspiring Liberal candidate. Completely unprepared for this description it took me several courses and glasses of wine to recover a degree of composure. The situation was not eased by the impression rapidly received that Hooson's admiration for JT was less than overwhelming. Added to this were his obvious skills as a barrister – an inquisitorial lightness of touch more JCB than QC. Somehow I managed to produce reasonable answers to questions about my age and county of birth, but when it came to expressing my views on Liberal philosophy I must have looked pretty pathetic. Happily my quick-witted companion was able to jump in and interpret my ramblings before all cover was blown. As luck would have it, Hooson was leaving early the next morning for his constituency and asked to be excused before the coffee was served. As he departed I couldn't help thinking that our leader's standing in the principality had not been enhanced by the evening's encounter. Jeremy, on the other hand, was elated by it all and demanded large brandies to toast our jolly jape. I vowed to myself not to dine with him in Pall Mall again.

One evening in his flat Jeremy announced that he was going to a meeting in Geneva in his capacity as Chairman of the British branch of the United Nations Association.

'Les Avants isn't far from there, is it?' he asked. 'What do you think the Master would say if I asked to worship at the Coward shrine during my stay?'

'I'm sure he would be delighted,' I replied. 'I will ring Coley tomorrow and see what can be arranged.'

I had not actually spoken to Coley for some time although we had exchanged letters and he had sent me a very warm reference. He answered the phone when I rang the next morning, and seemed pleased to hear from me. He was very intrigued when I told him about my new friend and did not attempt to conceal his enthusiasm when I explained the reason for the call. Apparently they were all enduring one of the Master's periodic bouts of depression and writer's block, and a new and amusing visitor was just what was needed. It was agreed that Jeremy would ring from his hotel once he knew what free time he would have.

Well, it turned out that Jeremy could find as much free time as he wanted. After all, even by Liberal standards the United Nations Association was not one of the world's great forums and the Chairman of the British Branch would not be missed at one fondue evening. During a jokey telephone conversation with Coley a date for dinner was duly arranged. He was the only guest, with Coley, Graham and the Master all on cracking form. The evening began with Graham's inhibition-shattering bullshots, proceeded with dishes of Guido specialities washed down with litres of local wine and culminated in the small hours with a sing-song around the piano in the drawing room. In his own words, Jeremy's only regret, apart from the quantities of booze, was that he had not been word perfect in a performance of 'Mad Dogs and Englishmen' sung in the manner of the composer, who accompanied him at the keyboard. The evening was a great success and as Jeremy left, the Master made him promise that they would lunch together during his next visit to London.

In no time at all dressing gowns and Salem cigarettes were being stowed away in a suite at the Savoy Hotel and a telephone call put through to the office of the Leader of the Liberal Party. I could not resist a wry smile as Jeremy told me that when he announced himself at the Grill at one o'clock on the appointed day he was told that Mr Coward was slightly indisposed and that lunch would be in his suite. Up on the fourth floor Jeremy found his host with a beaming smile, a glass of champagne and precious little sign of a migraine. In the sitting room beside the window overlooking the Thames a table, complete with exotic floral arrangement, had been set with two places. Gossipy conversation flowed easily between them as they enjoyed their drinks and moved onto a delicious lunch. With the cheese course, however, the Master's mood became darker as he talked of unfulfilled sexual desire and unrequited love. Although Jeremy, as much as any man, was in a position to empathise, he confided that he could not help feeling a little uncomfortable at the turn in the atmosphere of the evening. Anxiety developed when his host, rising unsteadily to his feet, suggested that their glasses of Armagnac would be enjoyed in more comfort in the bedroom. In turning towards the bedroom door, the older man failed to see that his guest was weaving his way in the other direction. Realising that he had not been followed the Master returned to find Jeremy climbing into his overcoat and mumbling about a vote in the House and letters to sign. A chase of sorts ensued, with the younger man dodging between easy chairs and coffee tables until he finally reached the safety of the door to the suite. With a breathless expression of thanks he fell out into the corridor. They never met again.

Some days before the announcement of his engagement to Caroline Allpass, Jeremy revealed to me his determination to make the wedding and reception as impressive as possible. To that end he had sought the permission of his friend the Archbishop of Canterbury to hold the service in the private chapel at Lambeth Palace. Lack of space would limit the size of the congregation, but this would be more than compensated for by the reception to be held two weeks later. The President of the Royal Academy had agreed to the use of Burlington House for the entertainment of five hundred of Jeremy's closest friends.

The Gods of media and weather smiled happily down on the great day. Evening television news programmes and the following day's papers were full of shots of the radiant couple posing for the press in the sunlit garden of the Archbishop's residence. I cannot remember where the honeymoon was spent but they were certainly back in time for the big bash in Piccadilly. I went to the reception with two of Jeremy's business associates, who were involved in television production. He had very kindly brought us together in case there might have been a role for me in their new company. Progress was slow in the receiving line as the queue of guests covered the length of the Academy staircase and meandered into the courtyard. Quite by chance I found myself standing beside a man in clerical dress who introduced himself as Leonard Tyzack, domestic chaplain to the Archbishop of Canterbury. He had got to know the newlyweds by being mainly responsible for the Lambeth side of things. As neither of us knew many people there we stuck together and spent as much time pretending to peruse the pictures of the Summer Exhibition as we did identifying the faces of the great and the good among the guests. Scrummy food came from a buffet of hot and cold dishes whilst nimble waitresses kept the champagne flowing.

At around midnight the offer of a nightcap at Lambeth Palace was too tempting to refuse, but we were both anxious not to leave before we had thanked our host. Jeremy was obviously surprised and delighted that Leonard and I had found each other, but as we said our farewells and turned to leave I glimpsed sadness in his eyes.

I saw Jeremy only occasionally after that evening; quite naturally his new responsibilities had radically changed his life. When he was on his own in London, old friends from his bachelor days, including me, would be asked for a drink at his new and much larger flat in Artillery Mansions. In fact I was with him there one evening when a call came through from the hospital to say that Caroline was going into labour.

In the run-up to the referendum on Europe I went one evening to a public meeting at Westminster Central Hall where the main speakers were to be Edward Heath, Roy Jenkins and Jeremy. I enjoy political debate but I was also interested to hear Jeremy address a large audience on an issue that was one of his celebrated hobby horses. I had planned to find a seat at the back of the hall, but I arrived late and the size of the crowd meant that the only available place was close to the front. For some reason I was nervous about being seen from the platform, which meant that by the time the political heavyweights made their entrance, to enthusiastic applause, I was slumped right down in my seat. Jeremy sat in the front row on the stage between Heath and Jenkins. The formidable figure of his mother was in place just behind him. During the introductory speech I watched Jeremy's face with great interest. It was arranged as an effective mixture of profound concentration and wry amusement. But what the casual observer might not have spotted was that his eyes were taking in everyone sitting in that vast auditorium. Although he had absolutely no idea that I would be there it did not take long for him to see me. Staring hard in my direction he almost imperceptibly inclined his head. From that moment on I got the impression that he was watching me the whole time. The discussion was very lively with some very good speeches, including Jeremy's. During the final ovation I joined several others in making a dash for the door. Looking back I was never sure why I approached the evening with such apprehension. Perhaps it was the fear of being embarrassed by him in public. I certainly did not want to be introduced to his mother.

For some years I have known Dinah, a delightful antique dealer who lives in Suffolk with her husband and daughter. Late one night after a very good dinner at their house it emerged in the course of conversation that she had not always earned a living flogging old furniture. Indeed, during the late sixties and early seventies she had enjoyed a promising career as a model. In those days she lived in London to be close to her work, sharing various flats with friends in the business. To my amazement she mentioned in passing that for a time one of her flatmates had been a male model called Norman Scott. My exclamation of disbelief prompted her to ask if I had known the gentleman in question. I replied by saying that although we had never met we had a mutual friend in Jeremy Thorpe. When I went on to explain how Jeremy and I had first come into contact I could see that I had her attention. At the end of my tale Dinah said that she had always thought of Scott as a sort of Walter Mitty character living in a fantasy world. She and her friends got very bored with his claims of a close relationship with the leader of the Liberal Party. One evening he returned to the flat in a great rage saying that Jeremy had fallen in love with a footman at Buckingham Palace and that their affair was over. At the time Dinah had dismissed this outburst as the product of a disturbed mind, little realising that one day the erstwhile footman would become a friend.

One Sunday afternoon during the summer of 1993 I was walking in Queen Mary's Rose Garden at Regents Park, picking my way carefully between picnicking families from the Indian sub-continent, when to my surprise I thought I recognised a woman just ahead of me whose nose was closely involved with a particularly lovely bloom. As I drew nearer I realised that it was indeed the ex-granddaughter-in-law of the woman after whom the garden was named, Marion Thorpe. She appeared to be in on her own, but as I walked past, a brown trilby caught my eye a few yards further on. A stooped figure, leaning heavily on a stick was sitting on one of the benches. Hearing approaching footsteps he slowly looked up and our eyes briefly met. My pace slowed for a moment but I carried on, turning my head just once to see him walking painfully down the path towards his wife.

My nightcap with Leonard at Lambeth proved to be the start of a richly rewarding friendship that continued through many happy hours spent in his flat overlooking the Palace gardens. Like everyone else he was devoted to his boss and Mrs Ramsey, but felt out of place in the rarefied atmosphere of the Archbishop's 'court'. The job of domestic chaplain was much sought after among the young high-fliers of the Church, as it represented a leap of several rungs on the promotional ladder. Leonard shared his duties with a very ambitious fellow who filled his apartment with fine furniture, and gave glittering dinner parties for the well connected. At the end of his tour of duty he went off to New York as a bishop. My friend, on the other hand, had entered the Church because he genuinely felt he had a mission to help people. His happiest times were spent as a young curate in an industrial area of the North of England. One day he told me that he had asked the archbishop if he could be released from his post, and return to parish work. The primate had reluctantly agreed, and in due course a selection of good livings was produced for him to choose. He rejected them all, insisting that he needed to get his teeth into a parish with poor housing and high unemployment so that his skills as a social worker could also be used. Eventually he was offered the incumbency, long vacant, of a parish on a huge housing estate in Dover. A couple of weeks after he made the move he rang to say that his induction was to take place on a particular Sunday afternoon, and would I be able to attend.

Finding Leonard's particular bit of housing estate proved to be more difficult that we had thought. The Dover of castle and port is only a tiny island in a sea of the dreariest urban landscape it was possible for 1950s architects to produce. But find it we did, and the rectory too. It was a shabby little council house at the end of a row of similar dwellings, right at the heart of the estate. Close by, the contemporary concrete church was the setting for the service conducted by the Bishop of Dover and Dr Ramsey. A congregation of about a dozen gave what it could to the rousing hymns, and afterwards we all repaired to the community hall – a blackened wartime Nissan hut. Mrs Ramsey, who had brought scones and cakes she had made, helped an elderly lady to dispense tea while her husband moved among us with cheery words and much laughter. What could have been a dismal affair, if surroundings were any influence, turned into a jolly party.

Staying with Leonard for a weekend some time later, I saw for myself something of the hard work he was putting into his challenging task. His home had been turned into an unofficial youth club, with table tennis in the sitting room and guitar practice in the kitchen. A spare room housed an unmarried mother and her baby. Only Leonard's own bedroom, with its moss green walls, bookshelves and four-poster bed, was representative of other vicarages in other parishes in less hostile parts of the Home Counties. The church was more than half full on Sunday morning for the eleven o'clock service, and as we filed out afterwards Leonard was thanked with warm handshakes by smiling parishioners as he stood in the porch. His efforts were rewarded some years later when the adjoining rundown parish was added to his, and more recently he has been made a canon.

By now I had moved out of my mother's house, as she was thinking of retiring and returning to Cornwall. At the same time my job at Fortnums had come to an end and I found yet more temporary work in the lighter (cigarette, that is) department at Aspreys. With brilliant timing a new friend called Richard Dallimore suggested that I share his flat at Lancaster Gate, just a skip across the Park from Bond Street. My new address was very smart indeed.

Hyde Park Gardens is a terrace of enormous stucco houses set back from the Bayswater Road, just across from Hyde Park. The mews behind it, originally designed to house horses and carriages, or more recently cars and chauffeurs, now provided bijou accommodation for the well off. I am not sure how 'well off' my landlord at number 43 actually was, particularly as he did not seem to earn much out of selling what his headed paper described as 'Grand Touring Cars'. The ground floor of the building was large enough to contain six cars and Richard had a short lease on the small flat above. My few pounds went towards the little bedroom at the back, and I also typed the odd invoice and letter for him. This arrangement was slightly complicated by the fact that a doctor friend of Richard's was also paying rent for my room. The theory was that he used it as a knocking shop when he picked up a bit of rough trade. But in practice the young men would normally need so much chat and drink before submission that they spent the night on the sitting room's pull-out sofa. The doctor was a very charming man, but he sailed very close to the wind in the sex department, eventually taking his own life as the police started showing interest in his activities.

Life in the mews was very convivial, with jolly friends in lots of the neighbouring houses. We occasionally had a drink with Leslie Mitchell, the veteran broadcaster, and his Danish wife, as well as chain-smoking Hugh and Jo Grainger who lived opposite. He was chairman of the Baltic Exchange. Alison, a great friend, lived in a big house at the West End and next to her by the arch were two unattached brothers; one with a limp and the other with a fondness for a drink, known as Dick the Stick and Bob the Bottle.

Richard was an interesting character about fifteen years my senior and with whom, on the face of it, I had nothing whatsoever in common. On the other hand we did laugh a lot and we both liked men. His background was Anglo-Irish, public school and a smart cavalry regiment. He was once famously described by Oliver Barnes, the bicycling bridge-player-about-town, as having had one elocution lesson too many. When it came to food and drink he enjoyed other people's enormously, although a second glass of anything invariably induced a sneezing bout. His favourite supper at home was grilled sausages, boiled potatoes and a curious mixture of tinned tomatoes mashed with white bread. This culinary masterpiece had to be followed by a tin of mandarin oranges. As far as his business was concerned the level of activity may have been low but the list of his clients read like the cast of *Sunday Night at the London Palladium*, and included Jimmy Tarbuck, Russ Conway, Jeremy Brett and Alan Bates. In categories of their own were the boxer Billy Walker, the Arsenal football team and composer Lennox Berkeley. They all sought his advice about their motoring needs and he bought and sold motor cars on their behalf. Although I met them all from time to time the only one I spent an evening alone with was Mr Conway. He had telephoned Richard one day to ask if he could come round that evening for a drink. Richard said of course that was fine, but that he had to go out to dinner at about eight p.m. When I got back from work Richard explained that he was coming and cautioned me that Russ was paranoid about his name. For some reason he only liked being called Terry, his real name, and woe betide anyone who called him Russ. The three of us talked happily for about an hour until it was time for Richard to leave. At that point Terry turned to me and asked

if I would like to go to a local pub. I said that I would and suggested
The Victoria at the end of the mews. My apparent enthusiasm masked
the fact that I was always incredibly shy and ill at ease with anyone
even vaguely celebrated. Bear in mind also that 'Terry' was at the
height of his fame, with records in the charts and almost daily
appearances on the telly.

A few heads turned and some did a double take as we walked into
the bar, but in fact it was the sort of pub whose patrons would rather
not be seen to recognise a star of light entertainment. We took our
drinks to a corner table and had another stab at conversation, but he
didn't seem to want to know anything about me or reveal very much
about his own life. It was quite difficult to reconcile the image I had
of the smiling and animated performer on the box with the obviously
troubled figure sitting across from me. After a second round of drinks
we decided to call it a day. As we walked away from the pub he turned
to me and said:

'Tell me, why have you been calling me Terry all evening?'

Changing flints and refuelling lighters was not a wildly interesting
way to pass a day, but I enjoyed the atmosphere of the old emporium
and the people with whom I worked. What I did like was being called
occasionally to do door duty, which meant greeting the punters and
conducting them to appropriate departments. Names that stick in my
memory are the imposing figure of the old Duke of Marlborough,
who needed picnic hampers for an African safari, and the diminutive
Wilfred Bramble from *Steptoe and Son*, who wanted an onyx ashtray.
But all in all I was not too sad when Mr Wilkinson, the personnel
manager, said that when my three months were up, Aspreys would not
be able to keep me on. However, if I was interested, he knew that there
was a job at The Dorchester where various shops, including Aspreys,
kept showcases that displayed items for sale, under the watchful eye of
a woman called Mrs Ross. On the way to meet her he warned me that
she had a reputation for not keeping her helpers for very long. With
this in mind I was pleasantly surprised by the big smile and bright
personality that greeted me. We hit it off at once and she asked me to
join her as soon as possible.

The showcases were situated in a vestibule by the main lift, between the hall and the lounge. Mrs Ross and I lay in wait behind a desk that was also a great vantage point for celebrity spotting. We were helped in this by a daily list of notable arrivals that was distributed by the press office. More detailed gossip about our guests was gleaned during daily visits to the staff canteen for coffee and lunch breaks. Even Mrs Ross's own secrets were not safe there. I soon discovered that she was actually Rossbottom, but had quite sensibly decided to manage with just one syllable. She was a wealthy widow and kinsman of the Duke of St Albans, with a valuable house in Gerald Road opposite a former residence of Noel Coward's. She had got the job through connections with the McAlpine family and had been there for many years. It didn't take me long to realise that although she was not universally popular, a number of the regular guests seemed to enjoy her company. The most extraordinary of these were the Misses Fox, elderly daughters of Mr 'Twentieth Century' Fox, the American founder of the film company. Although not twins, they were very alike, with dead white complexions, dark black hair and a taste for the sort of fussy Chanel suits much favoured by American women of a certain age. With failed marriages behind them they had both reverted to their father's illustrious name. The legacy of his enormous wealth allowed them to spend most of their time at a grand hotel near Lausanne, where Mrs Ross would visit them for weekends. She returned from one of these jaunts sporting a beautiful mink jacket they had given her as a birthday present. At the time I was pretty envious, without realising that I would soon be receiving presents of my own.

But for the time being I was happily enjoying my new surroundings. When the hotel was quiet I would wander into the entrance hall where three desks, the hall porters, reception and cashier represented the front line of the whole operation. But the one I went to most often was in the corner just inside the front door – the florist's domain. To begin with I went there to chat to the girls who were always fun and friendly, but after a while I stood among the buckets of cut flowers to gaze at Terry the young linkman whose looks were almost devastating. There were always two of them on duty and when the second one was John, his uncle, it was an added bonus. He was an ex-Guardsman of six-foot four and when he started work at the hotel the linkman's job was either passed from father to son or given to someone who paid for the privilege. John was a delightful man who deserved to do well out of his job. At the time of his retirement he was living in a flat in Richmond that had once belonged to Bud Flanagan. He died there and I went to his funeral. Terry had a lot of his uncle's charm and an attitude to life that he had acquired in the navy. We became good friends and remained in touch for many years.

Around this time two other people, Daphne Bywater and Marjorie Lee, also became important figures in my life. Daphne, who was number two in the press office under Marjorie, took me under her wing at a very early stage. The first person she introduced me to was a Dorchester regular called Maurice Thrift, whose office at the headquarters of the Rank Organisation was just round the corner in South Street. Happily, hardly a day passed without Maurice coming into the hotel for drinks or lunch, usually accompanied either by his boss, the Chief Executive Graham Dowson, or his fellow PR man Peter Lendrum. They were a remarkably entertaining trio and I was lucky that they sometimes asked me to join them.

In those days the Rank Organisation, with its interests in films and the leisure industry, was still clinging to its position as an important British business, even though the bulk of its income was derived from a partnership with Xerox the American manufacturers of the photocopying machine. It had at its head, in the nominal position of president, the gangly figure of Lord Rank, whose family had made its fortune milling flour. But the real power in the company was vested in its chairman, the disagreeable John Davies, who was known to the world at large as a former husband of the actress Dinah Sheridan. Graham, who as his deputy ran the organisation on a day-to-day basis from the palatial headquarters building near Berkeley Square, was in many ways the antithesis of his superior and as a consequence enjoyed a less than easy relationship with him. Graham was both physically enormous and larger-than-life. He was a bon viveur and raconteur with an incisive mind, benevolence and a brilliant sense of humour.

But these two disparate personalities did have one thing in common. Women. At the time we met, Graham had moved from two broken marriages to a long-term relationship with Pamela Awbrey, his former secretary. In everything but name she was Mrs Dowson. She had a figure that Wallis Simpson would have envied, and shared with Graham his vivacity and charm. Their life together revolved around film premieres, smart restaurants and continental weekends courtesy of the Rank jet aircraft. But it was a tempestuous relationship, not helped by Graham's wandering eye or Pamela's fondness for a certain admirer. Their many friends in the film business included Betty Box, whose family were involved in every aspect of movie making, and her husband Peter Rogers, the publicity-shy producer of the 'Carry On' films.

Through my friendship with Maurice and his with Pamela, she and I met often at parties. The most protracted of these that I can remember is the three-day series of festivities that launched the new Gloucester Hotel when Maurice arranged accommodation for me and some of his other friends at the Rank-owned Royal Lancaster Hotel. On her own Pamela was also a regular afternoon visitor to the Dorchester, where we would chat while she waited in the lounge to be joined for tea. With the arrival of a distinctive white Rolls-Royce at the door I would make my excuses and slip away. Very often she and Peter Rogers would sit over their Earl Grey until it was time for a glass of champagne, but sometimes they would move to an upstairs suite where they could take their refreshment in private.

The surprise announcement of an impending Dowson-Awbrey wedding was greeted with great delight by their wide circle of friends, who saw it as an event that was long overdue. But their joy proved to be short lived for, only a few weeks later, it emerged that the ceremony had been cancelled. Pamela was left angry and upset, with only Max her faithful hound for company. Graham went on to compound her unhappiness by marrying someone else with what can only be described as indecent haste. His bride, Denise, was a much younger woman, whose father owned a chain of cinemas. Somehow or other the *Sunday Times* latched onto this saga and included it in a lengthy and irreverent article about Rank's Davies years in the magazine section. It may have been purely coincidence, but Graham was asked to stand down as chief executive and lost his chance of succeeding the elderly chairman. His departure was regarded as a great loss, both for the organisation and for the sharp end of British industry. But happily there is always demand for a talent like Graham's and he went on to run several other companies and to lend sparkle to programmes such as *Any Questions?* Pamela has perhaps coped less well with her changed circumstances, but works hard and is resolutely independent. After many years I saw her again at a dinner party given by Alan Lamboll and Jonathon Wicks at their temporary flat on the embankment. She was on cracking form and as beautifully groomed as ever. We stayed late and I offered to drive her home. She sat in the car quite happily as I headed towards the West End and joined in my laughter when she confessed to a moment's amnesia when it came to the details of her address. But fortunately I had enough knowledge of London to know that there weren't many mansion blocks that stand at the corner of a five-way junction!

As the man at Rank most closely identified with Graham, poor old Maurice was also told to pack his bags. But in his case he was given a job with Southern Television, in which Rank was a major shareholder, based in Southampton. Although he was never known to complain, I know that his fall from grace was a bitter blow. He could see no reason to think that his job in South Street, working so closely with the chairman-designate, would not go on for as long as he wanted. He had also never saved a penny and was never happier than when spending his own money and generous expenses on dinner for friends in an Italian restaurant. His home was a tiny rented flat in Sloane Avenue Mansions and could not have been in greater contrast to the large South Kensington house, complete with resident chef, where his colleague Peter Lendrum lived.

After a brief and unsatisfactory spell at Southern Television, Maurice moved back to London, keen to find a media-based job that would allow him to utilise his writing talent. Although not ideal he quite enjoyed working for an old friend in Soho who sold advertisers the right to use their merchandise in big blockbusters, like the Bond films. For many happy years he shared a flat in Mandeville Place and dispensed delicious pasta to a small group of rummy players that included Stephen Barry, Michael Cashman and me. He ended his days as the poorly paid 'words' behind a Peter Stiles's successful public relations firm that ran the Berkeley Square Ball and organised conferences and product launches. I had moved to Scotland some months before his untimely death at the age of sixty-two, and was keenly awaiting the details of his planned visit courtesy of British Rail. In what was seen as a belated act of generosity his employer arranged the funeral at Golders Green and laid on cars and a lavish lunch. However, I discovered later that the bill for it all had been sent to Maurice's executor. I was bequeathed a large modern picture, which I have grown to love.

Through Marjorie I also met a couple of camp old American queens called Dick Hanley and John Lee, who were E. Taylor and R. Burton's secretaries. They had worked together for years in the service of their very demanding employers, organising every aspect of their lives. Such a claustrophobic existence was only possible because they were long-term lovers and shared an apartment in Los Angeles. They were also hoping before too long to move permanently to a house they had built in Palm Springs. One day Marjorie confided to me that one of their more serious shopping expeditions had yielded a Rolls-Royce, bought from a West End dealer. It seemed to them to be just the sort of runabout they needed for their retirement in California, adding a touch of gloss to their trips to the shopping mall, beauty parlour and shrink. When she said that they were going to look for a trustworthy person to drive their new toy across the States I volunteered at once. It just so happened that I had been thinking about making a change, so here was a great chance to take a working holiday. Fortunately, Marjorie thought it was a good wheeze, especially as John and Dick had already met me. Without further ado she went up to their suite to get their reaction. She rang me later to say that the idea was well received and that they would like to meet me again and go for a test drive.

A few days later I was sitting at the desk when one of the porters came over to tell me that the car had been delivered to the front door and that John and Dick were on their way down. As I went through the revolving door I saw the gleaming machine, in two tones of grey, waiting outside. It certainly was not one of the newer models, but I was also relieved that it was not a vintage banger either. I had already decided that if it had been a really old car I would not take on the responsibility. After all, a chap could have nightmares over a 'big end' biting the dust on a dirt road somewhere in the Midwest. I speak as someone whose only contact with an engine has been with a duster, but who could probably check oil provided a way was found to open the bonnet. When the proud owners arrived I congratulated them on the elegance of their baby and discussed the route we should take for the inaugural run. Something told me that a gentle glide would be preferred to a burn-up, so I suggested a turn round the carriage road in Hyde Park, which was very well received. As I helped them into the back of the car I saw for the first time that there was a major obstacle to my comfort at the wheel. The wretched car had been designed with a glass partition that separated the driver from the other occupants, with the lion's share of space going to the passengers in the back. Of course, had I been five foot-four and not six-foot four this would not have been a problem. As it was, I was only able to squeeze into the driving seat by being ridiculously intimate with the steering wheel. For our short run between the Bayswater Road and Hyde Park Corner my discomfort did not matter, but a longer journey would have been impossible. Safely back at the Dorchester once more, I was surprised to be complimented on my driving by John and Dick, who had sat through the jaunt looking very regal but not saying a word. I thanked them profusely for giving me the opportunity, but went on to explain that I could not possibly undertake a three thousand-mile journey feeling like a bird in a gilded cage that was built for a butterfly.

As doyenne of the press officers of grand hotels, Marjorie Lee had a rich and varied life and her story is certainly worth telling here. The Dorchester Hotel in Park Lane was built in the 1930s by McAlpines the builders on the site of one of London's great townhouses. In common with its neighbours, the huge mansions of the Grosvenor and Londonderry families, it had become too expensive to maintain at a time of economic upheaval. As a provider of considerable luxury it soon established itself as one of the key players in the big league, along with the Savoy, Claridges and the Connaught. When Queen Mary dined there, paying her first ever visit to an hotel, a seal was set on its social standing.

During the war it proved to be a popular bolt-hole with prominent hostesses such as Lady Cunard and Lady Colefax, who wanted to keep a base in the capital without the inconvenience of trying to obtain enough ration books to satisfy a temperamental cook, or replace a butler who had received his call-up papers. When I first got to know the place in 1969 – many years before it had passed through the hands of a couple of Middle Eastern potentates and had tens of millions of pounds lavished on it – it still retained an aura of gracious living from an era that had largely disappeared. To a great extent this atmosphere was created by the staff, of whom at least twenty had been there since the doors first opened – Michael the liftman, John the linkman, Joan the cashier in the Terrace and Roy who ran the American Bar, to name but a few. Having failed to find a buyer for their speculative venture, the McAlpines were still there, enjoying their ownership to the full. Various members of the family maintained suites of rooms and treated it rather like a private club or directors' dining room.

The three elderly ladies who, at the outset, had taken up permanent residence in small suites were still very much in evidence – their tariff, I suspect, having been frozen in the dim and distant past. Grander accommodation was kept for the sole use of two publicity-shy and equally wealthy families: the Breninkmeyers, Dutch owners of C&A, and a South African couple, Sir John and Lady Ellerman, of the eponymous shipping line. Somerset Maugham's sitting room was decorated with his own furniture and pictures for use during his London visits, and Elizabeth Taylor and Richard Burton filled up almost an entire floor when they and their entourage moved in.

Before the war the concept of public relations was almost unknown in this country, but one of its earliest exponents was a man called

Richmond Temple. At that time he was based at the Savoy Hotel, with his young assistant – Marjorie Lee. When he was asked to add the fledgling hotel in Park Lane to his list of clients, Marjorie was sent there to open a press office and deal with publicity and promotion. So successful was she in her task that her professional involvement with Elizabeth Taylor grew into the role of unofficial secretary and London representative. Not only did she plan all the Burtons' parties, she even acted as intermediary in personal situations of a delicate nature. A warm friendship was formed that weathered many a dramatic storm.

As Marjorie's skills in the sensitive world of public relations became widely known she was asked to take on assignments outside the hotel. One such occasion was the wedding of David Hicks and Lady Pamela Mountbatten. This was to be an enormous society affair at Romsey Abbey near Broadlands, the bride's family home in Hampshire. Because of the expected attendance of the entire Royal Family, and subsequent media interest, it was decided that Marjorie would be the right person to act as ringmaster. History does not relate the reaction to this decision of the Palace's own press secretary, an aristocratic retired naval officer. By all accounts, in spite of bad weather (over which even Marjorie had no control) the day was a great success and Marjorie's contribution much appreciated.

She enjoyed her job so much that she stayed in it for forty years, retiring for the first time in 1975. Unfortunately her departure coincided with the sale of the hotel to a buyer whose identity was supposed to remain secret, but who was generally thought to be the Emir of Kuwait. Inevitably a certain amount of chaos and confusion followed in the wake of the changed regime and Marjorie was persuaded to return and sort things out. This she did to great effect, and five years later she threw in the napkin for the last time and emigrated to Australia to start a new life with her great-niece and family.

Marjorie had never married, but her home life was shared by Bruno, the world's largest poodle. He burst onto the scene one day when she went to Harrods pet department to buy a puppy. She made it perfectly clear from the start that as her flat, just off Baker Street, was tiny she could only accommodate a very small dog. With this stipulation firmly in mind she was introduced to a little brown bundle, which was described as a miniature. At first sight love flowed between them and the poodle pup was whisked away to begin a new and much-pampered existence. At the outset everything went according to plan, with Marjorie sparing no expense for Bruno's comfort. He dined each evening on fillet steak or a couple of lamb cutlets, while his mistress happily ate a boiled egg or fish finger. The diet seemed to agree with him and he grew at a remarkable rate; so much in fact that by his first birthday he was taller than a golden retriever. With such a large and boisterous presence in what had always been a particularly small sitting room the disruption to Marjorie's well-ordered life was significant. It was no longer possible to invite more than four people to dinner, when the space for a fifth person was already spoken for. She also started to get pains in her arms, caused by the daily trial of strength when Bruno took her to Regents Park, or on the walk to the office. But in spite of all this Marjorie loved him dearly and resisted any suggestion that she should sue Harrods or get them to trade him in for a sensible little Chihuahua. They were parted when he finally went to that great kennel in the sky.

On the human side, Marjorie had a devoted bachelor friend called Alan Lamboll who was a magistrate and prominent City figure. Although the relationship was platonic they spent a lot of time in each other's company. She went as his lady to Guildhall banquets and livery dinners, and he would return the compliment by escorting her to parties at the Dorchester. I sometimes joined them, with Daphne, to make up a foursome for big events like Election Night or New Year's Eve, when the press office had its own table. Alan's enthusiasm for the traditions of the City, supported by a family wine merchant's business, took him to the Mastership of the Vintners Company and then a place on the Court of Common Council. At the same time, although a rather shy man, he built up a reputation as a gifted after-dinner speaker. On one memorable occasion he enlivened a dull Guildhall dinner by having a telephone secretly installed under the table. When it rang during his own deliberately pompous speech he answered it and pretended the caller was his irate wife demanding to know where he was, to the delight of his soporific audience. When it rang a second time and he had to deny being with another woman the sound of laughter was deafening. What started as a dull and predictable evening became, thanks to Alan's masterstroke, an event that no one present would forget.

In due course he was elected an alderman and subsequently served as sheriff during the Queen's silver jubilee year. Two years thereafter he would have taken his turn as Lord Mayor, the pinnacle of his ambition, and received the customary knighthood from the Queen. But by this time he had lost his heart to Jonathan, a younger man whose background was an exotic mix of East End beer retailing and American old money and much liked for his outgoing personality and wicked sense of humour. Alan moved in to Albany from his fusty old bachelor flat in Pall Mall and Jonathan joined him there. As they began to give dinner parties and meet each other's friends, Alan realised that the impending year of office in the Mansion House was not so important to him after all. The prospect of sitting through all those interminable civic functions (at the risk of sounding like the Duke of Windsor) 'without the man he loved at his side' filled him with gloom and he was aware that a role for Jonathan in such circumstances might raise a few eyebrows. Finally he announced to a disbelieving Court of Aldermen that he was withdrawing his candidacy.

Without doubt the subsequent fifteen years were the happiest of Alan's life. Jonathan turned the small Albany 'set' into a comfortable and slightly over-the-top home where the emphasis was on space for entertaining. On dinner party nights guests were often outnumbered at the dining table by candelabra, with sight-lines across almost completely obscured by plated objects from another era. Alan played the part of host with courtesy and charm, but always looked forward to retreating to the kitchen with the pudding plates and was seldom seen again. They spent many holidays on the island of Barbados, where they enjoyed the friendship of the small group of interesting ex-pats and 'natives' who lived there. On one of their trips they came across a badly neglected Jacobean plantation house that cried out for lots of tender loving care. They fell in love with it, of course, and decided to restore it and make it their home. But at the eleventh hour, just as all the negotiations were coming to a head, they both had a bad attack of cold feet and the move was abandoned. After much discussion they acknowledged that although they wanted to move out of London, island life was not really the alternative. They moved instead to an unpromising farmhouse on a wind-blown spit of land near Aldeburgh. To most of us it seemed to have only the advantage of an oblique estuary view, but by the time the builders left it had been transformed into a cosy and stylish country house. The two large guest bedrooms and bathrooms, including one on the ground floor known as 'the Marjorie Lee Suite', had weekend bookings for months ahead. Gardening in that part of the world, where the wind makes an uninterrupted journey from Siberia, is notoriously unrewarding, but Jonathan used hedges and statuary as windbreaks to great effect. There was even a decent-sized swimming pool. Before long they were pillars of local society and well to the fore when it came to raising money to restore the church at Iken.

After ten years of giving the Aldeburgh Festival a wide berth they decided, once again, to have a stab at living in a warmer clime. They bought some land on a hilltop in southern Portugal, bored successfully for water and commissioned a house in the style of a mini-colonial mansion, complete with flagpole and heli-pad. The British community was soon beating a path to their door. In spite of irrigation problems for Jonathan's cherished garden, delay in the arrival of Alan's newspapers and the loss of a Tibetan spaniel, they were happy there for five years. But by then Alan, who was in his early seventies and a dedicated hypochondriac, began to think that they should move a little closer to Harley Street. This idea was very much at the planning stage when Jonathan awoke one morning to find that Alan had died peacefully in his sleep.

I was fortunate enough to be invited to lots of Alan and Jonathan's parties, often at short notice – I was a dependable standby! But one of the best I can remember is a dinner for about twenty they gave in a private room at the Garrick as their way of celebrating the royal wedding. Jonathan told me in advance that on one side at the table I would have Camilla Dempster, who was delightful but very shy. Needless to say, she proved to be a charming companion and appeared to be greatly amused by my Noel Coward stories. When we moved around after dinner I bumped into Jonathan, who was keen to know how I had got on with Nigel's good lady. I explained that the combination of my nervousness and her diffidence produced an endless monologue about my life with the Master, which she seemed to enjoy. With much laughter Jonathan said, 'Well I am not surprised. I had warned her that you once worked for Coward but that she was not to expect any juicy stories as it was something that you absolutely never talked about!'

10

Without doubt the Dorchester's favourite guest was Alan Searle. Although not at all effusive he greeted the staff like old friends and rewarded even the smallest service with a handsome tip. Marjorie was very keen for us to meet and she chose the day of his arrival, when she traditionally gave him lunch, to introduce us.

As Marjorie made the introduction I couldn't help thinking that, in spite of the beautifully cut three-piece suit, I was actually meeting a sweet little apple-cheeked old lady. This impression was enhanced by a smooth and clammy hand, a gentle voice and wafts of scent. It was a perfume, fortunately more citrus than violets, that I soon came to recognise as his trademark. To be fair Alan was now in his sixties, and in spite of being severely overweight, the years had been kind. Closer acquaintance even allowed me to catch glimpses of the cherubic young man who had captured the hearts of Lytton Strachey and Somerset Maugham all those years ago.

At the time of our meeting Maugham had been dead for about three years, but Alan still adhered to the travel routine they had followed together for over half a lifetime. Marjorie said that he had been curious to meet me when she had told him that I had worked for Noel Coward, whom he had known quite well. It transpired that another common link was the fact that he had been secretary to an earlier archbishop of Canterbury, whilst I numbered among my friends Archbishop Ramsey's domestic chaplain. He asked me to dine with him that evening, and I arrived at the appointed hour at his small suite on the seventh floor. Although the rooms were not on the scale of the larger suites that he was used to, it was still a very elegant and comfortable place to stay. We talked incessantly and regaled each other with 'Master' and 'Willie' stories before going down to dine at his usual table in the Grill. It soon became clear that he missed Willie dreadfully and was terribly lonely without him. But what was remarkable was that, as with so many of life's great relationships, it very nearly didn't happen. He had been asked to a dinner party by someone he didn't much care for, and havered as to whether to accept or not. Eventually he did go and found himself sitting next to this brilliant but shy and stammering middle-aged playwright who was the toast of London. During the evening a close bond was forged between them and the course of Alan's life was changed forever when Willie asked him to be his secretary companion. It is hardly surprising therefore that Alan's advice to everyone was never turn down an invitation – just in case. We lunched and dined together many times before he had to return to Monte Carlo. Some days after he left he rang me from his home with an invitation to go and stay for a weekend. I leapt at the chance to continue our friendship and to see the South of France for the first time.

On his death, Maugham's famous house the Villa Mauresque on Cap Ferrat passed to his daughter Lisa. Alan was bequeathed the contents and Maugham's royalties for his lifetime. Rather than return to England after so long he decided to move into an apartment in the Avenue de Grande Bretagne, in the centre of Monte Carlo. I think initially his plan was to rent a small flat for a while before finding a permanent home in the hills near Grasse. This was to be a recurring theme in many of our conversations, but in fact he stayed at the same address for the rest of his life. His landlord was a formidable Englishwoman called Isobel Darley, for whom the epithet 'grande dame' might have been specially created. Tall and charming, she proved to be one of the many ladies who laid siege to Alan from time to time.

Although there was no denying that that apartment was small, it was light and airy with a pretty terrace that provided lovely views across the town and out to sea. And of course it was crammed with some of the best things from the Maugham collection. For various reasons a great deal had been sold, but the elegant drawing room contained fine pieces of Chippendale furniture, Henry Moore maquettes and valuable glass, porcelain and books. Guests were housed very conveniently in a quite separate flat a few floors above. Somewhere too there must have been a room for Henri, Alan's loyal manservant. Henri was a Pole who had been a footman at the Mauresque for twenty years. In that time he had managed to learn only a smattering of English and French. As Alan spoke no Polish either it meant that communication between them was conducted in a sort of pidgin, often with hilarious results. Transport was provided by a handsome, solid Monagasque called Louis, known as Loulou. I think he was actually a taxi driver, but his sleek machine always seemed to be at Alan's beck and call. Loulou said very little and just got on with the job. Even the drive to Venice was all part of a day's work. The other occasional part-time employee I never actually met. She was a wild Irish woman called Maria, with a reputation that made her one of the most sought-after cooks on the Riviera. Several uncorked bottles of wine were left in the kitchen for her on lunch party days and Alan claimed that the quality of the food was matched by the extent of the noise she made as she sipped and stumbled around her domain, breaking plates and dropping saucepans. Complete cacophony – guests hardly able to hear each other talk – was synonymous with gastronomic bliss. Perhaps not surprisingly Alan could only take so much of this and preferred to lunch or dine most days at rather quieter establishments. His favourite was the elegant dining room of the Reserve at Beaulieu, where he delighted in ordering bangers and mash. He demanded, slightly tongue in cheek, that the potatoes were always prepared with at least a pint of heavy cream. Slavish service was ensured by a bundle of notes being slipped into open palms as each course was served.

The Chateau de Madrid, perched on a rocky outcrop just off the grand Corniche, was another restaurant he also adored. It was run by two incredibly handsome brothers, and the clientele was probably evenly divided between those who came to gaze at them, others who looked at the amazing view, and yet more who had eyes only for the sumptuous dishes that were placed before them.

Alan and I unashamedly revelled in all three. I don't know if it is still owned by the family, as I gather it has been turned into a private house.

During one of my visits Alan told me one morning that he had just been thrown slightly into confusion by a phone call from a young man called Michael who was in Monte Carlo for a brief holiday. Alan thought he had been angling for an invitation to stay, but he was asked to lunch instead. The reason for his caution was nothing to do with the fact that he had never met Michael before; what lay behind it was the identity of the people from whom he had received Alan's phone number. Apparently they were a gay couple, involved in the theatre, whom Alan knew slightly. After staying as Alan's guests for two weeks they left, taking with them everything from the bathroom that didn't have to be unplumbed. Knowing the bathroom as well as I did I reckoned their hoard, which included a pair of towelling dressing gowns, must have required a suitcase to shift. Needless to say, they were not asked to stay a second time.

Michael Cashman proved to be a handsome eighteen-year-old actor – and probably rather a good one, if his flair for mimicry and way with a story were anything to go by. As lunch progressed it emerged that we shared an interest in politics, but with the added bonus of opposing views. In spite – or possibly even because – of his East End background, of which he was justifiably proud, he was staunchly Tory and right of centre to boot. For my part, I was going through a vaguely socialist phase, but went on to be a floater with Liberal leanings. I know that Michael's allegiance has changed too and that he is now something of a Green Room Keir Hardie.

After lots to eat, and even more to drink, Alan led the way to that part of the flat I knew least. No, not the kitchen, but his bedroom. While he encouraged us into a comfortable position on the bed, much to our amazement he busied himself setting up a projector and screen. Once everything was up and running he sat close to the bed and entered whole-heartedly into the spirit of the occasion. The film was certainly very exciting and like nothing that either of us had been treated to before. The naked beauty of the participants made me realise that, sadly, there was no role in it that I could have played. But for my young friend there were parts galore!

Following that first meeting I saw Michael quite often in London and was soon introduced to his lover, Lee, and the third member of the family, whose name was Rebel. True to his breed, Rebel, a large shaggy Alsatian, was devoted to his masters, but regarded every other living thing as either an implacable enemy or food. Michael began to be noticed by the profession in a number of small parts that included a film called *Zee & Co* with Elizabeth Taylor and a television series, *Sandbaggers*, that was known as *Handbaggers*. But he only reached a wider audience with his role as the misanthropic young homosexual in the new BBC soap called *EastEnders*. Sadly, it was a dull part and completely resisted Michael's attempts to give it life. As far as I can see, the rich vein of talent that was obvious in the South of France has, so far, remained untapped. Who knows, perhaps the European Parliament will prove to be a worthy stage for this gifted man?

In the early 1970s Monte Carlo was yet to become a theme park and still retained the last vestiges of its turn-of-the-century elegance. Very little land reclamation had taken place and the height of high-rise buildings was still strictly controlled. The cost of living had not soared dramatically and the dwindling band of elderly expatriates enjoyed a reasonably comfortable lifestyle. But where there was real financial hardship among the English community, Alan would always offer discreet help. I went with him on several occasions to visit a peer's octogenarian widow and former Gaiety Girl whose rather shabby surroundings did nothing to diminish her zest. For hours she would regale us with stories of the Riviera in its heyday between the wars. Sadly, one of her few remaining pleasures in life was to retire early to bed with a good thriller and, much to the alarm of her friends, a packet of Capstan Full Strength.

Another of Alan's oldest friends in the area was a fascinating man whose father had been the scion of a noble English family, married to a wealthy American. When I got to know him quite well he confessed that his beautiful house in the hills above Antibes was all he had left. Somewhere in London he had met and become besotted with a handsome young member of the fire brigade. A passionate affair ensued and Bill eventually lent him large sums of money to set up a business. When the venture collapsed, Bill lost everything and the fireman went back to his wife and children, leaving Bill heartbroken and virtually penniless.

Rory Cameron was the son of Lady Kenmare, one of the great society beauties of her day. When she died Rory inherited La Fiorentina, her enchanting property on Cap Ferrat. Although he loved the house he spent most of his time on his ranch in Australia, and came back for only a brief annual visit. Alan and I were bidden there to lunch one day and in the car he told me that Barbara Hutton had rented the house for six months, which meant that Rory was living in the dower house. We passed through imposing gates and stopped in front of a charming little bougainvillaea-clad cottage *ornée*. Our host, a tall man with rather cold good looks, led us to a table and chairs arranged under shady trees. Over a delicious lunch he told us a little about the temporary occupant of the big house. Miss Hutton had arrived three weeks before with a maid, a hunky hairdresser and mountains of luggage. She had immediately taken to her bed in his mother's old room and had stayed there ever since. The only visitor she had was Rory, who went for drinks each evening at six o'clock. To him the remarkable thing was not that she received him in her bedroom, but that she lay propped against her pillows wearing a negligée and a different suite of jewels each evening. As far as he could tell, the hairdresser's only obvious task was the daily arrangement of one of the tiaras from her seemingly endless collection. After lunch he suggested that we should go and see the house, but stressing that for obvious reasons he could only show us the ground floor rooms. As we strolled through the immaculate garden we could just glimpse the party clad figure of the artist-in-hair lying by the swimming pool. Each room was breathtakingly more beautiful than the last, and as we tip-toed into the drawing room Rory held a cautionary finger to his lips and pointed up to the ceiling. We padded quietly through French windows onto the terrace and stopped to admire the panoramic view. As I shielded my eyes from the sun I could not help thinking that the one person who should be enjoying all this beauty was lying just above us behind closed curtains.

Every time I stayed with Alan in Monte Carlo – and that was quite often, it has to be said – he marked the occasion by taking me to the little local branch of Cartier for the ritual trinket-buying ceremony. It would be vulgar to itemise or describe in detail those exquisite examples of the jeweller's craft, but a tiara was not among them – not even a circlet of rhinestones. However, I did at one stage feel obliged to sell a pair of pavé cut diamond cufflinks in order to have shirts made to accommodate a ravishing sapphire pair.

It was as a teenager that I paid my first to Venice, travelling in a party by coach and staying at a very modest hotel. That unique city, of course, worked its magic for me as it has done for ever other expectant visitor, and I vowed one day to return. In the summer of 1973 I flew there from London to be met by Alan in the Gritti Palace Hotel launch. We swished through the canals in our stately craft, overtaking the packed waterbuses I remembered so well. Alan, as always, was a brilliant guide, pointing out all the places of interest he had known for forty years. As we pulled up alongside the landing stage on the Grand Canal in front of the hotel, various figures in uniform and tailcoats emerged to take my luggage and usher us in. We were conducted to the Doge's Suite on the second floor, which had been Alan's home on all his previous visits. We discovered later than another regular visitor, Gianni Agnelli, had been forced to settle, rather petulantly, for slightly less sumptuous accommodation down the corridor. I would like to be able to describe our rooms, but sadly things seen through the inside of a wine glass leave only hazy impressions. However, I do recall acres of tasselled upholstery and gilded wood. And that was only my bathroom. Each day began in the sitting room with the arrival of breakfast, a signal for us to emerge from our boudoirs and plan the day's activities. Promptly at ten o'clock we would descend to find a gondola moored at the door, complete with two gondoliers awaiting Alan's bidding. He had decided that during my two weeks we would make a point of seeing as many of Venice's thirty-five churches as we could reach without walking too far. And this we duly did. Oddly enough, as there was no other gondola with two crew members we became something of a tourist attraction in our own right. Alan had an amazing knowledge of all that we saw and kept up a running commentary. Our two swarthy pole pushers joined in with big smiles and broken English.

By midday we were usually back on the floating terrace in front of the hotel enjoying a glass of champagne and plates of delicious nibbles. Too many of these very often meant that lunch was postponed until a turn round the piazza induced something approaching an appetite. Invariably the only other occupants of the terrace were two rather bored-looking women, identified by a waiter as the Queen of Greece and her mother, Princess Aspasia. When I remarked that even given their rank they received an awful lot of attention from the staff, it was explained that they kept a special watch because the princess was known to while away the tedium of most afternoons by trying to drown in the hotel swimming pool.

Most evenings Alan liked a leisurely dinner in the restaurant before retiring early. But one night as we were leaving the table he led me not towards the lift, but out of the front door onto the pontoon.

'It's a lovely evening for seeing Venice under the stars,' he explained, as we tottered carefully out into the night.

For once there was no gondola to be seen, but in its place a gleaming white speedboat. We were helped aboard by its driver, Giorgio, a good-looking fellow in a leather jacket and jeans. It was apparent from their friendly exchange of greetings that Alan had used his services before. No sooner had we settled into our seats than the engine purred into life and the boat nosed out into the Grand Canal. Some of the great houses lining its banks were beautifully illuminated, others ghostly silhouettes. As we gathered speed and sliced through the inky waters of the lagoon the historic buildings around St Mark's Square, bathed in mellow light, receded into the distance. By now the wind was rushing through our hair and conversation was impossible. Alan indicated that I should move forward and stand beside Giorgio. Gingerly I got up as he suggested, shouting in his ear that this was not the time to take the steering wheel. But when I turned to find Alan approaching on all fours it dawned on me that it was something quite different I was expected to grasp. Happily the boat did not lurch, even momentarily, as my fellow passenger's experienced hand connected with Giorgio's manhood. The many-horse-powered engine, and several vital organs, achieved flying speed once I had fallen to my knees and joined in the excitement on the deck.

Over lunch the next day Alan announced that he had always wanted to give a party for the gondoliers, many of whom he had known for most of their lives. Furthermore he said that this was the perfect time to arrange it. He envisaged having about thirty of them for a slap-up dinner, with masses to drink, in the Gritti's private dining room. When I returned from shopping later in the afternoon it was to find Alan not in mid-siesta, but furiously pacing the sitting room. It emerged that after lunch he had gone to see the manager in order to plan our *soirée de gondolier*, only to be told that it was not possible to hold such a party at the Gritti. Alan was completely taken aback by this reaction, not only because he thought it was ridiculously snobbish, but also because it was an insult to him and his forty-year association with the hotel. He was not even placated when I pointed out that the management of the Connaught might be a bit sniffy about London cabbies being given a bun fight in one of their private rooms. After some discussion he had a brain wave, saying that he would take over the charming little restaurant across the street at the side of the Gritti. The next day it was arranged with the delighted manager that the party would take place on Friday, the day before I left. In the afternoon we tracked down Paulo, our favourite gondolier, as he waited for customers alongside the Doge's Palace. At first he thought Alan was joking when the invitation was extended, as no one had suggested anything like it before. But once he realised that Alan was perfectly serious his enthusiasm knew no bounds, and he assured us that he would muster the cream of his fraternity, and would make a point of including the men we had got to know through our daily outings.

When we arrived at the trattoria on Friday evening we were amused to find the place hung with bunting and balloons, as well as the flags of our two countries. The manager and his staff had even gone to the trouble of dressing themselves in gondolier outfits. As the guests arrived they were offered champagne or the drink of their choice, and within no time at all the atmosphere was very lively indeed. All the small tables had been removed and replaced by a large T-shaped table that dominated the centre of the room. Although there was no seating plan as such, it was obvious that the gondoliers on either side of us had been selected for their charm and good looks, rather than their knowledge of the English language. Course followed course with amazing regularity and no glass was left empty for very long. The pleasure it was giving Alan was obvious for everyone to see. When he discovered that there were no cigars to go with the coffee and liqueurs he sent me to the Gritti to fetch as many boxes of their finest Havanas as I could carry. The unmistakable sounds of revelry followed me into the sober surroundings of the hotel, where the staff were eager to know how the party was going. A waiter eventually appeared with about a dozen boxes of Cuba's most famous export and I carefully retraced my steps. By this time one of the guests, a mandolin in his hands, was standing beside our slightly flushed and embarrassed host. The main business of the evening was temporarily forgotten as he was serenaded with traditional Venetian ballads. After several encores Paulo stood up and made a very moving speech of thanks to Alan, saying at the end that everyone there had subscribed to some presents for us both. Words were impossible as we were presented with replica gondolas made of brass and the gondoliers' uniform of straw boaters and striped shirts.

After a while I began to see Alan less often. However, although I no longer worked at the Dorchester I still saw him there from time to time and introduced him to several of my friends. He liked them all, but his favourite was Terry the linkman who used to go and see him in Monte Carlo and who remained a close friend until Alan died.

My last foreign adventure with my fascinating friend had San Francisco as its setting. I had gone there to stay with friends in the suburb of Palo Alto on a 'fortune-seeking' exercise. Alan wrote to me there to say that he would be staying at the Mark Hopkins for a couple of weeks and hoped to see me. I joined him there one evening in the hotel's restaurant and after dinner he took me up to his suite, explaining that he had arranged a surprise for me. We sat for a while with a drink, but before too long a very tall, thin youth was shown in who introduced himself as Brad. Naturally I wasn't sure what was supposed to take place – although I had my suspicions. Sure enough, all was revealed when Alan explained that Brad had been recommended to him as being the possessor of San Francisco's greatest endowment. And we are not talking here of philanthropy to Stanford University, although it appeared that he was an alumnus of that great seat of learning. As the drinks flowed so did conversation, reducing the awkwardness of this rather odd situation. A frustrated actor, Brad had a pleasingly broad grin and a great sense of humour. The latter was resolutely put to the test when Alan, acting like the chairman of an interview board asking to see an applicant's CV, suggested that the obviously bulging zip that he displayed before us might be opened so that assessments could be made. Without further ado the unveiling took place, and I saw at once that here was a candidate for one of Lucien Freud's more striking canvases. It was indeed a splendid sight, but experience over the years has taught me that doing justice to physical phenomena on this scale can be a lengthy process. Suffice it to say that for quite a while my part in the conversation was restricted to pretty primitive sounds.

When Alan died his ashes, in accordance with his will, were scattered from a boat onto the sea off Cap Ferrat. Terry, who was there, told me that at the high point of the ceremony a sudden sharp breeze blew the contents of the urn back into the faces of the mourners on board. The poor things didn't know whether to laugh or cry – Alan would have loved it.

His death produced the inevitable *Times* obituary. It trotted out the usual stories but emphasised the one about Willie's attempted adoption of Alan just before he died. For Alan it had been a terrible embarrassment, although he knew the old man had meant it as a tribute and token of his affection. I wrote my first ever letter to the *Times* in the hope that they would add some details of Alan's charitable work to what they had already published. But nothing ever appeared.

As well as Aspreys, several other smart jewellers including Cartier and Garrard had their own showcases in the hotel. Other luxury items were available from Loewe, the leather people, a cashmere shop and an up-market sari and beaded bag emporium. On good days Lorna Ross and I worked quite hard at the desk in the vestibule. On very good days we would be asked to take a selection of things to the weary and well-heeled in the rooms upstairs. But the long periods of inactivity were making me restless. Maurice and the other boys from Rank, who knew of my need for a change, often mentioned that there might be an opening with them in South Street, although nothing ever came of it. But Maurice did arrange an interview for me with a friend of his who worked for Eon Productions, the company that made the Bond films. Cubby Broccoli, the Big Cheese, was looking for a new assistant – a sort of Miss Moneypenny, I suppose. I was received in a panelled room at their offices in South Audley Street, but obviously I was alone in thinking that the interview went quite well. I never got to meet Mr Broccoli.

It was left to an ex-Asprey friend called Jill Weston to suggest my next move. She had recently started work at a Bond Street art gallery called London Arts and said that they were desperately in need of another pair of hands. I was seen by the director, an American called Raymond Danowski, who was well known in the art world, principally through his marriage to Henry Moore's daughter Mary. Much to my delight he was keen for me to join them as soon as possible: there was much work to be done for a new exhibition that was about to open. It was with very mixed feelings that I took leave of the Dorchester, but happily I am still close to many of the friends I made there.

I suppose if I am honest, working in an art gallery was on that short list of 'glamorous' jobs that I always wanted to try. By a happy coincidence the most glamorous gallery at that particular time was the London Arts, whose forthcoming exhibition 'Bag One' was the talk of London. The reason for the interest was that although the exhibitor was largely unknown as an artist, his work in the world of pop music had made him internationally famous. His name, you see, was John Lennon. The press had already revealed the controversial nature of some of the works that were to be displayed, which meant that tight security was in place while the pictures were hung. On the day of the private view, caterers and florists prepared for the party that was to give the rich and famous a first look at the artist's work. It turned out to be a huge success and we were besieged with orders for the sets of pictures. After the last guest had gone we stayed there well into the night sorting out the paperwork and sipping a little champagne. The newspaper publicity the exhibition received the next morning, with much talk of lewdness and pornography, proved to be a poisoned chalice. At ten o'clock we opened the doors to admit the general public and were greeted instead by a delegation of policemen, led by an inspector, who said that he was invoking the Obscene Publications Act and closing down the exhibition. Quite a baptism of fire for yours truly!

The London Arts Group (or Farts Grope, as it was sometimes known) was actually an American organisation run from Chicago, with another gallery in Manhattan. It specialised in contemporary works and also early twentieth-century artists such as Kandinsky, Arpel and Dali. As well as original pieces it also sold a vast number of lithographs, including a lot by British artists such as Philip Sutton and Julian Trevelyan. But by far the hottest seller while I was there was the prodigious output of a young American pop artist called Peter Max. He was obviously lucky enough to be in the right place at the right time – his brightly coloured images were all the rage. The selling side of the gallery was principally in the hands of two men, both quietly spoken, but otherwise completely different. Willy was German and spoke in heavily accented English. When asked by a visitor looking at a work of art, 'What is that?' Willy's reply would invariably be '\$125,000'. Edward, the young patrician English aristo, asked the same question would say, 'It's a very fine sketch by Chagall for a stained-glass window. Note in particular the inspired use of colour and light.' This difference in style meant, of course, two quite separate groups of clients, although, rather surprisingly it was Willys no-nonsense approach that was reputed to bring home more of the bacon. My own role in the proceedings was conducted at a much lower level. Although I did my share of gallery duty I also spent time at the offices in Lower Grosvenor Street, where prints had to be mounted and wrapped in nasty finger-cutting acetate. But my favourite time was spent with Vera, the little Ford van that bore me fearlessly round London making deliveries and running errands. She also ferried me from the mews each day and took me into the country at weekends.

After only a few months in the job I was surprised to be asked to take an exhibition of lithographs to a school called Atlantic College in Wales. Although it sounded like an exciting adventure, I felt obliged to protest that I really did not have enough knowledge to field questions from a lot of brainy kids. Pish, they said. All the students are sixth formers from all over Europe, with extremely wealthy parents. They'll be far too busy screwing each other and smoking dope to take much notice of you. Gee thanks, I thought.

On a bright spring morning, with a Vera full of acetated goodies, I headed west. But I had got no further than the top of the Chiswick fly-over when disaster struck. The wind somehow found its way under Vera's bonnet, lifted it up and slapped it against the windscreen. Blind panic and a very uncomfortable few minutes ensued before a kind fellow motorist helped me to wrench the blessed thing back into place. With that tiresome little incident behind me I scooted happily down the M4 until I reached Wales and the tiny village of Llantwit Major. From there I followed directions to the sea and the great castle called St Donats that had been restored earlier this century by an American industrialist. Atlantic College, which occupied it now, had once had Lord Mountbatten as its figurehead, but at his death Prince Charles took over. The pupils, mostly in their last year at school, came from all over the world, with the rich paying enormous fees for the privilege and the bright poor receiving scholarships. Among the former, apparently, were two sons of Stavros Niarchos the Greek shipping magnate. With the exhibition established in one of the recreation rooms I stood about waiting to introduce the *jeunesse dorée* to the delights of collecting limited-edition prints. Rather gratifyingly I was soon receiving a steady stream of visitors, and very charming they all were too. One of the most attractive was a Swedish girl called Ingeborg, who came a couple of times and then started popping in between classes. At first she gave the impression of wanting to know more about some of the pictures, but after a while it was obvious that she just wanted a chat. She told me about her family and where they lived. When I asked what her father did, she said he was involved in heavy industry. Naturally I assumed he was a steel tycoon or armaments king, but hope faded when she pointed out that her mother also worked in the same line of business.

'What work is it that they do?' I asked eagerly.

'They are both crane drivers!' She replied with a smile.

When a vacancy occurred at the gallery for a secretary/receptionist I passed on the good news to a friend called Sandra who worked in the Dorchester's banqueting office. She was eager for a change and joined us as soon as she could. Sandra had a great gift for friendship and her company, on form, could be life-enhancing. But she was also burdened with a feeling of unfulfilment and troubled in a way that was difficult to fathom. Our first meeting in the lobby of the hotel led to shared meals in the canteen and evenings spent together in Chelsea pubs. On one memorable occasion I joined her for supper at the little flat she rented in Chester Street. With Elgar playing loudly in the background we ate and drank extremely well and, to the strains of 'The Dream of Gerontius', made love on the sitting-room floor. To date, this was the last time I was seriously physically involved with the fair sex. But we did spend one more evening in bed together at the flat in Hyde Park Garden Mews. At her suggestion she came there for a drink, accompanied by the electrician who looked after the gallery's complicated lighting system. He was a handsome West Indian called

Mr White, after whom I had been lusting for some time. Although, to be fair, he gave no indication of being interested in me sexually, he seemed to enjoy my moments of mild flirtation. Sandra did her best to foster this relationship, even though we all knew that Mr White would not crawl over her to get to me. All too obviously aware of what was expected of him, it took a few drinks for Mr White to relax and even laugh at the novelty of the situation in which he found himself. Once we moved to the bedroom it was revealed to Sandra and I, to her relief and my disappointment, that Mr White without his clothes did not quite measure up to the legendary reputation of the Afro-Caribbean male. Nevertheless, it was still the sort of body that dreams are made of. In the first wave of enthusiasm lips and hands moved in every sort of direction, but after a while complications set in. Sandra, the effects of the wine having worn off, made it clear that she wanted me to have all the fun. Whereas Mr White, although prepared to allow me a peripheral role, wanted Sandra to have the most pleasure. In the end, a compromise was somehow engineered before we returned to the sitting room and a much-needed drink. The moral I drew from this little escapade was that sex with anyone other than yourself means never knowing what you are going to get. And who wants to look their best anyway?

Sandra stayed at the gallery for only a short time before working briefly for the musician, Gervase de Peyer and one of the McAlpines. She also fell under the spell of a popular singer/songwriter called Clifford T. Ward, whom she managed to meet a couple of times under the pretext of interviewing him for a magazine. But in spite of strong family support, she was unwell and far from happy. During a spell in hospital she met and fell in love with a fellow patient. When they were discharged they set up home together and to everyone's delight planned to marry. But it was not to be. An evening of celebration went tragically wrong and they were found together dead the next day.

The short lease on the mews had only a few years left to run and so Richard decided to sell what remained and move out of London. Although I did not see him as a country person, I could well understand that even with a large garage he needed much more space to accommodate his stock. Another reason for the move was that he had recently bought himself a Rolls-Royce and feared for its safety on the city's streets. With the idea that it was to be regarded less as a form of transport and more as an object of veneration he planned to rebuild it as a classic convertible of the 1950s. I went with him to Marlow to collect what I thought was already a beautiful car. It had a sand-coloured body, a pale pink leather roof and faded red upholstery. Many months and a great deal of money later it emerged in a two-tone livery of harsh black and red, with scarlet seats piped in black. Refinements also included doors with spaces for bottles and glasses and a pair of powerful lights mounted either side of the windscreen. The only subtle touch, albeit in dubious taste, was a tiny representation of his family crest on both doors. With its registration number, D 444, it could not help but be noticed wherever it went. Even the judges at the *concours des elegance* organised by the Rolls-Royce Enthusiasts Club awarded it prizes. But let us hope they were for craftsmanship rather than style.

Richard started buying *Country Life* to look at its property pages, and at weekends I went with him to see houses and to drive round the areas he had chosen. His first choice was Bath and the village of Castle Combe. A budget of £20,000 in those days (the early seventies) meant that, within reason, he could buy almost anything. It was Bath's fabled Royal Crescent that struck Richard as the perfect place to live – and number 1 was on the market. He fell in love with it at once and made an offer, but after months of protracted negotiations his bid proved unsuccessful. We looked at other houses in the area, but nothing else quite measured up. He lost heart and looked again at the map of England. With the M3 being extended and other motorways planned for the south, Richard decided to take his search to the area around Southampton and the New Forest. But he concentrated his search initially on that dotty, time-warped island called Wight. As it does not take too long to find anything there, Richard soon found an ancient manor house that suited his requirements perfectly. Quite sensibly he resisted the temptation to make an offer until he had looked more thoroughly at the island's property market and discovered the pros and cons of living there. It transpired that the manor, like some of the other bigger houses, had been on the market for rather a long time. Only bungalows and beach huts seemed to be selling and the blame was laid at the door of the weather. On foggy days the island was completely cut off from the mainland – ferries and hovercraft cancelled. Armed with this information Richard began to realise that he did not care for the idea of being quite so isolated. He switched his attention back across the Solent again, to the charming Georgian town of Lymington, where life revolved around the marina and yacht club. It was a well-heeled place, popular with senior retirees from the armed forces, and we both took to it at once. So keen was Richard that he decided to concentrate his house-hunting to the area within five to ten miles of the town. As it was a popular part of the world property was snapped up pretty quickly, but as luck would have it something that sounded suitable had just come onto the market. It was called Latchmoor House and situated on the edge of the village of Brockenhurst, about six miles from Lymington. As we turned the car off the main road we saw ahead of us, as we had been told, a line of trees and an extremely large thatched roof. Big wooden double gates stood beside a thatched two-storey lodge and beyond a short drive led to a broad gravelled area and stable yard. The house itself gave me the impression that it must have been built some time between 1900 and 1930 in a style that suggested arts and crafts without the stained glass and mock Tudor without the plaster. With the extensive use of dark wood and leaded windows the overall effect, unfortunately, was very gloomy. But at least the interior, with rooms on a generous scale, looked far more like the inside of a country house than an over-blown cottage. The present owners were an elderly couple originally from Glasgow, whose home it had been for many years. They were to be seen driving around in an old Rover with the registration number G8. (How odd that someone so numerically dyslexic as myself can always remember car numbers – though I suppose G8 is quite easy!) The house was too large for them now and they were preparing to move into something smaller they had built nearby. My reaction was that it was too large for Richard as well, but it soon emerged that he had great plans for it. In no time at all his offer was accepted and he made arrangements for the move. Naturally, while all this had been going on I thought a great deal about my own future. Working at the gallery was very pleasant, but I did not think it had long-term career prospects. And so when Richard asked me if I would like to move with him to Latchmoor, I said yes please.

The transition from a two-bedroom flat to an eight-bedroom house took place on a wonderfully sunny day in the spring. In the first few weeks there was so much to do that I didn't really have time to think about finding a job. I helped where I could around the house, but also used a spare car to explore the surrounding countryside. Richard, in the meantime, had engaged the services of Len, a local builder, who was soon to become a permanent fixture. His first tasks were to spruce up the gate lodge and the service wing of the house so that tenants could be found for them. Once the former was in a reasonably modernised state it did not take Richard long to find someone completely unlikely who was keen to move in. Her name was Joan Berker, the ex-wife of the founder of Berkertex the fashion business. Quite why she was moving from a swanky block of flats called Kingston House overlooking Hyde Park, no one ever discovered. But she arrived with Mabel the housekeeper, a great deal of luggage and an overwhelming desire to drink herself into oblivion. In spite of the cramped conditions Joan, at least, seemed to settle easily into her new home. Poor Mabel on the other hand, found the close proximity of her wayward mistress, whose motto was 'the bar is always open', almost too much to bear. With only one means of access, everyone living in the house had to pass the gate lodge several times a day, and it was jolly hard to do so without being hauled in for 'a quick one'.

Once the old staff wing was ready to be occupied, another sort of in-house entertainment arrived in the form of three young male students from Southampton University. Far be it from me to suggest that Richard chose them for any other reason than their obvious suitability, but as luck would have it they were all terribly attractive. As the house was laid out in the shape of the letter E, their rented accommodation was parallel to Richard's large kitchen and some of the bedrooms, providing endless opportunities for cross-observation – although I am forced to say that it was very much a one-way street. With the innocence of youth, the three newcomers eschewed the idea of dressing gowns and ignored the fact that their landlord had not yet got round to providing them with curtains.

To cap it all, no description of the early days of life at Latchmoor would be complete without mentioning Dick, the handyman, who arrived to join us from London. He had been a merchant navy seaman of long standing who was living in a Missions to Seamen hostel in Docklands. It was there that he was befriended by Richard Wood (hereafter known as Stupenda as a tribute to Joan Sutherland and to distinguish him from Dallimore of the same name). Stupenda at that stage had decided to forego buttling and take on the position of catering manager at the Mission. As anyone who knew him (renamed Stipenda by Sandra because of the size of his salary) would realise he spent more time as a missionary/Samaritan than he did ordering tins of baked beans. When he saw that Dick was down on his luck he rang Richard to suggest that for board and lodging and some pocket money Dick would work very hard. Richard, who had enormous admiration for Stupenda, agreed to take him on. All went well for the first few weeks and Richard was very pleased. And then things started to go wrong. Dick would spend the morning avoiding his boss, only to reappear after lunch looking for all the world as if he had been closeted at the Gate Lodge. Without further ado he would start up the powerful sit-on lawnmower and roar around the three-acre garden, aiming for anything other than long grass. Richard treated him with great tolerance and gave him several chances to reform, but in the end he had to go. By this time Richard had got used to having someone to look after the cars and help around the garden. He decided to find a replacement for Dick, by putting an advertisement in the local paper.

In the meantime, thanks to Richard, I had found a job. During one of his trips into Lymington he had paid a call on Corfields, the antique shop in the High Street. Mike Corfield, always the affable proprietor, had given him a cup of coffee, no doubt in the hope of a decent sale. But instead, Richard explained that he had a friend who was looking for a job and was there a chance that Mike had a vacancy? Indeed there was, thanks to recent expansion of the business that included a new picture gallery under the command of Stephen Garratt. When I joined them the only other employee was a glorious Liverpudlian lady called Pat Pugh, who was helped from time to time by Mike's wife Anne. As a young couple they had opened the shop as soon as Mike left the army. And in a surprisingly short space of time his knowledge of furniture, porcelain, silver and glass had earned them a splendid reputation with local punters and even with the trade. Stephen, an ex-Shell man, lived with wife Felicity near Lyndhurst. It was through their interest in English watercolours that they first got to know the Corfields, and how they eventually joined the business.

Mike went to great lengths to ensure that his antique shop was the antithesis of all those other unwelcoming emporia with no sign of customers, and where the cautious visitor is usually greeted with an unconvincing 'Can I help you?' from behind a beaded curtain.

When the bell rang to announce an arrival chez Corfield, one of us was expected to skip down the stairs from the first-floor office, ready to beam and charm. Newcomers were offered a guided tour, while old friends had tea or coffee thrust upon them. But more often than not, Pat and I would be lurking somewhere in the showroom, with a tin of Antiquax and a pile of dusters much in evidence. In fact this was a lovely excuse for a gossip and a chance to keep an eye on the activity in the High Street.

On one occasion I was rearranging the window, on Pat's day off, when a middle-aged man dressed like a farmer entered the shop and asked for her by name. He seemed very shy, but said that he was hoping Pat would help him to chose a present for his sister's birthday. I took him round our latest acquisitions and it did not take him long to plump for a small decanter. I wrapped it as well as I could and he gave me a cheque. With a smile of thanks and the assurance that I would see him again he left. As I closed the door behind him I looked at the cheque for the first time, and saw to my surprise that he had signed it 'Newcastle'. Now I know that is name-dropping of the worst kind, especially as he wasn't even my first customer. But let's face it, dukes are a dwindling band – not to say endangered species – and it isn't every day you get the chance to meet one. Certainly not one as delightful as Pelham Clinton-Hope. As a matter of fact he came into the shop quite often and we struck up a friendship. From time to time he asked me to call in for a drink after work. He lived in a little house on Quay Hill, the quaint cobbled street that runs down to the river. His sister Mary, who had once been married to Vic Oliver, lived opposite with a female friend. Over a glass of whisky one evening I asked him why he chose to live there when he had a farm near Salisbury that he visited every day. He thought for a moment before explaining that in a little town like Lymington he could be anonymous (before he met me, that is), whereas if he was known to be at the farm he would be expected to play a part in the community – and even open fetes, perish the thought! I know from our conversations that he had not always been reclusive. In fact he pointed out that one of the happiest periods of his life was when, as a young man, he spent some time in Hollywood. He hadn't at that stage succeeded his father, but bore the courtesy title of Earl of Lincoln. During his time there he was asked on several occasions why his parents had named him after a pub. When he heard that I too was going to California he gave me the telephone number of his daughter who lived in Los Angeles. But in fact I didn't get as far as that and never gave her a call.

Another of the shop's regular visitors was an Australian chum of Mike's called David Guthrie, who had a distinguished single-handed-sailing background. He had lived in Lymington for some time and had a part-time job with a firm of yacht designers. As an extremely eligible bachelor, he was a hot property in the fevered world of Lymington society. Although many invitations were turned down, he always enjoyed being entertained by his fellow Aussie, Marsali Barry, the widow of an admiral and by Pat de Trafford, a divorcée with an enormous collection of children. She and her brood lived in a huge house near Beaulieu, and in something slightly smaller in Fulham. I went once to a fancy dress party at the aptly-named 'House in the Wood' and met all seven or eight of the de Trafford young. During the same evening, their mother and I found ourselves standing in front of a portrait of one of her predecessors. When I remarked on the sitter's doleful expression, it was explained in mitigation that she had borne eleven children, and that like all other de Trafford women she was simply used as a breeding machine.

In spite of suffering from a depressive illness, David seemed to enjoy meeting for lunch at The Chequers, our favourite hostelry just outside town; and also coming to Latchmoor for supper. As his condition worsened I tried to lift his spirits by suggesting a holiday in Greece, which he seemed to think was a great idea. The thought had occurred to me because I had an open invitation from Alison in the mews to stay with her on the island of Spetsi whenever I chose. She had moved there as a result of meeting a journalist called Martin Leighton, with whom she wanted to start a new life. We made the journey sharing the driving of David's newly delivered Porsche, and achieving some amazing speeds on the way. Once we got to Greece, we made a detour in order to spend a couple of nights on Mount Athos where, in spite of being cold, uncomfortable and undernourished, we had the most extraordinary time. In those days access to the community was still very strictly controlled, and we were jolly lucky to get in. Our two nights were spent in a vast Byzantine monastery in the company of just twelve monks – one of whom was from Australia as luck would have it – where once upon a time over four hundred had lived.

When we got to Spetsi we found that the sleeping arrangements were completely reversed – too many people and too few beds. But David was quite happy to find a room in a nearby hotel, joining us for grub and the evening's activities. The other guests included the enormously sexy *Daily Express* football correspondent Ross Benson and his plain wife, Beverley, as well as two other journos, Nick and Wendy Worral. The island itself was quite a pleasant place, although I could well understand why Alison and Martin finally decided not to end their days there. The thing that I could not understand was why the authorities, who had gone so far as to ban the motor car, had not outlawed the scooter as well. The noise from those infernal machines was the biggest drawback to living there.

With the drive back to England to face, we could only stay there a few days. Our route home took us to Munich, where we saw the sights and had a good lunch. As we drove out of the city it became obvious that David was suffering terrible stomach pain, which he ascribed to the tiny morsel of cheese I had given him from my plate. He said at the time that because of his medication, cheese was one of the things he should not eat. After lying down for a while he recovered and we drove on.

Shortly after the holiday David decided to go back to Australia for a while. I received a couple of letters that suggested he was in good shape, but in fact he was soon admitted to hospital and never came out. Unfortunately I never got to the bottom of what happened, in spite of meeting his parents Sir Rutherford and Lady Guthrie – they were clearly reluctant to go into any detail about his death. They had come over to sort out David's affairs, meet some of his friends and get a flavour of his life in Lymington. As far as I was concerned that meant a bloody good lunch at The Chequers, which is exactly what David would have suggested.

I arrived back at Latchmoor one evening after work to find that Richard's advertisement had yielded one reply, and that applicant, in the person of Ian Macbeth, had already been signed up and moved in. Ian was about eighteen and had only recently left Pangbourne, the naval school. Officially he was still considering the next stage of working towards a place in the merchant navy, but realistically all he really wanted to do was to sail yachts – preferably big ones. To that end he had been living with his mother in her small house in Lymington, and offering himself as crew at the yacht club to anyone who needed a hand. But I think the attraction of the Latchmoor job was more to do with moving away from home than simply making a little bit more money.

Although I found Ian rather non-communicative to start with, I was determined to make him feel as comfortable as he possibly could in a house of queens. As I ran the kitchen I made it my business to find out about his favourite food, and dished it up from time to time; *all* the time, according to a rather miffed Richard. But in fact the two things he adored most were bread sauce and red cabbage (both very het, upper class and a bore to make), and I was not good at making either, in spite of long hours of perseverance. After he had been with us for a few weeks we started spending quite a lot of time at the Forresters pub in Brockenhurst, where the ex-navy landlord was very welcoming. And sometimes we went further afield, to the cinema in Southampton. As our friendship grew we even discussed the possibility of a hitch-hiking holiday in the States and visiting other places too.

At first I was flattered that a good-looking man, ten years my junior, obviously enjoyed my company. But in due course my own pent-up loneliness and frustration moved my feelings for him onto another level. I started buying him the occasional new shirt or book on sailing and, late at night and emboldened by whisky, sought to tell him how I felt. With a maturity beyond his years he coped remarkably well with my attentions, and expressed great sympathy, which probably made matters worse. And then one night as I lay in bed waiting for sleep he came into my room dressed in pyjamas and climbed in beside me. Although my own feelings were in a state of complete bewilderment, and it was plainly clear that he was more embarrassed then impassioned, he insisted on a few words of explanation. He said that for some time he had wondered if he was gay, and that a night with me would give him the answer. Well, he certainly stayed until morning. But sadly it was a one-off performance and one that was never discussed. Not for the last time, I was left to assume there was something about me that convinced men of their deep-seated heterosexuality!

While I had been preoccupied with my own emotions, Richard had been enjoying the company of a handsome Scotsman called Jim, who always seemed to come to the house at odd times, never joining us for lunch or supper. Both Ian and I were mildly intrigued by this state of affairs, and even more so when the plot began to thicken. One day Richard announced that he had found a young family from Totton to take the gate lodge in place of Joan Berker, who had moved back to London. And who should the new tenants be but Jim and his wife Pam with their two young children. Although I met them soon after they arrived, they were very unobtrusive neighbours and appeared to keep very much to themselves. The first indication I had that this was not necessarily the case occurred late one evening when I returned to Latchmoor after supping with Pat Pugh in Lymington. As I walked past the lodge on my way to the house I heard raised voices and lots of sssssshhhhing coming from inside. What stopped me in my tracks was that one of the voices was definitely Ian's. I moved towards a window where the curtains did not quite meet in the middle. Through the gap I could see into the brightly-lit sitting room where Ian and Pam were standing and facing each other in an adversarial sort of way. Jim was nowhere to be seen, which meant that he was probably with Richard. Feeling sad and rather lonely I continued my journey to the house and went straight to bed.

Not surprisingly perhaps, given the complexity of these relationships and the repercussions they might have on Latchmoor's inhabitants, the atmosphere in and around the house was a little strained for a while. But it soon improved with the arrival of Stupenda for a weekend. Although it was wonderful to have his jolly company, the presence of Davey his seaman friend was more of a mixed blessing. Davey believed that life should be rich and varied, with no hang-ups about sex. To that end his own orientation was more than a little imprecise, and by Sunday evening he was proclaiming to anyone who would listen that he fancied both Pam and Ian!

In spite of all the emotional upheaval Ian and I still went occasionally into Brockenhurst for a drink. While we were there one evening he confessed that he had been asked to join the crew of a yacht in Las Palmas and then sail her across to the Virgin Islands. He did his best to keep excitement out of his voice, but it was still perfectly obvious that it was the best bit of news he had received for some time. I too tried to disguise my feelings, and concentrated instead on some of the practicalities involved, with questions such as 'What will your mother say' and 'Have you got any money for the fare?' But in the end I gave him the money for the air ticket and drove him to Heathrow on the day he left. His first letter arrived many weeks later from Road Town, the capital of Tortola in the British Virgin Islands. After that I heard from him only rarely, but his letter describing a trip up the

Amazon was fascinating. Later still he was taken on by Peter de Savary to skipper his yacht. I have seen him once in London, although his home now is in Florida.

I first caught sight of Dudley Forwood at the quaintly named Spinster's Ball, highlight of the New Forest social calendar held each year at Rhinefield House. It would not be too much of an exaggeration to say that he shone in every sense of the word in those rather gloomy surroundings. The sound of laughter drew me over to the corner of a room where a group of people were clustered round a beaming middle-aged man holding court. As my curiosity got the better of me I moved closer and took in the details of his appearance. The first impression was that he was handsome and distinguished in spite of a physique that suggested years of good living. The fine head was thinning on top but held twinkling eyes. One ear was home to a hearing aid. In time I was to discover that his deafness was a real problem but his no-nonsense attitude to it might serve as an object lesson to other sufferers. This was best exemplified when he met new people. Grasping them firmly by the hand he would roar, 'You'll have to shout. I am stone deaf and nearly a hundred!' Although we were not to meet that evening I didn't have to get any closer to see that the front of his dress shirt was held together not with buttons but brilliant diamond studs. I moved away and rejoined my partner. Some time later, mid-waltz, I saw him again and enquired of my partner, Sue Russell if she knew who he was. 'Oh yes,' she said, 'that's Sir Dudley Forwood. He's the official Verderer and used to be equerry to the Duke of Windsor. He and Mary are great fun and have a lovely house at Burley. You must meet them.'

Some months later Richard told me one evening that through Edward Montagu he had met a sort of cousin of his called Dudley Forwood who wanted to trade in his old Bentley for a new, smaller car.

On the day Richard took delivery of the car I went with him to take it to Burley. Although it was an ordinary small family saloon there was something about it that gave it an air of distinction. That may have been something to do with the silver stag's head surrounded by a coronet sitting on the bonnet. The Forwoods' house was called Old House although it was built in the sixties. As we approached down the drive it certainly looked impressively grand, but to my eye it lacked the scale and proportion of the eighteenth or even early nineteenth century. It tried very hard to be Georgian but the reality was a good example of twentieth-century pastiche. Dudley's interest in gardening was much in evidence around the small lake and that in turn gave a lot of pleasure to assorted ducks and geese. The front door gave into an enormous double-height hall with a gallery all round it at first-floor level. The walls were panelled, and Dudley said he had bought the lot from nearby Brockenhurst Park when that house was demolished. I told him that at the Metropolitan Museum in New York I had seen the two complete interiors that had been bought at the same sale. The hall, with its blazing log fire, was furnished like a colossal sitting room and was used as such most of the time. Mary was very charming and gracious as she dispensed tea with a practised hand. She and Dudley had enjoyed a long and happy marriage, sharing a love of country pursuits – especially those involving dogs and horses. He kept a groom and horses whilst Mary bred small yappy dogs. Dudley was Mary's third husband. By her second she had a son. Her first marriage had been to 'Nigs' whose father, the Marquess of Willingdon, had been one of the last viceroys of India. A mischievous Dudley once claimed to have had Nigs before Mary did. But everyone knew that he loved shocking people with the occasional outrageous remark and being mildly flirtatious with good-looking men – the more so if they were pompous and stuffy. In the days when they found travelling less exhausting they went to stay each year with some horsey friends in Kentucky. After a lunch party one day given by their hosts, Dudley shared a sofa with a fellow guest. At one point Dudley's companion turned to him, pointing towards his feet, and said: 'You'll forgive me for saying so, Sir Forwood, but I guessed suede shoes were only worn by a queer or a cad.'

'Oh really,' replied Dudley, 'how funny, I'm both.'

Dudley returned to live in England soon after the marriage of the Duke and Duchess of Windsor, his tour of duty as equerry having come to an end. As a former major in the Scots Guards he had joined the Duke's household from the embassy in Vienna, where he had been on secondment. Although the duration of the job was not long it was a particularly sensitive and turbulent time for all involved. He had had to deal with endless and sometimes emotional communications between his employer and Buckingham Palace, most notably over the question of the Duchess's use of the title HRH. Another potential minefield was the Windsors' notorious trip to meet Hitler in Berlin —Dudley is much in evidence in photographs and film footage of the visit. No prince was ever served by a more loyal or devoted royalist, and I suspect that he was never happier than during that period in his life. Like so many of his generation he was saddened by the events that had taken place but those feelings did not preclude a certain affection for the Duchess. Apart from anything else he shared her enjoyment of the company of unattached young men, who paid court to her at every opportunity. The Duke, on the other hand, displayed true Windsor naivety about such characters. He didn't know what they wanted, he only knew he didn't like them and he called them 'flitty flies'.

When Dudley returned from France I think he very much hoped that he might be offered a job on the staff of the new king and queen. But in his heart of hearts he knew that he was probably regarded as having 'worked for the enemy'. He had to wait many years, and for a new sovereign, before his services were required by the Crown once again. He was offered the post of Official Verderer of the New Forest, which meant in effect that he was the Queen's Lord Lieutenant of that huge area of woodland and moor between Southampton and Salisbury. He presided over the Verderer's Court at Lyndhurst, whose task was to look after the maintenance of the forest and oversee the activities of the commoners who enjoyed ancient grazing rights there. It was a position that gave him enormous pleasure and never more so than on the day he acted as guide to the Queen and Prince Philip on an official visit. Further contact with the Royal Family took place when he accepted the honorary post of Director of the Royal Show, England's premier agricultural show. Each year the event was patronised by at least one of the Royals. When it came to the Queen Mother's turn I can only imagine that Dudley's emotions must have been at fever pitch. As the great day dawned the weather was blustery with a strong wind, but no sign of rain. It was decided to stick to the pre-arranged programme, the highlight of which was to be the arrival of the Queen Mother in an open carriage at the Main Ring accompanied by the Hon. Director. The Queen Mother's interest in using out-of-the-ordinary forms of transport is well known. After all, in the last quarter of the twentieth century she has been pulled along by horses more often than probably anyone else alive. By contrast she has also spent more time in helicopters than any oil-rig maintenance crewman in the North Sea. At the appointed hour she was conducted to her carriage by a very nervous Dudley Forwood. They set off round the Ring to the accompaniment of warm applause from the assembled crowds. Dudley did his best to sustain a steady flow of witty conversation and point out items of interest, but unfortunately his mind was on something else altogether. The object of his concerned attention was the wide-brimmed confection of straw and tulle that bucked and weaved on top of his companion's head. Although he was terrified that a strong gust would separate the well-known trademark from its smiling owner he was not sure what he could do about it. After all, there was a golden rule that royalty are only to be touched in a dire emergency. And then suddenly he snapped. Throwing convention to the wind (in a manner of speaking) he lunged forward, placing his hand firmly on the crown of the Queen Mother's hat.

'Oh Sir Dudley,' she exclaimed. 'How kind. In a more gracious age I should make you my Comptroller of Hats.'

At some stage in the early 1980s it was announced that a television company was planning to dramatise the story of the Windsors' relationship in an eight-part serial. The writers and producers were determined to portray not only the well-documented events, but also to give a flavour of what went on behind closed doors. In order to achieve this they set out to interview as many of the principal characters involved as possible. But they immediately ran into problems. For a start, it was a very small group that had comprised the Windsor 'court', and by then most of them were elderly or indeed dead. To anyone who enquired it was also made abundantly clear that talking to the media was not the done thing. Dudley, of course, was one of those approached, not only because he was a star player, but also because he was still only in his early twenties when it all took place. He too declined to help. How different things are today, barely twenty years later, when the Duke's own great-nephew stars in his own documentary on the subject. Interviewed by Prince Edward, Dudley treated him with typical deference.

The role of Duke of Windsor was to be played by Edward Fox, and Dudley was surprised one day to find him on the telephone. I am sure the Fox charm, seldom far short of overdrive, was deployed to great effect when suggesting that they met for lunch one day. Dudley countered by saying that he would love to meet him, especially as he had fond memories of his mother, Angela. However, although he was not prepared to spill the beans about his time with the Windsors he suggested that Edward and Joanna David came to stay at Burley for a weekend. Diaries were compared and a date was chosen. Richard had recently sold Latchmoor House at Brockenhurst and bought instead a mock Queen Anne house with sea views near Fawley. He suggested to Dudley that he should bring his houseguests to tea on the Sunday of their visit.

As they got out of the car Dudley left us in no doubt that he had slipped back into obsequious courtier mode. Richard and I went across the lawn to greet them as Dudley, ushering Edward and Joanne forward, said:

'Sir, may I present Mr Richard Dallimore and Mr Guy Hunting.' Followed by, 'Ma'am, may I present Mr Richard Dallimore and Mr Guy Hunting.'

The little tableau faltered slightly when Joanna caught sight of an old friend of mine from Bournemouth, called Chris Owen, who had been to lunch with us. They had been drama students together and hadn't seen each other for twenty years. Their warm embrace was gently curtailed by the equerry in waiting.

By way of an aside: a memorable line from Chris emerged many years later on the day of Charles and Diana's wedding. A crowd of us had watched the TV coverage of the ceremony at Jonathan's flat in Albany and then made our way to the Mall to witness the balcony appearance at the Palace. We were intent on fighting our way through the heaving throng right up to the railings. By the Victoria Memorial progress was almost impossible, until that is, Chris suddenly thrust his arm into the air and exclaimed, 'Let me through. I am one of the bridesmaids!' A hush descended on the crowd, all eyes focused on Chris, and then like a scene from the Bible an avenue opened up ahead of us and we made our stately way to the front of the Palace itself.

Back at Burley, as the 'royal party' of Edward Fox and Joanna David was conducted into the house, Dudley took me on one side and explained that he had thought it a splendid idea to treat them both exactly as he would have done the Windsors. Calling him 'Sir' and 'Your Royal Highness' was a way of easing Edward into his role and in certain situations Dudley could also give an impression of how the Duke might have behaved. Edward was obviously extremely happy with this, whilst Dudley was content that he was not really betraying the confidence of his revered employer. The subtlety of Dudley's invaluable performance was best illustrated when it came to the question of tea. To the question 'How do you like your tea?' addressed to Edward, Dudley cut in to say 'His Royal Highness prefers weak China tea, a finger of toast and gentleman's relish and a jam penny. The use of an ashtray would be appreciated if you have one.' When it came to Joanna's turn, 'black coffee and no food' were ordered on her behalf.

The afternoon progressed at a jolly pace, with the two main protagonists continually developing their relationship. At one stage 'the equerry' suggested to 'the Duke' that it might be time for a change of clothes as he had been wearing the same suit since before lunch Edward, obviously panicking slightly, admitted that if he didn't get into something else soon there would be very little time left before changing again before dinner. Joanna and Chris were reminiscing very happily in a corner of the room, but she suddenly announced that they should be taking their leave, as she was worried about seeing their young daughter before she went to bed. In response Dudley rose from his seat saying:

'With my humble duty, Ma'am, may I respectfully suggest that Her Royal Highness The Princess Royal, imbued as she is with the sense of duty she has inherited from your Royal Highnesses, will curl up with her teddy tonight comforted by the knowledge that the sacrifice she has made this evening means that Your Royal Highnesses are bringing untold pleasure to three of Your Royal Highnesses unworthy subjects.'

A parody perhaps, but Dudley knew that that was the sort of speech the Duke of Windsor's parents might have had to listen to when he was a child. After much laughter and a quick drink they drove away.

As well as the house in the New Forest, Dudley and Mary also owned adjacent houses in the busy one-way part of Addison Road close to where it hits Kensington High Street. A very good income was derived from letting out the rooms in both of them to students. As a pied à terre for themselves, the pair retained the ground floor of number 43, which provided them with a large sitting room, bedroom, kitchen, bathroom and lovely west-facing garden. When either of them stayed there Cyril, the general factotum who scrubbed, polished and weeded for both establishments, took care of their every need. He was a lovely, kind and generous man who had been plucked from a park bench at the age of fifteen by Ted, who was much older but who became the love of his life. He let me into the house one evening when I called round to have a drink with Dudley. When I enquired as to his health he told me with great glee that he was so happy because the week before he and Ted had celebrated twenty-five years together. Mary had been staying there that week and when he took in her breakfast tray one morning she sat up in bed and declared:

'Dear Cyril, many congratulations on your silver wedding anniversary. I hope you have many more years together.'

She gave him a card containing a five pound note. Cyril was thrilled, as he set great store by the love and friendship of Dudley and

Mary. However he was appallingly badly paid and confessed to me one day that with no pay rise forthcoming he would be forced to find a job elsewhere. He had occasionally plucked up courage to ask for more money but, as happens so often with the very rich, his employers had pleaded poverty.

Dudley used to come to London for two or three nights about every other week and we would make a point of seeing each other at least once during his visits. In spite of the great difference in our ages, class and backgrounds we always had lots to laugh about and topics to discuss. Not surprisingly the subject of the Royal Family featured prominently in our conversation, even though neither of us had much in the way of first-hand knowledge of the younger generation. He soon discovered that my only contact at the Palace was Stephen Barry, Prince Charles's valet, and he expressed a great desire to meet him. Of course I told Stephen all about Dudley and he was just as eager to make his acquaintance. I brought them together one evening in Addison Road and the chemistry was immediate. Having made the initial introduction I just settled back and enjoyed the show. Freshening glasses was my only contribution to the evening's entertainment. In hierarchical terms it is worth explaining the difference in their positions. Dudley was the first to claim that he was not well born in spite of being the third baronet, educated at Harrow, and with an income that most of us would envy. The family fortune was based on a Liverpool shipping empire created by two businessmen, his grandfather and great-uncle. In the days when British shipping enjoyed world domination, their business was a colossal success. This was acknowledged by a grateful nation with the award of a baronetcy to the former and a peerage to the latter. Political parties were eager for funds even in those days, and it may be that money changed hands before these big gongs were handed over.

Dudley's inferiority complex was pretty deep seated. Unlike his cousins, who were 'the Hon.', he had no title until, in middle age, he inherited one from his father. Instead of Eton he was sent to the number two school in the pecking order. In theory things looked up a bit when he was given a commission in the Scots Guards, arguably the grandest and most distinguished of regiments. But it was his membership of that elite organisation that caused him the most discomfort. Many of his fellow officers were scions of the richest and noblest families, whose estates covered thousands of acres, with lines of credit at Coutts that stretched into infinity. Although he may have felt like an interloper, I know that he commanded the respect of the rank and file, and was a sought-after companion among his peers. He was promoted to the rank of major at a very early age. From the British Embassy in Vienna, he was sent to join the household of the Duke of Windsor as equerry.

By royal standards the Windsor set-up was rather small. This meant that Dudley had to combine the duties that at Buckingham Palace were performed by the Private Secretary, Master of the Household and Comptroller. In effect he organised all the public and most of the private lives of his employers. His relationship with them was intimate, but always very formal. They discussed guest lists and seating plans together and he accompanied them on official engagements. To the Duke he was 'Duddles', a nickname no-one else would dream of using.

Stephen was brought up in Fulham as a result of his family moving there from Ireland. He was a bright lad and after leaving school went to work in a bank. After a couple of years he realised that the monotony of it all was too much for him. He needed glamour and variety. I cannot remember how he came to be a footman at Buckingham Palace, but I expect he did what I did, which was to apply to the Master of the Household. In those days the Palace more usually found its servants from the families of existing employees, or through discreet advertisements in Scottish newspapers. This system ensured that the majority of the members of the 'Footmen's Room' were porridge-swilling Celtic supporters from Musselbrough. How times have changed! I suspect that these days they are mostly chardonnay-sipping Streisand fans from Braintree. This difference in style among the skivvies has undoubtedly been spotted by that well-known observer of the natural world, the Duke of Edinburgh. He was heard to ask one day:

'What's happened to John, the footman? I haven't seen him for ages.'

'I'm afraid he had to be sacked,' replied a nervous underling. 'He was found in bed with one of the housemaids.'

'Sacked!' snorted HRH. 'He should have been given a medal.'

Taken at face value it was remarkable that Prince Philip had been aware of John at all. Unlike the Queen, who had at her disposal the services of two personal footmen, he had to make do with two Pages of the Backstairs on split shifts. However, his more intimate requirements were taken care of by two valets, one of whom would attend him each day. In the late 1960s his senior valet was James Macdonald, the quintessentially dour Scotsman. The position of royal valet was always treated with a great deal of respect by the other servants – it represented the pinnacle of achievement.

James's number two was Joe Pearce, a younger man from the North-East, whose sister cooked for the Queen Mother at Royal Lodge. He was very popular, even though he was regarded as taking his job too seriously. His duty days began at eight-fifteen a.m., with the dilemma of the temperature of the royal bath water. He knew full well that a wrong judgement could seriously unhinge his master. I don't know if he was an elbow or thermometer man, but he must have prayed that he got it right some of the time.

One day at Sandringham the Queen was following the progress of the guns at a pheasant shoot. In the distance she could see the figures of two men in the butts, her husband and Joe who did the loading. Suddenly one of them fell. The Queen gasped and ran forward, not knowing who had collapsed. She arrived to find Prince Philip bending over the lifeless body of his faithful servant, who had died of a massive heart attack.

At the start of his career at the Palace, Stephen was obviously regarded as not having a great deal of potential. To that end he was given to me to train. I told him what to do and he got on with it. After a few months I gave in my notice, and left in January 1967. We didn't keep in touch for a long time, but eventually he tracked me down and we became firm friends. He surprised me by saying that although he enjoyed his time as a footman, he kept a bigger goal in view. Sure enough, he heard one day on the super-charged grapevine that Prince Charles had decided to appoint his first valet. Up until then, although in his early thirties, he was still in Palace terms regarded as part of the Nursery. Even though his beloved nanny, Mabel Anderson, had moved on he was still looked after by the Nursery footmen. Exhibiting initiative I didn't know he possessed, Stephen put himself forward in a letter of application to Charles's equerry, Squadron Leader Checketts. Checketts carried out the initial interview and a few days later he was seen by the Boss. No one was more surprised than Stephen when he was told that he had got the job. The reason for his success always remained a mystery, but I suspect Stephen's easy manner and smart bearing played quite a part. After all, in the absence of a wife, Charles was choosing the person with whom he might conceivably be spending the rest of his life. It was also more than coincidence that Stephen bore a superficial resemblance to the heir to the throne. He was the same height, but without the muscular build, and was even rather challenged in the ear and hair department.

For twelve years Stephen played a part in Charles's life that could never be overestimated. From the moment he woke the Prince in the morning he was closely involved in almost every aspect of his day. As well as the purely domestic side of things, like choosing the suit and tie the Prince would wear and ordering his food, he liaised between the Prince and his private office, made telephone calls for him and showed visitors into his presence. Apart from his family, very few people got to see the Prince without checking first with Stephen.

Dudley and Stephen met quite often, usually at my flat, where I would try to produce something interesting for them to eat. They both had small appetites and, in Dudley's case, very little interest in drink. Stephen and I were very happy drinking for three! I would sometimes ask other people as well, especially when I realised how much Dudley relaxed in younger company. They were also drawn from many walks of life with a sense of humour and love of chatter in common.

I only went once to stay at Old House, and that was for a weekend during a long trip that Mary made to South Africa. Dudley was pretty lonely in that big house all by himself, particularly as he and Mary were used to spending so much time together. He allowed me to take with me an American called Patrick Walker, with whom I was having a bit of a fling at the time. Patrick and I had met one Sunday lunchtime in a famous gay pub in Chelsea called the Queen's Head. I was enjoying a drink there with Stephen and a group of friends when one of them suddenly exclaimed, 'Christ, have you seen what's just walked in!' Now as you can imagine, it is difficult enough at the best of times sustaining interest during conversation with a gay bloke surrounded by other gays in a gay pub. But it is well nigh impossible when a young man who looks like a cross between Anthony Andrews in *Brideshead* and Doris Day in *Annie Get Your Gun* walks through the door. He did look quite special, and what is more, he made a bee line for where we were standing. Stephen, whose network of social contacts was legendary, recognised him and said hello. Patrick smiled acknowledgement and, indicating me, enquired, 'Aren't you going to introduce me?' Completely taken aback, I looked behind me to see if his determined gaze was intended for someone else. Stephen effected the introduction and without further ado Patrick moved in for the kill. 'I haven't seen you here before,' he began. 'What are you doing this afternoon?' I mumbled something about having to collect a friend from the airport at four p.m., but I pulled myself together enough to suggest that we continued the conversation a little further away from all the fascinated observers. We moved out onto the pavement, where he continued to insist that we spend the afternoon together. My behaviour would have reminded a well-bred woman of her reaction to large, sweaty hands at her first dance. However, the excuse I presented him with was perfectly true. I was committed to picking up Philip Wade at Heathrow when his flight from Lanzarote arrived at four o'clock. The debate went on a bit longer, probably because I was not very good at concealing the fact that I was susceptible to his blandishments. But eventually he caved in, with the proviso that we met the following evening. When it came to the exchange of telephone numbers the situation was complicated by the fact that he didn't have a job that I could reach him at, and no fixed abode. He divided his time between the chambers of his 'godfather' in Albany and the flat of an old friend in Kensington Church Street. In the fullness of time we overcame these, and a few other small hurdles and in purely fun terms went on to have a great time together. It didn't take me long to see that he was a mercurial and complicated character, hopeless at time-keeping and wildly flirtatious.

Soon after he came to London from his native California at the age of fifteen he was picked up by (or probably picked up) the owner of a successful chain of restaurants called Michael Golder. Having met him, Patrick stayed on here and became the chatelaine of the Golder stately pile, Acton Hall in Herefordshire. Their affair lasted for about seven years, and he and I met soon after the relationship bit the dust. Poor Patrick missed Michael dreadfully, and I think his erratic behaviour dates from that time.

Michael Edwards, who had the Albany flat, spent a lot of time at his house in Provence, allowing Patrick the run of the place. Many years before this I had been staying in France with old friends who were his neighbours. One day he asked us all to lunch. The other guests proved to be Peregrine Worsthorne and his charming French wife, Claudia. It was a lovely old house with a terrific garden and a tennis court. When lunch was over Michael asked if any of us would care to join him for a game. My hosts Robin and Gerald, and fellow guest Jane, all declined, saying that it would be less embarrassing if we went for a walk instead. Perry accepted the challenge with alacrity and we all trooped down to the court to witness the early stages of the game. On the way through the garden, Gerald, who was beside me said he felt sure Claudia and he had mutual friends in London, a couple connected with the art world called Dunford-Wood. Even before the match began it was plainly obvious that what was about to take place was only going to be memorable for its complete lack of skill and grace. Both protagonists were about the same age, early sixties I guess, and old hands in every sense. Perry, with his wiry frame and unruly grey hair, threw himself around with abandon. Portly Michael, on the other hand, subscribed to the minimalist view of movement and employed a very peculiar wrist action. After not too long Jane, Gerald and I decided that the time was right to do a little exploring. As we headed back towards the house we bumped into Claudia, who was on her way to root for her husband in his moment of glory.

'You're just off for your walk, are you?' she asked, in her lightly accented English.

'Yes we are', Gerald replied. 'Tell me,' he continued, 'do you know the Dunford-Woods?'

She thought hard for a moment before saying, 'Yes, I think so. Turn left out of the drive, keep going for about a kilometre and you will see them ahead of you.'

One memorable evening at Albany, Patrick cooked dinner, and in the afterglow we decided to stay up all night and go to the Covent Garden flower market at about five a.m. Its days were numbered as it was soon to move to the South Bank. We sipped brandy and chatted, pausing only to look at the moon and to scan the sky for signs of first light. Alcohol-induced fatigue eventually took over and we both decided to close our eyes for an hour so as to be fresh for our jaunt. We entwined together on a sofa. Stiff limbs and furry mouths made their presence felt at about ten o'clock. As we eased ourselves back into life we decided to have Bloody Marys instead of going out.

Patrick likes to give a party on his Saint's Day, and April 1985 was no exception. With Michael away he invited about thirty people to celebrate with him at Albany. As well as his own friends, he had asked quite a number of people he had met through me. A memorable encounter was the one between Brian Wright, ex-naval commander and Assistant Private Secretary to the Lord Mayor of London, and Leslie Sympson, a Dickensian character who co-owned with his family an alleyway of houses called Goodwins Court off St Martins Lane. They had met before, but not for some time. Seeing Leslie, Brian moved towards him with his hand outstretched, saying, 'Brian Wright.' Leslie, all smiles, paused for a moment and then said, 'No.' In spite of the identity puzzle, he clung quite happily to Brian's hand, and said, 'It's very nice to meet you, but I think you have the wrong person. My name, you see, is Leslie Sympson.' A very English sort of confusion, but it was sorted out in the end.

The party went on until about midnight, although a lot of the older people, including Leslie, had left by then. With a small nucleus left, Patrick announced that they would all go off to a fashionable piano bar to carry on drinking till the small hours. He was most anxious that I should be included in the party, but when I pleaded old age and inebriation he conceded that I could stay behind and wait for him to come back. All he asked was that I should not attempt to do any of the clearing up. Most of all he made me swear not to try to take any of the glasses down to the kitchen.

Having sat for a while enjoying a nightcap and mulling over the events of the evening I gradually became aware of the fact that the shabby old room was not looking its best. Every surface was covered in wine glasses and dirty ashtrays. Heaving myself up, I found my way to the door to the stairway that led down to the kitchen. In daylight it all seemed so easy but in fuddled gloom it presented a bit of a challenge. Servants' quarters in Albany, whether in attic or basement, are notoriously primitive. I found myself confronted by a run of well-worn winding stone steps, with head height for a midget. Feeling my way down I reached a room that passed for a kitchen and found two trays. With these under my arm I climbed back to the ground floor. I had forgotten all about Patrick's entreaties and was determined to clear the sitting room of its debris. With trays full of glassware I made several journeys, my sense of balance similar in appearance to the first steps of an unsteady tightrope walker. After a while the tinkling sound of thin glass bowl hitting thin glass became rather seductive and I did very little to prevent it. When my task was complete I congratulated myself on the appearance of the drawing room and stumbled away to bed. Only the next morning did the full horror of my behaviour become apparent. According to a very agitated Patrick I had managed to destroy almost all of Michael's much-valued collection of old crested glasses from the Savoy Hotel. Although they were not eighteenth century or Bohemian, they had tremendous sentimental value.

I took Patrick to Amsterdam for a weekend. Our short flight with British Midland provoked the only letter I have ever written to an airline. Once airborne we decided to celebrate by asking for champagne. Our beaming steward was quick to oblige, although I suspected that his eagerness to serve was influenced more by the appearance of my companion than his devotion to the flying waitress's manual. Nevertheless his conduct was first rate, and as we were preparing to land he appeared in the aisle to ask if we would like to take some champagne with us for the weekend. Not expecting us to say no he produced a carrier bag containing six half bottles. I thanked him and asked his name in order to sing his praises to his boss. I had the opportunity some years later to repeat the story to Sir Michael Bishop, chairman of British Midland, who was a guest with his lover Martin at a lunch party in Shropshire hosted by Kate Vestey, my then employer. Kate had been looking forward to meeting Sir Michael, as she thought he might turn out to be a friendly party-giving neighbour. After all, his home was only a helicopter ride away, in the Birmingham suburb of Edgbaston. However, although lunch was a great success, he took his leave with no hint of a return match.

Soon after Patrick and I checked into our gay hotel in the centre of the Amsterdam we sallied forth again, armed with our guide, to find the fleshpots and drinking places. Unfortunately, as neither of us had any sense of direction we soon became hopelessly lost. In desperation Patrick approached a pair of patrolling policemen and explained our predicament. They studied the guide and gave him careful directions to what they assured him was the liveliest gay club in town. Armed with this information he set off with confidence and sped in the direction they had indicated. I tagged along behind. We talked of it later as a good example of the 'blond leading the blind'. The club itself was not my cup of tea at all – a dingy hole in which the noise levels made conversation virtually impossible. The rest of the weekend we spent largely apart. Patrick liked to take his pleasures after nightfall, whilst I enjoyed exploring Amsterdam during the hours of daylight. That one experience of standing about in a dark and noisy cellar, being ignored by all and sundry, was quite enough for me.

Our weekend stay with Dudley at Burley was a very different kettle of fish. The surroundings were very comfortable indeed. We both had a room and bath on the first floor, off the gallery that ran round the hall. However, we soon discovered that the appearance of gracious living was rather superficial, and that our host lived in a manner that can only be described as frugal. His one extravagance was horses, and as he still indulged in a daily ride through the forest a full-time groom was employed to care for the beasts. Although I certainly was not expecting to glimpse a bevy of black-clad housemaids, I thought we might catch sight of an ancient char with a stiff broom at some stage during the weekend. Although this figment of my imagination did not materialise, the house was obviously well kept and a certain amount of food had been prepared. Dudley clung to the centuries-old tradition that if you were lucky enough to live in a grand house in the middle of your own estate you lived off the land. Of course, he shared this belief with his fellow horse-lover and landowner, Sam Vestey. Fortunately for Sam, as one of the richest men in England, this indulgence was easier to satisfy. One Sunday during lunch at Stowell I asked him if the delicious beef we were eating was home-grown. He replied that it did indeed come from his own herd and that everything else we ate was the product of the kitchen garden. The list included asparagus, vegetables and large white peaches. We both thanked God that the wine was foreign. No mention of chickens, but I suppose it wasn't the sort of house that would have had hens rootling around the pleached hornbeams or clambering in and out of the ha-ha. Dudley, by contrast, had hundreds of the buggers. Noisy ones that woke you up before dawn; fat ones that laid brown eggs for breakfast; sage and onion receptacles for the table, and a whole tribe of scrawny little brutes with big feathers and blue eggs so small they were almost impossible to sell. Friday evening's dinner was cold roast chicken and jacket potatoes. Saturday dawned fresh and bright. After a boiled egg breakfast we walked round the garden and then drove into Lymington to see the sights. On the way home we stopped in Brockenhurst and devoured a particularly meaty pub lunch. It was not as if either of us was obsessed by food, but increasingly, when alone together, Patrick and I would place imaginary bets on the make-up of the menu for the evening. Our gastronomic hopes rested on the fact that as well as some wine we had brought with us a side of smoked salmon, duly presented to our host.

A glass of sherry at seven p.m. in the drawing room set the tone for the night's festivities. We moved on to the big farmhouse kitchen and laid the table whilst Dudley busied himself at the stove with saucepans and frying pans, accompanied by the comforting aroma of cooking bacon and sausages. We prayed, in vain, that they would be embellished by grilled tomatoes, or possibly even mushrooms. Our hearts sank when the serving dish was placed on the table, a mound of scrambled egg dominating its centre. Patrick and I drank a bottle of wine and repaired to our beds.

Some time during the night my slumbers were disturbed by a tap on the door. Fearing that it might be our impassioned host, my 'Come in' was less than whole-hearted, but I put the light on to reveal the grinning figure of my companion. He sat on the bed and explained as best he could, between giggles, that he had never been so sober or so famished. Sleep would be impossible until he had eaten something and had a glass or two of wine. Against my better judgement we decided to slink downstairs to see if a pantry of cellar might yield a bit of sustenance. The ancient wooden staircase creaked like a galleon in a force eight as we tip-toed down to the ground floor. Although I felt sure that Dudley rested his ears at night by switching off his hearing machine, I was anxious, because the sound of our combined 'ssshhhs' might have agitated a corpse. Beyond the kitchen we discovered a veritable warren of sculleries and larders lined with marble slabs and slate shelves, but all as empty as the cave in the Bible. Finally we reached a sort of strong room containing an antique refrigerator and lots of rusty cake tins. To my surprise the fridge wasn't locked and I opened it to reveal the mouth-watering sight of the missing smoked salmon. Under normal conditions vacuum-packed fish does not yield easily without scissors or a sharp knife, but nothing could withstand the full force of Patrick's well-flossed molars. We fell on it with gusto. I think I even ate some of the inter-leafed slivers of paper. After half of it had been consumed we called a halt, so that Dudley would be able to vary his diet for one meal at least. And then the search was on for a little liquid refreshment. Patrick, who had a pretty little nose for these things, groped in a cupboard until his fingers made contact with glass.

He clutched his find and brought it out into the open. Eureka! A bottle of 1947 pink champagne. While I flew to the kitchen for glasses Patrick brought quite a lot of his body to bear on the elderly cork and its rusty surroundings. Miraculously, and without drawing blood, a sturdy 'phut' slipped into the ether and our glasses were full. Wine for me usually means a pretty label at no more than three pounds a bottle, but 1947 may well have been a vintage year. At three o'clock in the morning we really didn't care. Our spirits soared as we sipped away.

Then Patrick announced that there was something missing. A rich pudding, that was the answer! But the question was, how we were going to find such a thing in the wasteland of our surroundings? 'The cake tins,' Patrick cried, as the image of sticky gateaux overwhelmed him. The next instant he was grappling with the first of these ancient containers. He prised off the lid to find not even a crumb. Shaking a few more proved to be just as unsuccessful, although one did rattle rather ominously. With the seventh he scored a bull's-eye. It was not only heavy, but sealed with sticky tape. Without giving his fingernails a second thought, Patrick wrenched it open to reveal a perfectly preserved Christmas cake. Carter and Carnarvon at Karnak had nothing on this. With the sensitivity of a gynaecologist he lifted it out onto the table and undid the red and gold frill. The soap powder-white icing was rock hard and did not take kindly to the knife's penetration. But once a cut had been made, the mixture inside was moist and shiny. Assailed by the aroma of matured alcohol and fruit and spices, my nostrils quivered. It was so rich that we were able to eat only a small piece, but washed down with the remains of the champagne it was the perfect climax to our midnight feast.

The most extraordinary part of our eventful weekend was due to take place on Sunday afternoon. A girl I knew called Lucy Payn had just qualified as a pilot and I had accepted her invitation to be her first passenger. At weekends she stayed with friends near Dudley's place at Burley and learnt to fly at Southampton Flying Club. We arranged to meet there at three o'clock. She assured me that I needn't bother with a flying jacket and goggles, but she made me promise to be sober and alone.

Dudley's habit of rising early was not influenced by the Sabbath or by the fact that his guests had slept for just a few hours. Soon after seven o'clock he tapped on my door and came in with a cup of tea. He sat on the edge of the bed as we chatted about life in general and my relationship with Patrick in particular. My fuddled brain had difficulty with word organisation, but I was striving to reassure him that I was not hopelessly in love with Patrick and that I was sure he wasn't a gold-digger. Struggling as I was to make sense, the possibility of subtly introducing the significance of Christmas 1947 into the conversation completely defeated me. I was curious to know why a bottle of that age had survived so long. I never discovered if it was special, and so the mystery remains.

The main reason for Dudley's early morning visit was to tell me that his much-loved niece, Edwina, was joining us for lunch and to ask me if I could please help with the preparations. The temptation to ask him what sort of ground-breaking culinary torture we were going to inflict on today's old bird was almost overwhelming. Holding myself back, I enquired sweetly instead:

'Is it going to be a roast?'

'Yes it is,' he replied with the merest hint of an old-fashioned look. 'I have taken a shoulder of lamb out of the deep freeze.'

What deep freeze, and where? I wondered. What a good thing we hadn't found it last night, or we might have licked it into being our nocturnal main course.

'I thought we might start with some of the delicious smoked salmon you very kindly brought down,' he continued.

'Oh Dudley,' said I hastily, 'what a lovely idea. Although I must confess, it is a little diminished. What happened was that Patrick and I quite coincidentally woke in the middle of the night in a blind panic. We both guessed that you would want to have the fish today and we suddenly remembered that as it was a special offer it might just be past its sell-by date. You will be comforted to know that having acted as your food tasters we could find nothing wrong with it all.' Dudley seemed quite pleased with this little story and went off happily to check on the daily bantam harvest.

Edwina proved to be a delight – extremely attractive and sophisticated and devoted to the pair of King Charles spaniels, her constant companions, who arrived in her wake. Lunch was hugely enjoyable, with lots of red wine and excellent roast lamb. With a wry glance in my direction Dudley pointed out that the first course was only intended to be an appetite whetter. As lunch progressed I got more and more excited at the prospect of the trip in Lucy's aeroplane. 'What fun,' cried Edwina, 'the dogs have never flown before.' Dudley was adamant that he wouldn't join in, as he loathed air travel.

Running a bit late, we set off after coffee for Southampton airport. With hangars in sight I suddenly became slightly nervous, but this feeling was as of nothing compared with the presentiment of catastrophe that assailed poor Lucy as her first ever passenger stumbled his way across the tarmac towards her, flanked by swaying figures and followed by two dogs. Even at the distance of fifty yards I saw her recoil and look round anxiously as if for a means of escape. She greeted us politely, but with a few muttered admonishments to me. Recovering her composure, she explained that the aircraft had room for only two passengers as well as the pilot. When she heard this, Edwina immediately offered to take the dogs for a walkies instead. She told us how excited they had been at the prospect of following in the pawsteps of that Russian dog who had been the first canine cosmonaut. But they were easily distracted and the search for a stretch of grass would do just as well.

Lucy checked her watch and pointed out that it was time we climbed aboard to get ready for take-off. As we walked towards the tiny aircraft I thought the moment was right to assure our intrepid pilot that I had been in a small plane before. The occasion was the launching by the Queen of a ship at Barrow-in-Furness. We had travelled there on the royal train, but as we had to get back to London quickly (probably so that HM could watch some racing on the telly) the return journey was to be made in a Heron of the Queen's Flight. Compared to the VC10 that the Queen used for long trips abroad, the Heron proved to be very small indeed. I seem to remember that there were about ten seats, and in accordance with strict protocol we sat one behind the other, by rank. It seems remarkable to me now that I was allowed a place at all! Naturally HM sat in front, and then behind her was a lady-in-waiting followed by the Private Secretary, the Equerry-in-Waiting, a detective, the Queen's Dresser and finally yours truly. Although we were only in the air for less than an hour I was disappointed not to have a tray of tasty morsels placed in front of me, and I expect a trolley full of duty free would have been considered infra dig.

Lucy seemed rather too preoccupied to enjoy my little story, busy as she was putting on headphones and twiddling knobs. I was given headphones too and was able to hear the man in the control tower telling Lucy to make her way to the take-off point. Poor Patrick must have felt rather left out of it, stuffed in the back with not much more than the backs of our heads to look at. After no more than a few bumps and judders we were airborne and heading up the coast. Lucy was very quiet, but the whiteness of her knuckles as she grasped the control stick, spoke volumes. Inland a bit she suddenly exclaimed, 'That's where we used to live!' We were somewhere over Sussex and looking down on what was probably quite a large house. We flew on to the Kentish border and then she turned the plane in a wide arc to take us back to Southampton. After about a quarter of an hour she was very much more relaxed and feeling, no doubt, a great sense of achievement. For my part the most dangerous moment was yet to come. The dreaded landing. But I needn't have worried as, apart from a few wobbles, she handled it flawlessly. I managed to resist the temptation to kiss the tarmac as we clambered out, but dear old terra firma felt pretty good. As we walked back to rejoin Edwina it dawned on me that I was feeling quite sober.

After that extraordinary weekend you will not be surprised to learn, dear reader, that I saw much less of Dudley. In fact, his visits to London became much rarer, as he and Mary found the pace of life too tiring. They eventually sold the two houses in Addison Road and in due course moved from Burley to a much smaller place near Ringwood.

Lucy gave up flying and changed to a more conventional way of life following her marriage at St Mary, the Boltons, and a big reception at Searcys in Pavilion Road.

Patrick, to everyone's surprise, got married as well – but in less predictable circumstances. He had become very fond of Barbara, an old friend of mine who shared a small flat in Barons Court with two wildly anti-social Siamese cats called Humphrey and Magnolia. After a rich tapestry of a life she had taken early retirement and a pension from a senior job in the health service in order to tend her exquisite little garden and fill her friends with food and drink. A blissful day would mean an afternoon weeding, and the evening spent cramming as many queens as possible into her minute dining room. A marriage, many years previously, to a well-known sprinter of the day had lasted for only a few weeks, and since then she had eschewed long-term relationships. But with Patrick things were different. As a couple they had enough in common, and individually they had a need. She accepted his proposal and a date for the wedding was set. Although many of her friends questioned the wisdom of the union they were all, to a queen, delighted to see her obvious happiness and showered the happy couple with presents. Probably the most unexpected gift came from an old acquaintance of Barbara's, Sir Ralph 'Kitty' Anstruther, Treasurer to the Queen Mother, and a gentleman not unfamiliar with that fine old Scottish tradition of parsimony. Another tight-fisted baronet, in fact! When not at court, or at his castle in the Highlands, Sir Ralph lived in the oddly-named Pratt Walk near Lambeth Palace. The house was part of a short terrace and had a separate basement flat. Fearing the possible consequences of appearing prosperous, he used the flat, pretending to be the tenant, when entertaining 'new friends'.

An unfailingly charming and generous friend, Michael Whittacker, offered as his contribution to give a party at his flat for the newlyweds on the evening of the great day. Two of the great tenets of Michael's life were loyalty to friends and a belief that the countryside should be covered in concrete. I was amazed on my first visit to his house in Fulham, many years ago, to find that the walls of his sitting room were lined from floor to ceiling with a collection of portraits of old ladies. I wasn't sure then, and I don't know now, what these images might tell me about my host, but I remember thinking that they could not all be Whistler's mother. Michael managed to juxtapose a very high-powered job with a large corporation and a compulsively hectic social life. Unlikeliest, perhaps, among his many friends was the actor Kenneth Williams, to whom he was close for many years. In private life Mr Williams was universally regarded as tricky, but he and Michael enjoyed a tremendous rapport. They came together to a dinner party one evening where a group of extremely amusing people had been assembled for the 'Carry On' star's entertainment. From the moment introductions were made to the time a cab arrived to collect him he completely dominated the proceedings. With no prompting – in fact, woe betide anyone else who dared to interject – his monologues and mimicry spanned the evening. Of course he was terribly funny, but I couldn't help thinking that he might have been a happier man if he had developed the art of listening.

Kenneth's sudden death at a comparatively young age was completely unexpected. So much so, in fact, that his will did not take into account the possibility that he would be outlived by his adored mother. Fortunately for her the main beneficiary was Michael, and he made sure that she was looked after in the way her son would have wanted.

Patrick and Barbara's wedding was due to take place at eleven o'clock at the registry office at Chelsea Town Hall and I, as best man, went to collect the groom from the Kensington Church Street flat. As it was only just after ten o'clock I resisted the offer of a drink and waited for Patrick to get ready. The minutes ticked by and I began to feel grateful that it was only a blue suit he was climbing into and not an Emanuel confection in ivory satin and yards of tulle. Nevertheless, we had precious little time to spare as we raced out into the street to find a cab. Pacing up and down on the corner of the High Street, Patrick suddenly exclaimed, 'My God, there's Michael Golder. I'll get him to give us a lift.' He gestured furiously towards a brown Bentley that was stuck in traffic just in front of us, and shouted, 'Michael, please can you take us to Chelsea Town Hall! I am on my way to be married!' At that moment the traffic lights changed and our only chance of arriving in style glided away into the distance. The departing car left poor Patrick in a state of emotional confusion. On the one hand he had glimpsed his old lover for the first time for years, and on the other he had been rejected in a moment of need. A truly bizarre incident to contemplate on the very threshold of a new life. A friendly cabbie with an appropriate sense of occasion eventually deposited us at the Town Hall steps just as the bridal party was beginning to get a bit restless.

The formalities were legalised in a vast room that had the decoration and atmosphere of a public lavatory. It contrasted sharply with the setting for the lunch that followed, which was held in the quite literally 'over the top' private room of the Tent restaurant in Elizabeth Street. Of the ten people that sat down only two, Barbara's sisters, were family members. No one from Patrick's had made the journey from California. I am ashamed to say that coherence has always been my yardstick when it comes to judging the success of a party, and by the time I staggered away from this one I was making very little sense at all.

Not many hours later I was back again in Chelsea for Michael's bash. Apart from greeting a few people, including Fenella Fielding who always reacts as if she has never met me before (could it be that with eyelashes like hers, seeing anyone at all is always a surprise?), the only conversation I remember is one that I had with the happy couple. They came over to me to announce that they intended to spend that night at my flat before leaving for Brighton in the morning. Delighted though I was to be their host, I thought it sensible to remind them that I had only one bed.

'Don't worry,' they cried, 'we can sleep on the floor.'

By the time we came to leave I had roped in my old naval 'oppo' Brian Wright to come and stay as well. I had a feeling that a hard-drinking buddy, always prepared to stay up all night, was just what the situation required.

When sparrows farted the next morning I prised my eyelids apart and found myself in bed with Brian, whilst Barbara and Patrick played dead in different parts of the sitting room. A scattered collection of empty bottles and glasses provided evidence of some sort of party, but the place in the proceedings of a pile of wood that had once been a coffee table, remained a mystery. Later in the day the *Evening Standard* reported that Fenella Fielding had been knocked down by a white Rolls-Royce in the King's Road as she left a wedding party. And she doesn't even drink!

Soon after Ian's departure for the Americas, I decided that it was time for a change in my own life. Even before he left I had begun to hanker after the bright lights again. London was the answer and I began to make some plans. The first person I contacted was Paul Clarke, who ran the antique furniture department of Aspreys. During my 'lighter' days he had been working in Mount Street for a distinguished firm of dealers called Pratt. (An unkind person has suggested that Paul was Pratt's prat.) But I got to know him at Corfields when the shop was a regular stop on his buying trips once he had joined 'Ashtrays' as number two to Guy Holland, who ran the department. Quite by chance my call coincided with Guy's impending retirement, which meant Paul taking his place and the creation of a vacancy. He very sweetly indicated that, subject to the approval of John Asprey, who oversaw such things, he could see no reason why I should not be the man for the job.

I also rang Lesley Browne, who had been travel secretary at Chatelard, the girls' school in Les Avants. She had come back to London at about the same time as me and was now running a lettings agency called Flatmates. Once again I struck lucky when I explained that I was moving back to town and needed somewhere to live. Lesley said that she was trying to find a tenant for a nice little flat in Hollywood Road. It belonged to a woman, Mrs Rowell, who lived mostly in Wales but who owned the two flats – one of which she kept for herself – above a well-known Chinese restaurant called The Golden Duck. Lesley said that she would happily plead my cause, and knew that Mrs Rowell was more interested in finding the right person than getting the highest rent.

Thanks to Paul and to Lesley I got the job and the flat. At long last, aged twenty-six, I had a home of my own although Lesley had to find me a co-tenant to rent the second bedroom. Fortunately the chap she found travelled a lot on business, which meant that for most of the time I had the place to myself. Far and away the flat's best feature was its sunny little roof terrace, where I was able to have a few pots and make a stab at producing some flowers. I also enjoyed the area very much, especially as Hollywood Road was not at that time the fashionable street it subsequently became. The Hollywood Arms, opposite, was anything but chic and the only mildly trendy place to eat was the great value Bistro Vino. Art galleries and wine bars had not yet put in an appearance. Most mornings I set off on foot at about eight o'clock to walk to Bond Street.

In those days the antique furniture department covered the whole of the first floor of the main part of the Asprey building, with a small section of it devoted to antique clocks and watches. To help us in our work we enjoyed the services of a secretary called Denise, and Wally and Sid the two porters. When things were quiet, which they were most of the time, Denise the archetypal Asprey girl occupied herself on the telephone planing elaborate dinner parties. It was not what she said, but the way that she said it that jarred slightly on the nerves. She was able to produce soft, abbreviated vowel sounds like no-one else I have ever known. We are all familiar with 'Cuventry', 'hise' and 'brine' but she managed to turn the street called Conduit into Cundit.

The leisurely pace of activity allowed Paul to spend the first hour of the morning scanning the 'hatches, matches and despatches' columns of *The Times* before moving on to the crossword. He arrived for work each day wearing a bowler hat – probably the last to be seen in the West End – but would exchange it for a straw boater on the hottest days of summer. Without a hat he looked rather like Winnie the Pooh, with the tubby silhouette of a serious bon viveur. But his appearance was deceptive and concealed a strength and energy that revealed itself in Scottish dancing and across open country in hot pursuit of a hare with the Trinity Foot Beagles. His taste in furniture and works of art, influenced perhaps by his study of classical architecture at Cambridge, was restrained and leant heavily towards the eighteenth century. The consequent lack of conspicuous decoration in the showroom was not always greeted with enthusiasm by the Asprey family, or the big spenders from the Middle East. Although the profit margins were pretty hefty, I suspect the sales figures were less than commensurate with the amount of space the department occupied. By contrast, I am sure the reverse was true of the comparatively tiny antique watch and clock corner of the floor. This was the domain of Sebastian Whitestone, a young man considered a leading expert in his field. He had joined the firm after a teenage spell in the merchant navy, and acquired his knowledge on the shop floor. An early marriage to a South American girl produced two children, but did not prove to be a lasting success. He was tall, handsome and amusing, advantages he shared with his musician brother, and his sister, who was for many years the companion of Artur Rubinstein before she married Lord Weidenfield. Their father had been naval correspondent of the *Daily Telegraph*.

The greatest advantage of working upstairs was that we did not have to see, or be seen by Mr Hubbard, who reigned over the showroom like a Roman emperor. At ten minutes to nine every morning he arrived by car from his home at the Oriental Club and made his way with the aid of two sticks to his place at the centre desk. As the clock struck the hour a signal from him caused the simultaneous raising of the vast creaky shutters on the Bond Street windows. For the rest of the day he directed operations with a steely glare and a pointed stick. During her time there one of my future employers, Kate Vestey, worked in the department to the left of the front door that was given over to handbags and scarves. This little empire was controlled by the bird-like figure of Miss Dublanski, who had a nervous smile and the English of Yvonne Arnaud. Kate said that she ruled with a rod of iron and could be extremely cruel. But the Margaret Thatcher prize for female domination would have to be awarded to Jan Langley, scourge of small leather goods, who dealt with both staff and customers as if they were stone-deaf and half-witted. In the face of all this hormonal activity, the only haven of peace was the cubby-hole under the stairs, known by me as the 'reliquarium', where icons, crucifixes and religious medals were displayed.

At that time the Asprey family was very much in evidence on the shop floor. Mr Eric, who wandered about, had taken over the chairmanship of the company from his older brother, Philip. Philip's son, the completely uncharismatic Maurice, ran the antique silver department; and Eric's son, the almost-glamorous John, dealt with clocks and watches. The stately figure of Mrs Eric would glide in from Edenbridge from time to time to play the lady of the manor, whilst Mrs Philip, who fancied she had an 'eye', created dreadful window displays and spent holidays on the continent buying vulgar objects by the crate-load that were left unsold in the shop. Far and away the nicest of the bunch was Mr Algy, the third brother, who had served in the Guards and lived grandly in Trevor Square. He was quite stylish, and ran the interior decoration department with the help of Tim Field, who had been famous as a member of the singing group The Springfields, along with the lovely Dusty. When the oil-producing countries of the Middle East started making more money than they knew what to do with, Algy, through his old army contacts, moved in to tender for the contracts to build and furnish palaces for the ruling families. More often than not he was successful, and the Asprey design team and workshops were at fever pitch. However, the story goes that Algy's costings had a fatal flaw, which was that although the sums involved were usually colossal that essential element, the profit margin, was overlooked. You do not have to be an economist to see that therein lies disaster and, it is said, the decline in the company's fortunes dates from that time. There were huge family rows, which culminated in the brothers going their separate ways. Maurice opened his own shop in St James's and Algy had a short-lived go at a mini-Aspreys in Bruton Street. In the meantime John took over the running of the old firm from his father, with the assistance of Naim Atallah, the Palestinian entrepreneur and publisher. The City watched with interest as blocks of shares changed hands and other jewellers shops were taken over. But in the end they fell prey to the seemingly bottomless coffers of Prince Jefri, brother of the Sultan of Brunei. The business that was established nearly two hundred years ago finally passed out of the control of the founding family. Legend has it that the Aspreys were Huguenots who came to this country early in the 1700s. To find out more about this Mr Eric engaged the services of a genealogist to research the family history. His first report revealed that he had got back as far as an Asprey who worked as a blacksmith in Peckham. Mr Eric thanked him profusely for his efforts, but said that there was no need to go any further.

No sooner had I started my new job than I began to receive regular visits from errand-running Stephen, who had never used Aspreys before on the Prince's behalf. When buying cufflinks or having leather or jewellery repaired, he had always gone to Garrards or Mappin & Webb, but he was very happy to switch allegiance. Eventually, of course, the Prince's patronage lead to the shop receiving his warrant. Whenever possible, Stephen and I would use his visits as an excuse to meet up for lunch with our great friend Johnny Lyon, a rising star in the world of publishing. If we didn't go to a pub in Albemarle Street we usually went to Johnny's club, the Saville, next to Claridges, where we could eat on the roof. Johnny and I met for the first time one particularly wet Saturday afternoon at Chelsea Town Hall where an antique fair was in progress. I had rushed there from a morning at Aspreys to do the afternoon shift on a friend's stand. Johnny was performing the same function for his sister, Mimi, on her country (or 'farmyard') furniture pitch next door. I said a quick 'hello', abandoned my umbrella and galoshes and dived into the Gents to dry off. When I emerged a few minutes later it was to find that my precious American rubber over-shoes had been filled with flowerpots, much to the delight of Johnny and his fellow perpetrator. It certainly gave a new meaning to what they say about big galoshes! Later in the day I had the pleasure of selling an elegant mahogany wine cooler to a Mr Roux, who bought it for his new restaurant, Le Gavroche in Lower Sloane Street. When Jan, my stallholder friend, returned in the evening I took the piece of furniture in a taxi to its new home, very much aware of Jan's exhortation to 'try and get the money'. Needless to say, the staff at the restaurant tried very hard to fob me off with excuses, even when I explained very politely that I was not prepared to leave without being paid. After quite a long wait my patience was rewarded when someone was produced who could sign a cheque, and I returned to the Town Hall in triumph.

I only wish that selling furniture at Ashtrays had been as much fun. The only transaction I can think of that I enjoyed from start to finish was the sale of a table to Mrs Drue Heinz. It was a circular mid-nineteenth-century mahogany table, and a perfect example of Paul's taste. At first sight it looked like an ordinary breakfast table that would seat six or eight, but its remarkable feature was a clever mechanism that allowed it to expand to take several large wedge-shaped leaves. At its greatest extent it could accommodate twenty-five or thirty happy diners. Mrs Heinz declared it to be the neatest thing she had ever seen and asked for it to be delivered to her house at Ascot. On the day she had specified for its arrival the big Asprey van was off the road, which meant bringing in a specialist firm to do the job. By happy coincidence the driver and mate who undertook the task were two of the best-looking blokes I had ever seen, and I was delighted that Paul suggested I went with them to show the butler how the table worked. It was an uncomfortably hot day, and made even more so by the close proximity of my companions in their skimpy shorts and tee-shirts. But I certainly did not complain as we squashed into the cab together and headed for rural Berkshire.

The butler, whom I recognised as an 'extra man' from my palace days, brought us cold drinks as soon as we arrived. Watched by him and his enthusiastic mistress, the boys erected the table in a corner of the splendid dining room, while I did my best to appear knowledgeable about its special features. Once it was working to everyone's satisfaction, we prepared to take our leave, but at that point Mrs Heinz made a suggestion. As it was such a hot day, she said, why didn't we have a dip in the pool before heading back to London? She pointed through the French windows and told us to head in that direction. With profuse thanks we did just that. The garden, not surprisingly, was enormous and full of wonderful trees and shrubs. A place of such beauty and contentment that we decided we didn't care if we found the swimming pool or not. But find it we did, and what a whopper it was too. As we got closer to it, my new friends started to remove their clothing, and then ran the last few yards before diving headlong into the cool water. In spite of their urgings I decided to pretend to preserve my dignity by remaining fully clad; and lolled by the water's edge – in fact, I was supremely happy just watching them in action. After a great deal of gliding elegantly through the water and splashing about they hauled themselves out of the depths and flopped down beside me on the grass. It was only then that they realised that there were no towels. I toyed momentarily with the idea of offering my services with a handkerchief, but suggested instead that they jogged for a while to let the sun do the drying. We eventually made our way back to London, fuelled by stops at a pub and a chippy.

The department was visited on two or three occasions by a well-dressed middle-aged man, who arrived alone carrying a carefully furled umbrella and a bowler hat. Paul and I recognised him at once, although we both did so for different reasons. Rather like a contestant in a TV quiz show, I remarked to my companion that 'I know it's King Olaf of Norway because he has a laugh just like his cousin the Duke of Gloucester.' For his part, Paul claimed to know who he was because he had met him before and remembered that he was a fellow bowler hat wearer.

Another VIP visitor about whose identity there could never be any confusion was Mrs Imelda Marcos. In stark contrast to the way the King of Norway materialised, her impending arrival was foreshadowed by the appearance of a group of thugs, some in uniform and others in suits. When the former Miss Philippines Dairy Products herself reached the top of the stairs she had around her a bevy of jostling courtiers and a bemused John Asprey. When the poor man tried to guide her towards what he considered to be an interesting object the cry went up, 'I only want Chippendale.' (How lucky for the strippers that they had not yet been born.) At that point Paul moved forward to explain that he had only one chair at the moment that was attributable to Chippendale. 'I want library, whole room,' the lady insisted, in her eloquent way. All Paul could do was to say that if something like that appeared, he would immediately contact the embassy.

Paul had lived for many years in a charming little one-bedroom flat in Maida Vale, and although it was crammed with furniture, he could not bear the thought of moving. But one day he fell in love with a wreck of a house in an enchanted spot close to the heart of Kentish Town. It was an early nineteenth-century terrace called Torriano Cottages and was approached along a narrow unadopted road that seemed more like a country lane.

As well as being colleagues at work, Paul and I had also developed a close friendship. One evening over dinner at the house, soon after he had moved in, he asked me if I would like to take over the top-floor flat. He pointed out that although we could lead completely separate lives under the same roof, dinner parties could occasionally be shared and the odd quiet evening be spent watching the telly together. It took me a while to consider my attachment to the Hollywood Road flat, but in the end I decided that life at the Palazzino Torriano would be a lot of fun. And so it proved to be. Paul was a great cook – particularly brilliant at making quiches – though I don't know if that is difficult or not – and loved to have people to supper at least twice a week. If I was free I was almost always included, which gave me the chance to get to know more of his friends. They came from every walk of life, but with a bias towards the arts. Among my favourites were the larger-than-life West Indian actor Tommy Baptiste (with the Paul Robeson voice), the mouse-like Roy Barling, who ran the family shop in Mount Street that dealt in unimaginably ancient furniture, and Boris Mylne, the patrician valuer of works of art whose recreational interest centred on a set of black leathers and a Harley Davidson. A German called Peter Claas, an occasional visitor from his home in Malta, was the person I looked forward least to seeing. It was not his old age and heavily-accented English to which I objected, but the fact that he liked to round off a perfectly civilised evening by dropping his trousers to show off his wizened plonker to the assembled company. But Paul was very fond of the old rogue and spent a holiday with him each year.

One day as we were driving in to work, Paul announced that a young Maltese friend of Peter's was coming to stay for a few weeks while he looked for a job. Imagine my delight when the young man, called Philippe Abela, proved to be wonderfully handsome, with curly black hair that shone *and* a matching beard. But best of all, he had love in his eyes and he was looking at me. One evening, with Paul out, we had an early supper and then went to bed together in the guest room on the first floor. At about midnight a commotion downstairs signalled the return of our landlord from his carousing. Voices grew louder, accompanied by footsteps on the stairs. In a curious way, the inebriated always make more noise when they go out of their way to be quiet. The door to Paul's bedroom, next to ours, closed, muffling any further sound. I lay awake for a while and then joined my companion in the arms of Morpheus. After what can only have been a couple of hours I awoke with a start and sat bolt upright. It took me a few moments to realise that the sound that had disturbed me was the creak of the floorboards overhead. I roused Philippe from his deep sleep, and as quietly as I could explained that someone was walking round my flat. We clung to each other for comfort and listened. And then the noise stopped. Suddenly, in the half-light, I saw that the handle on the door was turning. We both gasped as a thin sliver of light came in to the room, and then the door closed again. We stayed as we were, hearts pounding and not daring to move. But after what seemed like an eternity I was aware of a cold draught and guessed that our villain had fled. Even then, with fear rapidly turning to anger, it still took me a while to step out onto the landing. The first thing I noticed was the distinct rush of air, and the fact that Paul's bedroom door was firmly closed. I followed Philippe downstairs to find the French windows wide open. With a great sense of relief we spoke normally for the first time as we both expressed the hope that Paul was OK. I banged firmly on his door before entering to find him doing his best to come to terms with the world. Rather to my surprise his bed still held another occupant, snoring noisily beside him. I explained what had happened as Paul led us on a tour of inspection. As far as we could see, the French windows had been forced from the outside, and very little had been taken. Paul had lost some pieces of silver and I discovered later that the jacket of my very best suit was missing. Not surprisingly perhaps, I expressed the belief that the intruder had an eye for good things, especially fine tailoring. Paul, on the other hand, was convinced that my jacket was only taken as wrapping for his tatty old bits of Sheffield plate!

Happily for Philippe and me our relationship survived that little episode and we remain good friends to this day. I was also pleased to be able to introduce him to his next employer, and one that he remained with until his death eight years later. I had got to know David Carritt originally through meeting him at Tattersalls, the Knightsbridge pub, where he indulged his penchant for the armed forces. Although not a well-known figure he was highly-regarded as a picture dealer and a leading authority on the Italian old masters. His London base was a rambling flat in Mount Street and weekends were spent at his house in Deal. Philippe moved in and soon brought order and a degree of stability into David's domestic life. At the same time Philippe, who happened to share his employer's interest in the painted image, began to accompany him to exhibitions and on visits to art galleries. As their friendship developed they started having joint parties, where some of David's less exalted friends mixed easily with Philippe's younger set, and found that they had much in common. The onset of a debilitating and painful illness cut short the career that would have taken David to the pinnacle of his profession, and revealed in Philippe the nursing skills with which he was so naturally endowed. David died aged fifty-two in 1985. The important thing he left behind was not the business in St James's that was his brainchild, but the knowledge and enthusiasm for paintings that he inculcated into Philippe. For, in spite of many setbacks after David's death, Philippe has designed and decorated a flat in Earls Court that is not only his home but also a greatly admired gallery for today's young artists.

One of my best memories of Mount Street parties is of David and Stephen, helpless with laughter, performing a ridiculous dance to the music of The Smurfs. But under his own steam Stephen was also doing a great deal of entertaining at Buckingham Palace. Although he was still lodged in the room next to the one I had as a footman, his new eminence as valet to the Prince permitted him to make an arch through to the neighbouring room and fix it up for dining. Without the use of the Queen's heated trolley and with no kitchen within striking distance hot food was a problem, but thanks to a Fortnum & Mason game pie or the occasional casserole provided by Johnny Wood, everyone's favourite royal chef (especially mine), delicious food was readily available. The guest list would often include old stagers like Maurice and Johnny, as well as Lesley from Flatmates and Michael Cashman. These four had become firm favourites of Stephens, but his increasingly high social profile was bringing birds with more exotic plumage into his circle. Although there was no question that they were drawn to Stephen's effervescent personality, I could not help but think that his closeness to the Prince added a touch more lustre. One particular charmer was Dennis Pehrson, the Danish-born secretary to Bruno Heim the Papal Nuncio. Even with space at a premium room was always made for the glorious soprano Rita Hunter, not forgetting (and she never did) her husband, daughter and manager. Another regular, at the opposite end of the physical spectrum, was Barnsey from the Bahamas, the self-absorbed widow of Sir Victor Sassoon. By contrast, no one sang more lustily for his supper than the ubiquitous Christopher Biggins, whose friendship Stephen enjoyed even before it became compulsory.

One glorious summer's evening, Johnny, Stephen and I took a picnic to Henley for a concert that was part of the new music festival that followed the end of the Regatta. Thanks to Stephen's food and the contents of Johnny's wicker cellarette we dined magnificently and eagerly awaited the appearance of La Hunter, who was the main attraction. Whilst we in the audience lolled on a bank of the Thames, a floating grandstand was moored alongside to act as the stage for the performance. With the orchestra already arranged on its three tiers, only the diva was missing. And then, to enthusiastic applause, she passed among us and made her stately progress towards the water's edge. She paused briefly, accompanied by an expectant hush and a degree of bracing from the artists already in place, as she shifted her considerable weight onto the right foot and stepped aboard. The platform dipped perceptibly in her direction as the audience let out a collective sigh and thundered their relief. She went on to sing superbly and gave us an evening to remember.

Barnsey, who was Canadian, had arrived in the Bahamas to act as nurse to the elderly millionaire, Sir Victor Sassoon. A relationship developed and they eventually married. Photographs of them together show two supremely happy people. When he died she was left a great deal of money and all his bloodstock interests. As a widow she came to London several times a year, usually coinciding with the social season and important race meetings. She invariably stayed at a large house in Upper Grosvenor Street that belonged to Bronwen Astor who, although she was the ex-wife of Lord Astor, had eschewed earthly titles since her discovery of Christianity. At Barnsey's invitation I went there one evening with Stephen for drinks. Another time she took us both to dinner at the Mirabelle, her (outrageously expensive and not very good) favourite restaurant. Affected by this show of hospitality, I asked Stephen to bring her to supper in Kentish Town, hoping against hope that Paul (like me, a sucker for a title) would be prepared to cook. My only vivid recollection of that night is of Barnsey pressing a small package into my hand as she arrived. Deeply embarrassed though I was that she should feel the need to bring me a present, I still opened it with interest. Much to my amazement, the torn paper revealed not a Hermés headscarf, but a carefully folded 'Souvenir of London' teacloth – and I don't think she meant it as a joke.

In the spring of 1974 I decided to leave Aspreys. Although Paul took me with him to view sales at Sotheby's and Christie's, and even sometimes sent me to do the bidding, most of the time I paced around the department like an attendant in a little-known museum. I had begun to feel that I would like to deal more with people, possibly even doing something that would make a difference to their lives. But no, I did not become a social worker or take holy orders. In fact I became an estate agent – and in spite of knowing all the jokes, I firmly maintain that a bright and conscientious estate agent is a useful member of society. The firm I joined, Marsh & Parsons, had been based in Kensington since the end of the last century and also employed Lesley to run their lettings department. I am sure 'the good word' she put in for me with the senior partner helped to tip the balance in my favour. But I was not employed to be let loose on the elegant highways and byeways of W8. The office for me was the firm's furthest outpost in the Shepherd's Bush Road. Although it was a far cry from Bond Street, it could at least claim to have one or two interesting buildings along its length. At the top end, just off The Green, is a marvellous 1930s block of flats called The Grampians. Halfway down and backing onto the playing fields of St Paul's Girls School, the classical revival public library is a treat for the eye. And at the southern end, near the Broadway, stands the great lump that is the Hammersmith Palais.

One of the first telephone enquiries I took in my new job was from a woman who wanted to know if we had any two-bedroom flats for £15,000. Quick as a flash I explained that we had a very nice one in The Grampians for £14,500. She hesitated for a moment before pointing out that she was hoping to find something a little closer to London!

The office was run by a manager, two negotiators and a secretary. When the firm opened a new branch in Holland Park Avenue our boss was sent there to take charge, and his place was taken by a chap in his mid-twenties called Christopher Marlowe, who had experience of the market in Fulham. Christopher was overweight, shy, amusing and personable and it was only much later that I discovered his natural aversion to work and the general public. Competition in the area was almost non-existent, which meant that we had a large portfolio of good instructions in the better bits of Shepherds Bush and Hammersmith and a steady stream of eager applicants. Because of the presence of two popular schools, St Paul's and the little Lycée, Brook Green was the most desirable part of our patch. Shirley Williams, whose daughter had attended the former, sold her house on The Green through us in my early days. Another good instruction we received was a house on four floors in an attractive road called Aynhoe. It was informally divided into three flats and used as a source of income by its owner who lived, rather predictably, in Cheltenham. She was a very grand Englishwoman called Princess Imeritinsky, whose late husband was from an old Georgian family. Over the following weeks I went often to the house to show it to interested parties before we finally agreed terms with the brothers, John and Peter Hardyment, who were property developers. Their plan was to put central heating and fitted carpeting into each of the flats, self-contain them to please building societies and stick them back onto the market. Egged on by my colleagues in the office I began to seriously consider the possibility of making the Hardyments an offer for the ground-floor flat. All it really consisted of was one large room, which had originally been two, with an open-plan kitchen and the back overlooking the small garden. A corridor led to a cupboard under the stairs and a no-frills bathroom. There was no doubt at all that I liked it very much and it was only the prospect of a crippling mortgage that made me hesitate. But in the end, thank goodness, I came to terms with that and took the plunge.

Of course, it was all very well owning my first home, but apart from some pictures and ornaments I had bugger all to put in it. However, I need not have worried as very soon the flat became a very happy repository for other people's cast-offs. My mother produced a small dining table and two chairs, Lesley came up with two marvellous pairs of curtains and Richard Dallimore shipped in an Edwardian double bed and a divan. To cap it all, the office presented me with a large window box for the big bay in the front. An excellent second-hand furniture shop in the Shepherds Bush Road provided other things as time went by. At Corfields my only acquisition had been a glorious Irish Georgian decanter with a mushroom stopper that I bought before discovering the initials GH engraved on its base. From my palace days there was the framed card containing The Beatles' autographs, from the Master there was his signed photograph and from London Arts one of John Lennon's lithographs of his naked wife smiling contentedly as she pleasured herself.

With my creature comfort taken care of, all that remained as far as making the flat into a home was concerned was finding someone with whom to share it. But I did not hold my breath. Nevertheless, life has a habit of surprising you from time to time. Out of the blue I was taken to dinner by my friends Robin and Gerald to a remarkable Elizabethan manor house near Heathrow that was about the last surviving part of an ancient village called Bedfont consumed by the airport. Our host Derek Sherborn, who was an expert on old buildings, had as his lodger and erstwhile lover a young auctioneer called Tim Mear, who was not popular with my companions. But as we drove through the suburbs they explained that his younger brother Alex had recently joined the household and that we would all be meeting him tonight for the first time.

Looking back, it is true to say that Alex proved to be one of the most attractive and engaging young men I had ever met. He had an open face, hair the colour of charcoal and the height and build of a jockey. But by far the most noticeable thing was the ease with which he listened, the sensitivity of his smile and the delight of his laughter. When it also emerged that he too was an estate agent our encounter got off to a cracking start. As we sat round the table with coffee after dinner, Alex described some of the lovely things that formed Derek's collection of antique furniture and objects. Leading on from that, he sought Derek's permission to give me a guided tour of the house. He took my hand on the staircase, and when we reached the landing, tenderly demonstrated that our feelings were mutual.

In the months that followed that memorable evening he came to stay in Aynhoe Road at least once a week, giving me a chance to show him off to my friends and allowing us both to become well-acquainted. He had spent most of his twenty-one years in the unspoilt countryside of southern Shropshire near Ludlow, where his elderly father's family had been tenant farmers for generations. His mother, whose Christian name was Turley, was a great deal younger than her husband and dealt in antiques when she was not riding to hounds with the Ludlow hunt. Her two sons, who were close in age, inherited their mother's twin passions and used them as an occasional basis for their livelihood. Tim was employed by Sotheby's at their Chester saleroom, and Alex worked with horses until the low wages forced him to don a suit again and return to an estate agent's office.

All this excitement had not been confined to my private life. Changes in the Shepherds Bush Road office meant that Christopher and I were joined by a keen young negotiator from Northumberland called Richard Hanlon, and Cheryl Worsley as the rather over-qualified secretary. They arrived at a time when Christopher and I were considering the possibility of breaking away from Marsh & Parsons and setting up a rival establishment of our own nearby. It was an idea that we both approached from different angles. As manager with a head for figures, he knew that our branch was an outstanding success and had great potential in a strong market. For my part, I was beginning to realise that we were on the edge of an area with a great future that might even become the new Chelsea. The patch I had in mind was triangular in shape and bounded to the east by Holland Road, to the south by Hammersmith Road and to the west by the Shepherds Bush Road. A hundred and fifty years ago it was fertile land for market gardening and the growing of fruit trees; with one of the biggest employers being Birds – who went on to give us custard. Descendants of their workforce still live in some of the older cottages owned by the Bird estate. And in spite of the best efforts of Victorian and Edwardian builders, Hitler's bombs and the local authority, the central core of pretty streets is still intact. Long before estate agents debased the word 'village', this one was for real and living and breathing. After the demise of horticulture, local prosperity was very much in the hands of two large organisations; the Post Office Savings Bank headquarters, whose hundreds of employees patronised the local shops, and J. Lyons, whose office complex included England's first supermarket. But all that has gone now and corner shops (and even the odd pub) have been turned into houses.

Since the early seventies an estate agency called Pettigrews had been operating in Masbro Road, where I am sure a good living was made selling flats and houses to BBC employees and anyone else who was prepared to 'pioneer'. Among their early purchasers were various members of the Day-Lewis and Branson families. Richard Branson's sister Lindy Abel-Smith had a house in Caithness Road where John Osborne once lodged and is reputed to have written *Look Back in Anger*. During the course of my research I was happy to discover from one or two dissatisfied clients that although the owner of Pettigrews was shrewd enough to employ the right sort of girls, his own reputation was less than squeaky clean. With this information under our belts we decided to hang about no longer, but get hold of a shop in Blythe Road as soon as we could. Although several premises were empty at that time, only the one on the corner of Masbro Road was ideal for our purposes. It looked rather forlorn and had long since ceased to be a dairy, but by happy chance I knew the owners, a Welsh family called Davies who had lived in the area for years and had been prudent enough to build up quite a portfolio of properties. I had often stopped to chat with the matriarch, Elinore Davies, a larger-than-life chain-smoker who ran their little empire with her husband Ben and sister Dorothy. Ben had building skills that he put to good use, with the assistance of the two overall-clad ladies, on any of the dilapidated houses they bought. They were naturally delighted when I mentioned the possibility of taking the shop, and I duly arranged a meeting with Christopher so that turkey could be talked.

Once the deal was signed and sealed all sorts of decisions had to be made. The first one was that for the time being at least the business would not be able to afford anyone other than Christopher, Cheryl and me, which excluded Richard Hanlon, whom I had hoped to be able to invite to join us. He had exactly the right personality for the job and might also have fought in my corner occasionally against the other two, whose partnership had now moved beyond the professional. Somehow Richard managed to survive this crushing career setback, remained an estate agent for a while and then found success as an interior decorator. He later went on to conceive and direct the Barbados Arts Festival, now an annual event.

The next issue to present itself was how the business was going to be known. We agreed that it must incorporate our own names, if only because they were already known in the area. When Christopher came up with Marlowe Hunting & Worsley I had no reason to object, but it amused me to think of the other names we might have used. Had Christopher's father not adopted a stage name, my mother not changed hers by deed poll and Cheryl remained married, we would have been Peridita Jobson & Geldart.

Through the many weeks of preparation that ensued we managed to keep our plans a secret as far as the Marsh & Parsons bigwigs were concerned, which made the synchronised arrival of our three resignation letters all the more dramatic. As soon as he had opened them the senior partner telephoned the Shepherds Bush office and demanded both an explanation and our presence in his office. We drove to Church Street together and filed in to see him, one by one. When it came to my turn the only part of the conversation I can remember is his question, 'Is this a coup d'état?' To which the only appropriate response was, 'No it's a fait accompli.' Christopher and Cheryl, who appeared not to have contracts, were asked to leave at once, while I worked out my notice in the office in Holland Park Avenue. In that month that elapsed before I could join them my two partners supervised the builders, bought furniture and equipment and battled with BT. But an equally important contribution were the letters they wrote to friendly local estate agents with whom we had had dealings in the past. Fortunately for a new agency like ours, the market was depressed and very much in favour of the buyer. Frustrated vendors would instruct agents on a multiple basis in order to achieve a sale, giving new boys and the cowboys an equal chance to get lucky with a purchaser. Details of properties we could sell, sharing commission, began to cascade through the letterbox and by the time we opened for business behind our smart blue facade at 118 Blythe Road the window was full of temptingly desirable residences. Very much as I had hoped, we began to find that there was a great deal of 'brand loyalty' among the applicants who had found the area. Getting them to consider the neighbouring streets of Fulham was almost impossible. Apart from anything else there were extremely popular shops behind Olympia, including Dave the candlemakers (who eventually became 'by appointment' to Prince Charles), the antique shop next to us and even Mary's bread shop in Masbro Road where for the customer the onus was on appearance rather than ability to pay. Many's the time I have stood in front of Mary's counter listening to an account of her most recent visit to Sorrento when a perfectly normal-looking human being has come in and asked for a cheese roll. If the unfortunate person has a jib the cut of which she does not care for, even the prominent display of the desired comestibles will not prevent Mary from declaring, 'Sorry love, haven't got any at the moment.' But by far the biggest attraction was 'Buckinghams', the butchers shop run by Roy and Joan Saunders and their teenage son Alan. I first became aware of its existence soon after I arrived in the Shepherds Bush Road. On any given day a queue of people (very often including a number of queens) would be waiting their turn to pass through the doorway in order to chat to the senior Saunders, to receive a beaming smile from the son and heir or occasionally to buy meat. I alone, it had to be acknowledged, would be the one person for miles around who would find it difficult to pass through those portals. I knew for sure that if Alan favoured me with a glance my cheeks would enflame, the power of speech desert me and the reason for my being there fly out of the window. I was reconciled to the fact that I would only be able to observe him from afar, or at least from behind my desk across the street. But the Lord moves in mysterious ways and one evening at about six, soon after we had opened for business, I was locking the door for the day when Alan came across and introduced himself. In spite of realising at once that he was in the presence of a gibbering idiot, rather than making an excuse to leave he asked if I fancied a drink! Covered in confusion I strolled with him to the nearest pub and spent the next few hours drinking a great deal of beer and getting to know something about my handsome acquaintance. In spite of being only seventeen years of age and average height, he had the powerful physique of someone who played hard at rugby and football. Other details of his appearance, although that is hardly the word, included a mop of shiny black hair, dark eyes surrounded by long lashes and a sensitive complexion. His seasoned poise and confidence had presumably been acquired through customer contact in the shop during school holidays. He had joined the business, travelling up with his parents from Biggin Hill each day, as soon as was legally possible. The topic of girlfriends (his, you understand, not mine) came up in the course of conversation, but he appeared not to have one at that time. What social life he had seemed to revolve around David and Paul, his two younger brothers.

To my amazement, after that first evening together we became pretty well inseparable. But whether it was a pint at lunchtime, a drink after work or supper at my flat, I made absolutely certain that the suggestion always came from him. On his eighteenth birthday I was able to give him my good wishes when we met in the street. But not content with that, he said that he would like to share with me that evening a customer's gift of champagne. He didn't know at that stage that I had laid in supplies in case the situation presented itself. At about seven-thirty he made his appearance, having had a sip or two with his mum and dad. By eight-thirty our intimate little party was in full swing. We were recharging our glasses in the kitchen when he suddenly came up to me, kissed me on the lips and proclaimed, 'I want you to make love to me!' My state of bewilderment was not allowed to last long, for just at that moment Chris and Mike, my neighbours from upstairs, burst in to say that they had heard it was Alan's birthday and to insist that we went up to their flat for a drink. Mustering as much composure as possible under the extraordinary circumstances, we climbed the stairs behind them. Thanks to Chris and Mike's natural exuberance we managed to have a pretty riotous time, but after a while it became obvious that all was not well with Alan. He had taken up a position in front of the fireplace, legs apart, but as the bubbly flowed his posture became less rigid and he started swaying as if in time to imaginary music. The colour of his face began to change, first to grey and then to a delicate shade of green. I stood up and said that it was time to call it a day. I helped my stumbling companion down to the ground floor and suggested walking back with him to the shop, above which he had a bedroom. But he assured me that he would be fine and reeled away into the night. I needed several more cigarettes and glasses of Scotch before I saw any point in going to bed. And even then I couldn't help thinking about the events of the evening and their impact on my feelings. Sleep eluded me for a long time.

As I approached the office the next morning I glanced cautiously in the direction of Buckinghams, only to be greeted with a cheery wave from my white-coated friend. The temptation to have a drink at lunchtime was almost overwhelming, but I battled on, with the support of my colleagues who had 'seen it all before'. At six I left the office as usual without having had any further eye contact from across the road. In the midst of making some supper, by which time I had decided that Alan would never come to the flat again, he suddenly appeared on the doorstep, oozing the resilience of youth! His only concession to the excesses of the previous evening was a glass of lime juice rather than his usual gin and tonic. Conversation was rather stilted, as if we both knew that there was something that had to be said to clear the air. I had spent twenty-four hours rehearsing what I was going to say and when it should be said, but I suddenly heard myself getting straight to the point.

'I know you had a hell of a lot to drink last night, but just before Mike and Chris came in you...' I tailed off as he got out of his chair and disappeared through the kitchen. Minutes passed as I waited for the front door to slam. But moments later he called:

'Guy, can you come here a moment?'

The corridor was in darkness as I made my way along it towards the open bedroom door. In the half-light I could see him lying naked on the bed.

Time will never erase the memory of that evening. Alas, in spite of that night rather than because of it, our relationship continued to blossom. During the next seven years we only had one more bit of passion, but hope certainly sprang eternal. I maintained my policy of not making the first move, even though my feelings were way beyond friendship. We entertained my friends together and snatched sailing weekends with Robin and Gerald in Suffolk. Dudley had Alan to supper, as did Stephen at the Palace, and Brian gave us a guided tour of the Mansion House. One summer we spent a few days with Terry at his pub in North Devon and a night at Biggin Hill while his parents were away. By way of a change we went one evening to drink at a great pub called The Scarsdale in Edwardes Square. After a couple of pints I suggested that we should call and see an old friend I hadn't seen for ages who had a house in the square. Although I think Alan got rather bored with being paraded in front of complete strangers, however friendly they might be, he agreed. On the way there I explained that her name was Fleur Czartoryski and that she was a widow of a certain age, with three children. I had met her in Lymington where her brother-in-law, Stephen Garratt, was Corfields' picture man. I like to think that I did not mention the fact that she was another well-born Englishwoman who had married into a princely East European family. Her dead husband, Andrew, was a Pole. I also may have omitted to point out that appearances can sometimes be deceptive. In Fleur's case, what she lacked in looks she more than made up for in personality. Where the house was concerned the exterior was smart, but the council had condemned the basement.

In spite of the lateness of the hour and the time that had elapsed since we last met, Fleur seemed pleased to see me and made Alan very welcome. Over drinks we chatted about Lymington, Corfields and the Garratts and the time she made my wrist bleed when she brought her son Guy to lunch with me in Aynhoe Road. After a couple of hours we left, having first declared our intention of keeping more closely in touch. But, as is so often the way, another year was to pass before I saw her again.

In the months that followed that evening I began to come to terms with the fact that my life was going to have to change. It was ridiculous to spend all my time thinking about, waiting for or being with someone who was capable of an affectionate gesture but who probably only thought of me as a good friend. At the same time if I reduced my support system he would be forced to make friends of his own and consider his sexual and emotional future.

I made a start by offering to go and run the new office we had opened in King Street, Hammersmith. The original idea behind it was that it should be Cheryl's plaything, but she soon lost interest and decided that having babies was more fun. (By this time she and Christopher were married.) Its site on the corner of Ravenscourt Road was a good one, but it had the disadvantage of a southerly aspect and large plate glass windows. By two o'clock on a warm day the atmosphere inside was like a Turkish bath house. From the outset the lynchpin of this first and last imperial outpost was a delightful Old Etonian called Charles Stanton, who would rather have been a vet, or possibly a doctor. Although Charles was someone whose company I enjoyed enormously, I tended to leave him to his own devices at lunchtime, when a tub of taramasalata and a hunk of salami constituted his diet. I went once to stay for a bank holiday weekend at Charles's home in Derbyshire. They lived on the edge of the village of Snelston, which the family largely owned, in what had originally been the stable block of Snelston Hall. The house itself, designed by the architect of St Pancras Station and in a similar style, had been pulled down after the war. All that remains is the overgrown outline of terrace gardens and a wonderful oil painting that shows the Hall in all its glory. In his parents' absence he had arranged a small house party that also included another of our employees, called Philip Vaughan-Fowler. At our first meeting I remember asking Philip if his father was the squadron leader who drove helicopters for the Queen's flight. He replied that he was, but that he never flew anyone very important. Just people like the Duchess of Kent!

After about nine months in Hammersmith, where business was not exactly brisk, I left Charles to manage with the help of Carolyn 'Caro' Havers and Alison 'Ali' Trier. (Charles and I called each other 'Cha' and 'Gu' in a gesture of solidarity.) When the fortunes of the office declined still further we reluctantly decided that it would have to close. For the last few months of its existence it was run as a one-man band by William Worsley (a proper Yorkshire Worsley), nephew of the aforementioned duchess. It was with mixed feelings that I returned to a Blythe Road office that was virtually partnerless. Cheryl never came in at all and Christopher made only token appearances when there were accounts to send out or cheques to pay in. But Philip V-F (or von Fowler as he was sometimes known) was firmly at the helm, ably assisted by Amanda Harris, who was another refugee from Marsh & Parsons. In my absence, and thanks largely to their efforts, the Brook Green area had turned into an arts oasis and a haven for struggling young comedians. Caithness Road houses had been bought by Brian Patten, the accessible Liverpool poet who hasn't forgotten how to rhyme, and the writer Brian Masters, who churns out books on hedonistic duchesses and mass murderers. Across the Green in Rowan Road, a converted cottage provides shelter for a happy ménage that includes Clive Evans, enfant terrible of sixties haute couture, whose production company Nice Pictures will probably soon make its first film. It is ten years since he first started trying to raise the cash. But, as he says, 'If it was that easy everyone would do it!' In Aynhoe Road the two extremes of the entertainment business are represented by Richard Eyre of the National Theatre and the former MP Harvey Proctor, who must surely be eligible for membership of Equity.

Comedy had four standard bearers as newcomers to the area. The first two were Lenny Henry and Dawn French, who had bought their first home together, a basement flat in Sinclair Road. The other two were Rik Mayall and Billy Connolly, who could often be glimpsed pushing prams around the neighbourhood. They both had houses in a small road called Irving, the most celebrated inhabitant of which hitherto had been harpsichordist-in-residence at a Dutch university!

Back once more in the old patch, an early treat was the instruction to sell the bachelor pad in Girdlers Road that belonged to a handsome young banker called Jamie Grant. Early risers – and I was sometimes among them – had the pleasure of the sight of his legs-to-die-for as he cycled each day to his office in the City. The only drawback with taking people to see his flat was the likelihood of disturbing the sleep of his homeless and out-of-work actor brother, whose name was Hugh.

At around the same time, I made the acquaintance of another up-and-coming actor, Nigel Havers, and his wife Caro. Nigel had not at that stage made the film *Chariots of Fire*, which was to propel him to stardom, but he was beginning to be recognised as a young actor to watch. The couple had very little money and no home of their own. Instead, they lived in a friend's house in a pretty street quite close to my office. When the owner, who was abroad, decided that he might sell it, he asked Nigel to get a local agent in to do a valuation. I turned up to do the business and we hit it off straight away. Soon after that Caro came to work for us as a part-time secretary. She juggled her hours with her responsibilities to their young daughter, Kate. Caro proved to be a delightful addition to the office, even though it would be hard to underrate her secretarial skills; her handwriting was among the worst I have ever seen. With a bit more money coming in they were able to buy a flat in Shepherds Bush and I started going there occasionally for dinner. Their friends were drawn mostly from Nigel's world, but with the addition of young aristos like Lord Bruce Dundas and the Brudenell-Bruces. As far as I was concerned the acting fraternity was best represented by Martin Jarvis and his enchanting wife; Ben and Penny Cross and the zany wife of Jeremy Child. For reasons best known to themselves Caro and Penny were keen to see the micro-talented Molly Parkin in a one-woman show at the Latchmere theatre. The three of us went together one evening and managed to stay in our seats for a record-breaking twenty minutes. In that time La Parkin succeeded in lacing a series of boring anecdotes with more expletives than Billy Connolly could muster at a rugby club stag night. As we made our way to the exit she harangued us from the stage for being stuffy and pompous. Almost certainly her best lines of the evening. We lanced that particular boil by going on to have a good dinner at Marco Pierre White's Wandsworth restaurant.

With the success of *Chariots*, Nigel and Caro moved again, to a much bigger flat in Sinclair Road behind Olympia. At the same time their entertaining became more lavish. Once dinner was over, a ritual that was new to me took place around a glass-topped coffee table. It involved straws, a credit card and a small heap of white powder. Although encouraged to join in, I didn't do so with the idea that it was going to be a life-changing experience – after all, I had been left cold by marijuana, and fought an almost daily battle against the temptations of booze and fags. However it would have been churlish not to tickle my nasal passages or wipe a finger round my gums while everyone else was doing just that. I waited in vain for flashes of bright colours or a feeling of delirium and settled instead for earnest chat at four o'clock in the morning. As the night wore on, Caro's staying power proved to be more robust than her husband's and once he had slipped away to bed we sorted out the world. She always showed a great interest in what I was going to do with my life, but more often than not our conversations centred on the state of their marriage. The core of her concern was the fact that she was ten years older than him and not really as conventionally good looking. She was sure that now that he was famous and moving in ever more glamorous circles, temptation in the shape of a younger woman would make its presence felt. And sadly prophetic she was too.

Given that *Chariots* had radically changed their lives it was hardly surprising that they both became slightly obsessed with the film. More often than not its distinctive theme music would be playing when I went to the flat and a large framed photograph of the Queen Mum with Nigel at the premiere was on display. I was not a great cinema-goer and some months after its release I had still not been to see it. One day Caro announced that it was ridiculous to put it off any longer and that she would take me, as she didn't mind seeing it again. I had a brainwave and suggested that we should take with us an old lady called Jean Darwin, who lived in a house on Brook Green. She would sometimes invite me for supper and Scrabble, and in the course of one of our evenings together it emerged that Harold Abrahams (played by Ben Cross in the film) had been a friend of her husband's and best man at their wedding. It turned out to be an evening of modified pleasure. At first I was amused to think that I was watching it with two people who had different but compelling reasons for being there, but as the opening titles rolled I began to realise that I might have enjoyed it more if I had been on my own. Caro on my left, in thankfully whispered tones, regaled me with a running commentary, whilst Jean on the other side, her hearing impaired and mind confused, was not sure what was happening at all. At the first appearance of Ben, and having established rather too loudly for some of our neighbours that he was supposed to be Mr Abrahams, she declared, 'But he didn't look like that at all!'

Starring parts in two big films took Nige to India and Australia for long periods and Caro, quite sensibly, paid lengthy visits to him in both countries. She particularly loved India and came back brimming with ideas to import hand-woven rugs that could be bought there very cheaply. I thought they were rather dull, pale things; in any case, she soon lost interest in the scheme. As a thank you for keeping an eye on their flat, she gave me a leather-bound address book.

Before too long Nigel and Caro decided to make what would turn out to be their last move before their marriage collapsed. By buying a house in Wandsworth, they followed the well-worn trail of the upwardly mobile to the green pastures south of the river. The convenience of West London was sacrificed for bigger houses with large gardens. Nige exercised his decorating skills with customary flair, leaving Caro to work out the school run and the shortest route to Sainsburys. As ever, their new home was a great venue for parties, but unfortunately I was forced to miss the one I would have enjoyed most. It was to be held on Election Night and one of the guests was Nige's father, the Lord Chancellor. Unfortunately, as I had already accepted another invitation, Havers Senior's observations as the results came in were lost to me for ever.

An important person in the life of an actor is his agent. In Nigel's case this rewarding job had been entrusted to his great friend Michael Whitehall. I too became fond of Michael and also his young actress wife Hilary, and was a guest at two of their dinner parties. On both occasions my fellow diners included amusing people such as John Wells and his wife, as well as Mr and Mrs Peter Bowles. But sadly for me, the single women for whom my presence at the two do's, as a spare man, was required were charmless in the extreme. My female companion at the first bash, Lady Aitken – mother of Maria and Jonathan – has a silly nickname that does not linger in my memory, but displayed a frosty countenance that does. Some days in advance of the next party I was telephoned by my host, who was presumably anxious lest I had let the date slip my mind. I suspect he only provided this service when the guest list included the daughter of the prime minister, a girl with whom he had once 'sparked clogs'.

Carol 'Mummy of course is a lawyer' Thatcher – next to whom I sat at the table – went out of her way very early on to establish that I was colossally unimportant. With that business taken care of, she spent the rest of the evening with most of her back towards me, addressing her lisp at anyone who showed more promise.

As Caro had predicted, the Havers' marriage eventually foundered. After the divorce, she moved to southern Spain to live near Penny and Ben, who have a house there. Penny's parents have been there for years and one of her brothers runs an avocado farm nearby. He had reached one of life's crossroads and asked me to sell his house in Hammersmith. As far as I can remember, it sold for about £125,000 – a decent sum in those days, and more than enough to satisfy his desire to buy something different. Having looked far and wide, the list of possibles was eventually reduced to two: a run-down castle near Glasgow and a neglected avocado farm outside Marbella. Pressure from his parents made him plump for the latter.

When a large unmodernised house came up for sale in Sterndale Road, we sold it to the developers John and Peter Hardyment for conversion into flats. As the work neared completion Alan decided to buy the top-floor flat to replace the Shepherds Bush bedsit that he was selling. He and I were still meeting from time to time, even though he admitted to having had a regular girlfriend for quite a long time. Although more than a little jealous, I was curious to know who she was, but could only discover that she was fairly local. On one particular evening when we met for a drink it was obvious that he was far from happy, but he only told me why with great reluctance. It transpired that a serious row had taken place and he thought the relationship might be at an end. Naturally I made sympathetic noises and then, in an effort to cheer him up, suggested going to The Scarsdale for a change of scene. For a fleeting moment I thought the mention of that name made his face even longer, but he accepted the idea, albeit without much enthusiasm. When we got there and found a table near the open fire I reminded him that it had been about a year since our last visit, and that we had rounded off the evening by calling on my old friend Fleur. Warming to my theme I recalled what good fun she was and proposed the idea of seeing if she was at home. He thought for a moment and then said something like 'Why not', and so we did. When Fleur came to the door she looked positively taken aback, which made me think we had mistimed our arrival. But, as I went through the formality of reminding her who my companion was, she showed us into the sitting room. As neither of them seemed prepared to say very much, I did all the talking until Fleur turned to Alan and asked him to get the drinks. As I leapt to my feet and offered to do it I heard her say quietly, 'Don't worry, he knows where everything is.'

Alan crossed the room and took glasses from a corner cupboard before turning to face me, his body tense with emotion. Between sobs he blurted out, amongst much more, that he loved Fleur and wanted to marry her. Fleur remained very quiet while this was going on, but I do remember her repeatedly reminding him that he had promised to break the news to me on many occasions. I sat in stunned silence until Alan ground to a halt and then, with as much dignity as I could muster, announced that it was time for me to leave. In spite of their protests I mumbled my goodbyes and headed for home. Back in Aynhoe Road I hit the heather juice and attempted to calmly come to terms with the events of the evening. Some time later my musings were interrupted by a phone call from Alan, who seemed to be prompted by Fleur to show concern (I think) for my well-being. But, with my trusty bottle of Scotch beside – or was it inside – me, I survived that night and lived to get some answers to a few questions that were puzzling me.

In fact, in the cold light of day I was really only baffled by two things. In order of importance they were: how did the affair begin after their first brief meeting? And secondly, why Fleur? Alan's answer to the former was that after we left Edwardes Square together the first time he had dropped me at my flat and then driven straight back to Fleur.

He never divulged what it was that prompted him to do it, but I can only assume that it was some sort of chemistry or a sign that passed between them undetected by me. As far as the latter is concerned, I think I already knew what he was going to say. Regardless of sex he needed someone who was strong, and although he claimed to have been torn between us, after all those years with me he wanted to be led not guided.

Many months later, and with the dust firmly settled I went once more to Fleur's house for a drinks party. I met her daughter Anna, whose dishy young fiancé was the son of the back-bench MP Sir John Biggs-Davidson. Alan was there too, on cracking form and thoroughly at ease with Fleur's family and friends. More recently she has sold the house and moved to more modest surroundings in Brook Green. I see them both from time to time, but not together. Whether or not they still see each other, I would be the last person to know.

While I was playing my small part in a relationship that can fairly be described as ill-starred, Stephen had an important role in one that was equally troubled. And there were similarities between the two. But in his case the protagonists were a prince, rather than a princess, and with the much younger person working in a nursery rather than a butcher's shop. He hoped that with the announcement of the engagement of the Prince of Wales and Lady Diana Spencer the turbulence that had marked their courtship would be a thing of the past. For months he had been involved in parallel attempts at concealment. One of them was designed to prevent the outside world from finding out about the extent of the friendship between the Prince and Lady Diana; and the other, which required all his diplomatic skills, was designed to prevent Lady Diana from finding out about the extent of the friendship between the Prince and Mrs Parker Bowles. But his feeling of relief was short-lived. With greater access to the Prince's entourage, Lady Diana started to look for allies in what she thought of as the 'enemy camp'. The two obvious targets were Stephen and the Prince's detective, John Maclean, who between them were privy to most of his actions and some of his thoughts. They soon discovered that the blushing schoolgirl smile concealed a woman with a streak of determination and stubbornness. But of course in the case of Maclean, although biologically susceptible to female charm, she was dealing with a highly trained professional and a dour Scot to boot! Stephen, on the other hand, was perceived to be a much softer touch and indeed he was flattered at first that she sought him out for a chat at every opportunity. But Stephen was nobody's fool, and although he did not see the Prince through rose-tinted glasses (after all, who was it that said, 'no man is a hero to his valet'?), his loyalty was unwavering. Questions about 'old flames' in general, and Mrs PB in particular, were either parried or politely ignored. But it was the honeymoon on the royal yacht that presented the greatest challenge – and sadly not just for Stephen. As far as the Princess was concerned, it represented two weeks, largely spent at sea, in the company of a husband whose interests she did not share, two hundred men with whom she could not mix and a dresser she hardly knew. Given all that it is not surprising that she sought out the man who had known her husband and his secrets for twelve years. He showed her every kindness, of course, but her changed status played straight into Stephen's hands by ruling out any question of friendship. He bowed when she came into the room and never addressed her as anything other than 'Your Royal Highness.'

Soon after the honeymoon and with media interest in the Waleses at fever pitch, stories about Diana's determination to get rid of 'the old guard' at Kensington Palace began to circulate. Stephen's name, often accompanied by expressions such as 'fun-loving' and 'confirmed bachelor', was always well to the fore. Soon after one tabloid declared 'Di sacks Charles's valet', Stephen received a letter from another newspaper offering him £60,000 to reveal all. When he showed the letter to his incredulous employer his reaction was: 'I wonder how much they would pay me to write about you!'

At the time, Stephen, confident that the Prince would never deprive him of his job, rejected the offer but kept the letter – just in case. Not many days later he was sent for by the head of the Prince's household to be told that in the staff reorganisation that was being planned he was to be moved to a different post. A final decision had not been

Main Picture: Me in finest state livery.

Inset: Former Liberal Party Leader, Jeremy Thorpe, who I first encountered whilst working at the Palace.

Me carrying out my official duties. Pictured with me here are Princess Marina, Princess Alexandra and Eddy Meeks.

Scenes from my childhood.
Main picture: My mother takes a spin on the local transport in Egypt.

Below left: John and my parents.

Below right: Young Buster.

Left to right: **Graham Payn, 'The Master' Noel Coward and Cole Lesley.**

Main picture: Michael Crookes with Gyp, Harry and Jasmine.

Inset: Michael Cashman, former *Eastenders* star and prominent gay rights campaigner.

Above: Naim Manjaka

Below left: Rosemary Orde

Below right: Ian Macbeth

Scenes from my time in the Alps.
Above left: The Master's chalet in Switzerland.

Above right: Me, Cole Lesley and the Coward Mercedes.

Below: With Naim and Graham Payn.

Above: With Stephen Barry.

Below: With Kate Vestey.

taken as to the position he was to be offered, but the Prince and Princess were anxious to retain his services in whatever capacity. A sheepish Charles, the next time they met, mumbled something to the effect that 'Her Royal Highness, quite rightly, had decided to take charge of the Household and to run things her way!' He added that they both hoped Stephen would consider returning to a uniform job, possibly as Page. In the meantime it was announced that John Maclean had been promoted and would no longer be responsible for the Prince's protection.

For many years my friendship with Stephen had meant almost daily phone calls and an evening together two or three times a week, whenever he was in London. At our encounter that followed the bombshell he sought my advice as to what to do next. After so many years spent in the safe cocoon of royal service, he was understandably apprehensive about taking on the outside world. And of course, the Page's job would mean much less travelling and more time for a social life. On the other hand, if one newspaper was prepared to offer him £60,000 for his story, he was tempted to wonder whether another one might pay more. I could only add to his confusion by pointing out that if he was going to spill the beans it might as well be in a book, even if it could only be published abroad. After many hours of deliberation he decided to stay with the Prince and become his Page.

But that was not the end of the matter. Stephen rang me the next day to say that he had just been informed that he would not, after all, be offered an alternative post in the Prince's Household. Although Stephen's position in the Household meant that his departure did not merit an official announcement, it did not take the popular press long to latch onto it. In isolation it was a story that was never going to create national interest, but beefed up with the removal of John Maclean, it contributed to the perception of a power hungry new broom sweeping through the corridors of Kensington Palace. And in its wake, of course, came many more offers of lucrative writing deals from Fleet Street. But it was the idea of a book that appealed to him most. He saw it as a one-off project that might produce a lump sum to finance a business venture, such as a bar or restaurant. However, he knew that in order to create anything even remotely readable he was going to need an awful lot of help. An introduction to one of the great ladies of Fleet Street proved to be the answer to his prayers. Unity Hall had enjoyed a long and distinguished career in journalism. She had also had some success as a novelist and ghost writer. At the time they met she had just finished helping Jean Shrimpton with her autobiography, in spite of being fully employed as 'Agony Aunt' on the *News of the World*. They hit it off at once and never failed to find an excuse to celebrate their friendship – whether it was over lunch at Langans or a bottle of Unity's favourite champagne at her house in Islington. Happily, she also proved to be a brilliant interpreter of Stephen's ideas and a provider of shape to rambling stories. She agreed with him too that, overall, the book should be dignified, humorous and affectionate with only the merest hint of 'kiss and tell'. From time to time I joined them, sitting in on their sessions at the house in Alwyn Square that Unity shared with Phil, her fellow journo and long-time companion. In spite of bouts of uncontrollable laughter and endless glasses of bubbly, work progressed apace. When every 't' was crossed and every 'i' dotted, the finished manuscript was dispatched to the New York office of Lucianne Goldberg, the controversial literary agent who specialised in books of a 'revelatory' nature. She read it quickly, claimed to have enjoyed it and proceeded, in her own inimitable way, to flog it to the publishing house prepared to produce the biggest bucks. Ironically the winning bid came from the deceptively English-sounding firm of Macmillan, although they were no longer connected with prime minister Harold's old business. With an agreement pending, Stephen flew out to New York to sign on the dotted line. He returned a few days later in a state of high excitement and full of stories about La Goldberg. Stephen's contacts at Macmillan were apparently very up-beat about the sales potential of *Royal Service* in a country whose appetite for books about the British Royal Family knew no bounds. He was bidden to return again a few weeks ahead of publication day to prepare for the media onslaught that was being planned. Once the book hit the shops he was contractually obliged to criss-cross the country on a promotional tour. A thoughtful gesture from Macmillans was that he should take a friend with him on the trip to steady the nerve and lend moral support; he asked me if I would be that person. I hesitated only fleetingly, worried about leaving the business, before saying how much I would love to. I kept a bit of a diary during those three extraordinary weeks.

I flew in to San Francisco on a warm spring day in 1983. As my taxi from the airport approached the Hyatt Hotel in Union Square I could see Stephen waiting on the pavement outside. We embraced warmly, although my lips stopped short of his rouge-covered cheek. Sensing my surprise at this little embellishment, he hastily explained that although he was hot from a radio show the make-up had been applied much earlier in readiness for two television appearances. In fact I soon discovered that a typical working day could include as many as three TV shows, two radio slots and a newspaper interview.

San Francisco provided the first of something like six opportunities to enjoy and observe the Hyatt chain of hotels. Their idiosyncratic style of architecture, with atriums full of trees and external glass lifts, was something that we had not yet seen in England.

On Sunday evening, after a weekend of relaxation in the city, we set off by air for St Louis. An important part of these carefully planned journeys was that we were met at each airport by local escorts, who would drive us to the hotel and take us to engagements. Elaine was the first of these ladies whose twenty-four to forty-eight hours in our company we tried our best to enliven. As conversation flowed it emerged that she had written two books herself – guides to the city's restaurants and historic buildings. When asked to suggest a good restaurant for lunch, she surprised us by saying that it would be difficult for her to recommend one. Apparently this was because in compiling her guide she had simply requested menus from likely establishments and didn't feel the need to visit them. Quizzed about the old courthouse and two-hundred-year-old cathedral near the hotel, she had to confess that she had not been to them either. Leaving Stephen at a television studio in the clutches of yet another married couple with a chat show we set off – atheist and Jew – to see one of America's most venerated Episcopalian temples. Meticulous restoration and modernisation, which included under-floor heating and double-glazed stained-glass windows, gave it a rather antiseptic feeling. But at least it was not struck by a thunderbolt while we were there!

With the chat show under Stephen's belt we left after lunch for Milwaukee and his first close encounter with the general public en masse. The Friends of the Library had arranged a lecture and slide show, followed by tea for four hundred. We were told that the auditorium could actually hold seven hundred, but that the caterers could only provide enough scones, Maid of Honour tarts and Victoria sponges for the smaller number. The stage was got up as if for a presidential address – complete with podium and 'Old Glory'. But the event was almost completely disrupted by the presence of camera crews from several local TV stations who indiscriminately thrust lights and cameras into Stephen's face as he tried to speak. Under the circumstances he spoke well and when he had finished, found himself mobbed by elderly ladies eager for his signature on their copies of his book. One feisty lady on crutches said that she would have worn a plaster cast if she had known she could get his autograph. The tea itself yielded another innovation as far as I was concerned. It was served on a large plate that combined space for food and a saucer-like indentation for the cup.

The next day started in Cleveland, one of America's most avoided cities, known as 'the mistake on the lake'. A confrontation had been arranged with one of that country's journo legends, ninety-year-old Dorothy Fuldheim. In her office before the taping we managed to look suitably awestruck when she announced that she had just negotiated a new three-year contract with the TV station. She went on to tell us that before Stephen was born she had interviewed both Hitler and the Duke of Windsor. She certainly knew how to put Stephen at his ease! But in fact, although in private she had some fairly sharp things to say about the Royals, in front of the camera she was surprisingly gentle.

Stephen's fellow guests on the show were two remarkably successful authors. Shana Alexander had just published a book about the murder of the man who invented the Scarsdale Diet. She was accompanied by the novelist Barbara Taylor Bradford, whose first work – *A Woman of*

Substance – had sold 7 million copies. With a second novel zooming up the bestseller list, she was beginning to enjoy the fruits of her labours. Barbara was a Yorkshire lass who had lived in New York for twenty years and always dreamed of owning a penthouse with a large roof terrace. Although she had achieved her goal by buying a flat on the forty-seventh floor of a new block, she confessed that at that height she was too terrified to step outside. We were to meet these two ladies again later in the day, when they shared the platform with Stephen at 'The Plain Dealer' Literary Luncheon. When we arrived and saw tables laid for a thousand people we realised why it was described as the largest event of its kind in the country. Industrial catering rather than haute cuisine was the order of the day and my lunch companion, the wife of the paper's publisher, was so charming that I almost failed to notice the absence of alcohol. Stephen spoke first and with great humour, but he said later that concentration was difficult with a constant stream of people leaving from the back of the vast room. We put that down to Ohio Dodgy Bladder Syndrome. In his speech he had heeded the words of the old adage and left them wanting more, but this was in stark contrast to Miss Alexander, who regaled the audience with the seventeen pages of foreword to her book that the publisher had sensibly chosen to leave out. After lunch the three speakers sat behind tables signing copies of their works. The separate piles seemed to diminish with equal rapidity, and at the end it was neck and neck.

Later that day we found ourselves in Detroit, holed up in an hotel called The Book Cadilac – a vast rabbit warren of a place that proved to be the worst hotel I have ever known. For once I wished that the big city American rule, 'if it's twenty-five years old, pull it down' had been applied to this particular building. The rooms were a disgrace, and after waiting in mine for two hours the next day for breakfast I telephoned the manager to complain. His response was that if I was that desperate for food there was a drug store across the street. In spite of that setback, Stephen managed to hold his own on morning television in the company of ten women in various stages of pregnancy modelling swimwear.

So much of what we saw on morning television was bizarre in its own right, but it was made even more unusual for us because TV before lunch in England simply did not exist. It was also as distasteful as smoking before the Royal Toast.

Later that day we emplaned for Pittsburgh, a surprisingly fair city surrounded by industrial squalor. Its streets were in a state of complete confusion as the authorities were digging beneath them to extend the subway system. This state of affairs was planned to last for at least another year and would result in barely a mile of extra tunnel. While we were there Stephen sat through very jokey interviews on both country and western and rock radio stations. He also found time to rush into a few bookshops to damage with his signature any copies of *Royal Service* that might be lying around. Not only was there a chance that this would make them more saleable, but it also ensured that they were not returned to Macmillan. We managed to include stops like this on even the busiest days. His efforts were not in vain, for by now we had heard that the book had reached number eight on the bestseller list, just ahead of Norman Mailer's latest offering. 'Fellow from Fulham beats Bruiser from Brooklyn!' That night I accompanied my weary friend on a flight to New York for an engagement-free weekend. He had got into the habit of spending his rest periods in a haven of comfort and calm beside Central Park called the Ritz Carlton. Its English manager had become a friend and always gave us the same rooms on the fourteenth floor.

On Sunday night we left New York once more, for Toronto. The highlight of the visit was Stephen's appearance as a surprise guest on a TV quiz show called *Front Page Challenge*, which had been running for twenty-six years. The other participants included a fascinating man, who as premier of Saskatchewan during the war was Canada's first socialist prime minister. But the highlight of the evening was reserved for a more romantic piece of history. Two young men who met by chance when they worked together on a ferryboat came on to be interviewed. One was called Bligh and the other Christian, and they were direct descendants of the famous duo who sailed on *The Bounty*. Like their forebears, it was the sea that had brought them together – but unlike them, they had become firm friends rather than bitter enemies.

From Canada to Boston, where we were met at the airport by a glamorous lady who turned out to be the fashion correspondent for, of all things, the *Christian Science Monitor*. She guided us around that lovely city, the streets of which were lined with blossom-clad cherry and magnolia trees. At a television station we watched in the Green Room as Stephen was preceded on the breakfast show by a group of eight Vietnamese ukulele-playing children. They played very earnestly, but their sad little faces seemed to me more a reminder of a long voyage in a small boat than evocative of the spirit of George Formby. From there we drove to what was supposed to be a two-hour stint for Stephen on a lunchtime radio show. This proved to be a very laid-back affair, with the two other participants being an actress called Pam Grier, who played a witch in a new Walt Disney film, and a doctor who had sold an astonishing 32 million lifestyle books. The programme presenter had so much fun with these two that my poor friend was not called until a few minutes before the show's end. However, he had by this time become such a skilled performer that he still managed several plugs for his masterpiece. Outside a bookshop later in the day Stephen was approached by a man who asked, 'Didn't I see you on television this morning?'

'You could easily have done,' replied Stephen, preening slightly.

'I thought so – I recognised the shirt and tie,' the man remarked, and walked on.

When we arrived in Philadelphia that afternoon we found that our hotel was famous as the one that had been closed for three years following the death there of twenty-eight people with legionnaire's disease. But nothing daunted, I stuck firmly to my rule of not drinking any sort of water, or having any truck with the air conditioning, and got through the night unscathed. However, the next day I nearly drank myself to death celebrating La Goldberg's birthday. She had come down by train from New York to spend the day with us and to accompany us back there in the evening. While Stephen was left looking bewildered in a studio where small babies were learning how to work-out with their own keep-fit book, she and I went off to find a festive beverage in a nearby bar. We soon discovered that drinking in Philadelphia takes place almost exclusively in impenetrable darkness and freezing temperatures. But after several false starts we found a bar that was lighter and warmer than the rest. Over a bottle of Pennsylvanian champagne that was old rather than vintage, we set about getting to know each other.

Luci had been married to a successful businessman for many years and had two teenage sons, of whom she was inordinately proud. The special part they played in her affections was largely due to a remarkable set of circumstances. In the early years of her marriage she had given birth to two other boy babies, a couple of years apart. One day she left them briefly alone in her car while she dashed into a shop. When she returned she found the car flattened beneath a mountain of fallen scaffolding, her children dead inside. Although shattered by such a terrible loss, she eventually had the two boys who are the apple of her eye today. And both of them were born on the same days as the two that died.

On a lighter note, she has the distinction of being the first mounted policewoman to patrol Central Park. And, at a later date, she had a lover who was vice-president of the United States – Senator Hubert Humphrey.

After many hours, more revelations and an unconscionable number of bottles, we returned to something like the real world and collected our friend from his last gig. A short train ride, during which we all snored loudly, took us to New York for our second weekend break before we tackled Baltimore on Sunday evening.

By now, as far as American breakfast television was concerned, I thought I had seen it all. But Baltimore's diverse offering was arguably the richest and tawdriest to date. The programme's first guest was a butcher whose appearance on screen at eight-thirty a.m. was presumably beamed into the homes of thousands of viewers who could just about cope with digesting coffee and toast at that hour. Nevertheless, he was revealed standing behind a table that strained beneath the weight of glistening cuts of meat in various shades of gore. His aim was to promote the consumption of new and exotic carnivorous delicacies. Using a knife as a pointer he indicated chunks of camel, lion and ostrich, which he described as ideal for the barbecue. When he disappeared, to thunderous applause, his replacement proved to be the marginally more palatable Honey Bruce, ex-wife of Lenny Bruce the controversial sixties comedian. With total disregard to the entreaties of the interviewer she regaled us with the non-stop story of her life as a stripper, heroin addict and convict. When it came to her marriage it was obvious that Mr Bruce in private was not a barrel of laughs. The only enjoyable anecdote about him was one that featured his camp manservant. It revolved around the fact that to start the day Lenny required large quantities of liquid, particularly orange juice. But his daily request from beneath the bedcovers was usually met with the same response: 'Lenny, you know I am not a morning person and I can't get you a thing till I've got my eyes on!'

As she got to the end of her time-slot I thought to myself that at least, thank God, she didn't have an exercise book to flog. But I was wrong. With seconds to spare she flourished her contribution to the nation's well-being with the delight of a woman who had found her shopping list.

The American preoccupation with fitness was becoming a force that it was difficult to ignore. In our free time together Stephen and I agonised long and hard about what he was to do next to capitalise on his current success. Our first thought had been to go for a more serious book, something like an encyclopaedia of royalty, or more simply 'The Royals A–Z'. But we began to think that the exercise bandwagon was the one to jump on, albeit from a very British standpoint. How about, for example:

'Work-Out with the Waleses'. (Succeed where they failed.)
'Pump with the Palace'.
'Anne's Aerobics'.
'Activate with Andrew'.
'Energise with Edward'.
Chuck and Di – the ultimate exercise'.
'Philsical'.
or, my favourite, 'Running from the Windsors'.

In the end commercial good sense prevailed and a more predictable follow-up was produced.

Just before Stephen's appearance, which was billed as a question-and-answer session on the British monarchy, our host revealed that a section of the specially invited audience was made up of a group of ladies who were dedicated to the return of burlesque. Quite what sort of contribution a group of old strippers was going to make remained to be seen. For openers Stephen was asked if being valet to the Prince of Wales meant that he spent his time parking the royal Rolls-Royce. This was a constantly recurring question in a country where 'valet parking' was a much-advertised service. The answer to that was much easier to come up with than the next little teaser, which was whether it was true that Princess Margaret was a drunk! I won't tell you what Stephen said in reply – except that it was a lie. After that there were several others that had not cropped up before. They included, 'What is Prince William's favourite colour?' (the lad was ten months old) and, 'Does Prince Charles sleep in the nude?'

After all that, Atlanta was rather an anti-climax, although architecturally it was interesting. What struck me as odd was that in a city dominated by buildings that looked as if they had been made of tinted glass, the radio and TV stations were housed in replicas of magnificent southern mansions. These establishments, like so many that we passed through across the country, seemed to have a workforce at a certain level of cloned ladies with big smiles and even bigger hair. They were unfailingly charming and helpful to us and we did our best to entertain them with a bit of send-up and self-mockery. I also like to think that the little routines we went through were helpful to Stephen as he tried to keep his nerves in check and think funny thoughts. When I left a Green Room on one occasion to powder my nose I overheard an assistant director saying to a colleague, 'You must go into the Green Room. There are two English guys in there and it's just like Monty Python.' (Pronounced 'Pie-thon'.)

We flew south from there to a very humid Palm Beach, where the temperature was ninety degrees. The journey was enlivened by the presence of a vivacious stewardess who surprised us by serving Chablis in tins while berating Stephen for mumbling on *Good Morning America*. The highlight of our brief stay was a leisurely alfresco lunch at the venerable Breakers Hotel. Although cabaret was not part of the deal, we were treated to an amusing piece of street theatre. Just across from us an elderly motorist ground to a halt beside the sort of parking space that I would have been quite happy with. Not without effort, a dowager eventually emerged from the passenger seat and made it to the pavement with the aid of a walking frame. From there she shouted directions to the driver, whose hearing was presumably impaired. His first attempt at reverse resulted in a noisy encounter with the car behind. When a forward gear was engaged the same fate befell the vehicle in front. After several of these manoeuvres and the destruction of lots more bodywork the car was still some way from its destination, but the driver decided to call it a day and climbed stiffly out of his battering ram. As he did so he was greeted by a standing ovation from the waiters and lunchers on the terrace.

Our arrival in Miami for the last pause in the peregrinations coincided with an artistic event organised by Christo, the avant-garde artist, who is known for wrapping unlikely objects. As we flew over Biscayne Bay towards the airport we could see the latest results of his handiwork in the water beneath us. He had been given permission to enclose several of the small islands in a ring of brightly coloured material, best described as vivid fuchsia. From our aerial vantage point it was rather like looking down on six plump Barbara Cartlands.

We had come to Florida's throbbing hot-spot so that the veteran broadcaster could be subjected to the unpredictable host of an acclaimed late night radio show. We spent the afternoon doing a bit of sight-seeing, which didn't take long, and trying to find a decent bookshop, which took rather longer. After a good dinner and moderate intake of wine we allowed plenty of time to find the studio, where we were expected at eleven p.m. The show was very definitely 'on air' when we arrived and without any of the usual formalities we were both shown straight into the lion's den. Unforgivably I have forgotten the name of the presenter, although anyone within spitting distance of Miami will know who it was. When he saw that we had entered the room he broke off mid-sentence and announced to his listening audience that 'The Brits have arrived.' A loud burst of 'Rule Britannia' followed. After some introductory joshing he flicked on some music and explained that the price he paid for success was that lots of local businesses wanted to use the programme to advertise. He showed us the lengthy script for the commercial breaks and pointed out the one he had earmarked for us to read! Although I protested that I was normally well behind the plate glass at this stage, he would have none of it. After a certain amount of royal-talk Stephen went first with a piece in praise of a local bank. Several records later I was introduced to the unsuspecting public and proceeded to extol the virtues of a Miami auto showroom that had the Rolls-Royce dealership. The two hours we spent in the company of this remarkable man flashed by at astonishing speed and we were both very sad when the time came to leave. It was definitely a high note on which to end our marvellous three weeks.

But the fun wasn't quite over yet. As a treat before we went our separate ways, Stephen had arranged for us to spend the weekend in Key West, the furthest extremity of the United States. For him in particular it was an opportunity to relax after weeks of tension and anxiety. Small wonder that we had forty-eight hours of memory-numbing excess. Looking back there was just one tiny cloud that hovered over us, but so high up that it was easily ignored. Among the people we met stories were circulating about a mysterious new illness that was affecting gay men in cities such as New York and San Francisco. But no one had any reliable information about it, and some simply dismissed it as a sick joke.

We flew back to Kennedy together on the Sunday evening so that I could take the overnight flight to London. Macmillans had a lot more exposure planned for Stephen and it was to be many months before I saw him again.

T he many years of my devotion to Alan the butcher had produced
a radical change in my social life. When I was not actually with him
I waited around on the off-chance that he might call, and any
arrangement that was made to see other friends invariably included
him. Although the inhabitants of the gay world were always, not
surprisingly, happy to see him, among my straight friends his
presence was sometimes difficult to accept. My only other emotional
involvement was still with Alex, but it was a watered-down version
of our original relationship. His youth and good looks brought him
lots of admirers and I was soon to lose him altogether for a number
of years.

Alex had fallen for Richard, a man of about my own age, who was
ex-army and had been married. It is not for me to say what Richard's
attraction might have been, as I never met him, but a smart public
school background and private means are things that would have
worked in his favour as far as Alex was concerned. Like so many of us,
whether consciously or not, he needed a degree of status and a lot of
security and life with Richard held the promise of both. He broke the
news to me one day that they had decided to set up home together in
Yorkshire, where Richard had found a good job. They moved into a
small farm not far from Leeds, where Richard would work. Alex
managed to find employment too and set about decorating the house
in his spare time. But he derived most pleasure from fulfilling his
dream of returning the outbuildings and small area of grazing to their
original use. A dog and a horse came first, but they were soon followed
as funds permitted, by hens, a small flock of sheep and some calves.
Farmer Mear was in business! To the locals and interested observers

they passed themselves off as cousins sharing a house – a deception that probably fooled no-one, but which was regarded as necessary by both of them.

After ten years of happy 'bed and breakfasting' my mother, facing seventy, decided to leave Mevagissey and move closer to her offspring. But there was a limit as to how far she would go to be near John, his wife Susan and son, John Peter, who were at RAF Kinloss in Perthshire. Kent, she felt, was a reasonable compromise, and she settled into a little modern house at New Ash Green near Wrotham. I drove down to see her most weekends and took her out to lunch or to visit local places of interest. But after she suffered a mild stroke, which mercifully only slightly affected her left hand, we decided to go the whole hog and move her into London. The price she could get for her house meant that she could afford to buy a decent one-bedroom flat somewhere near me. Thanks to my privileged position and a depressed market I was soon able to put together a list of likely properties. She came to stay and I took her on a tour of inspection. Quite by chance the one she fell in love with, and far and away the most suitable, turned out to be a ground-floor flat with its own little yard just a stone's throw from me in Aynhoe Road. What had once been a house, was converted in the sixties to three separate units by a dancer with the Royal Ballet called Petrus Bosman, whom I had briefly known. Her new home was an immediate success and she soon became a well-known figure in the area, as well as a regular visitor to the office, where she enjoyed being fussed over by the girls. At her suggestion I gave her a key to my flat so that she could do a little tidying and take away the laundry she claimed to enjoy doing. At the same time I got into the habit of suggesting that she came over whenever I was having people to supper. She was obviously always thrilled to be included and accepted with alacrity, even though she knew that a boiled egg at six suited her better than something indigestible from a casserole at nine. The subject of mothers and their reaction to homosexual sons is one that has often been discussed, but in my own case – if we ignore the 'drag' of childhood – she had very little reason to be suspicious. After all, she knew very well that I had always numbered girls among my closest friends and enjoyed meeting them. But it was certainly the Aynhoe Road supper parties that gave the game away. It was not that they were always entirely 'stag' affairs, but I suppose there was usually a male bias. I remember once extending an invitation and being asked, with a degree of gleeful anticipation, 'Will it be all boys?'

When Stephen finally returned after his extended stay in the States his first priority was to find somewhere to live. It just so happened that Johnny, after far too long (I was a firm believer in everyone moving at least every two years!) in a flat in Barons Court, decided to house-hunt at the same time. More out of friendship than a burning desire to live in Brook Green they turned to me for help. But after several joint viewing sorties with me wearing my Marlowe, Hunting & Worsley hat (or more probably, pullover, as Cheryl had knitted me a striking little number in the firm's colours of yellow and blue, with a border depicting a row of assorted houses) they both decided that they preferred the idea of Fulham. Johnny went on to buy a four-bedroom house near Zoe in Parsons Green while Stephen splashed out a large chunk of his American earnings on a newly converted flat in Harcourt Terrace. The terrace was actually a continuation of Hollywood Road, where I had once lived, but the intervening years had seen a marked improvement in its social standing. Stephen bought the first floor, which had lovely high ceilings but a disappointingly small bedroom, kitchen and bathroom. But these were details that he happily disregarded, as the flat's outstanding features were the large sitting room and enormous south-facing roof terrace, two things he had set his heart on. He was thrilled with his new home and delighted that at last he had a base for the life he shared with Richard, his devoted young boyfriend. They soon made friends with Eric Morecambe's son Gary, who lived on the ground floor, and were treated occasionally to the wafted piano playing of John Ogdon, another near neighbour.

When a house-warming was planned, Stephen had the brilliant idea of tenting the terrace as a hedge against inclement weather and to double the space for serious partying. It made such a wonderful room that he even considered retaining it as a permanent fixture. The evening got off to rather a slow start and it looked at one stage as if guests were going to be outnumbered by staff. But by eight-thirty the ratio had changed and the waiters were hard pressed to slake some serious thirsts. Exactly as Stephen had intended, it was a gathering that brought together all the strands of his life. His family of four siblings was represented by his adored sister Titch and her handsome husband Malcolm, Unity arrived with Ingrid Seward, the indomitable editor of *Majesty* and her boyfriend Ross Benson, who had recently separated from Beverley, and there was a small group from a couple of palaces as well as two of the Prince's old girlfriends. I knew so many of the people there – and in a number of cases was the link between them and Stephen – that it was very late indeed before I got round to them all. Happily our host shared my belief that a party was not over until there was nothing left to drink, even though he was famous for taking a quick nap halfway through the evening.

The next day's hangover proved to be a big league job and with little chance of an early night to aid recovery. Thanks to a complete lack of forward planning I had saddled myself with the prospect of friends coming to supper. But fortunately I knew that my two guests, both remarkable women, would be sympathetic to my plight. In fact Jane had also been at the party, but her weakness was always plate- rather than bottle-driven, even though the slenderness of her figure would suggest otherwise. She and I had met when, after a long and distinguished service to estate agents, she fetched up at Pettigrews in the Masbro Road. In her spare time she did voluntary work for the Royal Marsden Hospital and was known to be interested in medicine generally. But she surprised us all one day by announcing that she was going to work as secretary on the AIDS ward at the Middlesex. In spite of poor pay and the deaths of patients who had become her friends, she found the work richly rewarding.

'Naughty' Jane Healing (her infant nephew George just failed to get his tongue round 'Auntie', hence the sobriquet) holidayed with me from time to time, twice in Provence and once quite memorably in Cyprus. We went there to take pot luck for a week with Robin Guilleret, hiring a car at the airport. I sensibly failed to take my driving licence, which meant not being allowed to drive and many happy hours lolling on the back seat – taking in the scenery and enjoying mid-morning siestas. We loved everything about the island except the food, which was undoubtedly a lasting legacy of British colonial rule. However, we did manage to find one restaurant that became a favourite, in spite of being called 'Old Salamis'. They had a way with a chip that no other establishment managed to achieve, but failed miserably with the king prawns. We ordered some as a treat on our last night, but found to our horror that they were served boiled. The highlight of our trip, though, was an after-dinner visit to a bar in the little town of Paphos, which was obviously popular with the local lads. The evening got off to a good start when we were greeted in flawless Cockney by the owner, who had been a Stoke Newington-based cab driver for twenty years. He sweetly gave us the first drink 'on the house' and then suggested that we ran up a tab to be settled by Jane, who had charge of the kitty, when we called it a day. We had only just begun to take in our surroundings when Jane, one of the few ladies present, was whisked away from us on to the dance floor by a solidly built native. Although there were already a number of male couples smooching around, Robin seemed to be too busy eyeing up the talent to do the decent thing as far as I was concerned. As the night wore on and perspiration flowed freely it became apparent that Jane's partner was not going to take no for an answer, denying her even the smallest break between dances. Robin and I watched all this with amusement, while at the same time trying to be witty and fascinating to two young men whose command of English left much to be desired. At last Jane dashed for freedom when her admirer answered the call of nature. Breathless with exhaustion she explained that she was too knackered to dance one more step and was running out of dry bits of her partner's body to hold. I told her that the only way to get rid of him was to plead old age and infirmity and point out that one of us was her boyfriend – however ludicrous either statement might seem. When they were reunited a heated discussion took place until Jane finally undid the sweater that had been tied round her waist and handed it over. My first reaction was that, as it was an uncharacteristic and particularly nasty pinky grey creation in shaggy wool, he had probably offered to dispose of it for her, but as he clasped it to his bosom I began to have second thoughts. He left the bar with a happy smile on his face and a greatly relieved Jane came to join us. She and Robin were convinced that he had gone off with a memento of the love that might have been, whereas I was sure that he had coveted the sweater from the moment he had first seen it. After all that excitement Jane was clearly ready for bed and so we headed for the bar to get the bill from our host. Having studied the long piece of paper at length our friend, who is normally rather sound where money is concerned, suddenly exclaimed, 'This can't possibly be right! It must be more than this', and proceeded to double the amount of drachma for which we had been asked. Robin looked distressed but managed to regain his composure and encouraged our new friends to join us as we headed for the waiting taxi.

The other lass who came that night to Aynhoe Road expecting supper was, among many other things, a glamorous grandmother with a particularly unlikely nickname. As far as her parents were concerned she was called Eileen Alice, but with James as her surname she was known to one and all as 'Jimmie'. We met for the first time at a supper party held by Robin and Gerald, who were her neighbours in Addison Gardens. She proved to be delightful and amusing company and our relationship blossomed until I had too much to drink and discovered that she had been married three times. Looking back I suppose the concept of three stabs at matrimony led me to a series of wrong assumptions, and it wasn't until I had quizzed her relentlessly on the subject that I realised how wrong these had been. As I sat shame-faced beside her she took the trouble not to tell me to mind my own business, but to explain that each marriage had been supremely happy and had only ended when her husbands died.

I soon discovered that Jimmie had a special reason for making an allowance for my drunken behaviour that evening. Although nothing stronger than a spicy tomato juice had passed her lips for thirty years, she had once suffered from alcoholism. Over dinner in her flat one evening she told me the story of the battle she fought and of how she emerged victorious. When her brother realised the extent of the problem he took her to see a fellow sufferer and friend of his in York, with a view to attending a meeting of Alcoholics Anonymous. In her hotel bedroom she was horrified when he asked her to hand over any bottles in her suitcase, and protested vigorously when he insisted on carrying out a search. She was very unhappy when he took away two bottles of brandy. After a dreadful night she got up early and went out into the city in the hope of finding some liquid sustenance. After a desperate and fruitless search she found a pub and roused the landlord from his bed on the pretext of feeling unwell. Confronted by an elegant lady in a state of some distress he invited her inside and asked if there was anything he could get her that might help. She sipped two large brandies with as much obvious distaste as she could muster and left the bemused publican to return to her hotel. Her brother and his friend had been searching for her frantically, fearing the worst, but after much persuasion she went with them to the meeting. It is an enormous tribute to Jimmie and to AA that she has not touched alcohol from that day to this. In the intervening years she has repaid her debt to the organisation by making herself available to support and advise anyone who needs help. (I have occasionally asked her about my own relationship with the bottle, but she has assured me that although bouts of heavy drinking should be avoided they do not mean that I am ill – just stupid!) She has also written a detailed and very moving account of her battle, which she hoped to get published for the benefit of the membership. With that end in view I introduced her to Unity in the hope that one of her literary or journalistic contacts might be able to help. They had several very happy meetings and Unity too was greatly affected by what she read, although she had to admit that from a commercial standpoint it was fatally flawed. The problem lay in the fact that when writing it Jimmie had adhered scrupulously to the AA code of complete anonymity, making no mention of her name, background or the fact that she was the granddaughter of Sir John Everett Millais the distinguished artist. Had those details been in place, however, what was undoubtedly a remarkable story, would soon have been in print.

I have never acquired much in the way of kitchen skills, in spite of bouts of relentless enthusiasm. Following even the simplest recipes, such as one for a horror called sausage stroganoff, has almost always led to the consumption of a lot of bread and cheese. I now know and accept my limitations and only open the oven door to slide in a hunk of meat or plump bird to be roasted, along with as many suitable vegetables as I can muster. The night that Jimmie and Jane came to feast was no exception, but happily for us all the prospects for the evening increased considerably when Stephen rang to propose a last-minute change of plan. He and Richard had decided to enjoy a few more hours under silk-lined canvas before the stately edifice was dismantled the next day. He said they had managed to round up some faithful regulars and insisted that I bring my guests to join the party. The girls seemed almost indecently delighted at the prospect of not having me to themselves, and it did not take long to re-equip Jimmie with her bottle of tomato juice, her cushion bag, Rosie the Tibetan spaniel and Rosie's rug, before bundling her into Jane's car and heading for SW10. We arrived to find a table in the tent laid with about a dozen places and other guests ready to party.

Marlene, who had a Rubensesque figure and a personality to match, was the one I was most pleased to see. Her career in selling had taken her from bondage to bonds and she had a passion for elaborate footwear, schnauzers and a saxophonist called Bimbo who was half her size. Once the party got going she and Jimmie, neighbours at the table, became best friends, although it is difficult to imagine what they might have talked about. Our hosts had cleverly augmented the left-overs with other delicious things to create a great supper, and everyone agreed that it was an even better evening than its progenitor.

In the summer of 1983 I was asked to value a flat in Matheson Road, West Kensington, just off the North End Road. It proved to be the ground floor of a corner house with its own entrance and an unloved garden dominated by an enormous plane tree. I met the owners there and they guided me through the hall and three empty but newly decorated rooms. I knew the moment I took in the high ceilings, original fireplaces and elaborate plasterwork that it was destined to be mine, and said as much to the vendors. They reacted favourably to my enthusiasm and expressed no interest, in spite of my insistence, in getting valuations from other agents. Back in the office I discussed my predicament with the rest of the gang, who all agreed that I should go in high and offer the asking price that I recommended. Later in the day I rang the owners at home and said that I thought the flat was worth something in the high eighties and that an asking price of £95,000 was worth a punt. I offered that amount, they accepted it and the deal was done. In the days that followed I found a buyer prepared to pay £60,000 for Aynhoe Road, my home for nine years. At the same time I was comforted by Amanda from the office, who liked Matheson Road, but said I was paying too much for it; Stephen and Richard, who loved it; and by Jane's dog Nell, who gave it her seal of approval by peeing over the hall's tiled floor.

As luck would have it, Marlowe Hunting & Worsley, after a long struggle, was beginning to make some money. Even after Cheryl had taken her cut and the nanny had been paid there was still enough left for me to buy some carpeting, a cooker and one of Mr C.P. Hart's lovely shower screens. But that did not mean that I was not grateful for the gift of a modern set of table and chairs and curtains for the dining room from Jane and Stephen Spencer, who were giving their house a facelift. Having a proper dining room for the first time was certainly one of the real treats of the new flat, and as Christmas approached I decided to put it to good use by doing lunch on Christmas Day for anyone who was around. Mama was the first to accept an invitation and had my room for two nights while I slept on the divan in the dining room. Daphne also expressed a desire to come as David Petrie, her long-term boyfriend and recent husband, would be working on the day. The other guests were Philippe and his Anglo/American boyfriend Chris, an old friend called David Clark and Derek, who worked as a graphic designer. My friendship with David reached right back to my Palace footman days when he was involved with Edward Jones, my handsome Welsh colleague. He was in his early twenties then, with angelic good looks and a reputation as the rising star of Sotheby's furniture department. After a long career in

Bond Street he went solo and used his wealth of knowledge as a freelance valuer of fine things. As his contribution to the festivities he offered to bring some serious wine to go with lunch. On the day he was as good as his word and presented me with two very impressive magnums of nineteenth-century Lynch Barges Bordeaux that he said were a gift from the d'Erlanger family, for whom he had done some work. Although I was a keen guzzler of wine I had always chosen quantity above quality and missed, therefore, the full significance of these two bottles. It was some time before I was told that they were worth a great deal of money.

By the appointed hour of one o'clock all the guests except Chris had arrived and were being subjected to the sort of champagne cocktails that were best consumed in the sitting position. Chris had telephoned to say that he was running late as he had been to see his mother and was having difficulty finding a cab. We all agreed that we should wait – although Mama was reluctant – and I recharged the glasses. Our main course, a fat goose, seemed, under the circumstances, to be chugging along quite happily in the oven, although as I had never cooked one before I was not at all certain what to expect. As two o'clock struck a hot and bothered Chris burst onto the scene and refreshed himself with mineral water while I topped up the other glasses with a final round of the lethal brew. Much to Mama's relief those of us still capable of movement made it to the table over an hour later than I had planned. Once the smoked salmon was polished off I heaved out the long-suffering bird and thought at first that it had not suffered unduly after its extended incarceration. But to my horror, with a fork in its breast it collapsed like an exposed Grande Marnier soufflé. All I could do was to remove the bones from the husk that remained and dish up what was left, which looked no more appetising than the meat of an under-nourished chicken. But at least it did have the advantage of blending perfectly with the sprouts that had taken on the appearance of mushy peas and the roast potatoes that resembled misshapen chocolate truffles. Fortunately the company was in such good humour that they would have forgiven me for making any sort of culinary cock-up. And in any case they had all – apart from Mama and Chris – had their taste buds annihilated by large quantities of brandy and champagne. At this point David began to make his unsteady way around the table with the first of the large bottles of claret. In spite of repeated requests for more generous measures he treated each pouring as if it was a token at a religious ceremony. Sadly, by the time the second magnum was brought into play we had all forgotten to sniff and swirl and simply downed the precious liquid like so much Ribena. My culinary adventure reached its climax when a nasty smell of burning wafted in from the kitchen, indicating that the saucepan containing the Christmas pudding had run out of water. Once the sticky brown substance was decanted onto a plate I doused it in brandy, never thinking for a moment that it would actually catch light. But as I approached it with a lighted match flames shot into the air, stopping just short of my eyebrows and fetching paper hat. It hardly needs saying that subsequent Christmases have always been spent in the homes of other people, where my presence in the kitchen has been restricted to post-prandial tasks involving hot water and Fairy Liquid.

After Stephen's success in the States with *Royal Service*, he and Unity were keen to capitalise on his fame there by producing a follow-up book as soon as possible. Any idea of creating a work of reference had long since been abandoned in favour of a gossip-laden tome with the shameless title of *Royal Secrets*. Like the first book (famously described by Stephen as the world's largest sleeping pill) it was to contain nothing of a scandalously revelatory nature, but just the lighter side of a spoilt and rather ordinary family. Stories about them all abound and Unity grouped them together in chapters bearing the names of individual family members. When I was roped in I was happy to contribute what I could, but mostly I reminded and cajoled the author. The finished manuscript was completed in record time and despatched to Villard in New York for their approval. Realising that they had a money-spinner on their hands they accepted it at once and soon came up with agreeable terms. The only departure from the first agreement was that at Stephen's insistence Unity was to receive a share of the royalties rather than the flat fee she had been paid for the other book.

With the announcement of a publication date the Villard publicity machine cranked into life once more – media slots were booked and arrangements made for another whistle-stop tour of the nation's bibliophile hotspots. Although I never thought for a moment that the publishers would offer to stump up for me to act as handmaiden the second time around, I couldn't help thinking what fun it would be to do it all again. But I was not to be disappointed. Stephen told me had insisted that he would put on a better show with a friend to provide support, and they eventually agreed to pick up the tab. However, I learnt from Lucianne Goldberg some years later during a lengthy lunch in London that Stephen had paid the bills for both my trips out of his own pocket. At the time she was sworn to secrecy and only revealed the truth after his death.

Maddeningly, I failed to keep any sort of diary during the second tour and only remember the occasional highlight. To be sure, I flew out and met up with Stephen this time in New York, where we were ensconced once again at the Ritz Carlton with its commanding views of Central Park. Much more time was spent in the Big Bagel on this trip, thanks to demand for Stephen to appear on high-profile TV and radio shows. With Lucianne we lunched and dined at the Tavern on the Green, Sardis and the Russian Tea Room, as well as taking in *La Cage Aux Folles*. One evening Luci, who was aware of my determination to find an interesting job, got us together with a friend of hers called John Kobal, whose archive of film and theatre photographs had become big business. She knew that he was on the lookout for a new assistant and thought that I might fit the bill. But sadly, we failed to click almost at once and it was obvious to me that he was looking for a relationship that went way beyond the professional.

As far as out-of-town journeys were concerned we followed very much the same route as before and enjoyed some very happy reunions. But one diversion that I greatly enjoyed was a two-night stop at a splendid hotel called the Hay Adams, right in the centre of Washington. (I shudder to think now how much that must have cost my long-suffering friend.) As before, we met all sorts of other authors 'on the road', but the only one who sticks in my memory is a man I sat next to at Stephen's second appearance at The Plain Dealer Literary Lunch in Cleveland. His name was Kliendienst and he was the fat, sleek and suave stereotypical corporate lawyer. He had written a book about the Watergate affair and his part in it. I sat nervously next to him for an hour and a half, saying very little, but it was long enough for me to conclude that he was probably guilty of far worse things than any part in the infamous bungled break-in.

At the end of the book tour Stephen asked me which Caribbean island I would like to go to for our last weekend. As part of his job he thought he had probably been to them all, although his favourite was Eleuthera, where he had stayed with the Prince a couple of times as a guest of the Brabournes. In the end we plumped for Antigua, but ruled out the St James's Club as being too expensive, and settled instead for a hotel called Curtain Bluff. Our flight there from New York seemed at first to be perfectly normal, although from my seat beside the window it did look as if we were sticking surprisingly close to America's eastern coastline. Sure enough, after about an hour into the journey the captain announced that his navigational equipment had collapsed and that we would have to make an unscheduled landing at Miami to change planes. That little setback cost us several precious hours and meant that we reached our destination in time for dinner rather than lunch. But at the end of a long day the island proved to be lush and beautiful, with the added bonus of a jolly taxi driver who claimed to be the husband of the Minister of Tourism. The hotel itself was right by the sea, surrounded by lovely gardens and we were shown to a little bungalow on the beach where the water almost lapped at the door. It was indeed an idyllic setting and one that, during the day, I enjoyed enormously. But at night, as the lightest of possible sleepers, I found that the rhythmic sound of the Caribbean washing over tiny pebbles rendered sleep almost impossible. Happily for Stephen, who was the proverbial sleeper on a clothes line and the one who really needed to rest, the problem was confined to me and he awoke each day refreshed. We returned to New York on the Monday morning and went once more on our separate ways.

Royal Secrets sold well, although no one was surprised that it failed to make the impact of the first book. But the interest it created was enough to convince Stephen and Unity to continue their collaboration in other areas. One of the projects they had in mind was a newspaper or magazine etiquette and manners column that might have lucrative syndication possibilities. Tragically, however, neither of them was to live long enough to carry this idea forward.

In the meantime Unity continued to beaver away at the *News of the World*, have a novel published and work on the idea for the story of the birth of the American wine industry. Stephen, back in London again, continued to enjoy life to the full while at the same time giving more thought to a wine bar or restaurant. For the purposes of what he quaintly called 'research' we met often at different establishments to sample what their kitchens could produce. One of these gastronomic outings took us to one of London's horticultural wonders, the roof garden at Barkers. Judging by the size and maturity of the trees and shrubs it had been established for many years, but as a restaurant it had never really made its mark. On the day we were there very few other tables were occupied, and there was no question of having to whisper. But as we finished our first course and the accompanying bottle of wine we were aware that the other lunchers had sought shelter inside. We chose to ignore the rain, however, confident that it would only be a slight shower. When the waitress paddled out with our main course and another bottle she did her best to get us to take cover, but we were much too engrossed in our conversation to move. From then on getting more wine proved to be a problem, as the staff had difficulty tracking down an umbrella. Only then did the situation seem grave enough to force us to move, but we were so wet by then that there didn't seem to be a lot of point. Eventually a brave soul brought us coffee, but suggested leaving the bill till later. In fact, by the time we went in the rain had stopped and we were greeted by the staff with towels and a round of applause. The management very sweetly only charged us for the booze – pointing out that the food must have been a washout!

Another occasion was a marathon Sunday lunch at Pontevecchio in

Earls Court. By the time we sat down the party had grown to seven or eight people and we were the last to leave at about six o'clock. From there I drove Stephen to Kennington, where he had arranged for us to call on Reggie, the Queen Mother's page, whose remarkable old father had just died. I had met Mr Wilcock on a previous visit to the flat, part of the Duchy of Cornwall estate, which he shared with his son. Although he was very deaf he loved company and enjoyed showing off the medals he had won for boxing during the course of a long army career. Billy Tallon, Reggie's colleague and constant companion, was also there that night and dispensed the strong drinks for which he was notorious. In spite of the fact that I had been drinking by then pretty solidly for six or seven hours the combination of my complete lack of will power and Billy's unwavering insistence soon found me getting the other side of a large whisky and water. As we talked about the deceased, Billy made sure that our glasses were kept up to strength, which meant that by about ten, when we got up to leave, I was making even less sense than usual. As I swayed towards the door Reg suggested that I should leave the car and take a cab, but with the resolve that only a drunk can muster I insisted that I was OK to drive. Against all the odds we made good progress towards Battersea Park and then, in two lanes of traffic, Stephen mentioned that I had just scraped the side of another car. I drove on regardless and negotiated the Queenstown Road roundabout, but emerged from it heading towards the bridge on the wrong side of the road. In the head-on crash that followed my passenger, who had made the mistake of not being as pissed as I was, saw what was about to happen and thrust his arm defensively towards the dashboard. We were helped from the wreckage by the police, who arrived promptly, and were breathalysed by them as we sat beside the road waiting for an ambulance. When it arrived Stephen was taken to hospital to have his broken arm seen to. Suddenly very sober and full of shame, I went home in a taxi.

I received my comeuppance only a few days later when the little Indian magistrate peered over his desk in the Lavender Hill court, said something about 'a great deal of alcohol', fined me seventy-five pounds and banned me from driving for two years. Stephen, in the meantime, coped whingelessly with life in a plaster cast, ordered bigger shirts from Turnbull & Asser (which he eventually gave to me) and made impossible demands on Richard's endless patience. But unfortunately the break took a long time to heal and his general health seemed to suffer as a result. I went to see him one afternoon at Harcourt Terrace when he was in bed with pneumonia and told him how much my conscience was troubled. He responded by clasping my hand and asking me to swear that what he was about to tell me was to remain our secret. He said that in spite of the anxieties of his family and those he regarded as friends his poor health was nothing to do with the broken arm. In fact, his doctors had told him that he had AIDS.

Once Stephen's arm was as good as new again everyone assumed, quite naturally, that his health would recover and that the weight he had lost would quickly be regained. But in spite of eating regularly and with meticulous care he remained a shadow of his former self. In-between long periods in hospital he was determined to resume his old social life and to see all his many friends, but he tired very easily, had difficulty walking and found swallowing an increasingly painful process. That said, he never allowed those handicaps to overwhelm him – quite the reverse, in fact. His dignity, humour and complete lack of self-pity were a shining example to us all. When I called at the flat to see him one evening he told me that he and Richard had been to lunch at a local restaurant. He explained that the food had been delicious, but that he had had even more difficulty than usual getting to grips with it. When they had finished eating a waiter handed him a card that he said was sent by a woman at a nearby table. Greatly intrigued, Stephen saw that the name printed on it was Ursula Vaughan-Williams, and that underneath she had written:

'I do not think we have met and I don't know who you are, but I just wanted to say how much I admire your courage.'

From time to time during Stephen's terrible ordeal I considered writing to the Prince and Princess of Wales to tell them how ill he was and to suggest that a basket of fruit or even a visit would mean so much to him. But, for whatever reason, I never did. However, that is not to say that they were not fully aware of his situation. Even if the Palace grapevine had not kept them fully informed, the press certainly would have done. Speculation about his health had appeared in a number of newspapers and one tabloid had even published 'before' and 'after' photographs of him. Let's face it, in the days before the AIDS-related deaths of high-profile celebrities, Stephen's suspected illness and his links to the Prince were news. Looking back, how marvellous it would have been if Stephen had been the first AIDS patient the Princess has visited. Such a gesture would have gone some way towards repaying all the kindness he had shown her. But the only contact was to be too late.

On the 4th July, 1986, Stephen's birthday, I had been persuaded to join a party at Henley Regatta. I had been to see him in hospital the day before and rang him in the morning with my greetings. Although I said that I would be back early to see him later in the day, he insisted that I should stay on and enjoy myself. Slightly the worse for wear I didn't in fact get home until about nine o'clock. The phone was ringing as I arrived, and it was Stephen to say that if I was not too tired he would love to see me. I caught a cab and was soon sitting beside his bed. At first he seemed uncharacteristically subdued, but keen to know how the day had gone. He even managed a smile when I conveyed the horror of it all. When I saw that it was time to grind to a halt he told me that he had some bad news. In a calm voice he explained that he had been seen that morning by all the specialists and that they had told him he had only three months to live. We sat in silence for what seemed like an eternity, both of us too choked to speak. He was the first to recover his composure and asked me if I would be his executor. We went on to discuss his will, to which he had obviously given much thought. And to talk about the funeral.

With Richard kneeling beside him and surrounded by his family and friends, Stephen died on the 4th October, three months to the day as predicted. At his request, the funeral service took place in a side chapel at the Brompton Oratory about a week later. So great was the crush of mourners that the authorities realised, too late, that they should have used the main body of the church. When the procession of cars containing his family and close friends drew up outside it was confronted by a wall of photographers, some clinging to railings and others standing on stepladders. As we alighted the flash bulbs went off, even though the distinguished mourner whose presence they had obviously anticipated failed to put in an appearance. The interment took place at a cemetery near Uxbridge, close to where Malcolm and Titch lived. A small group of us went to their house afterwards to join the family in some fortifying refreshment. If such a thing can be described as a party then it is not surprising that it got off to an awkward start, but as memories of the deceased started to surface and be exchanged it turned into the sort of occasion that was quintessentially Stephen. As the noise grew louder Titch took me off to a quiet corner, saying that she had something she wanted me to read. It turned out to be a letter from the Prince, passed to her by Billy, in which in his own hand and over several pages he paid a moving tribute to his faithful servant, confidant and friend.

After that remarkable interlude the rest of the day became a bit of a blur, for which I have only myself to blame. I should have taken note of the fact that my vodka and tonic was being kept at full strength by none other than Mr William Tallon, the demon pourer! However, I was eventually scooped up and taken home, having declared my love for Stephen's brothers, by my guardian angels Johnny Lyon and Margaret Hickey.

Richard stayed on at the flat in Harcourt Terrace, which he had inherited, but his life too was cut short at a tragically young age.

_16_

By the mid-eighties Marlowe Hunting & Worsley was firmly established and doing very well, in spite of the proliferation of other estate agents in the area. But my relationship with Christopher and Cheryl, who had by then produced a fourth son, was strained to say the least and I longed to get out. During that time I took a two-week holiday with Barbara in Morocco – a trip that was to have a great impact on our lives. Although Barbara, who at that time had not travelled much, had never been there, it was a country that I had visited twice before and greatly enjoyed. We chose our destination, Agadir, with great care as we both wanted to avoid the urban centres such as Tangier and Marrakech and explore the mountains and beaches of the south.

My first trip to Morocco took place in the early seventies, when I drove to Tangier with Richard Dallimore and a delightful American friend of his called Bob Filson. Through France and Spain we stayed in top-notch hotels that were way beyond my means, which makes me think that I must have been pretty heavily subsidised. On arrival we drove to the home of Michael Burn, an old chum of Richard's who was to be our host. He had a rambling house in a village just outside the city, which had the sort of spartan comfort that is only acceptable in a warm climate. I took to Michael, who seemed to me to be the archetypal Englishman abroad, at once and set my heart on using him as a role model. He had set the right tone from the outset by asking us to collect his new blazer from his tailor Henry Poole, quite the smartest in Saville Row. Even more Brownie points were earned when I found that his conversation was strewn with words like 'riveting', 'maddening' and 'strordinary' that went with a consuming passion for Scrabble. To cap it all, on day two of our holiday he scaled the heights by ploughing through sand dunes in his ancient grey Bentley to deliver us to a seaside picnic.

Michael, who was then in his early forties, had lived in Tangier for a number of years and made his living as a lettings agent for various flats and houses. His partner in the business, the Hon. Vere Eliot (known as Robert), was the larger-than-life brother of the Earl of St Germans. Although their relationship was turbulent and eventually disintegrated, they both worshipped at the altar of Englishness. In Robert's case it was manifest in his house, which was reminiscent of a Cotswold manor, complete with chintzy drawing room, open fires and a pair of pampered whippets. On Sundays he was to be found enjoying his role as sidesman at the Anglican church – a job he shared with a fellow old queen and younger son, the Hon. David Herbert, brother of the Earl of Pembroke. Sadly, their feelings for each other amounted to nothing less than cordial detestation – even in the sight of God – and every honorary Tangerine had to choose which camp they preferred to be in.

Inevitably, in due course both Michael and Robert returned to live in England and I saw them from time to time in London. But Robert, to everyone's amazement got married and moved to a house in Cornwall close to Port Eliot, his family home. Michael, in the meantime, established a superior delicatessen in Witney, although I last visited him at a caravan in a field in Hampshire where he served particularly potent Vodkatinis.

My second Moroccan experience also began in Tangier, but led to a hire car and a touring holiday. I was the guest and travelling companion of an old friend called Philip Wade who had taken early retirement after many years as Shell's man in India. He was in his mid-fifties and still good looking, but was tortured by his homosexuality and turned its concealment into an art form. Nothing gave him more pleasure than for us to be taken for father and son.

In spite of visiting places of historic interest, such as Fez and Meknes, I am ashamed to admit that the highlight of the two weeks, as far as I was concerned, was a furtive sexual encounter in the small fishing village of Essaouira. We arrived at our hotel late one afternoon to find the public rooms thronged with a collection of impossibly handsome and extremely well-built young men, later revealed to be the national football team. By the time we had unpacked and come down to dinner I assumed that they would be tucked up in bed like well-disciplined athletes. But to my delight, they were still very much in evidence and obviously not adhering too closely to the Muslim code of alcoholic abstinence. After we had eaten, Philip and I returned to the crowded bar and managed to grab a couple of chairs, but after one Scotch my companion announced that he was going to have an early night. I said that as I was not particularly tired I would stay on a bit longer. With his departure I was able to absorb even more of the scenery, without wishing to appear transfixed.

Clutching my second whisky and water I began to be aware that in one of the groups of roistering young bucks my glance was being returned with the hint of a smile. As our eyes met more often the smile of the tall dark stranger grew broader and I started wondering what on earth I was going to do next. Having weighed up the possibilities, and emboldened by heather juice, I got out of my seat and sauntered out of the bar towards the hall. I paused there for a moment to make sure I had been seen and then slowly climbed the staircase. On the first floor I went into my room, leaving the door open. Having paced about a bit and opened a few drawers I returned once more to the corridor and saw that the object of my interest was standing in a doorway at the far end. When he saw me I beckoned and he headed rather unsteadily in my direction. When I shut the door behind him we shook hands, exchanged names and soon discovered that neither of us had more than a little basic French with which to communicate. However, we soon got down to basics when a wad of dirhams changed hands (I am sure you can guess which way) and he suggested an act of intimacy that I thought was too much for a first date. But as his trousers were by this time round his ankles I decided to demonstrate the sort of tackle his counterparts in England always enjoy. For a while all went well, but just when I was beginning to wonder if either of us could think of the French for 'brewers droop' he removed himself and stumbled into the bathroom. There followed the sort of sound that made me realise that his position in the team can have had nothing to do with accuracy in front of the goal posts.

He emerged shame-faced and muttering apologies. With a gentle kiss on the cheek he returned my, by this time, rather damp collection of notes and beat a hasty retreat.

Alas no such excitement awaited us in Agadir, but Barbara and I had fun nevertheless, in spite of a disappointing first impression. Because the old town had been destroyed by a massive earthquake in the sixties the new one that had sprung up in its place lacked the ancient charm that came with narrow alleyways and a maze of souks. Old Morocco hands compared it unfavourably with the country's old cities and regarded it as brash and nouveau – suitable only for packages of German queens. But once we started exploring we soon discovered that it had a great deal to offer. For a start it sat beside a nine-mile stretch of perfect golden sand and enjoyed a winter temperature that never fell below seventy. The best place for lunch was in the heart of the truly bustling port, where the freshest of fish was served at trestle tables in small open-air restaurants. In the evening the small-scale centre of the town was the focus of activity, with crowded pavement cafes and good places to eat. At one of these we got into conversation with a young teacher called Mohamed, whose brother was married to an Englishwoman and lived in London. He soon became a great friend and enthusiastic guide. Sadly his school could only afford to pay him for about two days work a week, but at least that left him with lots of time to gallivant with us. When we hired a car he came on trips through the fertile citrus-growing area to the fabled walled city of Taradont and down the coast to Massa, the World Wildlife Fund's estuary haven for birds.

Late into most nights and over innumerable bottles of wine Barbara and I talked long and hard about life and what we were going to do with it in the future. She, like me, was looking for a change, and a radical one at that. For some time she had been considering the possibility of selling her Barons Court flat and moving out of London, an idea to which I had also given much thought. As the end of the holiday drew nearer we both agreed that in Agadir we had found somewhere that could make us both happy, and decided that once she had sold her flat and I had extricated myself from MH&W we would come back again for a much longer stay and look into the possibility of buying a house to run as a small hotel.

For about twenty years, from the mid-sixties onwards, I had an open invitation to Sunday lunch at a house in the heart of Covent Garden. My host, Leslie Sympson, had worked for years for Marley Tiles, but more recently had the unenviable task of flogging a pretty disgusting sort of 'Complan' substitute called 'Supro'. He and his four siblings had been born in the first quarter of the century at a house in Lincoln's Inn, where their father worked for a firm of solicitors. After the Second World War, Sympson senior had the good sense and foresight to buy, at a knock-down price, a row of houses in a picturesque alleyway called Goodwin's Court, just off St Martin's Lane, that were condemned and due to be demolished. Thanks to the old man's efforts the houses were restored and Goodwin's Court, with its gas lamps and bow windows, became one of the most attractive streets in theatreland.

When I appeared on the scene, thanks to an introduction from Malcolm Higgins, who worked with Stupenda at Kensington Palace, Leslie lived at the Bedfordbury end where the court narrowed to a passage, with brother Tony's house opposite. Leslie's neighbour was his identical twin Clifford, and the three boys shared with their sister Eve, who was married and lived in Liverpool, the ownership of the rest of the court. Brother Henry had lost his life during the war.

Tony was a character actor who, although he never made the big time, was well known in the profession and always in work. He and his wife Jill were famous for their theatrical parties, and the first one I remember attending celebrated the opening of the musical *Pickwick* in which Tony had a part. Their tall, narrow house with its small rooms was a difficult venue for entertaining a large group of people, but Harry Secombe, the star of the show, held court in the kitchen while

Dougie Bing, the legendary female impersonator, dominated one of the bedrooms. On the stairs Stupenda and I bumped into Dickie Davies, the sports commentator, and his wife, who were old family friends. We were on our way to the bathroom where we were told that Nancy Spain was being outrageous. Sure enough, we found her sitting on the bath eating cherries and throwing the stones down the plughole, whilst telling wicked stories to anyone who could squeeze between the loo and the washbasin. After we had paid rapturous attention for quite some time, she edged her way towards us so that we could exchange names. That meeting, despite the unlikely setting, was to lead to a friendship that lasted until the plane crash that snuffed out her life. She particularly loved Stupenda and revelled in his gifts as raconteur and mimic. The Ivy was her favourite place to meet us and she invariably arrived there with a rather limp photographer friend called Laon Maybanke, who contributed even less to the proceedings than I did. But one evening she appeared alongside a woman with whom, she said, she had just spent three days in bed – a blue-rinsed grandmother called Dolly Goodman with a big personality and a body to match.

I was otherwise engaged scraping mud off wellingtons and throwing logs onto fires at Sandringham when Nancy gave a house-warming for the new home she shared with Joan Wernher-Laurie. But Stupenda went and had a marvellous time, spending most of the evening in earnest conversation with a young pop singer called Paul McCartney and his girlfriend Jane.

I was on duty at Buckingham Palace on the Saturday afternoon of the Grand National when the news came through that Nancy had been killed. It was a short life and there was so much that she had wanted to say. The only thing I have of hers is a copy of the book she wrote about her forebear, Mrs Beaton. It is inscribed, 'Darling Guy, don't ask me why but I love you. Love me too, Nancy.'

Lunches on Sunday chez Leslie followed a time-honoured pattern. Guests were bidden to arrive at twelve forty-five and shown up to the first floor sitting room, where they were served a glass of sweet sherry. (In later years, and under pressure, Leslie also introduced dry sherry and a choice of spirits – as long as they went with bitter lemon.) Soon after one we were summoned to the ground-floor dining room to take our places at the large mahogany table. Young men like myself then leapt into action, washing the sherry glasses and dishing up the soup (or Supro!). Placement was pretty arbitrary, but Leslie always sat at the head, with Tony at the other end. In Tony's absence his place would be taken by David Dell, an ex-lodger of Tony's who became a big cheese in the civil service. If David failed to appear my long service was usually rewarded with an invitation to take the chair. In the early days numbers at these gatherings could be anything from eight to fourteen, but as Leslie grew older they were sometimes restricted to four or six. The hard core was always Leslie, Clifford, Tony and Jill – although the latter, who had a colossal timing problem, always had to collect her plated main course from the oven when she arrived at one forty-five. The latest arrival of all was the octogenarian concert party star, Gordon Henson, who lived nearby and whose darkly toupeed head was always awash with bay rum. From time to time the ranks of the young male guests, usually connected with the theatre, were swelled by theatrical friends like Wayne Sleep, Patricia Routledge, Judy Campbell and Roger Reece. Ralph Reader occasionally came too, to see again the elderly twin Scouts who were the stars of his early 'Gang Shows'. An actor called Tony Warren was also sometimes among the guests. At the start of his career he had been obliged by Equity to change his name from Simpson to avoid confusion with his older colleague. But he will go down in history as the originator of *Coronation Street*, and still gets a mention in the credits.

The main course was always a joint of lamb or pork, roast potatoes and white cabbage. When it was ready – which was more likely to be closer to eleven than one, as Leslie only enjoyed eating meat and vegetables that were either completely limp or rock hard – everyone trouped into the kitchen and attempted to control the quantities that Leslie happily piled onto their plates. At the same time the more active among us would wash up the soup bowls. Wine was never served, unless a guest happened to bring some, but jugs of lemon cordial were placed on the table. Clearing up after the main part of the meal, including saucepans, invariably meant that the unlucky washer and dryer missed pudding, and possibly cheese, altogether. But at least it meant that by the time we got to the coffee stage the kitchen was immaculate, with very little left to do. The very last job of all was the ritual polishing of the table, when an ancient electric floor-polisher was hoisted on to the surface to restore the gleaming patina.

Nature had ensured that Leslie and Clifford could be cast in the roles of Tweedledum and Tweedledee, for not only were they physically identical but they also tended to wear similar double-breasted suits and bow ties. But anyone who got to know them well soon saw that there were differences. Basically, Leslie was a worrier who believed in God and worked hard for the church of St Clement Danes. Clifford, on the other hand, had anger and was famous for firing off ill-conceived letters to those in positions of authority. Part of his basement was arranged as a comfortable and well-stocked bar, while Leslie used his to store his bottles of largely undrinkable home-made wine.

At one of Leslie's lunches I made friends with a young Guildhall School music student called Ashley Barrow who, with his friend – a tenor called Laurence Dale – had been brought to the house by Malcolm. Ashley lived with a Royal Ballet dancer called Michael Crookes, who never appeared, but who was described by Leslie as being extremely handsome. At the time Michael's absence was explained by the fact that he was often on tour, but I subsequently discovered that Leslie's lunches were not really his scene. When I heard from Leslie that Ashley was very ill and in hospital, I went to see him. I arrived bearing an unsuitably weighty biography of Truman Capote to find that Michael and his mother were at the bedside. I remember thinking at once that he was one of the most handsome and charming men I had ever met. Poor Ashley had lost a lot of weight and looked far from well.

My mother died aged eighty-two in the spring of 1988. John and Sue and young John Peter came down from Scotland for the funeral, which was held at Golders Green crematorium. In the presence of a remarkable turnout of friends her ashes were scattered where other members of her family had been laid to rest.

Later that year MH&W was approached by a large building society, through a Fulham agent, with a view to buying the business. Negotiations were protracted in the extreme, but in the end a deal was concluded and a date in October agreed for completion. On the morning of the fateful day I travelled with Cheryl and Christopher to our accountant's office in Aldwych to collect the money. At lunch time I walked in to Marlowe Hunting & Worsley for the last time to say goodbye to Amanda, Melanie and Caroline, who were staying on with the new regime. I found it very difficult to speak when they presented me with a suitcase as a farewell gift.

Barbara, in the meantime, had sold her flat and was staying with her sister Pauline in Portsmouth. There was now nothing to prevent us from carrying out our plan to go off to Agadir for three months and discover what destiny had in store. But before the adventure began I decided to give a party, and rather unwisely chose the eve of our departure as the date for it. Invitations were despatched and a pleasing number of acceptances returned. One that gave me a lot of pleasure was from Alex, who was going to make the journey from Ludlow for the occasion. Some months before it had become apparent that life on the farm had turned sour. I had started to receive gin-fuelled late-night telephone calls during which I was spared no detail of the breakdown of his relationship with Richard. During the course of one angry monologue I agreed to go there for a weekend when his erring partner would be visiting his elderly parents in Devon. In fact, the couple of days I spent there were a great success – quite like old times. It was great to be introduced to the farm's four-legged inhabitants and to be shown something of the beauty of the Dales. Some weeks later I went again when Richard was once more away from home. But in spite of the fun we had together it was obvious that Alex was deeply unhappy and I could only suggest that he made a clean break. Soon after that he moved back to Shropshire to begin a new life, accompanied by his faithful friends Nero the horse and Ben the Great Dane.

Barbara came to stay for the party and did a lot to make it a success. Alex stayed too and joined in the stumbling attempt at clearing up when the last guest had departed, though more than three months later I was still finding forgotten glasses in overlooked corners! Feeling as rough as old buggery we sent off the next morning in the VW Golf that I had taken with me from the business. Our destination, Plymouth, had been chosen because we had decided not to drive all the way, but to cut out France. Later that day we sailed for Santander. The journey through Spain was dull and uneventful but, as luck would have it, we hit Madrid at the height of the rush hour. Although Barbara had received detailed directions from the friend she had arranged to meet there, I had the greatest difficulty finding a way of leaving the many-laned motorway that raged through the centre of the city. We were swept along on it first one way and then the other, engulfed in a tide of Madridois whose aim was to get to their homes as quickly as possible. After several abortive attempts I managed to turn into a side street and, with no sign of a parking space, double-park the car while we fell into the nearest bar. A couple of nourishing glasses later Barbara's shattered nerves were sufficiently under control for her to try to reach her contact by telephone. But to no avail. In the end we sought sanctuary in lots more wine before booking into a nearby and decidedly over-starred hotel.

Moderately refreshed, we found that leaving the capital the next morning was a markedly less gruelling experience, especially as our route to Valencia was clearly sign-posted. We were on our way to spend a couple of nights at a little hotel that was run by two people I knew only slightly, in the village of Gauchos.

The owners, Bill Job and Jose Gonzales, had built up the business over a number of years, having moved there from a highly regarded antique shop in the Pimlico Road. They had been partners – in every sense of the word – for over thirty years although Bill, who was a very dignified Australian, had also had some success as an actor. This remarkable relationship began one evening when, quite by chance, Bill wandered into a restaurant called The Eyebrow on his own to have some dinner. He enjoyed the food so much that he asked to be able to thank the chef personally. As he was shown into the kitchen he came face to face with the man who had made his evening so pleasurable – and who was destined to transform his life henceforth. I like to think that if there had been a sunset they would have gone off into it.

I came to know them through Johnny Lyon, whose sister Mimi was Jose's devoted friend and mimic. And I soon discovered that Jose is someone it is impossible not to love. Not only does he have an outrageous sense of humour and gift for plain speaking, but he is also fluent in four languages and extremely well read. Oh, and then there is the cooking!

The little white-walled village of Gauchos is high in the Sierra Nevada, with a fine view of the distant sea. It is also, for the uninitiated at least, completely impenetrable by motor car as I eventually realised after several attempts at squeezing the VW into some ridiculously narrow streets. I gave up in the end and retreated to the car park on the edge of the village that had presumably been provided for dizzy English queens. We were given two lovely rooms, and spent what was left of the day admiring the garden, which was Bill's pride and joy. That evening, after a delicious dinner, we joined our hosts in their private sitting room for a nightcap and a good chinwag. Barbara and the boys soon became firm friends and the gales of laughter reached a climax when Jose asked her about her place of birth. He said he thought he detected a slight accent and wondered where it came from. Linguistic confusion briefly took hold when she explained that she was from Gower, leaving poor Jose with a very puzzled expression. Bill and I soon realised that purposes were crossed when they went on to discuss the golden beaches and dodgy food that Jose remembered from a holiday there. By now it was Barbara's turn to look surprised, but also very defensive of the attractions of her homeland. At this point Bill entered the fray; quietly asking his lover if there was the remotest chance that he was muddling a popular Indian seaside resort with a well-known Welsh beauty spot.

We spent the remainder of the evening having the peaks and troughs of hotel ownership pointed out to us. Not only was this a subject with which the pair of them were all too familiar, but at that stage it was even more pertinent, as they were seriously considering jacking it in. Although they loved La Posada very much they were tired of sharing it with strangers and at the same time witnessing the disfigurement of the surrounding countryside by the increasing use of plastic sheeting. We saw exactly what they meant the next day when we walked in the hills around the village, with the fields below us shining like pools of water in the sunlight.

A ferry ride the next day took us across to Tangier and just about the most northerly tip of the continent of Africa. After an overnight stop we continued to head south until we joined the procession of charabancs on the outskirts of Marrakech as they headed for the magnetic heart of Morocco. After a simple lunch we headed out of the city again towards the snow-capped range of mountains that stood proudly against the clear blue sky. We were on our way to spend a night at the Hotel de la Rose – a treat we had promised ourselves from the moment our odyssey had begun to take shape. After climbing for several hundred feet we reached our destination, which proved to be a charming combination of alpine architecture and English horticulture. The only disappointment was that, it being December, even in North Africa the roses were not at their Chelsea Flower Show best. Nevertheless, we were soon made comfortable, dined well in front of a log fire, and slept like lambs. Onwards and upwards into the Atlas Mountains the next morning until we eventually started the long descent towards the wide coastal plain and our ultimate goal.

It was lovely to be back again in Agadarling and the first thing we did was to ring Mohamed from a call box. When we met up with him he took us to the little hotel he had organised as our temporary bolt-hole until somewhere to rent had been found. Refreshingly, Agadir was not a town with too many estate agents and we soon found one that was run by a jolly queen and had the best selection of properties on its books. He arranged for us to take a month's lease on a relatively modern flat on the top floor (there were six) of the town's tallest building. In spite of draughty, ill-fitting windows we were very happy there and soon got involved with the local market and any number of cafes and bars. On Christmas Day I rose early in order to get some flowers for Barbara, who shared her date of birth (but not the year, you understand) with Jesus Christ. In the evening we carefully avoided any

Christian festivities when I took her and Mohamed to our favourite restaurant for a bibulous dinner.

Large chunks of most days were spent on the beach, where Barbara touched up her tan, read her book and swam in the warm sea. Being a more restless spirit I occupied myself with long beach walks, pattering across the sand where it was washed by the water. But the rest of the time was filled with exploratory trips to nearby villages and the surrounding countryside within a wide radius of Agadir. We were by now very attached to the town and wanted our house to be as close to it as possible. We had also worked out how much, with our combined resources, we could afford to spend and had been advised that the sum involved would buy us something suitable.

On the way back from one of our outings we saw ahead of us beside the road a couple of strapping hitch-hiking lads, and agreed without hesitation to give them a lift. We discovered in due course that our two new friends, Brahim and Hassan, were delighted that we were English and that one of us was female. They came from a large village called Tikuene, close to Agadir, and were eighteen-year-old students with English as one of their subjects. Before we dropped them off in the town they accepted our invitation to sup with us at the flat that evening, thereby setting a precedent that was to endure for the rest of our stay. Sometimes they would come by arrangement, but they would often call on the off-chance that we would be at home. The only certainty was that their visits would always include a long session of a fiendishly difficult card game called '8 Americaine', which they patiently taught us to play. We still continued to see a great deal of Mohamed and he often cooked for us at his flat, but he and the boys never became close friends.

It did not take long for Hassan and Brahim to suggest returning our hospitality by taking us to Tikuene to meet their families – an invitation I knew to be inevitable and one that I looked forward to with dread. On the appointed day we drove the short distance to the village and were surprised to see what looked like the entire population milling around. When we tracked down our hosts we asked if it was some sort of public holiday, but were told, amid much laughter, that everyone had turned out to meet the visitors from England. My companion immediately rose to the occasion, diving into the crowd shaking hands and kissing babies like a girl who was running for elected office. (I had forgotten of course that Barbara, in her National Health days, had been active in her trade union and had once addressed the TUC's annual congress!) I could only follow in her wake, feeling decidedly uncomfortable. Once inside the cool and comparative calm of Brahim's house we met both families and were served cups of unbelievably sweet mint tea and plates of even sweeter biscuits and pastries. Eventually Barbara was whisked off to a room with the giggling womenfolk, while I was left, trying to appear interesting and amusing, with the crowd of dour men who spoke no language but their own. After what seemed like an eternity dishes piled high with hot food were placed in front of us and Barbara returned with the boys to join us for lunch. Although all I wanted to do was to go home without eating, I followed our hosts' example, tearing off a hunk of bread and using it in my left hand to scoop up dollops of unidentifiable meat and vegetables. In fact the food was delicious, but I yearned for a fork – or even chopsticks.

As we drove home, exhausted, later that evening I vowed to my friend that I would never again go through such an ordeal. But of course I did – although I did feign illness to miss one visit, from which Barbara returned with her feet covered in weird henna stencilling.

When our month in the 'high rise' came to an end we moved into a cosy flat in an older building close to the beach. Various people came from England on holiday and some, like Ba's sister Pauline, stayed with us. I telephoned Alex to get him to come out, but he made the excuse that he had only ever been on a day trip to France and didn't possess a passport. With quite a lot of comings and goings we discovered, rather alarmingly, that getting a flight from Blighty that was not part of a charter or package was both difficult and expensive. A little hazard for which we had not bargained, but it came at a time when we were beginning to despair of ever finding a house in the right position that provided enough accommodation. It had begun to look as if our only option was to buy some land and throw up our own creation – but that possibility was too daunting for words. With heavy hearts we both decided to stay as planned until the end of February, but to abandon any idea of moving to Morocco lock, stock and barrel. Once the heat was off, our last few weeks were spent very happily and I even allowed myself a fling with Karim, a young waiter at a beach cafe. Fortunately Ba approved and he spent the night with me quite often. We never declared anything approaching love for each other, but he did exhibit a passion for my possessions. The radio/cassette player I could understand, but his interest in my clothes was more puzzling – he was, after all, about twelve inches shorter than I was. In the end I topped up my usual contribution to his outgoings so that he could buy the shirts of his choice, rather than wear something of mine that looked ridiculous even on me. As the date for our departure drew nearer he pleaded with me to allow him to come with us via his village, the name of which sounded remarkably like Hammersmith – but was in fact Amizmiz – so that we could meet his family. (You can imagine how that prospect appealed!) In the end I agreed but with the proviso that I should get Ba's approval first. Now as it happened, Ba was suffering largely untold discomfort from a very heavy cold, and was positively not in the mood for jolly diversions of any sort. But even after making the point that space in the car would be at a premium, she finally relented. When the day dawned it found us both with monster hangovers following an emotional farewell dinner with Mohamed, Brahim and Hassan. Feeling like death I began to fill the car, and was soon forced to acknowledge that Ba's prediction was absolutely right. Two of the largest space fillers were a couple of 'antique rugs' I had bought in Marrakech under the guidance of Mohamed's uncle, who was one of the souk's official guides. Although I am sure I paid too much I had decided to use some money left to me by Stephen for their purchase. We were also taking back carefully wrapped packages containing tagines and other assorted bits of pottery as well as raffia baskets and the sort of brightly coloured blankets that were destined to look horribly out of place. The back of the car was so full that I found other uses for the rear-view mirror and there was only a tiny space for my small, but exquisitely formed friend Karim.

The details of our one-night stand in Amizmiz should have a veil drawn over them. But if I had to choose two words to sum it up they would be 'embarrassing' and 'uncomfortable' and they both describe the fact that Karim's parents gave up their bedroom for us, thereby obliging Ba and I for the first time to occupy the opposite edges of the same mattress.

We left predictably early the next morning for Marrakech and a rendezvous with some friends of mine from London. Although by the time we arrived a degree of good humour had returned, Maggie and Phylip confessed to detecting a hint of perma-frost in the warm air as we got out of the car. After a night on the town that included belly-dancing cabaret in a restaurant we started the next day on the long haul that would take us back to Santander and the Plymouth ferry.

Barbara settled for a while in a house she bought in Southsea and then succumbed to wanderlust once more, sailing to the West Indies firstly by banana boat, and then a second time with Pauline on her boyfriend's yacht.

I returned to Matheson Road, delighted to have missed a winter, but not at all sure what to do next.

After three months away it took a little while to get back into touch with people, but one or two old friends were soon on the telephone. One of the first to ring was Leslie Sympson, who liked to spend his evenings lying on the bed with the TV control in one hand and his phone book in the other. But on this occasion he had some sad news to impart. In my absence Ashley had died after a painful struggle with AIDS. Naturally my first reaction was that it was a tragedy he died so young; then I thought about Michael, who had put his own life on hold in order to devote as much time as possible to the lover he had lived with for five years. Leslie gave me Michael's address and I decided to write to him at once, but gave up after destroying several attempts that were woefully inadequate. A few days later I thought of trying again, but before I could do so, the phone rang one evening and I heard Michael's hesitant voice at the other end of the line. After a slightly awkward chat about my trip we both talked fondly of Ashley, and I concluded by suggesting that when Michael was up to it he should come to me for supper.

He came about a week later and, on our own for the first time, we had a gentle evening with the emphasis on an exchange of interests – none of which we seemed to have in common. My only obvious cock-up was to serve something vulgar – perhaps fillet steak – only to find that it was not received with squeals of delight by my vegetarian guest.

In the hope that Michael would be ready to pick up life's pieces – in the narrowest sense – I asked him to supper again a short time after that first evening, but this time with other people present. The other guests included David Denning, one of the sweetest people I know, whose salon floor in Chester Row is no stranger to the split ends of both

Michael Heseltine and David Steel. With Michael on cracking form the evening went well and he asked if he could stay the night rather than face an uncertain journey back to his flat in Colliers Wood. When everyone else had gone we cleared away, without attempting the washing-up, and I made up the old day bed in the dining room. With teeth cleansed I paused on the way back from the bathroom to kiss him goodnight as he lay with his head on the pillow.

Not only did our friendship continue to blossom, with almost daily phone calls, but he also took up his career again by joining a small and impecunious ballet company, run by a woman called Janet Lewis, which was dedicated to touring. One weekend he arranged some time off so that he could slip away with Jane and myself to spend a couple of days with our friends Martin and Tony, who had a cottage in a village in South Wales called Newcastle Emlyn. Having collected Jane from her Ladbroke Grove flat, Michael spent the best part of the next four hours closeted in the back of the car with Jane's dog Nell as his close companion. In wakeful moments, with his guard down, he would gently tease his fellow passenger, only to be rewarded quick as a flash with a rapier-like tongue sambo. He cemented that relationship very quickly and went on to do the same with Tony's handicapped son, Andrew, for whom face painting and dam building were the greatest excitements.

After that weekend, when we had shared a room, and following much discussion, Michael made up his mind to sell the Colliers Wood flat and to move in with me. His arrival with numerous portraits of ladies diva and assoluta and books referring to the same, transformed the appearance of my shelf and wall space – to great effect. He also brought with him some favourite plants to enliven the little back garden, the only other thriving resident of which was a fecund fig tree.

Looking back on those early months of our relationship I remember nothing but undiluted pleasure, but it soon became apparent that as far as Michael was concerned, one ingredient was missing. He had always wanted a dog – and not just any old dog, but an Irish wolfhound. I sympathised of course, having grown up with Fritz and Franz and lived in later life with Tarquin and Cleo in the New Forest. But more recently I had satisfied my canine urges by acting as temporary guardian to

Effie, Gerald's extraordinary four-legged friend, when he was out of the country. She had come into his life quite suddenly one day when he was walking along a street and became aware of something at his side. Looking down he met the gaze of a dog neither corgi nor Labrador, but a cross between the two. With no indication from whence she came or what she might be called, she followed him home; he called her Effie, after Jimmie's grandmother, and allowed her to take over his life. During his many absences from home she would walk with me each day to the office in Blythe Road and take up a position under my desk. On warm days she liked nothing better than to sprawl on the mat outside the open door. Never on a lead, she also came with me on valuations or to view a house, waiting quietly outside until I reappeared. She was a sea-dog too, and spent what must have been agonising hours on Robin's boat while we were sailing or stuck on a sandbank. I was inspired once to write a poem about her, but nothing remains on paper and all I can remember is:

> *'Effie doodle dandy, queen of all the world*
> *Robin brings you from the shore when you've walnut whirled.'*

When she stayed with me for the last time she was very slow and obviously in some distress. Soon after Gerald collected her he rang me to say that she had passed away, and speech became impossible for me.

Michael and I went off to Battersea to see if we could find the dog of our dreams. As I fully expected to fall in love with at least half a dozen, I was ill-prepared for the scene with which we were confronted. Narrow aisles ran between long rows of large cages, the occupants of which were the most unattractive collection of animals I had ever seen. As we passed by, wild-eyed Alsatians jostled muscley Rottweilers to get our attention while angry Dobermans bared their teeth. We did pause briefly in front of a quivering greyhound sitting forlornly in a corner, but soon moved on. Increasingly depressed, we quickened our pace, the search obviously hopeless. But just as we were approaching the exit I spotted an avenue that we had overlooked. I persuaded Michael to follow me down it, just in case. Although most of the cages were empty I could see that one at the end was occupied by a little white figure that was watching our every move. Drawing closer I saw that she was some kind of terrier, with a rough coat and very bright eyes. When I knelt down an arrow struck my heart as she licked my finger and wagged her stumpy tail. A notice fixed to the wire declared – 'GYP, 5-year-old female, well trained and good with children'. In spite of mutterings from Michael about wolfhounds, I rushed to claim her at once and discovered that she was actually a Parson Jack Russell and had only arrived that morning. The sad story of her presence there revealed that her five years to date had been spent as boon companion to an old age pensioner whose health had begun to deteriorate. Gyp's elderly mistress was forced to leave her flat and move into a nursing home – an institution that did not allow its residents to keep pets. I often used to think about that poor old lady, but I knew she would be happy that Gyp had gone to a good home.

Without further ado we bundled Gyp into the car and drove to Wimbledon Common to see how she would react to a major frolic. I parked behind the windmill and then we headed across country with Gyp off the lead and making all the running. But she stopped every few yards and turned her head to make sure we were close behind. She showed a restrained interest in other dogs, though she relished a quick flirt with larger members of the opposite sex. However, the most welcome surprise of all was that she came at once as soon as she heard her name. Gyp proved to be the perfect companion and we were very soon inseparable.

After several months of inactivity I had recently joined forces with an old gardening friend called Henry Alexander who, after a useful apprenticeship at London Zoo and Clifton Nurseries, had gone into business on his own. Thanks to his charm and ability he soon had more work than he could handle and was ready to take on another pair of sensibly gloved hands. He knew me well enough to know that I could contribute nothing but enthusiasm and was prepared to let me have a go. It took a little while to adjust to being ready to clamber into Henry's van at six a.m. for the daily dash to Covent Garden Market, but it was lovely to be able to reach for old clothes rather than something newly pressed. By ten o'clock we were always famished and I easily understood why manual workers are often seen eating large quantities of food at that hour. I was very happy to join them. As far as clients were concerned our starting time was eight, whether the destination was an exquisite Hampstead garden belonging to a member of the Guinness family or a well-planted rooftop owned by a property company in Manchester Square. We also devoted a day each week to a popular Marylebone florists called Flowers by Florence, the eponymous patronne of which could often be glimpsed at dawn in the market dressed like an extra in the Ascot scene from *My Fair Lady*. Our Thursdays with Florence were spent watering and replacing house plants and window boxes in offices all over Central London. But as well as lots of little jobs she had an important contract to look after the horticultural needs of a smartish hotel called The Clifton-Ford. I was there on one unforgettable occasion, about to revive the hall's drooping palms, when my brimming watering can fell apart and shed its load all over the marble floor.

But by far Florence's most prestigious client was a member of an Arab royal family who owned a large house just off Belgrave Square. Although there never seemed to be anyone in residence the wide area either side of the porticoed front door had to be constantly supplied with anything in a pot that was big and flowering. The same was also true of the interior, where an enormous artificially lit garden played host to all manner of exotica.

On other days the variety of our work was breathtaking. A particular challenge was a small garden right beside the Thames on Chiswick Mall that was submerged twice a day at certain times of the year. But in terms of sheer hard graft there was nothing to equal the contract we won (sadly, I suspect, with the Algernon Asprey system of pricing) to landscape an office development near Banbury. Getting there each day was one thing, but then we had to find the muscle to plant semi-mature trees and spread several tons of mushroom compost made sticky and leaden by days of driving rain.

Closer to home, we also provided a weekly maintenance for a ghastly firm of Kensington High Street estate agents called Regal Estates. On my first visit, watering can at the ready, I gave everyone a cheery good morning, which was ignored, and went about my business. It was only when I was about to trickle new life into a vulgar display in the window that I heard someone addressing me.

''Scuse me,' it said, 'can't you see that those are all artificial?'

Of course, I should have realised that anything that looked so healthy couldn't possibly have been planted by Henry.

After about nine months of pretty constant work business began to drop off and I decided it was time I did a bit of drumming up. The first step I took was to place an advertisement for our services in *Gay Times*, the best-known way to attract the pink pound. Although at that time they had a small section devoted to legal advice, poodle grooming and aromatherapy, ours was the first ever horticultural ad. In it I proclaimed that 'no job was too mucky, whether it was a small paved patch or rolling acres'. Rather naively we sat back and waited for the work to flood in. Sure enough Henry took a call on the day the magazine was published, but it was from someone who only wanted to know what he was wearing. The first one I received was from a man with a husky voice who asked if we liked being watched while we were doing it, and how late at night would we be available. When half a dozen more in the same sort of vein came through we could only assume that either we had tapped unwittingly into some sort of code, or that there were an awful lot of desperately lonely queens out there. Unfortunately we only had one genuine request for a spot of gentle gardening and that proved to be from an old friend whom I had not seen for years.

Bloodied but unbowed, I turned my attention next to some of the West End's smarter florists. In fact they all sounded very interested on the telephone, but the only one to come up with the goods supplied the greenery for the Barbican concert hall. It was in the middle of December, and for £60 (which I never received) they sent me there for the day to erect and dress a Christmas tree on the side of the stage. But it was not just any old Christmas tree, it was a nasty old artificial one in interlocking pieces that stood about thirty feet high. Although the various sections had been kept in boxes, presumably since the previous year, it had still managed to attract to itself great clouds of dust with which I was soon covered. After six hours of performing a precarious balancing act I was past caring whether or not the whole edifice came crashing down mid-concert.

By now almost bereft of ideas I had just two final stabs at success. The first was a letter to the American ambassador welcoming him to his new posting and pointing out that the front of his embassy was rather letting the side down. Had he noticed, I asked, that the great concrete barrels outside the main entrance (presumably there to prevent tanks from driving up the steps) contained nothing more interesting than a few scraps of tatty ivy? I went on to point out that I represented an organisation that, for a comparatively modest sum, would be prepared to fill these vessels with the sort of flowering blooms that would be appropriate to their important setting. My letter was ignored and the ivy still sits in solitary splendour.

Nothing daunted I tried a similar tactic in a letter to the manager of the recently refurbished Ritz Hotel in Piccadilly. Was he aware, I asked, of the fact that the splendid colonnade on the north side of his landmark building was grimy and neglected? Had he considered that this architectural feature of some importance could be greatly enhanced with the addition of tubs containing small ornamental trees and colourful hanging baskets (yes, there can be a role for these questionable objects) suspended from the arches? Henry Alexander Landscape Gardener would be happy to advise. Although this letter was also treated with indifference, I couldn't help noticing on my next stroll along the 'dilly that the arcade had been tarted up a bit. But the only real change was that the door and window frames had received a fresh coat of paint in a regrettable shade of blue.

By now I had to accept that my talent did not lie in generating new business and that Henry's workload did not bring in enough money for two. Reluctantly I withdrew from the partnership. But at least I had gained a love of gardening from the experience and went on to tackle my own patch in the challenging shade of the plane tree with increased enthusiasm. With no other work on the horizon I even toyed with estate agency again, embarking on a six-week temporary stint for Maggie McKenna at the Wandsworth office she ran for John D. Wood. Although I enjoyed seeing so much of Maggie, the best part of the job was being able to drive there each day with the Gypsy Cream, aka Gyp – a treat she was used to by now – and take her for walks on the common at lunch time. JDW suggested taking me on permanently at their Chelsea office, but I was not too disappointed when it was discovered that by working there I would be in breach of the stipulation that I should not sell property within two miles of the old Blythe Road office.

While all this was going on, Michael was still gamely tutuing the length and breadth of the kingdom, although he was finding the work increasingly unrewarding. When the company was performing close to home, in places such as Dartford and Watford, I loyally – and often with Jane – went to watch his *Nutcracker* and *Sleeping Beauty*. We also had a couple of hilarious supper parties, one for the entire company and another for the colleagues to whom he was closest. As a matter of fact, in his breaks between engagements we entertained quite often. One memorable evening brought together the aforementioned Michael Cashman and two other actors with much longer careers behind them. The first was a man called Alan Mclellan who had lived for years in a rented flat near Brook Green. When, out of the blue, he inherited some money I was able to find him a much better place to buy. He took me out to dinner to celebrate and then I returned the hospitality. During the evening it emerged that although he had worked in the theatre for about forty years, it was a part in a classic film that found him his biggest audience. He appeared in *The Importance of Being Earnest* with Michael Redgrave and might easily have uttered the famous line about the handbag. But in fact the part of Lady Bracknell was played by Edith Evans and Alan, in fleeting appearances, added lustre to the role of the footman. Our other thespian guest, Annie Gough, was a distinguished actress whose brother, John Standing, was also in the profession. Since the end of her long marriage to the actor Michael Gough she had lived in a small flat in Fulham and had become one of our regular and most popular guests. As long as she was warm and allowed to smoke her More cigarettes she made no demands. But she did saddle me with the name Gaylene when she heard that Michael had been christened Cindy by his mates in the Royal Ballet.

Our first ever meeting had taken place in a departure lounge at

Heathrow, as we waited to board the same flight to Skiathos. She was in a large party that included her old friends, Annie and Peter Wigzell, whose house, by chance, Marlowe Hunting & Worsley were attempting to sell. As their agent I had been to see the Wigzells some days earlier to be briefed on their holiday movements, only to find that their plans coincided exactly with mine. I was travelling with Zoe, who had rented a house on the island, and her childhood friend Sarah Geogehen (or Gorganovitch, as she was known by Michael). With Annie and the Wigzells were Annie's daughter Emma, her husband Charlie Ainley and their three children, as well as Annie Wigzell's naughty septuagenarian step-father, Stewart. As luck would have it, the hotel they were all staying at was very close to our villa and we were able to share the same beach. We also met up most evenings at any one of a variety of local restaurants where the numbers round the table were fairly evenly divided. In other words, Sarah, Peter, Charlie and I enjoyed drinking far more than was good for us and the other four didn't. But it was all very happy and harmonious, with only a hint of recrimination the next day.

One evening by way of a change the girls and I decided to stay at home and cook our dinner from food we had bought earlier in the day at a local market. All three of us were used to living on our own and to exhibiting varying degrees of skill in the kitchen. My ability, of course, could not be underestimated, although I firmly maintain that I am as good as the next man at French dressing and gravy, as well as a powerful Pimms and throat-numbing Bloody Mary. When I was told that none of those delicacies were required that evening and that I might as well go and read my book, I reacted by accusing them of treating me like an elderly maiden aunt. And so another nickname was born, although when Sarah uses it the sound is more like 'Arnteh'. Long after I – of course – had been allowed to wash up and Zoe was between the sheets, Sarah and I contemplated the future of mankind and poured each other 'just one more'. It was only then that we saw the full significance of the large map of the island that decorated one of the sitting-room walls. To our amazement, it seemed that it was completely made up of bits of donkeys. The more we examined it, with excitement mounting, the more we noticed that what at first appeared to be a bay or rocky outcrop was actually the outline of a donkey's head or hind quarters. When Zoe, woken by the din, stumbled in to see what all the fuss was about she was singularly unimpressed by our explanation and refused point-blank to see any of our four-legged friends.

Fortunately, by the time Sarah and I were ready to face the world the next morning Zoe had been on the beach for some hours. Over mugs of black coffee my fellow reveller and I tried hard to revive ourselves and to remember what it was that had kept us up so late. She had no recollection at all, and although I could remember some of it there was certainly one thing that puzzled me. As I got out of bed I was aware of some soreness around a red mark on my leg. At first I thought I had been bitten by a mosquito, but when I looked at it again with Sarah we both agreed, after much giggling, that it could only have been made by teeth. By now helpless with laughter we could only conclude that either I was capable of something I had only ever seen a photograph of Nijinsky doing or, at some stage Sarah's mouth had been dangerously close to that area of 'Arnteh's' body that is known as the Radish.

Everyone agreed that the holiday was a great success and plans were made to do it again the following year. Although, sadly, that did not happen, during the next two or three years we had any number of 'reunion' lunches and dinners at each other's houses. Not the least of these gatherings was spent at the Wigzells' new home, a lovely old farmhouse near Frome in Somerset. The girls and I valued their friendship enormously and I very much regret that through my own stupidity we have lost touch.

To date I have only had one other holiday with my two 'nieces' and that consisted of a four-day spring trip to Champery in the Swiss Alps, where Zoe has a share in a chalet. A highlight for me was a pilgrimage to Les Avants, where I pointed out landmarks and the narcissi that were enjoying a last gasp.

More recently, and to my great delight, they presented me with a small oil painting they commissioned from Johnny's talented artist sister, Mimi Roberts. Against a dark background and in striking colours it depicts an inordinately long radish.

Michael arrived home one day with his arms straining under the weight of a reddy gold bundle of hair that answered to the name of Jasmine. She was in fact a very large and extremely beautiful standard dachshund that he had just collected from a breeder near Watford. I had known for some time that as it had been his idea in the first place to have a dog he was disappointed that Gyp had become such a one-Guy girl. In an attempt at redressing the balance he had even briefly owned a rather well-born kitten, but she had long since disappeared into the night. It was only after I had expressed my approval and she and Gyp had exchanged cursory sniffs that he revealed his even bigger surprise. Jasmine, it appeared, had a distant cousin called Harry, to whom she was devoted and he too was due to join us.

Although in my own mind I questioned the wisdom of taking on the responsibility of three dogs when I was without a job and Michael was planning to leave his, I had to admit that our extended family was a constant source of pleasure. In appearance the latest addition had the head and body of a golden retriever, but with only dachshund-type legs as support. He may indeed have lacked height, but he wanted for nothing when it came to personality and sweetness of nature. His relationship with Jasmine was the essence of tenderness and devotion, and together they did their best to be friends with Gyp – however much she chose to pretend that they didn't exist.

Whenever possible we set aside part of each day to take advantage of our close proximity to three of London's premier parks. On foot and paw Holland Park took fifteen minutes to reach, and if time allowed we could go on from there to Kensington Gardens and Hyde Park. These three great green oases provided everything that a dog could want – including the pleasure of the hunt. As a seasoned campaigner, Gyp would respond at once as soon as the cry 'Squirrels!' went up and, with only a moment's hesitation, the Flubbies (as Jasmine and Harry were collectively known) would follow in her wake. However, it took them quite a lot of practice before they could work out precisely what it was they were supposed to be pursuing.

On one of our outings we decided to walk in a different direction altogether and crossed Hammersmith Bridge onto the towpath that leads to Barnes. The plan was to follow the path along the south side of the river until Barnes Bridge and then cross over onto Chiswick Mall for the journey home – a lovely hike of about three miles. But as we approached the outskirts of Barnes I suggested paying an unscheduled call on Penny Kegerreis, who lived with her dog Betsy in a house between the river and the village centre. My friendship with Penny dates back to Lymington days, when we met at a dance at the Beaulieu Motor Museum. Sadly only two things stick in my memory from that evening. The first was being terribly impressed that she wore an Ossie Clark dress, and the second was driving her home in my old green Jaguar and getting inextricably stuck in a water-logged ditch. Before her marriage we used to see quite a lot of each other, and she even very bravely entrusted to MH&W the sale of her fascinating house in Peel Street. (To be fair, it was outside our area and we only succeeded in selling it by enlisting the help of Aylesford's Kensington office.)

Ever since that first meeting I had always associated Penny with counselling work and charities for the homeless, so it came as rather a surprise to discover that she had recently bought a clock-making business. It was a venture, she said, that had introduced her to a completely new environment – a world of craft fairs and commerce, the like of which she had never known before. As we were by now consumed with curiosity she took us into her 'horolarium' so that the goods could be inspected. I suppose in my mind's eye I had visions of the carriage clock and bracket clock I had been given by my mother, but Penny's timepieces proved to be very decorative and extremely simple. They were just single pieces of board shaped like the face of a longcase clock with a small unit at the back that housed a control knob, a tiny battery and a hook for hanging. Michael was obviously very intrigued and asked her all sorts of questions, including whether she might in the future need some help. She seemed to like that idea and undertook to telephone Michael to discuss it. With that we retraced our steps to Hammersmith – Gyp and the Flubbies thrilled to be on the move again.

In no time at all Michael's tutu was not just hung up but locked away in a trunk for positively the last time and he joined forces with Penny. Using the skills he had learnt on a course at Wimbledon School of Art he spent hours in the dining room working on designs for something stronger and more interesting than the slightly Laura Ashley look the clocks presently had. Every surface was soon piled high – for Michael was a great hoarder – with his old sketches and pictures, as well as posters and programmes recalling long-forgotten opera and ballet productions. His first attempts, most of which depicted scenes from well-known ballets, had artistic merit but lacked dramatic impact. He persevered however, and eventually came up with the brilliant idea of concentrating not on particular aspects of Covent Garden's output, but portraying all the personalities who were part of the Opera House's history. He used as background the familiar image of the proscenium arch and crimson curtains, with likenesses of the famous – some from the end of the last century – superimposed on top. The overall effect was quite stunning and we both knew at once that he had produced a sure-fire hit. Sure enough, when he and Penny revealed the prototype to the manager of the Opera House shop he was so impressed that he placed an immediate order. Some weeks later the clock was the centrepiece of the new catalogue, with sales booming.

Although Michael continued for a while to help Penny with fairs and the production of her existing models, he began to feel the urge – inspired of course by the success of the Opera House clock – to concentrate on specialised pieces. He also liked the idea of something we could do together and thought I should tackle the selling side. When he broke the news to Penny she perfectly understood and accepted his offer to churn out Opera House clocks whenever she needed them. And so, suddenly, I had a new career in sales and marketing with a two-man band called And The Clock Struck One.

With the memory of my disastrous touting for gardening letters very much in mind, I decided this time to approach potential clients by way of jaunty, hard-sell phone calls. And to my amazement it paid off. But quite why non-theatrical establishments like the Science Museum and Greenwich Observatory were chosen as early targets I simply can't remember, even though they were numbered among our first customers. For the former, Michael used a striking picture of a steel foundry and produced another that was a tribute to Mr Babbage and the first computer. Clocks for the Observatory concentrated, not surprisingly, on Greenwich Mean Time and the Meridian Line. A Charing Cross Road ballet bookshop took a Fonteyn and Nureyev clock, whilst Liberty's accepted something awfully esoteric for its little arty department. (But probably only because the manager fancied my partner!) Happily, all of these commissions sold well and yielded repeat orders. However, the successes were matched with an equal number of failures. Of these the most disappointing, from a sentimental as well as an economic point of view, was the Queen's Gallery at Buckingham Palace. From the outset things went remarkably well, when I established a good telephone relationship with the woman in charge. When we went to see her she was very taken with Michael's portfolio and spent a great deal of time choosing pictures for him to experiment with. Greatly encouraged by this, he spent the next few days attempting to make the best of some of the more prominent members of the House of Windsor and their palatial surroundings. Pleased with the result, he left the best of the bunch at the gallery, where he was warned that approval might take a while to come through. When the friendly lady rang a week later it was to say that in spite of the clocks being well received by people more important than her, the decision to reject them had been taken 'at the highest possible level'. A case, perhaps, of the Queen's unerring good taste revealing itself yet again. Who knows, if the clocks had been less attractive she might have wanted to wear them. Miaoooow!

Harrods, surprisingly, proved to be another disappointment in spite of the fact that the colossal souvenir department stocked nothing resembling a timepiece. From what we could see on a tour of inspection it must have been the only inanimate object left on earth not marked with the ubiquitous logo. Michael submitted various versions in the obvious colour scheme, but they were all rejected. However, we had more luck with the Historic Houses Association, for whose one-day conference we shared a stand with Penny. A number of commercially minded aristo owners of stately piles expressed enthusiasm for our wares and one couple even invited us to lunch to talk about a project.

On the day duly appointed we found ourselves trundling up the drive of a house called Rotherfield Park, where the Lord Lieutenant of Hampshire and Lady Scott were waiting to greet us. Whilst guiding us around their enormous home Sir James explained that in order to keep it going a wing had been divided into flats, and they were looking at ways to beef up the little shop that was open on days when the great unwashed were admitted. A tasteful clock, they suggested, might be a good seller. Over drinks (in which our host showed a keen interest) before lunch we pored over innumerable images of the house and gardens until a final selection was made. By this time Lady Scott was very keen on the whole idea and insisted on presenting Michael with a hefty advance for the work. Encouraged by Sir James we carried our glasses through to the dining room where, in a bay window, the smallest of three tables had been laid for lunch. The table that dominated the centre of the room could have accommodated Mr Blair's entire cabinet as well as the Manchester United football team, while Jeremy Thorpe's old Liberal Party would have had space to spare at the smaller one. Food was brought in by what looked like a lady from the village and the Queen's representative busied himself with bottles. Lunch proved to be a very jolly affair and I had no hesitation in accepting several cups of coffee before thinking of driving back to London. In fact, with the thanks and farewells taken care of I parked the car just outside the main gates, giving the dogs a chance to pee and me to have a tiny nap.

With the business up and running we decided to take a few days off to visit a part of the world that neither of us knew, to stay with two friends of Michael's from Opera House days. Uncharacteristically he had kept in touch with an acclaimed soloist called Vergie Derman and her husband Stephen, who had been a behind-the-scenes man. They had left the company to move to south-west Scotland, where they ran an hotel in a large village called Creetown. In fact this was to be the second of the expeditions we had made, not just as a jaunt but with a view to finding somewhere different to live. We had both grown weary of London and went initially to see what our money would buy in Northumberland. We based ourselves with friendly B&B providers near Alnwick and carried out a serious exploration of the area. The grandeur of the coast and the stark beauty of the rolling countryside captivated us both, but habitable dwellings that were neither castle nor terraced cottage seemed not to exist. At the time this was seen as a great pity, especially as our hosts, mindful of Michael's background, predicted a great future for a ballet teacher in the town. Quite what role I would have played – short of taking money at the door – was open to question. However, we decided in the end to look elsewhere.

Our journey to Scotland, with breaks on the motorway every two hours for rubbish-bin sniffing, leg lifting and water guzzling, meant turning sharp left at Carlisle, gliding past Gretna Green and following the Solway Firth to our destination. Creetown itself, in the manner of so many small Scottish towns, proved to be less than lovely, but the hotel was a fine early nineteenth-century building with a respectable drive and decent garden. Later that evening, after Vergie had cooked and Stephen had served a delicious dinner, we left the other guests to their coffee and joined our friends in the kitchen. Over a bottle of wine it emerged that a year into their new life running a hotel was not exactly a bed of roses. Stephen even confessed to dreaming of stacking shelves at Sainsburys or a small house that did bed and breakfast. 'No more breakfasts!' cried his wife with passion.

I set the alarm for an early start the next morning. The object of the exercise was to get Michael's dogs (how soon they became his when things started to go wrong!) downstairs and out of the front door before the day's first bowel movement. We had learnt from past experience that the control they demonstrated at home did not necessarily extend to strange surroundings. After three nights in Creetown it began to look as if I had misjudged our hairy friends. However, on the morning of our departure curiosity got the better of me and I poked my head round the half-open door of the room next to ours, which I knew to be unoccupied. What should I see but a smart new carpet dotted with piles of poo. Coincidence? I hardly think so.

In the time at our disposal we covered a lot of the old county of Wigtownshire, including the market town of Newton Stewart and the port of Stranraer. Every estate agent's window revealed attractive houses in good positions and well within our price range. But quite by chance the one on which we had set our hearts was the little lodge at the bottom of Stephen and Vergie's drive. They had not bought it when they took over the hotel and so, boarded up and neglected, it was still for sale. Having borrowed the key from the agents we spent several hours trying to assess what work would be required and the sort of space we would end up with. Although it was small we reckoned we could fit in two bedrooms, a studio for Michael and a sitting room big enough to double as an antiques showroom. Although we were both becoming increasingly excited about the project our main stumbling block was the fact that we were powerless to take matters further until the London flat was at least under offer.

As soon as we got home one of the first things I did was to call in two of the local agents to get a valuation and to instruct them to put the flat on the market. The men in sharp suits were quick to point out that what had been seen in the mid-eighties as the inexorable rise in house prices was now very much heading in the other direction. I was forced to accept that I would be fortunate to make a profit on the price I had paid for Matheson Road four years earlier. Bearing that in mind it became obvious that the downturn had happened almost within days of the sale of Marlowe Hunting & Worsley going through. Perhaps I do, after all, have a guardian angel.

Having for the first time entrusted someone else with the sale of a property I rapidly began to realise why estate agents are sometimes accused of not providing good service. First off, letters confirming instructions failed to arrive. Detailed particulars had to be asked for and, once received, gave the impression of having been written by someone who had never seen the flat. And, most surprising of all, a For Sale board was *not* put up, even though I had specifically requested one. After all, it wasn't as if I had asked for a full page in *Country Life*, just the most basic form of advertising. With my own experience not yet a distant memory, I tried so hard not to be thought of as 'that difficult old cow in Matheson Road', especially as both firms were run by friends of mine. In the end, however, the goods were delivered and a very nice girl made an acceptable offer. It was only then that I rang the agent in Newton Stewart to explain that having agreed terms on my sale I was now in a position to go ahead with the purchase of The Lodge. Knowing how keen we had been, it was difficult for the woman at the other end of the telephone to put the bad news into words. But the upshot of it was that in the true manner of Sod's Law a second interested party had appeared soon after us, even though the house had been rejected and ignored for many months. As contracts had just been exchanged there was bugger all we could do about it.

Quite naturally we were both very disappointed, but there was never any question of not going ahead with the next part of our grand design, which was to go back to the area and buy a house. For our second visit we decided to forgo the comfort provided by Stephen and Vergie, plumping instead for a more modest establishment in Newton Stewart that was also run by a couple of Sassenachs. Using the B&B as our base we set out to explore the other side of the River Cree, a peninsular that culminated in the Mull of Galloway, Scotland's most southerly point. After about three miles we reached a small bypass and a large sign that urged us to consider the historic delights of Wigtown. Unlike, sadly, most visitors to the area, we decided to do just that. I parked the car in the deserted square and we set off on foot to explore. It soon became apparent that although only a very small town, its centre was laid out on a relatively grand scale. The broad expanse of the square itself had at its heart a rather under-planted garden next to the ubiquitous and immaculate bowling green. Evidence of wealth in the nineteenth century was provided by an imposing town hall and there were also one or two fine houses from an earlier period. It seemed that day-to-day life revolved around a post office and general store, a SPAR supermarket and more gloomy little pubs per head of population than even the mighty town of Windsor. Further afield we followed a sign proclaiming 'Martyrs Stake' that led us down a hill towards the sea. On the way we passed the church's forbidding presence and came upon a terrace of three cottages, the first of which was for sale. Without further ado Michael declared, 'This is it!' and hauled the Flubbies up the steps behind him into the garden. Gyp and I followed more cautiously, but having admired the view, agreed that he was probably right.

Armed with the agent's key we returned to the cottage, called 'Moss Cree', later in the day for our first look inside. Happily the house was well within our price range and was being sold complete with contents, including – hallelujah – a washing machine. The owner lived abroad and only used it for holiday lets. Once bitten, twice shy, we returned to the agent, offered the asking price and spent a very solemn hour or so with a local solicitor.

Although I am the first to admit that there was more than a hint of madness involved in making the move at all, it was not in fact as irresponsible as it might have seemed. For a start, with a full order book The Clock Struck One could be run from virtually anywhere. Moreover, Scotland was an untapped market, with every prospect of new commissions. As far as my own livelihood was concerned I had just been taken on by an organisation called The Wayfarers to act as a guide on their walking holidays – seasonal work, but quite well paid.

Our last few London weeks were spent divesting ourselves of unwanted or unsuitable possessions, with a break in Bromsgrove for Christmas with Michael's parents. A last flurry of entertaining reached its climax with a heavily congested farewell party at which Alex made a surprise appearance. He had managed at the last moment to escape for twenty-four hours from the demands of a small newsagents shop and a business partner whose social life revolved around the lonely hearts column of gay magazines. He had also recently moved from rented accommodation into a house of his own in the tiny village of Munslow. He had been to supper with us on an earlier visit to London when he had spent the night at the Shepherds Bush flat of a friend called Sophia Wilberforce. Alex had made a point of getting to know Sophia and her two brothers, Sebastian and Nicholas, soon after their mother, Baroness de Stemple was charged with appropriating cash and gold bars that belonged to her aunt, Lady Illingworth. This crisis in their lives came soon after the children's father was found murdered in circumstances that have never been explained. Although Alex's interest initially was focused on Nicholas, in the hope of a little bedroom activity, he actually became a friend to them all by taking in their disagreeable cat and keeping the lawns in shape at their Shropshire house.

20

With the worst of the winter out of the way, we moved to Scotland in March 1991. All our worldly goods were transported by the local carrier and, much to my surprise, fitted into the house with remarkable ease. I even managed to find room to display my growing collection of camels – a hobby I had started with the Agadir venture in mind. Although the house was smaller than the Matheson Road flat it was, to use a ridiculous estate agent's phrase, 'deceptively spacious'. There were two double bedrooms, a big bathroom, a kitchen/breakfast room clad in nasty pine and a large sitting room with the later addition of a bay window and window seat. We were still unloading when we received our first visitor, a delightful woman called Rosemary Bythell who was related by marriage to the previous owner. She and her husband David and their three teenage children lived nearby in what had once been a farm, but which had been converted by them to create holiday cottages. They proved to be enchanting and incredibly hospitable neighbours.

As spring was around the corner we elected to make the garden a priority and, as at Matheson Road, Michael took on the back part while I concentrated on the bit at the front. We started with almost a blank canvas, but also the undoubted advantage of rich soil and the presence of the Gulf Stream. In spite of all the horticultural activity Michael was not neglecting the clocks, particularly as they represented our only source of income. Since before the move we had been in telephone and postal communication with New York's Metropolitan Opera House, whose director of publicity was thrilled with photographs of the Covent Garden clock. Michael had already submitted some attractive designs for a clock of their own, and they were talking in terms of a large order. But sadly they were never able to produce the photos and pictures that he needed and all his hard work came to nothing.

To make up for this setback I set up appointments in Glasgow and Edinburgh with the buyers for a number of the leading museums and art galleries. In the course of a great deal of mileage we had only limited success, as well as a first encounter with the Scots' legendary reluctance to part with money. Unfortunately 'sale or return' was very much the order of the day. It was a rule that even applied to the small craft shops we called on, as well as the Wigtown Post Office, for whom Michael covered a dial with a scene from a football match! And no, the players were not wearing ballet pumps.

But we did have one day that was pure undiluted pleasure. A trip to Sir Walter Scott's home, Abbotsford, in the Borders was a jaunt I had been looking forward to for some time. With the Flubbies in their accustomed position on the shelf behind the rear seat and Gyp on Michael's reluctant lap, waiting like a coiled spring to thrust half her body out of the side window, we set off. We were thrilled by the house and its setting and, as luck would have it, we had chosen a day when there were very few other rubberneckers. An unexpected bonus was that Scott's great-granddaughters, Jean and Patricia, were selling tickets and guides at the door. I remembered the tall, thin figure of Dame Jean from my Palace days. Her marathon stint as lady-in-waiting to Princess Alice Duchess of Gloucester had recently been acknowledged with the honour of a DCVO. But recognition was one-sided – which probably meant that I had never thrown peas down her cleavage. A table in the corner of the hall displayed prints of the house, some tea towels and oatcakes, but apart from that there didn't appear to be much in the way of a souvenir for the rapacious public to buy. When one of the ladies casually asked what it was that had brought us there Michael explained the nature of our business, boldly flourishing his portfolio and the designs he had produced for Sir James and Lady Scott at Rotherfield Park. Bull's-eye! Dame Jean was obviously impressed that we had been commissioned by one of the Queen's anointed. Scenting success, Michael said at once that he would be delighted to produce a sample clock for Abbotsford – possibly something depicting the Great Man and some of the characters from his novels. They appeared to be delighted with the idea, and after much rootling presented him with some pictures of Sir Walter and a print of the house. A personally conducted tour then ensued, followed by tea in their private sitting room. Encouraged by this level of intimacy, I felt the time was right to take the relationship onto another level. However, my revelation that I was linked to their family by marriage did not receive the rapturous reception that I had anticipated. I told them that my mother's maiden name was Jobson, and that it was part of the family folklore that the Jane Jobson who had married Sir Walter's son was a kinswoman of hers. With a pronounced straightening of her back Dame Jean declared, 'Her name was certainly Jobson, but I doubt there is any connection. In any case, she died childless!'

In due course a Walter Scott clock was produced, and a very colourful effort it was too, though unfortunately the central figure of the author looked rather too much like Marlon Brando in *Mutiny On The Bounty*, while all the other characters bore a striking resemblance to Michael. Soon after it was finished a major upheaval disrupted our lives and no copies were ever made. The original hangs on my kitchen wall.

In May I was bidden to Cheltenham for the start of the first of my Wayfarers' walks, but in the same phone call I was also told that as a result of the recession demand for the holidays had collapsed and I would only be needed for two that season. At the hotel I was met by an old friend called Robin Edleston who had been with the company for a year, and through whom I first heard about the job. During my time at The Dorchester he had been a junior manager, but had then gone on to run a successful herb farm in Somerset. As we waited for our party of Americans to check in we were joined by a young chap called Geoffrey, who was also there to learn the ropes. He and I became quite friendly in the days that followed, but the only clues he gave to his background were that he lived in Devon and had recently inherited a large house on the coast. Then, when it came to the part of the walk that featured a visit to Lord Dulverton's arboretum, he let slip another nugget of information. As we arrived I claimed, quite casually, that I thought the noble lord had recently died. Geoffrey looked startled and said, 'I don't think so. I am sure I would have heard, as he is my wife's uncle.'

When I got home I satisfied my curiosity by looking him up in *Kelly's Handbook*, only to find that he was listed as the third baronet. This news would certainly have amused the walkers. One or two of them had been so impressed with my knowledge of the Royal Family (although I did not reveal from whence it came) that they asked if I was a 'Sir' or a 'Lord'!

The object of the holiday was for the unencumbered guests to walk the Cotswold Way from Cheltenham to Burford, averaging about eight to ten miles a day, and with overnight stops in places such as Broadway and Winchcombe. While the other two acted as guides, my role was to drive the estate car, ferry the luggage and settle bills. I also had to provide cold drinks and refreshments when I rendezvoused with the party at pre-arranged spots. After feet had been revitalised and corn plasters applied, each day ended with a very jolly dinner party.

Later in the summer I took part in my only other walk, which was much closer to home. On foot this time, I accompanied the guide as he led us through the beautiful Borders country south of Edinburgh. The meticulously planned route meandered through forests and beside rivers, reaching its climax at the top of a hill with a heart-stopping view of fairy-tale Floors Castle. A journey like that convinced me that Scotland is definitely Britain's best-kept secret.

Back home once more at Moss Cree we began to receive visits from our London friends. Among the first to arrive was Jane, who had never been to that part of the world, but who came armed with maps and addresses. These had been provided by her mother, whose very grand family had once lived in various parts of the area. We spent one whole day in pursuit of these ancestral homes, and could not have enjoyed it more. The first one to be tracked down was an enormous pile just outside Newton Stewart. Since the Heron-Maxwell family had moved on it had become an extremely vulgar and deservedly empty hotel. Although we explained our reason for being there, they were obviously not impressed by our appearance and only grudgingly allowed us a tour of the public rooms. By contrast, the occupants of the next house could not have been more welcoming – in spite of the fact that it was one of Her Majesty's prisons! Although the rules prevented us from seeing beyond the hall, we were given a guided tour of the prize-winning walled garden. When we exclaimed at the beauty of it all a friendly inmate, knee-deep in cabbages, asked if we knew anyone who might be interested in the job of resident gardener. He also pointed out the charming little house that was provided. We were both very tempted.

Another exceedingly welcome house guest was Helen 'Digger' O'Keefe, a talented artist and painter of miniature furniture, famous amongst her friends for calling nice things 'Christmas Pie!' Her reward for being such a joy to have around was the subsequent introduction to the man who was to become her husband. But more of that later.

Although it was lovely having people to stay, the downside was that it obliged Michael and I to share a bedroom – a thing we had not done for some time. Another indication that all was not well were the long periods of silence between us (usually initiated by me), a sign perhaps that we were preoccupied with worries about the future. Certainly the continuing recession was affecting the demand for clocks and with very little money coming in the loss of the Wayfarers job was the last straw. My daily walk to collect the newspapers took on a greater significance as we began to study the advertisements for jobs. Michael boldly struck first in response to an ad by Butlins, who wanted new Redcoats for their holiday camps. Although it clearly stated that show business experience would be an advantage, the fact that they did not reply implied that a chap who had spent most of his life in full make-up and leotard was not what they had in mind.

My turn came next when I rang a firm who needed car owners to work from home, selling an 'ethical' product, with no cold calling and good commission. It turned out to be a Yorkshire-based company called OBAS who manufactured orthopaedic beds. Influenced, perhaps, by the knowledge that it was a product I might soon require,

I asked when I could start. Some time later I found myself in Wakefield ready for a week of intensive training. I chose not to take advantage of the long list of bed and breakfast establishments they sent me and stayed instead just outside the town in the picturesque village of Hooton Pagnell. My base, Church Farm, had been for many years the family home of Johnny Lyon and I had often been a guest. Since his mother's death the house had been unoccupied, waiting to be let or sold, and he was happy for me to stay there.

On my first trip to Yorkshire with Johnny we had stayed at their much larger house, Burntwood Hall, close to the mining town of Barnsley. In those days his mother Betty and stepfather Doug were still remarkably active supporters of the Conservative Party at a pretty senior level. Tory bigwigs were often present at weekend lunch and dinner parties, where Betty's cooking skills and Doug's no-nonsense approach to the consumption of alcohol were displayed to best advantage. On one such occasion I remember sitting next to Tony Barber, Ted Heath's Chancellor of the Exchequer, who was an old family friend. The poor man's monetary policy was rather unpopular at the time and, fired by too much gin and not enough tonic, I set myself the task of quizzing him over it. Well I can only say that since he stood no chance of making sense of the questions and I could not begin to understand the answers it was an exchange that he handled with astonishing patience.

Burntwood Hall's fabled reputation for hospitality reached its peak on the day of Lucia's marriage to Reid. As she was the first of the three children to wed, the boat the parents pushed out was the size of an aircraft carrier. The tiny church nearby was the scene for the ceremony, and the reception took place in the garden that surrounded the house. Music for the occasion was provided by Yorkshire's most famous brass orchestra, The Grimethorpe Colliery Band. Among the guests was a large contingent from Reid's home, the island of Bermuda, for whom he had used his sailing skills to compete in the Olympic Games. As their first home was to be his yacht *Chicane* they had left their list of wedding presents at a well-known chandlers called Captain Watts in Albemarle Street. In the weeks before the wedding, guests responded to their suggestions and they were bombarded with innumerable objects made of cork, rope and plastic. But as the day drew nearer Lucia noticed sadly that one rubber item had been overlooked. However, as guests for the reception started to arrive, Stephen stepped forth to fulfil the role of her knight in shining armour. He approached her across the lawn, grinning from ear to ear and holding in front of him a natty pair of ladies' sea boots.

When Burntwood Hall was sold and subsequently turned into offices, Doug and Betty moved to the smaller house at Hooton Pagnell. Although it had fewer rooms, the emphasis was still on comfort and space for entertaining. Whereas ordinary mortals have a cupboard that is used for drinks, Doug had an entire room that was set aside for this purpose. Nevertheless, the arrival of an enormous double-fronted American refrigerator, which dispensed ice at the touch of a button, presented them with a serious space problem. In the end it was consigned to one of the sculleries, but not before someone had suggested fitting it with a loose cover and standing it in the drawing room.

The last time I saw Betty was on a Friday evening when I had driven there with Johnny from London. It was typical of her generosity and urge to nourish her only son that dinner that night consisted of a Dover sole each, followed by large fillet steaks.

After a hard day in Wakefield it was marvellous to have Church Farm as my retreat. The OBAS advertisement in *The Times* had attracted a disparate bunch of people, about a dozen altogether. Among their number was a redundant master of foxhounds from Northumberland called Valentine, a miner from one of the recently closed pits and a man from Scrabster who ran the most northerly shop in the British Isles. Our days were spent being coached in the art of bed selling. And the horror of it was that each presentation had to take not less than two hours, using only the script that we were supposed to commit to memory. Our guide through this arcane ritual was OBAS's top salesman who had probably spent more time at sea, thanks to winning so many cruises, than most ratings in the Royal Navy.

I spent each evening at Hooton Pagnell walking in the garden and in the country round the village trying my best to memorise the pages of the script that were my homework. Mercifully, the terrifying tests the next morning indicated that I was not alone in finding the task beyond me. Nevertheless, at the end of the week I was told that I had learned enough to qualify and went back to Moss Cree to await my first assignment.

As luck would have it I didn't have long to wait, thanks to the fact that OBAS had recently exhibited at Edinburgh's large agricultural show. In fact, my first customer, a distressed cowman near Stranraer, was a bit of a cheat as he only wanted to replace an existing mattress that had collapsed. My second call was a new enquiry and would require all my oratorial skills. When I arrived at the house in Ayr and found no one at home I heaved a sigh of relief and took the dogs for a long walk. Although I did ring the doorbell again about an hour later, I knew deep down that I wanted there to be no response. I went home after that, threw away all my OBAS literature and reconciled myself to the fact that I would never meet a rich widow on the *Oriana*.

Soon after our move to Wiggy, I arranged to meet a gay couple we had met in London chez Alan Lamboll and Jonathon Wicks. I drove to Crossmichael, a little village about fifteen miles away, to pay a call on Roger Cave and John Jarvis Smith, who had recently bought a house there. During the dinner party at which we had met there was great excitement when we realised that we were all moving to the same bit of Scotland within a few weeks of each other. Roger, who was in his mid-thirties, ran an extremely successful travel agency in, of all places, Penge. John, who was retired and in his mid-sixties, had apparently made a stack of money during a long career with Mr Latsis the Greek shipping tycoon. The gay gossip had it that John added his mother's name, Jarvis, to his surname at Roger's behest. As if John Smith alone was not distinguished enough. A steep and narrow winding road led to their house, which was large and plain but had beautiful views. They made me welcome and took me on a guided tour. In order to put you completely in the picture I should be fair and explain that this was not their only home. They also had a flat in Marsham Court, a large house in Brighton, a cottage in Dorset, a flat in Nice and a small house in the hills above Nice. And how could anyone expect to have enough interesting furniture to fill all these places? Well of course they couldn't, and that is obviously why Roger chose to ransack the showrooms of the retailers near his office to find the three-piece suites and other items he thought would be in keeping.

In spite of having lived there only a short time, and with a lifestyle that in modern parlance can only be described as alternative, Roger and John were already a force in local society. This social success was probably a marked contrast to the way they lived in Brighton, a place that had been their main home for many years. That was a big-pond town, and as it became more and more popular with well-heeled gays John and Roger's piece of the action got progressively smaller. Rural Dumfriesshire, on the other hand, was a very smart tarn for brown trout with money and social aspirations. Also, rather like parts of East Anglia, it played host to a surprising number of gay couples. With its three or four large reception rooms, Walbutt provided ample space for buffet parties or sit-down dinners for twelve. The back lanes and byways of the county were a much-needed route home after a convivial evening spent as guests of Messrs Cave and Jarvis Smith.

Although I knew that Kate Vestey was an occasional attraction on gala nights, the way she was often referred to by Roger intrigued me. Usually in exasperation she was mentioned in connection with weekend visits that were cancelled at the last moment, or travel arrangements he had made that overlooked an important hairdressing appointment. But no matter how serious the outburst, in the next breath he always spoke of her as a much-loved friend.

I began to learn more about this enigmatic figure when Roger rang me one day to say that Kate, in her search for a house in Scotland, had received the details of a small estate near Kirkcudbright. It transpired that since her divorce from Lord Vestey she had been looking for somewhere north of the border that would allow her to continue the lifestyle she had enjoyed at their Cotswold home, Stowell Park. Roger explained that he often looked at houses on her behalf, but that he would be tied up with visitors for the next few days and could I suss it out instead?

I found it the next day, and a rather sorry sight it was too. Beyond the little rustic gate lodge and past a range of stable buildings the pot-holed drive stopped in front of a square grey block of early Georgian domestic architecture. Using the keys I had collected from the estate agent I went inside to see what joys were to be found. The rooms were disappointing. Not much in the way of cornicing and large holes where chimney pieces used to be. How sad to see a once fine house so neglected. In Sussex or Hampshire it would have been worth a fortune, and much cherished too. A tour of the garden revealed terraces behind crumbling balustrades and a small lake choked with weeds. Sadly I was going to have to report that in my view, although the house could be marvellous, it was going to need a Sam Vestey fortune, rather than the Kate Vestey version, to lick it into shape.

When I got home I rang Roger to report on my visit, and he responded by saying that I must meet Kate when she next came to stay. As far as the old house was concerned I was later to discover that it was never in with a chance anyway, as she had no intention of living that close to Walbutt or indeed in that part of the country. I had some sympathy with her view that it was not 'proper' Scotland.

Some time elapsed before Roger rang me again to say that Kate was paying a flying visit, and would I join them for lunch at the chintzy Knockinam Hotel in Port Patrick. Unfortunately I had to decline as my car was receiving a major service and I could never get there without my own transport. Our meeting was postponed for another day.

Michael, in the meantime, had had no luck at all on the job front. His attempts at finding work locally – where there was almost always a need for bar staff – were complicated by the fact that he couldn't drive and public transport was virtually non-existent. Over supper one evening we had one of our rare lengthy discussions and covered the subject in some detail. Although we both accepted that as a last resort we could always cut our losses and return to London, in the end we reached the decision to have one more crack at gainful employment. I declared my intention of contacting a firm of auctioneers in Dumfries to see if they needed a porter or even someone with a minuscule knowledge of antiques. At the same time Michael vowed to abandon his prejudice against the tutu and telephone a friend at Scottish Ballet in the hope that there was a gap in the corps de ballet. Much to our delight his call was well received and before you could say 'rosin' he was dusting off the *Bayadere* head-dress, re-ribboning his pumps and winging his way to an audition in the big city.

He started work as soon as the job was his. For the first couple of weeks he commuted, not an easy exercise when the only railway station in the area Dr Beeching left untouched was twenty miles away. But thereafter he stayed during the week with kind friends called Bernard and Andrew who had a fine house near Kilmarnock, which was only a short train ride from Glasgow. In the early days he came back to Moss Cree every weekend, but after a while his visits became less frequent. However, he telephoned quite often and occasionally mentioned an old friend from the Royal Ballet, confusingly also called Michael, who was now working as a physiotherapist in the city. They had apparently bumped into each other by chance and were meeting for a drink from time to time. But one evening when his call came through he sounded quite distressed, confessing eventually that he had something difficult to tell me. I knew at once what that was going to be, but shed a tear nevertheless as he broke the news.

Even though we had been drifting apart, the fact that he was leaving me was still a terrible blow after two and a half years of life-sharing. But it was not the bombshell it might have been, largely because we both knew that I was pretty set on returning to London anyway. This solution to my problems took on a greater significance when I discovered that the tenants in my mother's flat in Aynhoe Road were due to leave at the end of October.

At about this time a call came through from Roger to say that Kate's arrival for a five-day stay was imminent. As he was at a loss to know how to keep her amused over such a long period, he asked if he could bring her over to lunch. Naturally I said I was delighted to help him overcome this very real problem. He had, after all, often regaled me with stories of meticulously planned visits to Scotland's grandest stately homes and finest gardens. Kate was a pretty fast mover at the best of times, but presented with three drawing rooms, a long gallery and a bedroom that briefly accommodated Good Queen Bess and her feet would hardly touch the ground. She never noticed how many Holbeins were waiting for her inspection of whether, more surprisingly, the bed hangings were Osborne & Little. What is more, anything dug, planted or filled with water by Repton or dear old Capability received the same whirlwind treatment. Lunch was usually his last resort, but even there he sometimes faced defeat. On a good day this little pastime could happily fill three of four hours, but on diet days the plate of freshly sliced oranges and glass of non-sparkling water took only minutes to consume.

Roger advised me beforehand to keep lunch simple, as Kate was notorious for toying with even the finest food. As it might be a day for sticking to her not-drinking-at-lunch-time routine, I was only to buy a couple of bottles of wine. The thinner and drier the better. I shopped in Newton Stewart that morning, but finding something simple and delicious wasn't easy. Eventually I settled for some fish paté and a selection of cheeses. As it didn't take long to arrange the food and lay the kitchen table I decided to use the rest of the morning to attack the weeds in Michael's overgrown garden at the back of the house. I have always found that sitting at a typewriter and kneeling in a flowerbed obscure the passage of time more than anything else I know. That morning was no exception. One minute I was choking ivy and in the next instant scraping mud off my hands to greet my lunch guests, still in my tatty clothes.

Many months later Kate confessed that although she had been made aware of the fact that I was tall, what she had not been prepared for was the size of my Wellington boots. My riposte was that proportions like those can sometimes be misleading!

I escorted them from the car straight into the house, knowing full well that there was little point in guiding them round my cherished garden. Fortunately Roger was on splendid form and got us through the initial slightly nervous stage. But this soon evaporated once we were all sitting down with a glass of wine in our hands saying silly things. Moss Cree itself invariably provided rich pickings for Roger's wicked sense of humour and, true to form, he began by pointing out to Kate that it was a cross between a railway carriage and an early nineteenth-century bungalow. He turned his attention next to the view, which for many months of the year, he claimed, required a vivid imagination. But I suppose the source of most amusement sat on the muddy foreshore of the estuary just below us. This strange but much-venerated object was the martyr's stake, a grisly reminder of religious dissent several hundred years ago. Unbeknown to the hordes of pilgrims who made the journey to see it, the poor old thing had to be regularly replaced, rather like the sceptre held by Queen Anne outside St Paul's.

Whilst Kate was enjoying these revelations I had the opportunity to size her up. Although I thought she looked no younger than her forty-eight years, she was certainly well preserved. But what struck me the most was that her natural good looks were rather obscured. An attractive face with good bone structure was not set off to best effect by gold-rimmed spectacles and a frumpy hairstyle. Rather a lot of bright gold jewellery (sent away to be cleaned at least once a month) decorated her neck and wrists and a claret-coloured corduroy skirt covered too much of what were obviously a decent pair of pins. But she had a lovely laugh, which she used a great deal, and showed a keen interest in whoever was speaking at the time.

During lunch, which seemed to meet with approval, Kate and I found to our great surprise that we had mutual friends from our salad days at Aspreys and Fortnum & Masons. Although we did not actually overlap at either establishment, our memories of the rich casts of characters involved were much the same. Aged eighteen at Fortnums her best friend was Tom Lewis who ran the tea counter, and he has remained close to her ever since. I had known him too, though I had to admit to a stronger attraction for the young man who worked beside him. But we both agreed that the outstanding personality in the shop at that time was the manager of the grocery department, Mr 'Dolly' Hobbs. With his matinée idol looks, silver hair with a hint of blue and ever-present carnation he could persuade even the most formidable dowager to part with large sums of money for ridiculously exotic hampers. But I would occasionally see him passing through the staff door after work, hurrying home to his partner Ron and the little flat they shared in Kings Cross. After his tailcoat was exchanged for an old raincoat his off-stage persona was quite different. When it came to pickled kumquats and preserved ginger, no one else alive had sold greater quantities than Mr 'Sally' Lunn, who had joined the firm as a boy and was now reputed to be in his eighties. His huge following of loyal customers refused to be served by anyone else. Nestling among the shelves of delicacies with her ancient cash register was the all-important figure of Joan, the cashier. For as long as anyone could remember she had reigned supreme from her rostrum-cum-pulpit. Every purchase had to be wrapped with brown paper and string in the cramped space beside her and under her eagle eye. For those of us with thumbs instead of fingers this ritual was a nerve-wracking ordeal.

After lunch we took our coffee through to the sitting room. By this stage we were all very relaxed, and Kate led the conversation with questions about Michael and my plans for the future. She explained that she used to go to the ballet at Covent Garden quite a lot and even fancied the male dancer 'look'. The idea of blokes in make-up apparently attracted her. In view of that it was not surprising that she looked with approval at photographs of Michael. Without going into too much detail I told her that I had decided to put Moss Cree on the market and once it had been sold, move into my mother's soon-to-be-vacated flat. I could not say what I was going to do when I got back to London, except that I would have to find work in double-quick time. As I had not been in a proper job for five years this was causing me some concern. The very thought of having to wear a suit and clock in at an office every day filled me with gloom. And there was also the Gypsy Cream to consider, especially as we had not been apart since the day our eyes met at Battersea Dogs Home. With heavy hearts, Michael and I had already decided the fate of the Flubbies. As neither of us could cope with them in our changed circumstances, they were going to be returned to their breeder.

Right out of the blue Kate suddenly exclaimed, 'Why don't you come and work for me? You could be my PA/companion and help me organise the new flat in London, and come with me to find a house in Scotland.'

Well, I was completely taken aback at this suggestion and momentarily lost for words.

'What a fabulous idea. Of course I'd love to,' was all I could think of to say. With a mixture of relief and excitement I visualised a regular income, an unconventional job and no problems for Gyp. Looking back, it is impossible to say what Roger's reaction was. Could it have been through gritted teeth, or with a sense of release that he said, 'That would be terrific, you will get on so well together.'

Two days later I received a charming letter from Kate, in which she told me how much she had enjoyed lunch, and how sure she was that we were going to be friends. She added her telephone number in Eaton Place and stressed that she wanted to hear from me as soon as I arrived in London.

I was advised by the estate agent in Newton Stewart through whom I had bought the house to put it on the market at £52,000. A thousand pounds more than I had paid for it nine months before. With remarkable luck the first people who came to see it agreed to pay the price – and they were keen to move quickly. As I could see no further reason to stay there I arranged for the canny old local removal man to take my things into store, as I didn't know when I was going to need them again. My most precious plants were decanted into pots and given a temporary home with Rosemary and David at East Kirkland. When removal day dawned I filled the car with suitcases, a few camels and the Gypsy Cream and set sail for Hammersmith.

I was very happy to be back in London and soon felt at home in my new abode, surrounded by all Mama's things. A phone call to Kate was high on my list of things to do, but it was several days before I summoned the courage to dial her number. In the weeks that had elapsed since we met I had thought a great deal about her proposal, and was nervous now it case she had had a change of heart. But I needn't have worried. Instead of the expected 'Guy who?' she greeted me most warmly and invited me for a drink the following evening.

Her rented flat in Eaton Place was on the ground floor of an ugly post-war block that sat oddly between its stuccoed nineteenth-century neighbours. Another resident of the building turned out to be a by now very elderly Joyce Carey, whom I had got to know when she came to stay in Les Avants. Kate came to the door looking every inch the society lady, in a smart black dress and high-heeled shoes. I followed her into the kitchen as she asked if I would like a glass of champagne. Producing a bottle from the fridge she cautioned me to open it with great care as she had once been hit in the eye by a wayward cork. Although she had luckily not lost her sight, her vision had been permanently damaged, requiring the use of spectacles or contact lenses. As a rule she wore very little war-paint, which I thought suited her well, but on party nights she went to the other extreme and needed help with eye make-up. A professional beautician was wheeled in to do the business and the pudding was sometimes over-egged, in a manner of speaking.

We took our glasses into the sitting room and chatted quite happily about our lives and her plans for the future (I hadn't really got any). It emerged that she had been divorced from Lord Vestey for about eight years. Younger daughter, Flora, was at a smart school called Tudor Hall near Banbury and Saffron, nineteen, was spending a year in Australia having fun and vaguely doing something for one of her father's companies. Thanks to her Australian paternal grandmother it was a country with which the family had close links. Pamela Vestey's own grandmother was Dame Nellie Melba, one of the world's first opera megastars.

Kate told me that her house in Seymour Walk had been sold and the contents put into store. A flat in Campden Hill Gardens had been bought and was being torn apart even as we spoke. She also said that since we had met she had made an offer for a house near Forfar in Angus, on the east coast of Scotland. But unfortunately another punter had also put in a bid for it, which meant that Kate would have to wait on tenterhooks for a few days to see if she had been successful. Her search for a house to buy in Scotland had apparently taken her the length and breadth of the Highlands. She said she had fallen in love with a succession of castles on clifftops and been the under-bidder on several loch-side laird's houses. Not surprisingly it was the rugged beauty of the west coast that attracted her most. But she soon realised that nature's biggest help in the creation of that glorious countryside was rain. Gallons of it sweeping into the hills and valleys in great misty waves. Even ground that wasn't officially a bog would be pretty soggy going for months on end. After seeing a particularly lovely house near Fort William in driving rain someone suggested she should get some figures for annual rainfall from the Meteorological Office. For a girl who prefers velvet pumps to waders the information she received made up her mind in very short order. It was the east coast for her and no looking back. This meant exploring the area north of Perth, which is famous for its vast estates and the little-known fact that it has more butlers per head of population than any other part of the United Kingdom. Her favourite and extra-long suffering Edinburgh estate agent, Andrew Rettie, had sent her the brochure for a house called Kirkbuddo, near Forfar. She went to see it and decided at once that it was the house for her. The only doubt in her mind was whether or not she could persuade the trustees to buy it. Lengthy consultations with trustee Tony Goode then ensued.

He in turn reported to fellow trustee Mark Vestey who liked to keep several steps removed from the trust's principal beneficiary, his ex-sister-in-law. Although the trust finally agreed to buy it, that was certainly not the end of the story. With someone else equally keen to make it their home the outcome was still unknown.

That evening I also had my first encounter with Bumble, the West Highland terrier. He was Kate's first dog and meant more to her than almost anything. After a pet-free childhood Sam had given her a black Labrador called Taxi to keep at Stowell, but as it was very much a gun dog and lived outside a close relationship had never been forged. When I came on the scene Kate was in the advanced stages of anticipating Bumble's every desire. He only had to change his position on the sitting-room floor before he was whisked outside for yet another pee. Sometimes the poor little chap would stand on the pavement trying to decide what was expected of him and wondering why his dreams had been disturbed. Anyone within hailing distance was called upon to perform this task, but the obvious candidates were usually Irene or me.

Irene had been Kate's housekeeper for twenty years. She travelled to work each day from the home in Wandsworth she shared with her English husband Michael and son Paul. Although it was many years since she had left her native Portugal, her command of English left something to be desired. This little failing, particularly when it came to telephone messages, was the source of a great deal of barely controlled exasperation on the part of her employer. She was meticulous in her work and never complained, even when obliged to wash and iron clothes that had hardly been worn or wipe a damp cloth over paintwork that had not had a chance to get dirty. I sometimes used to think that mishearing a name or pronouncing it incomprehensibly was her way of getting her own back. If it really was a ruse it was most effective when her mistress was attempting communication by car phone from somewhere north of the border, where reception was particularly bad. 'Mr WHO?' she would cry, or 'Why didn't you ask him to spell it?' (As if it would have made any difference.)

Irene's name cropped up when we got down to the nitty gritty of my new job. Kate was most anxious that I should call her nothing but Lady Vestey in front of Irene, a rule to which I adhered for the most part. But in the four years we were together I may have lapsed from time to time, especially since in private I addressed her as Katerina Valente, Kathryn Mary, which she liked, or Old Girl, which she didn't. The sordid question of money also involved Irene. The plan was that once Kate had bought somewhere in the country she would only need Irene on two days rather than the present five. As her salary would be adjusted accordingly she could then afford to pay me 'properly'. In the meantime she asked if I would be able to manage on £100 a week – cash, of course! Now as it happens I had never earned very much money, apart from during the last years of the estate agency. But I had been looking forward to receiving a little more than that from the ex-wife of one of England's richest men. In discussion with friends they had all said that I should hold out for £20,000–£40,000, but of course this was before they knew that I would be eating a lot of free lunches and dinners! However, as I very much needed the job – any job – and was more than a little intrigued by its possibilities, I accepted.

It was agreed that I would start my first day by meeting her at the new flat in Campden Hill Gardens at nine o'clock. The twenty-minute walk with Gyp from Aynhoe Road taking in Holland Park was a lovely way to start the day. As I arrived, Kate drew up in her Range Rover (sprayed a special shade of navy blue). I was introduced to Cedric the architect and swept my eye over the builders, of which there were many. Although this was now October and the flat was due to be ready by Christmas, the scene that presented itself was reminiscent of the Blitz rather more than an article in *Interiors*. In an effort to save money she had decided to do without the services of an interior decorator and relied instead on the advice of an antique dealer friend called Dorothy Ratcliffe. Dorothy was a plump, jolly divorcee in her sixties when she and Kate met in Egypt at a performance of *Aida*. They were both there on their own and soon struck up a friendship. Since that time Kate had been matron of honour when Dorothy married Leonard Ratcliffe, a wealthy widower and retired businessman with a house at Halstead in Essex (or 'close to the Suffolk border' as Kate preferred to describe it). The year I met him he was also High Sheriff of the County. Between them they had gone for off-white and pale biscuity tones as a colour scheme, thereby avoiding the cost of expensive fabrics. My first few days were spent driving them round the shops that supplied material and wallpaper. Lunch was provided for us either by Irene at Eaton Place or with a picnic in the car. But at least two hours each day were spent giving Gyp and Bumble a good run in Hyde Park and Kensington Gardens. By six we were usually back at the flat so that Bumble could have his supper and his mother a glass of wine. I would very often join her for a drink before heading for home.

My first evening 'on duty' loomed large. Kate had asked me to go with her to a big bash at the Hurlingham Club organised by Louis Vuitton. It was to be a black-tie affair with old motor cars, celebrities and food by Anton Mossiman. I thought at first I could get out of it by explaining that I no longer had a dinner jacket. With the move to Scotland I had happily consigned my old one, which I had owned since I was fifteen, to the rubbish bin. But Kate would have none of it, insisting that I buy a new one, as it would have lots of outings in the coming months. Rather rashly she even said she would pay for it, but I was destined to remain £500 worse off.

It was a balmy night by the river in Fulham and the grounds of the Club looked magnificent. We met up with Tom Lewis, who at that time was working for Vuitton at their Bond Street shop, and some of his gay friends. Also in the party was Diane Wilson, a wealthy widow friend of Kate's with a flat in Cadogan Square. She was great fun, but rather quietly spoken. Her only known outburst was directed at a hapless taxi driver late one night as we left Annabels. We had been celebrating Kate's fiftieth birthday and I had offered to drop her off on my way back to Brook Green. Having given the cabbie her address we set off. Before you could say Jack Robinson we had stopped in Trafalgar Square. 'What number did you say it was?' the driver enquired. 'Not Trafalgar Square, Cadogan Square you ARSEHOLE!' screamed my normally subdued companion.

Armed with our glasses of champagne we wandered through the

gardens, carefully avoiding the vintage cars and picnickers lolling on the grass. At one stage we encountered another peer's ex-wife, but one for whom Kate had no great feelings of kinship. She was the fearsome French-born Lady Ampthill. Pausing to chat, she asked me to hold her little gold pochette while she lit a cigarette. I don't know if it was made of solid gold, but it was certainly heavy and metallic with a lid on a spring. Having lit up she put the cigarettes and lighter back inside. At that moment the lid snapped shut, clamping in the process a rather fleshy bit of her arm, causing her to cry out in pain. Once the jaws were prised apart she regained some of her composure and beat a hasty retreat. Suppressing our giggles as best we could, Kate and I continued our perambulation. We stopped again when Kate whispered:

'Do look, there's Nigel Havers. I've always wanted to meet him.'

'Ah,' said I. 'In that case I can introduce you. Although I haven't seen him for ages we used to be quite good friends.'

As subtly as we could, Kate and I moved closer to our prey. It may of course have been my imagination, but I got the distinct impression that young Mr Havers became more animated as the corner of his eye filled with our presence. Notwithstanding the fact that his interlocutor was extremely attractive, I waited in vain for that moment when he would swing round, exclaim and embrace me like the long-lost friend that I was. Meanwhile it must have begun to dawn on my restless companion that I was a pathetic wimp when it came to confidence and bravado on social occasions. Exasperated, she hauled me off towards the house, from whence came the sound of a traditional jazz band. That was the moment we realised we shared a fondness for exuberant dancing.

Sadly, that was not to be the last time Kate must have wondered why she had employed me as a companion in the first place. I saved my worst ever performance for a terribly grand drinks party at Guildhall in the City. She had been bidden by stiffest of stiffies to attend some sort of celebratory rout given by her investment bank, an organisation she took very seriously indeed. Although very keen to go she expressed her familiar horror at the prospect of going somewhere on her own. Having checked first to see if I was free, a courtesy that was sometimes overlooked, she contacted the man in charge of her portfolio to ask if she could bring a friend. How could the poor man say no?

We arrived to find that colossal room, familiar as the setting for lord mayors' banquets and state occasions, stuffed to the gunwales with every imaginable City and Westminster bigwig. Our host, standing near the door, greeted us and introduced his chairman and the Governor of the Bank of England. After that we were on our own. Plates of delicious finger food (a term that makes me uneasy) and glasses of champagne arrived from all sides. But Kate asked for mineral water, as she had declared beforehand that she was not going to drink. Just in case. We had agreed many months before that the people we admired most in the world were the ones who toyed casually with a glass, sometimes making one drink last an entire evening. To our constant regret she and I were both guzzlers and one glass was never enough. I started quaffing for two as we moved into the throng. Famous faces hove into view, but no one that I actually knew and could latch on to. Kate, on the other hand, spotted a number of people from her Establishment past. An obvious one to greet should have been Sir Mark Weinberg, husband of her one-time friend Annoushka Hempel. But she didn't want to approach him. True to form, my only contribution to social intercourse was saying 'please' and 'thank you' to the ever-present waitresses. After a couple of circuits of the room and no contact at all with our fellow guests we decided to call it a day and head for Campden Hill Gardens. In the taxi we convinced ourselves that they were all ghastly people anyway and not worthy of our attention. Besides which, going home meant a reunion with her beloved Bumble – the only 'man' she had decided whose affection she really wanted. Once inside the flat Bumble treated us to his usual whole-hearted welcome and was rewarded with a 'schnoogie' (more formally known as Smacko dog biscuits) and lots of cuddles. The Gypsy Cream was also often present for these nocturnal revelries as Kate had sweetly suggested that they would be company for each other if we were out having fun. But poor old Gyp, much though she adored Kate, had very little time for Bumble at all. To be fair there was a ten-year age difference, and Gyp really only liked sniffing the bums of the big boys. She was long past the boisterous whippersnapper stage.

As there was no chance of Campden being ready until well into the New Year, and with the short lease on Eaton Place about to expire, Kate had no choice but to take up temporary occupation of a suite at the Capital Hotel in Basil Street that was owned by her old friends, David and Margaret Levin. With Christmas approaching most of her time – and therefore mine as well – was taken up with the buying of presents. On her behalf I was permitted to use her credit cards, for all of which I had been made a signatory.

In mid-December I went with her to a carol concert organised by Carolyn Parker Bowles at the Guards Chapel, at which Prince Charles was the guest of honour. Poor Flora made the mistake of being home from school and was dragged along as well. The grey and featureless chapel – rebuilt in the sixties after a direct hit during the war whilst a Sunday morning service was in progress – was full to overflowing with the great and the good. I sat on the aisle and Flora was between us. Suddenly in the reverential hush that preceded the royal arrival, the sable hat in front turned round and enquired, 'Has Daddy by any chance got a spare pair of glasses I could borrow? I seem to have left mine at home and can't read a thing.'

As I explained that I only had one pair and had need of them myself I could feel Flora beside me doing her best to suppress her laughter. It seemed as if the idea of someone thinking I might be her father was just too much.

After the concert we left the chapel, with Kate seeing but avoiding many Establishment old friends of Sam's, and made our way to Greens Restaurant in Marsham Street, which was owned by Simon Parker Bowles. Simon and his brother Andrew were old friends of Sam's from their days together at Eton. Although the brothers were very close, this could not be said of Carolyn and her sister-in-law Camilla. We were joined there by Carolyn's Australian mother Lady Potter and their two sons, one of whom was Kate's godson. Lady Potter was a larger-than-life character with an obvious taste for jewellery and gin. She had been married more than once, and hit the headlines a few years ago when another of her daughters was abandoned at the altar as her intended ran off with the best man. I found her a very amusing companion, but her behaviour was apparently a cause for concern for her younger grandson. Towards the end of the evening he was heard to enquire of his mother: 'Is Granny drunk yet?'

In due course the move to the new flat finally took place and I was able to see it in all its splendour. Using estate agentese I would describe it as follows: 'Campden Hill Gardens is a small cul-de-sac of late nineteenth-century terrace houses, close to Holland Park.'

Kate's flat comprised the raised ground floor with a large staircase hall suitable for dining, a big sitting room, kitchen, understairs loo and a walled patio garden. The first floor had a huge bedroom as well as a smaller one. Another flight of stairs led to a bathroom. Although the work had taken far longer than predicted and gone way over budget, I must say the end result was magnificent. Fortunately Kate was thrilled with it too.

No sooner was her London base established than she had to decide what she was going to do with Kirkbuddo. After sealed bids she had emerged triumphant. Although she had no plans to start work on the house at once, she was naturally terribly keen to see it again after so long. It was arranged that she and I with Dorothy in tow would fly to Edinburgh and be met by Roger, who would motor across from Walbutt. We spent the night and a great deal of Kate's money at the Caledonian Hotel, where a lavish dinner was enjoyed by all. The drive to Kirkbuddo the next morning took about an hour, and we got there in time to meet Cedric the architect and two men from a security firm who had flown up from London to be there.

Our route had taken us through Perth and some glorious countryside, but as we approached our destination the scenery became less attractive. Only the distant snow-capped Grampians reminded us that the grandeur of the Highlands was not far away. Glamis was the last village we passed and that was dominated by the colossal presence of the Queen Mother's birthplace. The sheer scale of the castle might easily have suggested to her that by comparison, Balmoral looked more like a croft. There was no village at Kirkbuddo and the house itself sat in the middle of twelve acres of ground. There was no sign of gates at the entrance and one of the gateposts looked as if it had been hit by an armoured vehicle. But at the end of the five-hundred-yard drive it was perfectly possible to see why Kate had lost her heart. First impressions were of a house, or possibly even a rectory, that could have been at the heart of a Hampshire village, hard by the church. It was low and wide, built on just two floors, with lots of big windows at the front that were surrounded by Virginia creeper. We all congratulated Kate on her choice (even though there were those in the party who wondered how she was going to run it) and followed her inside for a tour of inspection. The large hallway at the centre of the house had an elegant staircase at one end. A door on the left led to an enormous drawing room, with two smaller rooms beyond. To the right of the hall was a dining room that led through to the kitchen breakfast room. Beyond the stairs was a much older wing, containing a number of small rooms, that made the house a T-shape. The half-landing was occupied by a billiard room, the centre of which was dominated by an appropriate green baize table. Upstairs there were eight bedrooms and four bathrooms. Although it was clear that such a house should have had a history, Kate was never able to find out anything very interesting. All she could discover was that the previous owner had not owned it for very long and had never even moved in. The only information she could get from him was that he had bought it from a successful wholesale plumber who had filled the kitchen and bathrooms with his unspeakable wares and presented the house as a sort of showroom. Sure enough, every item of plumbing and sanitary ware was the wrong colour, the wrong size and made of the wrong material. It was sad that such a fine house had been so badly abused.

While Kate consulted with her small band of advisers I went off to have a look at the state of the garden. At the front of the house was a large and badly neglected lawn that was struggling to keep massed ranks of rhododendrons at bay. There were one or two fine trees, but a vast number of badly planted and undernourished ones. The only pleasant surprise was that behind the house was a large walled garden, open on one side in the Scottish manner. Loose boxes had been built and it was mostly laid to grass, but there were still some healthy espaliered fruit trees and a bed containing leggy old-fashioned roses. Later in the morning Roger and I drove the few miles into Forfar to get sandwiches and soft drinks for lunch. Before we left I took Kate to the walled garden and showed her where we could grow our first vegetables among the roses. An exciting prospect and one we took with us as we flew back to London.

With plans for Kirkbuddo on hold for a while, life with Kate slipped into a daily routine. I would take the Range Rover back to Brook Green every evening and return with it at nine the next morning. More often than not I would arrive to find Irene busily preparing breakfast. Having observed the house rule and removed my shoes, I would climb the limed oak staircase and wait to be allowed to enter the principal bedroom. On good days I was greeted cheerily from the bed by the lady of the house as she leafed through the *Daily Mail*, tore advertisements from magazines or looked with horror at a bill that had arrived by post. In planning our programme she would sometimes announce that it was a day for pursuing a particular quest. During my time in her service there were two that became a relatively major preoccupation. Happily for me they both entailed lunching in a variety of establishments. The first was the search for the pepper mill with the coarsest grind, and the second was the discovery of perfection in calves' liver. This harmless form of entertainment took us to restaurants as diverse as Chutney Mary, Foxtrot Oscar and Quaglinos. But in the end it was Simon PB's other establishment in St James's that came up with the goods – scoring maximum points for having both things under the one roof.

On other days I arrived to find Irene quietly squeezing oranges for juice and laying the breakfast tray. She said that as there had not been a peep from our mistress she would creep upstairs and collect Bumble. A few minutes later she reappeared with the dog in her arms. Once I had placed him on the back seat of the Range Rover and he had been snubbed by Gyp, we headed off towards the wide open spaces of Kensington Gardens. With fine weather my morning walk across to the Italian Garden at Lancaster Gate, under the bridge and round the

Serpentine would take about an hour and a quarter. Of course, I would only be away for as long as that if I knew that Kate was sticking to her usual routine. After breakfast in bed she would invariably be visited at ten by Sally and her Black and Decker-esque machine. The whirring, pummelling and kneading took the best part of an hour and was set against the background of Sally's carefully controlled gossip about her other clients. When some of this was relayed to me later it amazed me that her extremely spicy stories stood on their own without any names being mentioned at all. A source of some comfort perhaps to Kathryn, Lady Vestey.

After a few weeks of pretty much the same route the dogs and I began to recognise and acknowledge other canine walkers, and sometimes their handlers as well. The story goes that one day driving through Windsor Great Park the Queen and Prince Philip found themselves in a similar situation. On the road ahead of them was a man and a Labrador.

'Oh look,' exclaimed the Queen, 'there's Aspden.'

'Really,' muttered the Duke with ill temper, wondering how his wife recognised a man who had been one of their senior chefs for thirty years. 'How do you know?'

'Know the dog, of course,' she replied tartly.

One tracky-bottomed owner trying to cope with five stubborn Pekinese who looked as if he did not want to be subjected to the early morning combined Hunting/Vestey charm offensive was Nigel Dempster. However, we usually had a reasonable response from Lord Carrington and his dachshunds, Michael Berkeley with his black Labrador and the ever-so friendly yellow Labrador of Norman Tebbitt.

Early spring in the park and gardens meant bulbs and buds, my walk taking me from the sunken garden by the Palace to the daffodil-planted verges by the Wet Boat House. A long pause to take in the lovely little garden of the lodge just south of the police station and then on to the Dell at the easternmost end of the Serpentine.

Late spring saw a sudden burst of activity on the human front. Men and horses from the Royal Mews began to limber up for the summer's showpiece spectacles by trundling up and down the Carriage Drive;

gleaming black-and-chocolate wagons complimented by the grooms' matching greatcoats and top hats. On a parallel course the sand of Rotten Row was thrown up by individual officers and men of the Household Cavalry as they took their shining mounts through their paces. As time went by the great wooden doors of the barracks would swing open to allow groups of new recruits to strut their stuff across the vast open space where once the Great Exhibition had stood. A source of curiosity for the straggle of tourists from Okinawa, who were trying to find their way through the trees to Harrods, was the fact that the cavalry's drab khaki uniforms were embellished with burnished plumed helmets and gleaming swords. But the real treat was the rehearsal for the Musical Drive and the stirring strains of the *Rodetzky March* from a mounted band in full fig.

Kate was rather taken aback one day when her neighbour, Barbara, emerged from the house next door, gave her a big hug and said:

'So long since I've seen you. Come in for a drink soon.'

'I'd love to,' Kate responded, 'but we can't stop now as we are off to watch Flora jumping at Stowell.' With that she climbed into the car beside me and, as I drove off, asked, 'Do you think Barbara is a lezzie? That was a very passionate hug!'

'I wouldn't have thought so,' I replied, 'she doesn't strike me as the sort of girl who wants to get her head into your knickers.'

'She'd have a job, I'm not wearing any,' she retorted.

In spite of helpless laughter I was slightly shocked to think that she would be pantyless if felled by a horse in front of that formidable trio of her enemies – the ex-husband, ex-mother-in-law and her successor.

I headed towards the M40 while Kate beside me sorted through her usual pile of newspapers and periodicals. Once in a while she would read out an amusing snippet, or toy with Radio 2 or a cassette. She was soon bored and restless on any journey and really happier in the driving seat. For my part I disliked being behind the wheel and was delighted that our journey today would take no more than one and a half hours. Our destination was the glorious five-thousand-acre Stowell Park estate near Northleach, which had been bought by the present Lord Vestey's grandfather from the Howe family at about the time he had purchased his title. As the scenery began to change and red brick became Cotswold stone, Kate started to express her familiar nerves and anxieties. These were the legacy of the difficult years she had had with the Vestey family since the divorce. This was the second time I had been with her into the lion's den, and she admitted it was less of a 'nightmare' if I was there. Along with that admission came a warning not to be seduced by the charm and hospitality of our hosts. An added worry for her today was the possible presence of Princess Anne, whose son Peter was competing with Flora.

'I hope to God she doesn't stay to lunch,' said Kate. 'You've met her, you know how ghastly she is.'

Yes I had met her, but not since she was a tomboy teenager. I didn't relish the thought of seeing her again either.

Instead of making for the main drive at Stowell, Kate guided me round the edge of the estate to reach the field where the jumps were arranged. The setting was magnificent. The course was laid out in a river-fed meadow in a valley beneath the house and terrace gardens. Small groups of wax-jacketed figures stood around in a confusion of lurchers, Labradors and Landrovers. A few yards from where we parked Kate spotted Sam and his wife Celia with Sam's mother and Mark Phillips. Not far away Princess Anne was talking to Tim Lawrence and Peter Phillips. As we approached Sam indicated our presence and proclaimed: 'As the Princess is here with both her husbands, I have sent for another of my wives!'

Much laughter from everyone, but with some staring at shuffling feet from Capt. Phillips. After the obligatory exchange of noisy air kisses, Kate made finding Flora an excuse to set off round the course, with me and Bumble and Gyp in tow.

Following in the family tradition Flora was devoted to horses and had even thought of working with them as a career after school. She was becoming an attractive girl, with her father's dark good looks and the beginnings of a wicked sense of humour. We traded nicknames when I called her Florinda Jane and she christened me Guyrena. The family adopted this name with relish, although it sounded completely ridiculous when used by Sam. We joined Sam's younger brother Mark and his wife Rosie to watch Flora's first attempt at the course. Mark had been a fine horseman and polo player until a bad fall caused paralysis from the chest down, confining him to a wheelchair for the rest of his life. Although of course a terrible tragedy, his cheerful demeanour would suggest that he copes very well, always protected and supported by his devoted wife. They have three delightful children of whom the eldest, Tamara, takes after her father on the polo field. Foxcote, their house near Stowell, enjoys the enviable atmosphere of a supremely happy home. Dinner parties are presided over by the host and hostess sitting together, side by side.

The jumping continued for what seemed like an eternity, with Kate and I desperately trying to create an impression of interest and enthusiasm. She had learnt to ride in the early days of the marriage, but a nasty fall gave her the excuse of never having anything to do with horses again. Even her own colours and some of her doting husband's best bloodstock competing in her name did not encourage her to make more than a token, elegant appearance in the winner's enclosure.

Just before one o'clock we were rounded up by Ce and told to head for the house for lunch. A small procession of gleaming Landrovers climbed through the fields towards the two-hundred-year-old house that was a landmark for miles around. The last stretch of the drive, lined with pleached hornbeams, took us past an imposing stable block that was home to horses and an array of motorcars, as well as flats for the stable staff. Other buildings nearby included a small chapel, the nanny's cottage and the Agent's handsome house. The walled gardens, I later discovered, contained every conceivable vegetable, flowers for the house and hothouses full of peaches and other exotic fruit. No leaf dared to be out of place. This air of order and attention to detail was carried on into the house itself. Boots in the entrance hall, Wellington and riding, arranged in neat rows. Only the children's toys and bicycles looked as though they had been abandoned where they had fallen. Further into the house the impression of great, but understated wealth, was confirmed by the sight of a pair of unlit Canalettos hanging on the staircase. In the half dozen times I went to the house I caught only a glimpse of the small army of people who must be employed to keep the show on the road. Charles, the butler, and his assistant appeared briefly but did not take coats. Sam served drinks from a vestibule outside the drawing room, and when we went in to lunch the dishes were already sitting on the sideboard on hotplates for us to serve ourselves. Apart from the family, the only other guests were Lord and Lady Banbury and Simon and Carolyn Parker Bowles. Although the Banburys sounded as if they should have stepped out of a nursery rhyme, they were in fact rather normal and natural. They lived locally and he had a stammer and framed pictures. She was pretty and Scandinavian with a baby daughter. Simon was there as Flora's dutiful godfather, although his approach to the role could sometimes be a little eccentric. One Christmas she was horrified to find that his present to her was a pair of baggy shorts.

At the table I was between Ce, who sat with Mary her two-year-old daughter beside her, and Pamela, Lady Vestey. She was paying her annual visit from Australia, where she still occupied Nellie Melba's old house. I suppose I had imagined she would be a cross between Joan Sutherland and Edna Everidge, but in fact she was demure and shy and quite difficult to engage in conversation. Her husband had died at a relatively young age and she had been left to bring up two small boys on her own. They all shared a love of horses, but I think that was one of the few things that brought them together. She did eventually show a bit of spirit by telling Sam he was name-dropping as he regaled Bill Banbury with his Princess Anne quip, and she laughed like a drain when I wondered aloud if Mark Phillips had understood. All in all I was having rather a good time at my end of the table, but I could see that Kate, beside Sam as convention required, had decided on 'grin and bare it' as the best policy. They were both quite animated as far as the table in general was concerned, but between each other no word or glance was exchanged. In the years since their divorce a certain amount of communication had had to take place – usually in connection with the girls' schools, holidays and travel arrangements. Money was never discussed because her settlement involved a one-off payment into a trust, from which she derived her income. Although the amount ran to several million pounds it was way below the sort of figures achieved today by the ex-wives of enormously rich men. A possible explanation for this is that the female lawyer acting for Kate had a habit of saying, 'Well we don't want to upset Lord Vestey, do we?' whenever a new restriction was placed on her room to manoeuvre. The poor thing emerged from the debacle without a single piece of family jewellery or as much as a wedding present toast rack. To cap it all, Sam announced his engagement to Celia Knight in *The Times* even before the divorce became absolute.

After lunch some of us went into the drawing room for coffee, while the others repaired to the library to watch the racing on television. Quite a bit of traffic between the two rooms meant that I tried to do the polite thing and stand up whenever a woman appeared. After a while this became too much for Sam, sitting resolutely in his seat.

'For God's sake stop jumping up and down!' he roared. 'The trouble with this house is that there are too many women in it. There are three Lady Vesteys for a start!'

22

It was obvious from the start that being employed as Kate's 'companion' was going to mean far more to both of us than simply acting the role of hired hand. The very nature of the job entailed spending a lot of time alone together, a proximity that inevitably led to friendship. There were sometimes companionable silences, but we were never at a loss for something to talk about. We got to know each other extremely well.

Looking back, I think she enjoyed the first few years of her single status. After all, an attractive woman with money and a title is always going to be courted by certain sections of society. However, a lesson she learnt very early on is that once you are cast out by a rich and powerful man you are on your own as far as his friends are concerned. Most of them had probably thought she was an upstart in the first place, but feelings like that were suppressed when her flare as hostess at Egerton Crescent or Stowell Park became apparent.

Although Kate had been to a reasonably posh public school, her background was firmly middle class. The Eccles family came from Lancashire, a source of great pride to her parents. A pride that did not, however, extend to their elder daughter's strong regional accent, for she was forbidden to answer the telephone until she had taken elocution lessons. John Eccles worked for H.J. Heinz, travelling the world to buy the ingredients for their tinned products, and retiring as a director. His job enabled them to live comfortably in a West London suburb. Kate left school with little in the way of academic qualifications, but with a good record on the sports field. She had also blossomed into a considerable beauty, with fair hair and a figure of which to be proud. Extra polish was provided by a cordon bleu course, as well as the sort of undemanding selling jobs at Fortnums and Aspreys taken by girls not quite bright enough for secretarial college. Her social life took off when she moved out of 4 Astons Road and into shared flats at good addresses in SW7 and SW3. Unusually, she did not smoke or drink, but her sense of humour and vitality ensured a constant stream of well-heeled admirers. Good connections were made whilst using her domestic skills in grand houses in the South of France and at a smart pub in Oxfordshire run by her friends, David and Margaret Levin, who went on to own the Capital Hotel in Knightsbridge.

She had always enjoyed fast cars and the company of the men who drove them. Such an interest inevitably led to her regular attendance at motor-racing events and trips to continental Grand Prixs. Pretty soon she got to know the stars of the track like Graham Hill and James Hunt, as well as her fellow enthusiast, Prince Michael of Kent. But her sights were set on that arguably most handsome and charismatic of British racing drivers, Jim Clark. As a shy and diffident Scot he must have presented quite a challenge for even the most determined groupie, but our Kathryn was up to the task. Not surprisingly, he very soon fell for her charms and they began an affair that was to last until his untimely death on the race track. The passing of the first great love of her life left her devastated.

At a party in London she met a young ex-Guards officer called Robert Fellowes. After they had known each other for a while he invited her to a weekend house party in Gloucestershire, to the home of his best friend Sam Vestey. Sam and his younger brother, Mark, were probably the most eligible bachelors in England at the time. Both were titled, dashingly handsome, extremely rich and brilliant polo players. Kate, with her well-known obsession for cleanliness and order, was rather put off by the state of Stowell Park, the boys' bachelor pad. But she could see that it had possibilities. Invitations to more weekends soon followed and before long she was acting as hostess for young Lord Vestey in London and the country.

In spite of her parent's strong misgivings – for Sam and his future father-in-law were never to hit it off – they married in Northleach parish church and cruised the Greek isles on honeymoon. As well as the happiness of her husband, Kate saw as her main task the complete overhaul of their much-neglected stately home. To that end, and with the complete indulgence of the doting Sam, she engaged the services of leading interior decorators Nina Campbell and David Milinaric. At the same time they moved their London base from a small mews to a five-floor house in elegant Egerton Crescent, a perfect setting for weekday entertaining. A limitless budget, combined with her perfectly pitched taste and understated style shot her to the top of the society hostess league. But all was not what it might have seemed. Day-to-day living with her hard-drinking and gregarious husband was proving quite stressful for a woman, shy in those days, and lacking in self-confidence. They were both keen to start a family, and as the cracks appeared the prospect of a child – preferably a son and heir – seemed likely to be the panacea for all their ills. In due course Kate was able to announce that she was pregnant, but sadly the baby did not survive. This great loss was a terrible blow to her, though at least it had the effect of uniting the young couple once more. She was to endure several more miscarriages before finally she gave birth to beautiful and perfectly healthy Saffron. Having had the advantage of a wonderful mother herself, Kate approached her new role with love and enthusiasm. Saffron soon grew to inhabit an idyllic world of ponies and parties, watched over by a succession of nannies who came and went with some regularity. The fleet of helicopters, at least, were constant and reliable and she spent as much time in them, winging her way between London and Gloucestershire, as she did in her pram in Kensington Gardens. On one turbulent flight the poor infant was spectacularly sick all over her mother's full-length silver fox coat. On arrival, this unhappy garment was despatched not to Sketchleys, but to the dustbin, whilst another one took its place.

In those days Sam Vestey's chairmanship of the family firm gave him autocratic power over the lives of thousands of people, and control of a budget that would have gladdened the heart of many a South American dictator. His land holdings in countries like Australia and Argentina ran to many hundreds of thousands of acres. Routinely every year the company jet would head off to the far outposts of his empire, where he and his wife would be regarded like minor members of the Royal Family – meeting senior executives, station managers and the ubiquitous babies held up for a kiss. At almost every destination a certain amount of time was set aside for his all-consuming passion, polo. To the uninitiated, and therefore unrich, it is probably the world's least spectator-friendly sport. The action always seems to take place at the far side of a vast field, where a small group of men and horses become a blur of flailing legs and sticks. Sometimes a body is hurled to the ground (usually that of the Prince of Wales), but more often than not the excitement is confined to the colourful language (usually that of the Duke of Edinburgh, in his playing days) that wafts across the greensward. The game's saving grace, as far as most women and gay men are concerned, is the bodywork, charm and sheer masculinity of the players (with the obvious exception of the D of E and, of course, Kerry Packer). Naturally enough, Kate was also vulnerable to the blandishments of these male icons, and her blonde good looks as well as a title and untold riches made her a target too. Sultry afternoons at the polo ground, particularly in Buenos Aires, were made tolerable for her by their presence. She looked forward to the season in England when selected teams were invited to stay at Stowell.

Sam and Kate decided to try a year's separation to see if a time apart could save their marriage. By now she began to suspect that all Sam's many friends showed allegiance only to him, and that if for some reason she was no longer by his side they would drop her like a hot potato. In order to escape all that, she took a large house in Barbados for the winter. She took another in Majorca for the spring and moved to Long Island for the autumn. She travelled with as many friends as she could muster, as well as a personal trainer, a nanny and a housekeeper. At the end of the twelve months she moved back to Stowell, determined to play her part, but probably resigned to the inevitable.

She became pregnant again, but this time enjoyed the services of the Queen's gynaecologist, Sir George Parker. She gives full credit to him for the success of the birth of her second child, Flora. In 1995 a surprise party to mark Sir George's retirement was held at Grosvenor House. All the mothers and babies, known as 'Pinker's children' were invited to lunch in the ballroom. It was impossible for Flora to get away from school and so Kate asked me to go in her place. Quite how my presence was going to be explained I have no idea, but fortunately at the last moment Saffron left work early and went with her mother instead. They clearly had a marvellous time, and when I picked them up afterwards in Park Lane Kate was determined to carry on with the party. She announced that champagne cocktails at The Capital were what was needed. Through a painstaking process of elimination we had agreed that these were the best drinks of their kind in London.

Once we had settled in the bar I heard all about the party. Hundreds of people had turned up to honour this distinguished man. Princess Michael was among them. After a delicious lunch David Frost appeared on the stage, and to the guest of honour's complete surprise, presented a sort of 'This Is Your Life'. Colleagues and patients came on to pay tribute and by the end there was not a dry eye in the house. A standing ovation brought the proceedings to a close. Saffron left us after several glasses and her mother and I decided to stay on for dinner.

When Sam and Kate announced their formal separation with a view to divorce they were living in an enormous house in Upper Philimore Gardens. Sam moved out and its ownership passed to the Upper Philimore Trust, from which Kate was to derive her income. And so began the difficult state of affairs whereby Kate was rich, but had no money of her own. After a while she decided that the house was far too big to live in on her own and asked the trustees to sell it. At the time estate agents said it was the first house in London to sell for more than a million pounds. With part of the proceeds something much smaller was bought for her in Seymour Walk, a cul-de-sac of attractive houses just off the Fulham Road.

One of the few society friends Kate had in her own right was Lord Bradford's sister, Serena Bridgeman. When Serena's father died he left her a small estate near Fort William, on the west coast of Scotland. I only went there once with Kate, but it was a lovely house in a perfect rural setting and Kate became very fond of it. To look after the sporting side of it Serena employed a ghillie called John, who lived with his wife in a scruffy wee cottage near the big house. It was difficult to put an age to John. His rugged outdoor existence had given him a weather-beaten face, but I suspect his legendary attachment to the national brew had added to the colour of his complexion more than somewhat. He looked about sixty, but may well have been in his forties. His wife, Rene (pronounced Reen), on the other hand was definitely old enough to be his mother. Kate and John got on very well together, particularly once she had taken the trouble to understand what he was saying. A sort of Queen Victoria/John Brown relationship began to develop, but without any question of impropriety. He always addressed her very firmly as '*My* lady'.

On one of her many visits, Kate asked John if he would teach her to fish on the loch. He proved to be a considerate and patient tutor, and they spent many hours together on the water, at all hours of the day and night. This new interest, the only hobby she has ever had, added to her feeling of contentment in that part of the world. Serena stayed at the house only occasionally and tried to let it out for large parts of the year. When Kate asked if she could take it for a couple of the winter months, including Christmas, she readily agreed. For some time Kate had been toying with the idea of keeping a small flat in London and having a proper home in Scotland. A prolonged stay at the worst time of year to test her reaction was eminently sensible. The experiment turned out to be a great success. The house was warm and comfortable and the presence of Serena's 'couple', as well as Irene and her husband from London, ensured fresh sheets every day and starched napkins by the yard.

The first stage in Kate's planned re-location was to sell the Seymour Walk house, of which she had become very fond. The eventual buyer was Peter de Savary, who had obviously come a long way since Ian Macbeth left Latchmoor to go and skipper his yacht all those years before. From there she moved into the Eaton Place flat, and that closes the circle.

With Dorothy's help the final touches were added to the decoration and furnishing of the new flat. The search for particular items had been concentrated on that part of East Anglia near her home that Dorothy knew well. These trips often entailed overnight stops at the Ratcliffes' beautiful Georgian house, set in a large walled garden on the edge of the unremarkable town of Halstead. The house was a tribute to Dorothy's decorating skills and overflowed with the fruits of her years as an antique dealer. If any object looked out of place it was usually because it pre-dated Dorothy's arrival on the scene. She solved this problem in the next house to which they moved by grouping together Leonard's knickknacks and ornaments in a shed in the garden! They both went out of their way to make me welcome and comfortable, even though Leonard was probably not at all sure why I was there. But he was clearly very fond of Kate and included her on fishing trips to the Tweed, where the Duke of Roxborough charged them vast sums of money for the privilege. Our excursions from Halstead sometimes took us to an architectural salvage emporium, or more probably to Long Melford where almost every shop was given over to the sale of antiques. The main attraction for us was the largest shop in the town, which was run by a pair of handsome and unscrupulous queens. Kate and Dorothy enjoyed an easy, jokey relationship with them and bought some of their goodies. We called several times to see them, but gave up in the end when we were always told that they were on holiday. One day we discovered the reason for this change in their lifestyle when it emerged that the brother of one of them had been the close companion of the artist Francis Bacon. When Bacon died he copped the lot.

By now Kate was turning her attention to the next part of her grand design – doing something about Kirkbuddo. We had agreed that I should have my belongings sent there from Newton Street and take up temporary residence. She was concerned that the garden needed urgent attention and, more importantly, that the house should be treated by Rentokil to rid it of any small furry rodents. For she was a serious miceophobe. But before all this happened I asked if I could honour a commitment and have two weeks' holiday – unpaid, of course.

Maggie and Phylip had been my last friends to stay at Moss Cree, and while they were there I had agreed to join them, with Jane, at a friend's house they were going to rent in the Auverne. While they were with me we indulged our joint passions for garden visiting and long rambles, and they also took it upon themselves to completely redecorate the kitchen – the orange pine which they knew I hated. My contribution to their efforts was to provide them with hot and cold refreshments and to spatter every item of clothing in my possession with blobs of white paint. But, let's face it, the house did sell to the first people through the door!

The four of us had an idyllic time in the rather dank and hilly boar-sustaining countryside of that part of France. The house provided us with all the comfort we needed, but for my part I never felt entirely at ease in it. The problem was that although the owner had insisted we treat it exactly like our home, she did make one stipulation. The *spiders* were not to be disturbed! Now, although I am far from arachnophobic, I really don't care for the beastly things – especially when they are big and fat and black (and presumably French). After a while I tried to pretend that they weren't there, and they certainly didn't seem to move very much. But it didn't take long to notice where they all lived and if I happened to glance at a corner I knew to be a dwelling place and it was empty! You can probably imagine how I felt.

Most days we availed ourselves of delicious lunches, for not much money, in nearby towns and villages. Afternoons were spent reading or being guided on long walks by Phylip and his detailed map of the area. We came across acres of spring flowers and collections of marvellously decaying farm carts and old implements. But we avoided, where possible, the farms themselves after a first encounter with an over-zealous Alsatian.

Once the fire was lit, evenings were given over to bacchanalia, with hysterical games of Scrabble rounding things off. Before retiring I would often stumble into the night with something from the table as a treat for a neighbouring horse. During the day he happily crunched his way through our Fox's Glacier Mints, but I couldn't help thinking that those and grass alone were not enough to keep those rippling muscles in shape. He always rushed over to greet his nocturnal visitor but, equally, never hesitated to express his disdain for the salami and Toulouse sausages I thrust in front of his ultra-sensitive nose. We returned refreshed from our break and waited with trepidation for the arrival of Philip's photographs.

Soon after I got back, Gyp and I were despatched to Kirkbuddo with Bumble to begin the process of turning the house into a home. Kate was always keen that instead of tackling the long drive I should make the journey from Euston on the overnight train. That was fine from the timing point of view, but it meant a pretty uncomfortable few hours for the dogs in the guard's van and me in a sleeper. Even alone in a first-class compartment I found sleep quite a problem and always had to have one of Kate's sleeping pills to get me through the night. But the bonuses were that by eight o'clock I was tucking into a 'full' Scottish breakfast at the Cally, and by nine-thirty I was breathing quite different air, opening the back of the Range Rover to allow the dogs to charge across the lawn, with the cry of 'bits!' ringing in their ears. During the next few days my Moss Cree things arrived and were mostly used to make the breakfast room more like a cosy sitting room. I also hung pictures in the hall and on the stairs to make it more welcoming. By the time I collected Kate from Dyce, Aberdeen's airport, the laurel hedges had been clipped and the rose bed dug over, ready for seed sowing. Accommodation had been arranged for her at the first of a series of hotels in the area she was to use, before moving into the house. She put up no resistance at all when I showed her the job I had saved for a two-pronged attack. We spent a whole day with stiff brooms clearing the drive of every last vestige of moss and lichen, the accumulation of many years. Although it was back-breaking work, it was something that I knew would please her. Equally appealing, I hoped, would be the opportunity to grow her own vegetables. At Forfar's garden centre the next day we duly bought seeds, half-barrels and plants for the front of the house and an enormous motor-driven lawnmower.

Kneeling carefully between the rose bushes we committed to the ground rows of lettuces, peas, carrots, onions and broad beans. As it was Kate's first venture into the world of horticulture she very determinedly gave each of the tiny seeds her individual attention, making the operation a back-breaking process. When we finally stood back to admire our handiwork we noticed at once that, in the excitement of the moment, I had failed to allow enough space between the rows for access. But as the little green shoots began to appear in the weeks that followed we had to come to terms with the fact that this was the least of our problems. What we had fondly imagined to be a small family of Flopsy, Mopsy and Bobtails was in reality a vast marauding tribe of ruthless veg eaters. What is more, we were told that the county of Angus has a larger rabbit population than any other part of the kingdom. To protect our precious crops men were brought in to construct wire fences that had their roots buried two feet into the ground. But even defences like those did not keep out the most single-minded of our furry foes.

With the arrival of summer another monstrous pestilence was visited upon us. As old Scottish hands we were both prepared to be bitten by the country's national creature and best-kept secret, The Midge. But what we had not expected was that it would join forces with Kirkbuddo's own variety of nasty blackfly to make our outdoor lives a misery. I have never been so heavily veiled as I was on lawn mowing days, and for Kate there was no chance of sunbathing. More men were brought in to spray the woodland with a powerful insecticide, but to no avail.

All in all, keeping the fauna at bay had become a major preoccupation. But at least, thanks to Rentokil, Kate had accepted that the house was mouse- proof enough for her to take up residence. However, as a last precaution before her bed arrived yet more men were recruited to cover her bedroom floor with securely fixed hardboard. Between trips to London she spent quite a lot of time with me at the house during the summer months. We passed the time exploring the area and looking for redeeming features in the little towns of Brechin and Arbroath. Sadly, the coast too was fairly uninspiring, apart from one glorious stretch of sand called Lunan Bay, where the dogs were dive-bombed by seagulls. With such an outdoor life we were quite happy to spend most evenings on our own at home, only venturing out occasionally after dark to a couple of local restaurants. Cravings for shellfish were satisfied at one of these, whose speciality was lobster. This has always been Kate's favourite crustacean, and one she can handle with aplomb. In fact you might say she had a lobster grip.

Flora came for a few days and so did Saffron, fresh from her year in the Antipodes. We had both heard a great deal about each other from her mother and soon found that with a shared, and rather mucky sense of humour, we were firm friends. Although they were both delighted to see that Mama was happy in her new home, they made it clear that the long journey would preclude regular visits.

As the summer wore on Kate began to feel the need for some serious sunshine and announced that she had taken a house in the South of France for two weeks in August. She chose that time deliberately in the hope that at least one of the girls would be able to go too, but they had already made their holiday plans. In the end we went on our own by air to Nice and hired a car at the airport. Fortunately it was a house she had rented once before and remembered how to get there. Although it was hideously hot, by the time we reached our destination in the hills near Grasse we began to feel a slight breeze. The house was not only very comfortable, but luckily quite cool and was surrounded by a shady garden. When the trip was first discussed she had said that she might get in touch with her old friend Joan Collins, who had a house not far away at Porte Grimaud. But this idea was never mentioned again and we spent the two weeks making our own amusements. Most days we drove the short and horribly congested distance to the beach at Juan les Pins, where Kate soaked up the sun and practised her 'Monte Carlo Crawl'. I, on the other hand, kept firmly out of the water and wherever possible the sun too, taking long walks dodging from tree to tree like a randy Labrador. Although we only went out to dinner twice, the cost of both meals would have paid for two package holidays to Majorca. The name of the first place escapes me, but it is a restaurant where you are given the choice of only two breeds of meat and whichever you have chosen is thrown onto a blazing fire in front of you. The other venue, to which neither of us had been before, was the unbelievably chi-chi Moulin at Mougins whose speciality, as far as I was concerned, was intimidation. By contrast, the hatched-faced old crone sitting alone at the next table was obviously completely at ease. She spent the duration of a five-course dinner feeding the contents of her plate to the Yorkshire Terrier who sat at her feet. When it came to paying the bill at these places the signature may have been mine, but mercifully the credit card was my companion's!

As soon as we got back I had urgent business to attend to that required yet another Range Rover/overnight train journey to Kirkbuddo. The reason for the haste was that in our absence someone had been found who would water the garden, and Kate was concerned that we might have missed the start of the broad beans. We had already enjoyed the other fruits of our labours before we went to France. But I got there to find that the wretched things were still not ready to be picked, even in extreme youth. However, the trip was not entirely wasted as I just had time to cut the grass before retracing my steps to Edinburgh and the train back to Euston. At a cost of the best part of four hundred pounds it was not the most financially effective way to not obtain vegetables. But at least we now knew that things reach fruition a little later in that part of the world, and that there would be a need for lots of parsley sauce in October.

I spent that Christmas with Alex in Munslow. Festivities centred around lunch on Christmas Day, when I cooked a brace of pheasant and we were joined by his mother. Although the house was slap-bang on the busy main road between Craven Arms and Much Wenlock he had made it very comfortable and distinguished with the furniture and pictures he had collected over the years. We also saw quite a lot of his neighbours, Murray and David, who lived at the other end of the row of five houses. They had for many years taught at primary schools in Wolverhampton, but with one long break when they took over the town's celebrated gay pub. Munslow had a pub too, but with a more conventional clientele, and happily it was within easy tottering distance.

The time I spent with Alex was always very special, even though I competed for his attention with the black beauty who shared his life. Last thing at night she was always quicker than I was to reach his bed and his arms, but I was usually allowed to perch on the edge of the mattress. In spite of this nocturnal battle of wills she loved me for the walks we shared, a treat she was seldom given by her master. But I knew that lurchers love exercise, even though they don't demand it. Gyp, of course, thought Rush was a pushy old bag and treated her with her usual total disregard.

Kate started the New Year determined to resuscitate her social life and to start entertaining again. Among the first dinner parties she gave was one for friends she had met through me. The guests were Maggie and Phylip, Zoe and Sebastian Whitestone. I was thrilled to see Kate's dormant flair as a hostess in action and between them, she and Irene, made the flat look magnificent. The menu she had chosen, caviar followed by bangers and mash, was one she had enjoyed at the home of her old chum, Ned Ryan. (The only real difference was that at Ned's house the food was served by a footman loaned from Princess Margaret. Although I suppose my presence made up for that!) The evening was great fun and a colossal success – with old Whitestone on cracking form. But the high hopes I had entertained for his meeting with Kate sadly came to nothing.

Several other dinner parties were to follow, including one at which Ned himself was a guest. His Irish wit and charm were much in evidence, even though he was enduring his annual three months of total abstinence. For many years he and Kate had belonged to the same group of friends that included Rowena Cotton, a woman for whom Kate had considerable affection. In due course I went with Kate to spend two weekends at Rowena's house, Tythrop Park near Thame. She lived there with her husband, Jeremy, who was the son of Jack Cotton, the enormously rich property developer and 1960s partner of Charles Clore. The house was vast and Carrollean and filled with marvellous pictures and furniture. As a child, Rowena told me, she had often seen it from the road and been impressed, never dreaming that one day she would be its chatelaine. Over the years she had used her skills as an interior decorator, and Jeremy's money, to great effect.

More recently she had turned her attention to the outside of the house and recreated the original parterre and knot garden.

Kate had often enjoyed their hospitality and sometimes used the house as a retreat when the going was a bit heavy at Stowell. The Cottons were well established in the area and enjoyed entertaining neighbours such as Lord and Lady Carrington and Robin Gibb of The Bee Gees. Another occasional house guest was the hostesses dilemma, Princess Margaret Rose. According to Kate, their visits often coincided, with disastrous consequences for her nervous system. Rather than relaxing, PM liked nothing better than to emulate her grandmother by leading the house party on a tour of local antique shops, where there was little to admire, let alone purchase. By the late afternoon she would be firmly ensconced in the library's most comfortable armchair beside the fire reading a racy novel. As her fellow guests feigned interest in copies of *Country Life* and *The Field* all they could think of was escaping to their rooms to prepare for the ordeal of having to sit next to her at dinner. When the strain became too much for Kate, she suddenly stood up and said the first thing that came into her mind: 'Well I suppose I had better go and bath Saffron (who was ten) before dinner.' She fled the room just as PM was heard to mutter, 'I should have thought she was old enough to do that for herself by now!'

The ritual of Sunday evenings at Tythrop revolves around the fact that the 'couple' are 'off' and leave a cold supper to be eaten in the kitchen. In a house where the Queen's sister is a guest this level of informality presents everyone with a sartorial dilemma. After great deliberation Kate plumped for a very short skirt and began the journey from her bedroom to the back of the house. On the way, who should she bump into but the mother of the Queen's only nephew and niece. Poor flustered Kate, feeling an explanation was necessary, said;

'Oh Ma'am, it's so difficult. I didn't know whether to wear a skirt or jeans.'

With a glance at Kate's exposed legs, PM retorted witheringly, 'I should have thought both would have been more appropriate!'.

I arrived at the flat one morning to be greeted with the disappointing news that Kirkbuddo was going to have to be sold. I had been aware, of course, for sometime that a battle was raging over its future. The last straw came when Tony Goode paid a flying visit and saw for himself how much money was going to be needed to get it done up to the Vestey stratospheric standards. When this was added to the estimated annual running costs the trust simply put its foot down. I was sad because I had been looking forward to occupying my little bedroom and bathroom that was to be created on the ground floor behind the drawing room. However, the agreed timetable was that Kate would continue to enjoy the house during the summer and use it as a base from which to look again for something more suitable. In September the house would be put on the market, with me in place to show people round.

Happily Kate soon recovered from the Kirkbuddo setback and began to talk enthusiastically about showing me the beauty of the west coast. Secretly this was where her heart had always been, and she had never really taken to the less dramatic landscape between Edinburgh and Aberdeen. With our two furry white companions we spent many happy days following up advertisements for houses in *Country Life* and brochures from agents. For someone who had never been beyond Argyllshire on that side of Scotland (except in *Britannia*, but that doesn't count), the scenery was a revelation to me. After all our wanderings, particularly in the area around Fort William, two places emerged as distinct possibilities. Kate went so far as to make an offer on one of them, but as there was lots of interest from prospective buyers who were able to move quickly, nothing came of it. In the end, the launch date for Kirkbuddo was brought forward and I stood by to point out its special features.

At Kate's suggestion Alex came up for some holiday and to keep me company for a week. I had brought together these two people who were so important in my life some months earlier. On one of Alex's trips to London I took them both to lunch at the Greenhouse in Hays Mews, where a good time was had by all. It meant a lot that we all got on so well, and that she became forever his KV.

Later in the summer Kate's housing problems were put on hold when, at last, she became romantically involved. The object of her desire was a six-foot three Canadian chiropractor of about her own age who, in his youth, had been a considerable sportsman. And very charming he was too. His name was Chris Moffat (although Kate had to add the '-topher' and remove the identity bracelet) and they had met through a mutual West Indian friend called Noel who had once run a famous nightclub in Barbados. Noel's other claim to fame was his serious involvement with Carina Fitzalan-Howard, daughter of the Duke and Duchess of Norfolk. The story goes that the relationship had reached the stage where the dutiful daughter felt it was time to take her beau to meet her famously Roman Catholic parents. The encounter went well, with both sides turning on the charm. But the last word on the subject from the ducal pair was that the liaison should go no further. They had no objection to Noel at all, but the fact that he was a Protestant made marriage impossible. Carina went on to marry David Frost.

In a re-run of the year before, Kate began to feel the pull of the South of France as August approached. Thanks to a late cancellation Roger satisfied her need by coming up with what he described as a 'good deal' on a 'stunning' house near Eze. I got the impression that she and Christopher were going to share the cost which meant, I hoped, that I would have two weeks with the dogs walking the Shropshire Hills. But that was not to be. Instead of being romantically à deux, a ticket to Nice was produced for me, and Roger came along too.

In the bright Riviera sunlight it was plain to see that the only stunning thing about our holiday home was the view from the very large terrace. And it was truly spectacular. But the house itself was modern and undistinguished, with very cheap furnishings. However, it did have the advantage of enough space to preclude unplanned encounters. We were met on arrival by a friend of the owner who acted as resident caretaker. Middle-aged and English, he bore a marked resemblance to Anna Massey in one of her spookier roles. From the outset he did his best to help in every way, but with one broken wrist and another that looked distinctly wobbly there was a limit as to how much he could do. The accident happened, apparently, when he stumbled on some rocks (late at night, according to Roger), but what we all wanted to know and dare not ask was – did he fall or was he pushed?

In spite of the blistering heat I managed to do a certain amount of walking – including a great big circular hike with Roger around Cap Ferrat. As a foursome we also went to Juan les Pins and to Roger's house in the hills. But the best day for me was a nostalgic trip to Monte Carlo that culminated in drinks at La Reserve. We sat in the bar I remembered so well and got into conversation with an elderly waiter who had fond recollections of Alan Searle.

Unlike our last French holiday we avoided expensive restaurants and spent far more time buying food for home consumption. The local markets were a rich source of delicacies and a magnet for any girl with the urge to shop – and three men to carry the bags. Tasks in the kitchen were shared between us, although Kate had overall control of presentation. But her efforts were often frustrated by a shortage of dishes and the existence of only one dinner service. Things came to a head one day when a cold lunch was being arranged on the alfresco dining table. With a wide range of meats, salads and fruit already assembled the hunt was on for a suitable receptacle for the apricots, figs and grapes. When a shallow pie dish was found for the role it was immediately christened 'the platter of tiny fruit'.

Back once more at Kirkbuddo, interest in the house was hotting up. Among the people I showed round was a young local couple whose faces were somehow familiar. I thought at first it was the husband who was famous – but he proved to be just extremely handsome. When I checked with the agent I was told that it was his wife who had the fame, and presumably the money. She was the runner Liz McColgan. Although they made interested noises, nothing more was heard from them. But, hot on their heels, there came a maker of greetings cards from Dundee and his extended family. When they paid a second visit it was obvious that they were considering an offer very seriously indeed. In the end I think it was the billiard room that sold it to them, even though the house was perfect for three generations of a family who wanted to live separately under the same roof.

Looking back, events that year also included two more invitations to lunch at Stowell. The first, inevitably, revolved around Flora doing something with horses. But instead of returning to the house to eat we sat on the grass for a picnic. Happily the House of Windsor had not sent a representative and I was the only outsider. As ever, Ce went out of her way to make me feel relaxed, while her husband was positively matey. With increased confidence I even felt able at one stage to make a remark to him about a horse! As a pretty young filly was trotted past I observed:

'Gosh, that's a fine-looking specimen.'

To which he responded, 'Well, Guyrena, all I can say is that you are to horses what Cyril Smith is to ballet dancers.'

I recovered my composure sufficiently some time later to point to a combine harvester that was at work in the next field. 'Is that something you hire?' I asked, 'or do you own it? I know they are enormously expensive.'

'We own it,' he said. 'But you are quite right, they are expensive and always have been. I remember many years ago my mother buying a Rolls-Royce. Do you know, we bought a combine harvester at the same time and they were both the same price.'

The next time I went there was with Kate to celebrate her elder daughter's twenty-first birthday. How she was to spend it had been left entirely to her, even though both parents had suggested every sort of ball, dinner and reception. But having reached her majority Saffron Vestey was very much her own woman. To a great extent she was embarrassed by the family name (particularly when 'the Hon.' was put in front of it) – not because of what it was, but because to most people it smacked of great riches. Although I'd not known her before she went to Australia, I knew that she had worked for a time in an estate agent's office. After Australia, that sort of job was anathema to her and she worked instead, unpaid, for a charity that cared for the homeless. With a trust fund at her disposal she had quite naturally used the money to buy her first house (only a short walk from where her mother lived) and she used it to provide food and lodging for any of her friends who were in London. As well as anything else she had brought back from Australia, the most tangible thing was an extraordinary little dog called Bee. She had lots of character, was utterly obedient and very shy. On many a morning I would collect her to join Bumble and Gyp for our daily assault on the Royal Parks. On one particular day we had got as far as the middle of Hyde Park when I noticed that Bee was lagging behind. When I called her she shot off, without hesitation, in the direction from which we had come. I ran after her for as long as I could, but she was jet-propelled. Defeated, I went back to gather up the other two and made tracks for the car. After driving frantically around for a while I returned to Saffron's house in the hope that Bee might have, against all the odds, got back there in one piece. Sure enough, she was fast asleep on the doorstep.

Saffron's birthday lunch proved to be a low-key affair, even though she had chosen the guest list as well as the menu. The Banburys the PBs and Tim the agent were there, but the star performers were Saffron's best friends from schooldays – four glorious girls called Cack, Willie, Em and Tilly. Carolyn PB recorded the occasion with her camera, with the best photograph being of Sam on a sofa in the drawing room, with a wife on either side and surrounded by his five children.

Alex came to say at Aynhoe Road for Christmas and we started the festivities by supping with Kate on Christmas Eve. Dorothy and Leonard had also been invited as well as Margaret and David Levin and their three children. Instead of going to Stowell, Saffron was there to give her mother moral support. Once the guests had departed

Saffron and Alex decided to go to Midnight Mass in the church just round the corner. I stayed behind with our hostess for a nightcap. In due course the dogs became restless and so I took them out for their late night pee. Not only was there Bumble, Gyp, Rush and Bee but also Fred, who had recently been bought by Saffron from a man in Battersea Park. With a profusion of leads all went well until we approached the church. As we passed the door the voices from within reached a crescendo and Bee, Fred and Rush obviously heard the unmistakable sounds of their owners. With no regard for the sanctity of the occasion they burst through the double swing doors with me, Bumble and Gyp in helpless pursuit. With commendable sang-froid, the vicar treated the visitation not as the second coming, but as an outrage to be ignored. But to the amusement of the congregation I gathered up my wayward flock and beat a hasty retreat.

Alex and I eventually returned to my flat and spent what was left of the night very happily watching wicked videos and drinking great quantities of heather juice.

Christmas Day itself was uneventful as far as I was concerned. With a hangover that had destroyed my senses there was very little part that I could play. But on Boxing Day I drove Saffron and Alex to Sandown Park, where they joined her father to watch some racing. We paused en route for Bloody Marys at the sort of rough pub where they ask if you want Worcester Sauce with them, and I spent a non-equestrian afternoon walking the dogs.

Ever since the party at Hurlingham Kate had wanted us to spend another evening dancing. The opportunity to do so presented itself when New Year's Eve came round again. We checked with all the big hotels to see what sort of entertainment they were offering, and plumped in the end for The Lanesborough in spite of the ludicrous cost. The attraction for us was the idea of dancing to the Confrey Phillips band. I was also curious to see the inside of the building as I had only been there once many years before to visit a friend whose hip had been replaced. We dined in what I think had been the mortuary, a setting alas, where some of our fellow guests would not have looked out of place. Younger people (apart from us) were presumably put off by the prohibitive cost. But the food was perfectly decent and Mr Phillips certainly had a way with a tune. We managed to stay just long enough to see in 1994.

Kate's decision to give up the idea of a house in Scotland was influenced largely by her concern for Flora. Her daughter had reached the age at which as well as spending time with her pony at Stowell, the bright lights of London were becoming increasingly attractive. Her Kate had taken great pains to ensure that Flora's bedroom at Campden was just as she wanted it. Another, and very surprising, factor in the equation had been a chance remark from Ce. Watching Flora on horseback at Stowell one day, her stepmother turned to Kate and expressed the opinion that it was a shame she didn't live closer so that she could come to Stowell more often when Flora was there.

Fired with new enthusiasm we consulted a map and decided to see what north Oxfordshire had to offer. It was an area that had the advantage of close proximity to London, Flora's school and, of course, Chateau Vestey. There were picture-postcard villages in profusion and quite a number that had houses for sale. But it soon became apparent that Kate was dead set against the idea of a village house and was handicapped by a budget that bought a lot in Scotland, but much less in the Home Counties. Probably because she regarded me as a bit of a dimwit she didn't seek my advice very often, but after this setback she asked me where I would live, given a choice. Without hesitation I explained that in recent years, and thanks entirely to Alex, I had become particularly fond of South Shropshire and North Herefordshire. He was devoted to his home patch and spent hours showing me isolated churches and countryside that was reminiscent of Scotland. That did it for Kate; using my name rather than hers, I registered her interest with all the appropriate estate agents and waited for the brochures to arrive.

To start with we followed one false trail, thanks to an illustration of a pen-and-ink drawing in *Country Life*. It was the work of an artist called Simon Dorrell whose boyfriend, David Wheeler, was an occasional contributor to the magazine. With cats and dogs in the foreground, it was a depiction of their house in Wales, which they were trying to sell. From Kate' s point of view the house proved to be a disappointment from the word go. The outside of it was the colour of butterscotch, which did not encourage us to penetrate further. But we took to the owners at once, even though they were (to use Kate's oft-repeated phrase) 'two of your lot!' We kept in touch and when they eventually sold they moved to a larger house near Presteigne that had the amount of land they wanted. Both house and garden required a lot of attention, but the first thing they did was to paint the exterior a remarkable shade of blue. A lot of the work they did themselves, even though David was heavily committed to *Hortus*, his erudite gardening periodical, and Simon always seemed to be preparing for another exhibition. As a surprise for Kate's fiftieth birthday I commissioned him to draw Bumble and she was thrilled with the result.

Parties at their house always attracted a marvellous mixture of people. One day at lunch I got into conversation with an attractively young bohemian couple. At one stage the girl asked me to guess what her boyfriend did for a living. When I was forced to admit defeat she told me with great delight that he worked as a white-faced clown, and was much in demand for children's parties. She then asked me politely what I did, sure in her own mind that I drove a lorry or sold insurance. So when I confessed to 'companion' they both seemed rather amazed. At that point the clown chipped in to tell us that as a teenager he used to go and stay with his grandmother who employed a young woman to act as her companion. Although there was a big difference in their ages an intimacy developed and his grandmother's companion eventually deprived him of his virginity. When the grandmother found out, the woman was dismissed and was last heard of being companionable with a peer on his estate in North Devon.

Our only other excursion into the principality was for an extremely indulgent two-night stay at a hotel called Llangoed Hall, owned by Bernard Ashley. One of the house rules was that dogs were not allowed into the building, and had their own accommodation in a converted stable. It was most unusual for Kate to stay somewhere that prevented Bumble from sharing her bed, but in this case she made an exception. After dining well on the first night we went to see him and Gyp in their suite, where they appeared to be very comfortable. Having kissed them and each other good night, we retired. But no sooner had I put out the bedside light than the door opened to reveal my wide-awake employer. Without Bumble sleep was impossible, she said. And she couldn't bear the thought of him pining for her in that draughty old stable. A heated discussion ensued, but in the end I climbed back into my clothes and made my way through the eerily silent building, hoping not to be taken for an intruder. The dogs, of course, were fast asleep, with Bumble showing no interest in being disturbed. But I gathered him up and crept cautiously back to Kate's room, without seeing another soul. Well before sparrow fart she re-appeared with her little bundle of fur and begged me to return him before the crime was discovered. Mercifully, once again I saw no one. But at six o'clock in the morning the corridors of a luxury hotel are not likely to be thronged with people.

Once Kate had decided to concentrate her search for a house on the area around Ludlow and Leominster our sorties slipped into a regular routine. She and Bumble would book into an hotel either in the centre of the former or in the county just outside the latter. Having made sure she was comfortable I would then go on to Alex, and we would meet up again in the evening for dinner. Over a period we went to see a fair number of desirable and not so desirable residences, but none of them quite fitted the bill. But among the pile of brochures and particulars that travelled with us, the details of one house were always pushed to the back. The house in question was called Oldfield Farm, at a place called Richard's Castle. An unflattering photograph showed a half-timbered building that might have been in Hampstead Garden Suburb. With a dearth of things to look at, we decided one day to see what it really looked like. However, even with an ordnance survey map on which it was marked, pinpointing its location proved to be a problem. After several false starts we drove through a place called Wooferton and headed for an area that was described on the map as The Goggin. As the road narrowed and became steeper the woods closed in, creating an impression of a private drive rather than a highway. At the end of a level run we saw sunlight ahead and, turning a corner, we emerged into an open valley. The house nestling in the middle of it, surrounded by sloping fields, was Oldfield Farm. I drove slowly past and stopped just beyond the entrance. By this time my passenger was starting to make very interested noises, but as no appointment had been made we had to content ourselves with seeing what we could from the road and an adjacent field. It was clear that the agent's photograph had done the house no justice at all. For a start it was no younger than sixteenth century and had been created without the help of Norman Shaw or any other architect. The front faced south and overlooked a stream and lush garden. There was a collection of attractive outbuildings and a tiny cottage beside the house that had once been the granary. Of all the houses we had seen this was the only one that stirred the Vestey juices. Without further ado we returned to Kate's hotel and made an appointment to meet the owner in the morning.

Mrs Brindley assumed that Guy and Kate were Mr And Mrs Hunting – a mistake that neither of us corrected (especially as it caused us so much amusement). She and her husband, who was ex-army, had lived in the house for many years, but since his death her children were anxious that she should move to somewhere less isolated. She hated the thought of moving and leaving behind the collection of old roses that were the garden's pride and joy. After a tour of the house she took us over to the granary, which was let to a young couple. As this was likely to be my home I took more notice of it than I did the house (particularly as I guessed that Kate had gutting in mind). There were two good bedrooms and a bathroom upstairs, and on the ground floor a decent sitting room, kitchen and cloakroom.

Shortly after that first visit we went again when Mrs Brindley ('call me Gaynor,' she insisted, which was confusing for a chap called Guyrena) asked us to lunch. Once I remembered to remain permanently stooped, except of course at the table, lunch turned into a remarkably jolly occasion. She had set the scene so that we moved from the blazing log fire in the drawing room, into the sepulchral gloom of the dining room, where the table was laid and the aroma of fresh mushroom soup wafted in from the kitchen. She pointed out that if we bought the house she would be delighted to introduce us to the locals, all of whom were charming. Our nearest neighbours, she stressed, were the Dunnes – Thomas and Henrietta, who lived at Gatley Park. This piece of information was not music to Kate's ears, as she knew that Henrietta was a close friend of Ce's.

Nevertheless, she asked the Trust to buy Oldfield Farm and after the usual procrastination, they did. In spite of agreeing with Gaynor Brindley, as you do, that the house was almost perfect as it was, Kate knew that her plans for it would render it uninhabitable for months to come. The main jobs would be digging eighteen inches out of the ground floor, replacing the floor of the main bedroom – which resembled a ski-slope – building a new kitchen/utility room and a garden room, adding a couple of bathrooms and completely re-decorating. As all this would take some time to plan, she chose to move in and get the feel of the place before the work started.

Once Rentokil had done their stuff, and TV points had been added to every room, she took up residence. At the same time I glided seamlessly into 'the bit on the side'. At first we were only there at weekends, but with the onset of summer we often left London on a Thursday and returned on the following Monday. Social activity got off to a slow start but Alex, who was a regular visitor, did his best to help. We went with him to a number of events connected with the Ludlow Hunt, of which he had been a member since childhood. Closer to home we met other horsey people who divided their time between a house nearby and their daughter's farm in Zimbabwe. Patience Worthington rode past the house most mornings and introductions were soon effected. My initial impression was of a woman with enough drive and personality to run the Conservative Party, an armoured battalion and a multi-national company on a part-time basis. This view was underlined one day when she strode mounted into the forecourt where I was doing a little gentle gardening. I don't think she slapped her thigh, but she certainly addressed me as if I was a Sandhurst Passing-Out Parade.

'Can't remember your name. Come to lunch on Sunday!' was the immortal line.

Kate and I did go to lunch that day, and on many other days, and for dinner too. At home with her husband, David, Patience was a complete pussycat and dutiful wife. On one particular occasion they came to lunch with us when Johnny motored over from Gloucestershire with his sister Mimi and her husband and stepson. I got the proceedings off to a rip-roaring start with jugs of artery-exploding Bloody Marys. Johnny and Patience soon discovered that they had publishing in common when it emerged that he knew her writer sister.

Help in the kitchen on party days was provided by a freelance cook and Rosemary, the Rubenesque cleaner, for whom I sometimes had to interpret. In spite of twenty-five years of Irene's pidgin English, Kate found Rosemary's dialect difficult to unscramble. Only once did we understand what she said first time round. It was during a giggling session in the kitchen after another lunch party when she suddenly turned to Kate with a grin and asked, 'Do you and Guy like getting drunk, Lady Vestey?' She came from a family that had lived in The Goggin for generations. Her powerfully built brother Mike brought us logs and chopped down the occasional tree.

Our grandest neighbour, the Lord Lieutenant, drove by regularly in a pony and trap and always gave me a cheery wave. One day when I was in the garden he and Henrietta and a black Labrador walked towards me looking for all the world like an advertisement for Burberrys. They knew all about the farm's new owner, but quizzed me with regard to her plans for it. Some time later Kate and Flora and I went to Gatley to lunch. We had seen the house from afar on one of our walks. It was Jacobean and sat on top of a broad escarpment, with the ugly scar of a quarry close by. While we ate (roast chicken with grilled tomatoes as a substitute for potatoes in deference to our hostess's diet) Thomas told us that the quarry provided a lot of the hardcore that went into new roads (and presumably made masses of money). He also pointed out that Oldfield had originally been part of the Gatley estate. After coffee the girls were taken into the garden while I went with our host to his muniments room, where he showed me old maps that had Kate's house on them. Kate returned their hospitality by having them to a dinner party where, in an attempt to make them feel at home, the other guests included Jeremy Lywood, High Sheriff of Shropshire and his wife Anne. They were friends of Alex's of whom Kate had become quite fond.

But in spite of Kate's best efforts, her relationship with the Dunnes was always going to be cordial rather than close. She rang Henrietta one day to ask them for drinks at the weekend, but was told that they had a house party. When Kate suggested that they should bring their guests as well, she was told that 'they were the sort of people that didn't go out much'. (Kate could only think that it must be the Queen – she was known to be an occasional visitor.)

Kate received a telephone call one day that took her completely by surprise. It came from Diana Beamish who, with her husband Richard, had known Kate slightly in Spain. In the course of conversation it transpired that they lived only about three miles from Oldfield and had heard of Kate's arrival through Serena Bridgeman, their mutual friend. It was some years since they had met, but Kate recalled that Diana was South African and Richard Irish – a jack of all trades with a colourful past. Soon after that call we went to their house for dinner and what proved to be the first of many happy evenings in their company. Richard, at that time, was working as a gardener and although they were short of money the food was always delicious and one's glass always filled. Among our fellow guests, we met two couples who were to become the lynchpin of our social lives. Three and a half of them were refugees from the big city who had jumped off the treadmill. The remaining half, Fiona Annesley, still worked in London three days a week, where she lodged with her mother. Her husband, Rory, was alarmingly bright and the possessor of a devastating sense of humour. He had dabbled in the theatre and run the hotel on Mustique, before retiring early through poor health, with the whippets Parsley and Pfiefer. They lived in a rather yellow double-fronted house, with an equally colourful garden, in the centre of Presteigne.

David and Susie Scott lived with their two young daughters in a hilltop house a few miles from Leominster, where David was in the final stages of running a picture gallery. He had spent some time in the City in the days when his charm and laid-back approach would have been thoroughly in keeping. Susie taught at a local school, but her manner and appearance suggested an earlier life that was much more interesting. Sadly, her natural reticence prevented me from finding out more about it.

When an architect and builders were appointed to start work on the house its contents were moved into two of the large barns. At first Kate was inclined to use The Marsh, her favourite hotel, as her base. But I eventually persuaded her that the larger of the granary's two bedrooms could be made comfortable enough for her own use. To everyone's surprise, not least her own, this arrangement worked remarkably well and did so for many, many months.

The last visitor to the house before the move was the interior decorator David Hicks. In spite of the fact that Kate was not the biggest fan of his designs, she was convinced by Dorothy, their mutual friend, that his newly established skills as a garden designer was just what was required to get Oldfield's three acres into shape. He was invited to lunch and I guided him by telephone to a large pub called The Salwey Arms on the A49 where I arranged that we should meet. This became a popular method of getting people to the house, as the last couple of miles were so complicated.

David Hicks proved to be an amusing lunch guest, even though Kate was not impressed by his confession that as far as the garden was concerned he was not a 'plantsman'. For a girl who, by her own admission, needed her hand holding every step of the way, this bit of news was a body blow. Nevertheless, after his hearty consumption of food and drink, we tottered round the garden while he scribbled away on a notepad. With bated breath Kate met him again in London and collected the fruits of his labours, for which he charged her £2,000. What she had purchased for this not inconsiderable sum was an A4-size piece of paper that was covered in the sort of watercolour daubings that an untalented eight-year-old might have produced. Although disappointed, Kate was determined to put it to good use, and had it framed with the lavatory in mind. There was never any question of referring to it as far as the garden was concerned.

Some weeks later the maestro invited us to lunch at his house in

Oxfordshire. Roles were reversed when he gave me directions on the telephone and insisted that we arrive no later than one fifteen or the French chef would go berserk. In the course of our chat we discovered that we had a mutual friend, Mark Carlisle, whose firm of land agents looked after his estate.

More by luck than judgement we arrived at the house from Shropshire just before one and were immediately taken on a tour of the garden. Old-fashioned bits like herbaceous borders were certainly very impressive, but the rest, for my taste, was too cluttered and compartmentalised. In the distance I spotted a couple of earth-moving machines hard at it and asked our host what they were creating.

'Pammy has given me a lake for Christmas,' he replied.

We had drinks before lunch in a wonderfully elegant drawing room (presumably decorated by his wife) and met the other guests, who were a charming local couple. The room was dominated by a collection of beautiful oval portraits, which Kate admired.

'Yes,' he said, 'they are lovely and rather fun that they are all by Romney.'

Lunch was served by the chef's young wife in a small dining room whose walls were covered in a mural that was a representation of Broadlands and its gardens. In fact what we saw of the house and garden was awash with Mountbatten memorabilia – a veritable shrine to the in-laws.

By now the wicked month of August was approaching yet again and I began to hope that Kate would be content to spend it quietly in the country. But it was not to be. She had an overwhelming desire to return to Greece, a country she had not been to since her honeymoon. When brochures were perused, the place that caught her eye was a large villa with its own beach and whose only access was by sea or along an unadopted track. Once again she and Christopher shared the cost, and I was given no choice but to tag along. Happily, Roger was pressed into service once more, but could only come for a week.

We flew to Salonika, where we hired a car for the two-hour journey to our destination in the south of the country. In the spring the setting must be glorious, but after a long, dry summer the countryside was parched and dusty. Our track was strewn with boulders and potholes and covered with a deep layer of pernicious red dirt. By the time we had bumped our way along it to the house we were all spluttering and covered from head to toe. After an experience that we all vowed never to repeat, we were grateful to find that the house and its beach lived up to the description. Although none of us admitted to knowing anything about boats, it was clear that the one that was provided was going to be our lifeline. The next day Christopher and I chugged around the headland to see what delights were in store. Much to our relief there turned out to be a small resort that contained a cafe and a bar. However, we had to break the news to Kate that the assault course was the only way to shops and restaurants. When Roger arrived we attempted some exploring on foot and even the occasional dip in the warm sea. We left our redoubt for only a couple of nocturnal visits to local restaurants, and made the journey covered in towels and at a snail's pace to minimise the effect of the sand. During one of these outings when the wine had flowed a little too freely, the happy harmony of the holiday suffered a bit of a setback. Christopher and Roger had a silly misunderstanding over dinner, with the result that Roger left us early the next morning. But before he went we discovered that a number of glass-topped tables on the terrace had been used as missiles at some stage during the night – an act for which Kate was later to take full credit. When we told the letting agent in the local town about the accident he said that he fully understood. Apparently a number of tenants had had breakages, though never before in such quantity. I received a withering look from my employer when I said blithely, 'I know it does seem ridiculous, but it is not as if Lady Vestey broke them deliberately!'

By the end of the fortnight order and calm had returned. In fact we had so much fun on the flight home that none of us remembered to collect the large jars of honey and olive oil that had been stowed away for safe keeping. But at the end of my third August holiday in a row I made a vow never again to leave these shores between July and September.

During the year Kate's mother had died after a long battle with cancer. She was one of the sweetest and most delightful women I had ever known, and I shared the family's grief.

That year she asked her father and sister, Susie, to come to Campden for Christmas lunch. Saffron and Flora were there too, as well as Christopher, my friend Digger and a friend of Kate's called Peter Williams. Alex was not on the guest list, as he had left me yet again for another saddle-soaping faggot. Kate and Christopher had met Digger once before when they came to my flat for supper. Johnny had been the other guest and everyone got along famously.

When the news of Alex's defection became common knowledge I received messages of sympathy from three of the Vestey women. Pragmatic as ever, Saffron was quick to remind me that there were 'plenty more fish in the sea', and said she had a man in mind who might be a suitable replacement. She also told me that Ce sent condolences and was keen for me to meet an old friend of hers who could be boyfriend material. Not to be outdone, Flora was also eager to help. The bloke she suggested as a possibility was the young undergraduate cousin of one of her best school friends. Apparently he had just 'come out' and was looking for a partner. Although I was touched by the thought, I had to point out that at the age of nineteen he was unlikely to find a crabby old queen like me at all attractive. Ever since we had first exchanged nicknames I had become terribly fond of Kate's younger daughter. Although her mother made a point of collecting her from school whenever possible, there were times when I had to make the journey on my own, giving me a chance to get to know her chums. If the dreaded Sunday evening was when she had to be back Kate would make us a delicious mixed-grill high tea before we set off. One year I attended the Tudor Hall sport's day, as well as Flora's confirmation service in Banbury parish church, which was followed by lunch at Stowell. I drove to the church on my own from the farm, while Kate came independently from London. As I got out of my car the Vestey Bentley drew up and Sam and Saffron emerged.

'Where's Kate?' asked the anxious ex-husband. 'Is she already on her knees inside?'

'I am sure,' I replied. 'You know how devout she is!'

In the New Year Kate and I agreed that I should move into The Granary permanently so as to be on hand while the work was going on. I decided to let my flat, as I could always use Flora's room if I needed to be in London. In order to avoid driving for two and a half to three hours Kate began to make the journey by train to Leominster. Christopher, who was working as a locum in London, would often come and stay as well, which meant that they would drive down together. I would often use his visits and the subsequent lack of space in The Granary to have a weekend away. Until his recent abandonment of me, my destination would usually be Alex's house, the other side of Ludlow. But since that happened I invariably accepted Jane's open invitation to stay at her cottage near Malvern. Our many shared interests, which included Scrabble, garden visiting and walking the dogs, meant that going there was something to which I looked forward.

However, there was one particular weekend when I remained at The Granary, keeping out of the way as much as possible. The reason I stayed was that we had been invited to dinner by old friends of Kate's, Theo and Louise Fennell, who had a weekend house near Hereford. She had got to know them through Joan Collins, with whom they were still best friends. Louise had been in touch with Kate soon after she heard about her move to the area. We had dined there once before and met the Cotterell family on whose estate, Garnons, the Fennells rented a house.

Fortunately for me, Christopher (or Chrissy Crumble as I chose to call him) elected to drive, as I vividly recalled the extent of Theo's hospitality. Once again the Cotterells were there with two sons and a delightful daughter, who was lady-in-waiting to the Duchess of York. Apart from Louise's delicious Thai food, the highlight of the evening for me was a snippet of conversation I overheard during drinks before dinner. Sir John Cotterell and Chrissy Crumble were talking in general terms, when the older man suddenly asked CC what he did for a living. In his rich Canadian accent CC replied:

'I am a chiropractor.'

'How fascinating!' cried Sir John, turning to find his wife. 'Darling, you must come here and meet this interesting man – he's a car parker.'

For the rest of the evening, which was downhill after that, I sat at the table between the Duchess's handmaiden and her mother. On my right, Lady Cotterell did her best to convert me to Christianity, while on the other side her daughter tried just as hard not to answer any questions about her royal mistress.

On the way home through the back lanes of Herefordshire our headlights suddenly illuminated a car and its four occupants standing on the side of the road. It says something for my condition at that time that I suggested that they might be having a barbecue. But as we pulled up beside them it emerged that they had suffered a puncture and had no light at all. Our hero at the wheel immediately positioned the jeep so that all was revealed, and did what he could to lend a hand.

In spite of the lack of space, Kate and I managed to co-exist quite happily at The Granary. However, we were both very conscious of the other's presence and stuck to a routine whenever possible. My day would begin at whatever getting-up time was appropriate. If Kate had been sleeping badly – and sometimes I would hear her downstairs during the night – she would ask not to be disturbed until about nine. At first I found that the stairs were impossible to negotiate without making a noise, but after a while I learnt which bits to avoid. My first task was to drive the three miles to Orleton, our nearest village, where I was always assured of a cheery welcome at the post office from Ruth or one of her lady helpers. The core of the village, centred on the church, was old and quite attractive, but lots of new housing had changed its character. The only pub, The Boot (or 'Sling Back') was constantly changing hands, with unpredictable consequences for the food. But there was a brief time when the dining room was worth patronising, and we did so quite often.

Armed with two copies of *The Times*, one *Daily Mail*, milk and bread I would return to make breakfast. Squeezing oranges and grapefruit was the first operation, followed by laying the tray so that I could take my mistress her boiled egg in bed. On weekdays the peace and calm of the morning was shattered by the arrival of the builders. Fortunately they were a very nice bunch and well aware that pop music was forbidden. As with all groups of men, some were more attractive than others, but in this case at least they had one thing in common. They showed not the slightest interest in me at all. Only once did one of them approach me in a way that could have been thought suggestive. I was in the kitchen one day when very much the least attractive of them appeared in the doorway holding a paper bag. Nervously, he asked 'Could I warm my pie in your microwave?' I *think* he only wanted hot food!

With Kate happy in bed surrounded by crumbs and the papers I devoted the next two hours to Bumble and Gyp. But before heading for the hills I would pause to inspect the greenhouse and terracotta pots, where tomatoes and sweet peas were doing well. The farm had never had a vegetable garden and, unlike Kirkbuddo, there was no obvious area that could be cultivated. But I was determined to grow sweet peas, Kate's favourite flower, and with bamboo pyramids in three large pots there was a constant supply of sweetly smelling flowers for the house.

Walking from the farm was a great treat, not only because of the beauty and peace of its setting, but also because no roads had to be crossed. One of my favourite routes, in the direction of National Trust-owned Orleton Common, took us past a remarkable house that had been built in the sixties by Thomas Dunne's mother. Known locally as a folly, it was in fact a very striking round tower on three floors. The commanding position it occupied made it level with her son's house and provided glorious views. The owner used it only occasionally, but Kate and I went there once to drinks and had a guided tour. We also met her collection of four-legged friends, amongst whom was a sweet little chap with a coat like a mole's who was a Lancashire Heeler, a breed of which I had never heard.

One morning in the summer I set out as usual, with Bumble following a scent ahead of me. When I turned to see what had happened to Gyp I saw to my amazement that she was sitting just outside The Granary door, showing no sign of wanting to follow. Even when I called she made as if to come and then sat back again on her haunches. I urged her on again and she moved forward, but very slowly, by which time I was running back to see what was wrong. As I stroked her she looked very uncomfortable, her body slightly shaking. Whispering sweet nothings and pressing my nose into her face, I saw for the first time that her right eye was strangely discoloured. With some alarm I told Kate what had happened and drove Gyp to the vet in Ludlow. After examining her carefully he broke the news that she had lost the sight in one eye and that the other one was at risk. He said that there was nothing he could do to help and that at the age of thirteen, things do start going wrong with dogs. After eight years of unimaginable companionship, this was a shattering blow.

A few weeks later Gyp was completely blind. She seemed to adapt to her handicap remarkably easily, and certainly with great courage. As ever with pets, I think I was more traumatised than she was. And as one wise person pointed out, it was not as if she didn't know that it wasn't supposed to happen. In the months that followed she pursued the sound of my voice with no regard for her safety. On one occasion I was talking to Henry in the garden outside his house, when we looked up and saw her on the balcony above. Quick as a flash Henry shot forward and caught her as she plummeted through the balustrade.

By a strange quirk of fate Gyp's disability occurred at the same time that Nell, Jane's dog, lost her sense of hearing. From Jane's point of view this meant a great saving on tranquillisers when thunderstorms were in the offing, even if it also allowed Nell to sniff and rootle largely unchecked. When Zoe and I went to spend Christmas in Boston with Johnny a couple of years ago Jane agreed to have Gyp at the cottage for those five days. By the time we were reunited she had some amusing tales to tell. When she announced that their supper was ready, Gyp would somehow make her way to the kitchen, even though she couldn't find her food. Nell, on the other hand, could get to the kitchen okay, in spite of not knowing that she had been summoned. When the three of them went walkies Jane said that it was almost like being with one complete dog.

Alex, by this time, had ditched his most recent floozy and we were seeing each other again. Apparently the crime that caused his dismissal was an uncontrollable urge to be beside the sea. For Alex, who had

been born and bred close to the middle of England, this idea was
anathema. Added to which he had always disliked water in any of its
guises. My little friend had surprised everyone by fulfilling what he
described as a long-held ambition. He had taken a job as a care worker
in a residential home for the mentally handicapped in a tiny village
miles from anywhere. It was poorly paid and involved working long
shifts, but he loved every minute of it. The only problem he had to
face was his own little handicap – he had been banned from driving
for a year thanks to an eight-thirty *a.m.* breathalyser test that had
proved positive. With public transport in that part of the world merely
a distant memory, he had to rely on friends and colleagues to ferry him
to and fro. I was happy to play my part whenever I could.

Flora came to stay from time to time, and was happy to sleep on a
camp bed in the sitting room. Saffron also paid the occasional visit,
but with Fred, Bee and boyfriend Matt in tow her arrival meant that
a room at The Marsh was booked for use by either Kate or me. Matt
was charming and dishy – in fact, to my eyes he was more attractive
than either of his film star sisters, Kristin and Serena. What is more,
he coped remarkably well with the complicated lives and strong
personalities of his girlfriend's family. It soon became apparent that
their intentions towards each other were serious, and the
announcement of their engagement was received with much rejoicing.
When a wedding date was fixed for the following May I was promised
a leading role in the proceedings. They knew that I already had the
hoop and only needed a length of peach satin to bring it to life. Kate
took the three of us to Marks Club in South Audley Street for a
celebratory dinner.

Work on the house was making slow progress, and for some weeks
nothing at all was done while a new architect and builder were being
chosen. At the same time the situation was not helped by the fact that
the house was Grade II listed, and every alteration to its appearance
had to be agreed with the authorities. The budget, of course, was the
other great worry and it was being exceeded with every day that
passed. Kate was urged to cut down on her expenses and decided that
I was a luxury she could no longer afford. This struck me as strange

reasoning when I considered that my cost to her each week was the equivalent of one crimping session with Nicky Clarke. However, she stressed that she would like me to stay on at The Granary, rent free, and I agreed.

With my only income being the rent I received from letting my flat I had to think quickly about finding alternative employment. My first thought was to trawl the local sale rooms for antiques that I could sell on in London. The area was rich in such places and I had often been to sales out of interest. With the local paper as my guide I started attending them regularly and made one or two purchases that were not likely to upset the very busy 'ring' of dealers. After a couple of weeks of relatively feverish activity I had collected enough stuff to fill my car, and set off one day to dazzle the antiquaries of London with my goods. I saw no point in making for the West End and headed instead for the more approachable shops at the top end of Wandsworth Bridge Road. Dauntingly, the three proprietors I spoke to all stressed that business was going through a bad patch, but they all came reluctantly to cast their eyes over the contents of the car. After much haggling that left me only marginally better off than breaking even I managed to off-load a Lloyd Loom linen basket and chair and a collection of clay pots. With my car still surprisingly full, I called it a day and drove eagerly towards the M40.

Having put that little exercise down to experience, and one that I would never repeat, I looked for solace in the company of Rory Annesley and David Scott. We were in the habit of meeting from time to time for a pub lunch and a wide-ranging discussion of affairs. They were both very sympathetic to my plight and keen to offer suggestions. Since the demise of his gallery, David had also been looking for something else to bring in some money. His wheeze of the moment was a plan to supply pubs with nuts and nibbles, but we also went together to meet a friend of his in Cirencester who ran a successful sandwich shop. Rory, on the other hand, had altogether more ambitious ideas. We found some empty restaurant premises close to the centre of Ludlow and considered the possibility of running it as a wine bar. In those days that ancient little town made no allowance at all for sophisticated night life – fish-and-chip shops, dreary pubs and ethnic restaurants were all it had to offer. We both agreed that with a certain amount of alteration the site in Broad Street would be idea. I began to get terribly excited about it, and thought of the name 'Critchleys', in deference to Julian of that name, the MP and long-time Ludlow resident. Quarterly literary lunches were envisaged, with famous authors as guest speakers and JC himself as master of ceremonies. Even Kate became keen on the idea and offered to help at any time. But in the end neither of us was prepared to take the risk. Sadly, the streets of Ludlow were destined never to echo to the sound of pixilated 'Critchleyarians' – their bellies full of monkfish thermador and oak-tinged Pinot Grigio.

With my fiftieth birthday approaching I knew that on the open market I would be regarded as largely unemployable. Nevertheless, I registered with an employment agency in Hereford, where my CV generated a few giggles. I also sought work at a very well-run garden centre near Tenbury Wells, but found that they had no vacancies. The only hint of an offer I received was a suggestion from Stowell that Ce's widowed mother might appreciate someone to take the sort of role that I had played in Kate's life. However, I explained that having 'given myself' to one woman I was not, at that stage, ready to do it again.

Until something turned up I spent a certain amount of time ferrying Alex between Munslow and his work at Bishop's Castle. On one of these journeys he told me in the course of conversation that he had taken as a lodger a young stable boy called Chris. I was intrigued by this piece of information, particularly since I knew that Alex was drawn to almost anything in trousers. However, he said he was fairly convinced that Chris was not gay. Moreover, there was the fact that he was under-age and the son of a woman Alex had been to school with. Nevertheless, my curiosity was seriously aroused and when Alex suggested a cup of tea at the end of a return trip, I readily agreed. As he opened the front door my nostrils twitched at the scent of polish and fresh flowers that greeted us. Such a change, and not necessarily for the better, from the cocktail of smells – of which stale cigarette smoke was the most attractive – that usually assailed me. The interior of the house was almost unrecognisable, with no assault course of abandoned shoes to negotiate. Fortunately, Rush was the same as ever, although I was surprised not to see a ribbon in her hair. As I had feared, Chris (or Lolita, which was how I began to think of him) looked wholesome, sturdy and terribly poised. Needless to say, I didn't stay long. But after a cup of tea I made nose-powdering an excuse to slip upstairs, only to find cleanliness and order there as well. The last straw was net curtains at the bathroom window – when I didn't even know the bathroom *had* a window!

In spite of all that rampant home-making, Alex continued to deny that there was anything going on. He still came over to join us for supper and stayed the night. But he always had to ring 'the lodger' during the evening to make sure he was all right. Even with my rose-tinted spectacles firmly in place I could see that that was not standard landlord/tenant behaviour. When I discussed the situation with Kate she was quick to suggest that Alex probably regarded me as a very good friend, and nothing more. I could only speculate as to who might have put that idea into her head.

With no job and a dismantled relationship my thoughts became a re-run of the last days at Moss Cree. As then, I decided that the only course of action open to me was to look for a new beginning in London. The long arm of coincidence struck again when I learnt from the letting agent that the tenants in my flat would be moving out in the middle of September. With the certainty of a home to go back to I broke the news to Kate giving her, effectively, six week's notice. Her first reaction was that I was leaving her in the lurch and had not tried hard enough to find a job. She refused to see that I loved our life together and being part of her family, but without a job or money I had no choice but to move on. In the ensuing month and a half life at Oldfield Farm was not a lot of fun, and we kept out of each other's way as much as possible. Kate still came down at weekends, but only to meet the architect and to monitor progress on the house. On the Sunday of our last weekend I was invited to a farewell lunch by David and Patience Worthington. Kate was asked too, but she had already accepted another invitation. On the Monday morning I loaded her car for the last time. She kissed me on the cheek and said goodbye, rather firmly. Later in the day I went to lunch with the Annesleys, where the party included Richard and Diana Beamish and David Wheeler and Simon Dorrell. I left for London on Tuesday 19th September.

Soon after my return I wrote to Kate to thank her for all her kindness during the four years we were together. I also explained again why it was I had to leave. On reflection, I suppose it was not the sort of letter that required a reply.

In November I went with Matt and Saffron, at Ce's invitation, to an evening in aid of St John at The Draper's Hall in the City. On the way there in a taxi we joked about the match-making Ce had planned, but none of us knew whether her antique dealer friend had been told anything about it. On arrival we met up with Sam and Ce and the rest of their party, which included Lady Jane Fellowes and Colin Anson, whom I had known many years before through David Carritt. Colin had with him the tall bearded man whose acquaintance Ce was determined I should make. It turned out, of course, that we had known each other by sight in his pre-beard days when he was at Sotheby's and I worked at Aspreys. Watched discreetly by the Vestey girls, we greeted each other cordially, but without the chemistry for which they were looking. After drinks we went through to an enormous chamber where we watched a performance of *The Magic Flute*. It was a magical and very intimate production, with the cast in full costume and not confined to any sort of stage. When it was over and Sam had made a typically witty speech, we moved into another room, where round tables had been arranged for dinner. The seating, I was not surprised to discover, had been planned so that I sat between our hostess and the 'date'. Although conversation flowed, that was mostly because Ce and I were having such a good time. After dinner Ce drew the prizes for the raffle, leaving me in charge of her tickets. When one of hers was picked, a weekend for two at a Scottish hotel, she insisted on giving it to me. When a lot of the guests had gone Sam came over to sit with us for a nightcap while I explained to his wife that I was grateful for the trouble she had taken, but that I was still a childless one-parent family!

When my invitation to Saffron and Matt's wedding arrived I rang her to say how pleased I was to receive it. However, I added that I would not go if I thought for a moment that my presence would upset or annoy her mother. Saffron, in her usual no-nonsense way, replied that if Mum saw me she would probably be both. She knew that I had been invited and reacted by saying that it was Saffron's day and she could ask who she liked.

The weekend in May that was chosen for the wedding produced the nastiest spring weather that anyone could remember. On Saturday morning I set off from Jane's cottage in driving rain, armed with the small map that had been provided. Knowing that I was completely devoid of a sense of direction or bump of locality, that important piece of paper was kept within easy reach. The problem was that the service was being held at a church in a village close to Stowell, but not one that I had been to before.

After a little back lane confusion I arrived at my destination and found a place to park with only minutes to spare. As it happened, I was pleased not to be early so that I could slip into a pew without being noticed. However, what I had not bargained for as I hurried towards the church door, was the sight of Kate standing alone in the porch. Too late to hide or turn back, I propelled myself forward, saying the first thing that came into my head as she offered her cheek to be kissed.

'You look very lovely,' I claimed.

'Thank you, sweetheart,' she responded, while my lips touched her foundation.

In point of fact she did look terrific, but I was surprised that she was wearing a colour that might have been more appropriate for the leading lady in the proceedings. Or is it considered chic now for the bride and her mother to both be in white?

As the service drew to a close I caught my first glimpse of Saffron.

Radiant she was, with her hair piled high as I had never seen it before. Outside the church I caught sight of some familiar faces and bumped into others that I knew, like David and Margaret Levin. Being six-foot four, my problem at weddings is that I only ever see the crowns of girls' hats, and find recognition a problem. However there was no identity crisis with the next person I encountered. Sam strode towards me with a glint in his eye:

'You must be a friend of the bride's,' he declared.

'Yes, I am,' I replied 'but I am not a friend of the bride's mother — and we've got that in common!'

'Oh Guyrenu!' he roared, and rushed on.

In what had previously been a paddock at Stowell I ran into Richard, the chauffeur from Miles & Miles, whose lucrative work for Kate I had deprived him of for four years. At the front door the stream of guests was guided through the house and across the terrace into a huge marquee. Without the formality of a receiving line (which was presumably why Kate hovered in the church doorway) we were all thrown straight into the melee. In the distance I caught sight of a group of Kate's Praetorian Guard: Roger and John, Tom Lewis and his mother, Diane Wilson, an old friend called Janet Clarke and Irene. With their leader nowhere to be seen I flew over to greet them. In spite of being, in their eyes, a traitor they were all very friendly. But my encounter was cut short when, out of the corner of my eye, I spotted Kate heading our way. Although she had been sweet to me earlier, I didn't want to risk embarrassing her. I moved instead to speak to the Parker Bowleses, although Carolyn's hat ruled out any intimacy.

My place for lunch was beside Emily, Saffron's old friend and the person charged with looking after Bee and Fred during the honeymoon. Other people at the table also included the business associate of Sam's whom Saffron thought was both suspect and suitable. Certainly, if jewellery was a pointer Saffron's judgement was spot on, for he sported a ring that would not have looked out of place on the hand of the Vicar of Rome. Sam and Flora both came to the table for a chat during the feast. She was no longer the cheeky schoolgirl, but beautiful and elegant in a blue suit and wide-brimmed hat, with a hand displaying a cigarette. Not surprisingly, Sam and Kate sat at separate tables – she surrounded by the group I had met earlier and he with Ce and a group of toffs that included Lord and Lady Hartington. With a lot of traffic between the tables I tried to summon the courage to go over to Ce, whose very presence there was remarkable. Since I had last seen her at the Draper's Hall she had been through an appalling illness that had endangered her life. But with brilliant medical attention, her own determination and family love and support she had made a complete recovery – as everyone there could bear witness to. In due course, and to the delight of everyone at the table, she came over to see us and was as sweet, charming and naughty as ever. When I had a drink with Saffron one evening after the honeymoon she told me that at one stage the family had considered engaging a companion for Ce in case mobility was a problem. When my name was mentioned as a possible candidate Sam and Saffron both agreed that with my recent experience I had demonstrated that I had the patience that might be required. However, Sam's only reservation was a concern for the sexual well-being of the men on the estate. Quite a compliment, I thought!

After the speeches I decided to slip quietly away while I was still capable of finding my car. I returned to Hanley Swan, where Maggie and Phylip were also guests. We spent the evening in overindulgence and lengthy games of Scrabble.

More than a year passed before I had any news of Alex. It was our longest period without communication in a friendship that spanned two decades. I had a phone call one evening from Chrissy Crumble, whose relationship with Kate had finished long since. He said that he had heard from Kate that Lolita had left Alex for another man, and that Alex had attempted suicide. Apparently he had been in hospital and had his stomach pumped, but was now out of danger. CC promised to ring me again if he heard any more. Naturally, this news came as a terrible blow and left me at a loss to know what do to. I saw no point, at that stage, of making the long journey to try and see him. So I settled instead for a cheery card and a large bottle of health-giving herbal tonic, which I despatched by post. Knowing how appalling his diet was – usually booze and fags – at the best of times, I thought that might be a sensible supplement. Some days later I answered the telephone to hear his familiar voice, and within seconds it was as if time had stood still. He told me that he had moved into the groom's flat at Ashford Court, the Lywood's house near Ludlow, and had gone back to his job with the handicapped. Soon after that conversation I went to stay with him for a weekend, and exactly like old times it was too. I went again in August for his birthday and took him to Erdigg as a treat.

Gyp, 'the girl of my dreams', died in October at the age of fifteen. She had been unwell for a few days, and was so uncomfortable one evening that I took her to the emergency clinic in Elizabeth Street. After extensive tests they broke the news that all her vital organs were packing up. It took me only a minute to accept the vet's advice and she administered a painless injection. Gyp died peacefully in my arms as the tears streamed down my face.

Fearing the worst, I had phoned both Henry and Jane before setting off for the clinic that evening. Although I had hoped that one of them might have been able to come with me, I was only able to leave messages on their answer machines. Jane got home in time to telephone me while I was there, and also appeared on my doorstep the next day with a bottle of whisky and a bunch of flowers. Among the other expressions of sympathy I received, none meant more to me than a phone call from Kate who, more than anyone, knew how I was suffering.

Much to my amazement, I had two more phone calls from her before the end of the year. The first was from her holiday hotel in Florida and the second came in December, for my birthday.

Saffron rang me in January to invite me to supper. She explained that her mother was coming up from the country to stay overnight and that they would love to see me. Since I had last seen them they had moved to a bigger house with room for a nursery off Kensington Church Street. The family had grown to include not only a son and heir called Alfred, but also a scrumptious black Labrador called Jesse. Although I took the wee lad a silly present, I did not see him that evening, as he was confined to his room with a bad attack of asthma. But Kate I did see, and Flora – in fact, it was a glorious family party. After we had eaten Flora went off to a party in a discotheque and Matt and Saffron retired to bed early, having had very little sleep since the baby's illness. That left Kate and me to chew the fat. She did not drink alcohol during the evening but made very sure that I was well supplied. As quietly as possible (although I suspect I was shouting) we took my glass up to the drawing room and talked non-stop into the small hours. By the time I left we had agreed that I would ring her to make a date for a weekend visit.

For no particular reason we chose the St Valentine's Day weekend – the fourteenth February 1998, a date that will be etched forever on my memory. Kate was keen that I should arrive on the Friday and stay through until Monday morning. However, I pleaded pressure of work and said that I would be there by lunch time on Saturday.

I drove first to Ludlow's marvellous open air market where I assembled a large bunch of flowers in the pastel shades Kate liked so much. From there my route to Oldfield Farm took me past any number of favourite walks and brought back a myriad of memories. In the more than two years that had elapsed since my departure I had cautiously driven by the house a couple of times during weekends with Jane or Alex. As I drew up, Kate and Flora emerged for big hugs and kisses. They introduced me to Beetle, Bumble's West Highland companion, and opened the door of the large kennel to allow Baggage, the young German Shepherd dog, to throw her front legs round my shoulders in what I hoped was a greeting. Instead of lunch, in true Kate fashion we went off to Safeway in Leominster to get those little half-forgotten extras. We ate sandwiches in the car on the way back, worried lest the light would go before our walk. Back at the house I left Kate and Flora to sort out our purchases while I went off to collect Rush, whom I knew would be sitting, walkless, at home while Alex was at work. With all the dogs eager and assembled we set off through the main gate, across the stream and through the meadow where I had been known to find wild orchids. We climbed across a steeply grassy field and, as the gradient increased, through the sad remains of what had been a neighbour's attempt to grow sweetcorn. On more open ground I threw a stick to the delight of all the four legged except Beetle, who quite sensibly stayed close to her mistress. Close to the top of the hill we lost Bumble, but were made aware of his presence, as Kate predicted, deep inside the tunnels of a badger's set. For an hour or more we strained to hear his muffled barks as he rushed through the empty chambers. By now an old hand on these occasions, Kate finally insisted that we all went home – Bumble, she was sure, would follow.

I was unpacking my suitcase when, to the sounds of modified retribution and much rejoicing 'the little feller' returned. Caked in mud, looking guilty and wagging his tail furiously he waited expectantly just inside the kitchen door. With Brownie point-earning the name of the game I set about giving him the bath of a lifetime.

Supper on trays – roast chicken and spring greens, a Vestey speciality to make me feel at home – was produced by Wendy the cook so that television viewing (another Vestey peculiarity) was not interrupted. As I sat in my chair the long, muscular body of Baggage lay beside me allowing easy access for big strokes – something, according to Kate, she had never seen before. Before retiring I said that I would take the dogs for a long walk in the morning. That was fine, said Kate, but I had to be back in time for lunch as surprise guests were expected.

The morning dawned with no sign of February at all. I saw a sharp, clear sky as I opened the curtains. After creeping quietly downstairs I made a frugal breakfast before returning to my room to get ready for the big outdoors. However, on the landing I was stopped in my tracks as the cry 'Guyrena' rent the air. I opened the door of what I thought of as the old ski slope to find Kate and Flora in a four-poster bed, surrounded by Bumble, Baggage and Bee. After big kisses I whisked the dogs away, stuffed them into my car and headed for our starting point. Ten minutes later we left the car and made our way down a Forestry Commission track. To avoid a repetition of his disappearing act I was advised by Kate to keep Bumble firmly leashed, but Baggage and Beetle forged happily ahead. As the walk turned into a climb we saw ahead of us a lone man heading in our direction. Too late to stop her, Baggage leapt forward with a roar and jumped at the walker in the way she had tackled me the day before. Startled, but not obviously nervous, he shouted a few oaths and pushed her off. I could only apologise as he looked at me darkly and continued his journey. We re-grouped and carried on to the top of the hill where the views towards Wales and the Malvern Hills were breathtaking. An hour later we were nearing the end of our outing, with the car in sight. Ahead of us a small group of people and a yellow Labrador on a lead were coming in our direction. Growling, Baggage edged forward in spite of the leash I had rapidly applied. Her fierce pulling only subsided when the enemy disappeared into the distance. With the danger past I let her off the lead, and she turned in a flash to grab Bumble by the throat. With those huge jaws clamped round his windpipe the poor little thing couldn't even make a sound. After a moment of frozen horror I shouted and tugged at the big dog's coat, but in vain. It was only with a frenzy of kicking that her grip was finally slackened. As I pulled her away Bumble tried gamely to get to his feet, but couldn't find the strength. He lay panting on the ground as I rounded up the other two and pushed them into the car. By now Bumble was barely breathing as I picked him up as carefully as I could and placed him in the boot. It was only by the grace of God that there was no other traffic on the road as I drove like the wind to the farm. I leapt from the car by the back door, yelling for Kate. From her bedroom window she asked what was wrong. As I outlined what had happened she started screaming – a sound that will live with me for ever. By the time I placed Bumble on the mat inside the door the life in his body had almost ebbed away. At that moment all hell was let loose. With Kate wailing uncontrollably a shattered Flora began to make a series of phone calls. The first was to the vet and the second to Jackie, the housekeeper. When she got hold of Saffron in London I described to her what had happened and she said she would leave straight away. As I put the phone down I heard the sound of cars and went outside to see that the Scotts and Annesleys had arrived for lunch. They stood awkwardly by the gate, aware that something was amiss by the clearly audible sounds of their grieving hostess. After a slightly surreal exchange of pleasantries I told them the story and likened the scene in the house to a Greek tragedy. 'It sounds more like Irish famine,' said one, producing the only smiles of the day.

As the newcomers were obviously not going to be fed I produced a bottle of wine and some glasses from the kitchen and joined them in a much-needed drink. By now more people had arrived and a sensible neighbour took charge. After being comforted by Fiona and Susie, Kate was taken into the garden and asked to choose a spot for Bumble's burial. The last thing I did for him was to help dig his grave.

Before I left, Kate had calmed down enough for me to tell her exactly how the tragedy occurred. Given time she might even stop blaming me for it, but whatever happens my name will always be linked with his death.